Prehistoric farming in Europe

D1345643

NEW STUDIES IN ARCHAEOLOGY

Series editors
Colin Renfrew, *University of Cambridge*
Jeremy Sabloff, *University of New Mexico*

Other titles in the series include

Graham Connah, *Three Thousand Years in Africa*
Richard Gould, *Living Archaeology*
Ian Hodder and Clive Orton, *Spatial Analysis in Archaeology*
Kenneth Hudson, *World Industrial Archaeology*
Keith Muckelroy, *Maritime Archaeology*
Stephen Plog, *Stylistic Variation in Prehistoric Ceramics*
Peter Wells, *Culture Contact and Culture Change*
Ian Hodder, *Symbols in Action*
Geoffrey Conrad and Arthur Demarest, *Religion and Empire*
Patrick Kirch, *Evolution of the Polynesian Chiefdoms*
Dean Arnold, *Ceramic Theory and Cultural Process*

Prehistoric farming in Europe

GRAEME BARKER
Department of Archaeology and Prehistory
Sheffield University/British School at Rome

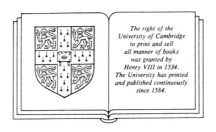

The right of the
University of Cambridge
to print and sell
all manner of books
was granted by
Henry VIII in 1534.
The University has printed
and published continuously
since 1584.

CAMBRIDGE UNIVERSITY PRESS

CAMBRIDGE

LONDON   NEW YORK   NEW ROCHELLE

MELBOURNE   SYDNEY

Published by the Press Syndicate of the University of Cambridge
The Pitt Building, Trumpington Street, Cambridge CB2 1RP
32 East 57th Street, New York, NY 10022, USA
10 Stamford Road, Oakleigh, Melbourne 3166, Australia

First published 1985

Printed in Great Britain at the University Press, Cambridge

Library of Congress catalogue card number: 84–17451

British Library Cataloguing in Publication Data

Barker, Graeme
Prehistoric farming in Europe. – (New
studies in archaeology)
1. Agriculture, Prehistoric – Europe
I. Title II. Series
630'.936   GN803

ISBN 0 521 22810 7 hard covers
ISBN 0 521 26969 5 paperback

CONTENTS

ILLUSTRATIONS

LIST OF TABLES

To Miranda, with love

Fig. 1. Prehistoric farming in Europe: the regional studies. Numbers in brackets refer to chapters.

My concern in this book has been to attempt to describe and analyse (if only partially to explain) the development of European farming from its origins until the close of the prehistoric era – a task which has seemed increasingly foolhardy as my publishers' deadlines have remorselessly slipped by. There are two introductory chapters describing the intellectual development of the subject, the kinds of information available for its study, the resources available to prehistoric farmers, and the constraints within which they had to operate. The bulk of the book, Chapters 3–9, consists of a series of regional studies, the geographical boundaries of which are shown in Figure 1. The timescale of the book is some 10,000 years, from the beginning of our modern climate some 12,000 years ago (the Holocene, or Postglacial, or present interglacial) – an early starting date for most studies of prehistoric farming, the justification for which is given in Chapter 1 – to the end of the prehistoric period, a date which varied widely from region to region but which was generally towards the end of the first millennium b.c. (Table 1, pp. xvi–xviii).

The only general study of the subject previously available has been contained in Grahame Clark's *Prehistoric Europe – The Economic Basis*, published over thirty years ago and still a monumental landmark in the development of our subject. As I describe in my first chapter, the justification for attempting a new survey lies in the fundamental revolution in prehistoric archaeology since then – in chronologies, theoretical principles and methodologies – and in the huge expansion in subsistence data that has occurred in its train. However, one major problem that confronted me has been the bias of most agricultural research in the intervening period on the questions of the origins and initial development of farming (Dennell, 1978, 1983; Higgs, 1972, 1975; M. R. Jarman *et al.*, 1982; Murray, 1970), and we still have far less information about later prehistoric agriculture than we would wish. In particular, for the later prehistoric periods it is increasingly clear that the control and manipulation of an agricultural surplus must have been a cornerstone of elite power in most if not all of the complex stratified societies we can recognise; yet in some cases, although the rest of the archaeological record left by these societies may be both prolific and spectacular, virtually nothing can be said of the agricultural system beyond the fact that the people grew crops and herded animals. Therefore, in my selection of material for the regional studies, I have said little of these societies and concentrated instead on those for whom the archaeological record is adequate for profitable analysis. Some familiar and illustrious names have had to be left off the roll call for this reason; and I am also aware that European Russia has rather unfairly received short shrift because of my lack of Russian; but I think that the material I have selected is sufficient to illustrate both the origins and then the further development of the major farming systems of prehistoric Europe. Whilst in this sense there ought to be something for everyone, I am also uncomfortably aware that in any survey of this kind there must be something somewhere for everyone to object to as well!

I have not assumed any familiarity with European prehistory, and have therefore tried to place the agricultural data within the context of contemporary ecological and social history, relationships which are in any case essential to any understanding of how and why prehistoric farming developed as it did. The chronological framework for the discussion is the uncalibrated radiocarbon chronology throughout, except in the case of those final prehistoric societies conventionally linked by their trading relationships to the historical chronologies of the classical world. I have also made some use of the terminology of the Three Age system as a convenience even though the main technology for food procurement for most prehistoric people in Europe throughout the Holocene almost certainly consisted of stone tools, and organic materials (wood, leather, basketry and so on) which have hardly ever survived – the Bronze Age and the Iron Age were as relevant to the farmers of those periods as the Space Age is to the modern farmer. Certainly it is impossible to equate stages or sub-stages in the Three Age system with stages in a cultural, social or economic sequence, as the proponents of the model in the last century believed. Of course 'mesolithic' and 'neolithic' are definitional nightmares, as the following discussion will make clear, but these and the rest of the Three Age terms remain in some circumstances useful (and primarily chronological) labels of a very general kind and a lot less clumsy than some of the alternative terminologies – for example, linking blocks of time with sometimes unfamiliar site names as Burgess (1980) has proposed for British prehistory: the Age of Stonehenge is one thing, but the Bedd Branwen period quite another, and Heaven forbid the Age of Spišsky Štvrtok or the Age of Tjikkiträsk.

Whilst I must take full responsibility for what follows, it is a very great pleasure to record the debt I owe to many people in the production of this book: to my teachers at Cambridge – John Alexander, Grahame Clark, Glyn Daniel, and the three who probably influenced me the most: David Clarke, who in eight short lectures in my final undergraduate year gave me perhaps the clearest grasp of the fundamental patterns of European prehistory; John Coles, who convinced me of the excitement of later European prehistory despite the weight of archaeological evidence to the contrary which we had to study; and Eric Higgs, also my Ph.D. supervisor, who set me on course for research into the archaeology of agriculture in general and European economic prehistory in particular that has guided me ever since. Whilst I sometimes think he would have heartily disapproved of the result (and dismissed it in that inimitable ESH style), I hope I have held to the strongest principle he taught which so captivated a generation brought up on Gravettians and Urnfielders, that prehistory must be about real people and real issues or it is about nothing;

to my colleagues at Sheffield, from whose ideas, enthusiasm and researches I have derived so much profit: Keith Branigan, John Collis, Robin Dennell, Andrew Fleming, David Gilbertson, Richard Hodges, Paul Mellars (now at Cambridge), Pat Phillips, Robin Torrence and Marek Zvelebil; and the postgraduates and undergraduates over the past decade who have borne my protracted investigations into prehistoric subsistence with good grace, healthy scepticism, and (Nigel Mills especially) with a fund of new ideas;

to European colleagues for their kindness and often marvellous hospitality when I have visited their excavations, museums or institutes, and who have been so generous with offprints of their work including copies of unpublished material; above all those who were so helpful to me in Holland – Peter Brinkhuizen, Aneka Clason, W. Groenman-van Waateringe, G. F. Izjereef, Sander van der Leeuw, Wietske Prummel, J. van der Waals and Louise Wijngaarden-Bakker;

to local farming families in Edale and the Hope Valley for their patient and good-humoured advice, particularly Cedric and Val Gilbert, John and Sue Hall, and above all Oliver and May Archer;

to Derrick Webley, ever generous with his fund of wisdom both archaeological and agricultural;

to Cambridge University Press for supporting the project throughout its protracted incubation, particularly Clare Davies-Jones, Robin Derricourt, Kate Owen, and Caroline Murray; to Debbie Hodges for compiling the indices; and to Barry Vincent at Sheffield for preparing the illustrations so attractively, often from some very unprepossessing originals;

and finally and most of all to my wife Miranda, who has had to live with *Prehistoric Farming* as much as with me these past years, often in the mud and muck of the real thing outside my study window. To her I owe everything, and to her I dedicate this book.

Oaker Farm
January 1984

Table 1 *Simplified chronological chart with traditional terminologies and (italics) major subsistence stages, according to uncalibrated radiocarbon dates; some major cultural names are given in brackets.*

b.c.	GREECE		ITALY, S. FRANCE, SPAIN		BALKANS AND MIDDLE DANUBE BASIN	
0						
	classical Greece		Rome		iron age (Dacian state etc.)	*mixed farming ?exchange of agricultural surplus*
	archaic iron age		Etruscans late bronze age	*first systematic polyculture in Italy*		
1000					late bronze age	
	middle/late bronze age Minoan–Mycenaean states	*'palace economies': redistribution of agricultural produce*	early/middle bronze age, (Polada, Apennine, Argaric)	*mixed farming, some specialised herding; polyculture and irrigation in Almeria*	early/middle bronze age (Otomani)	*mixed farming ?exchange of agricultural surplus*
2000						
	Aegean early bronze age	*first systematic cultivation of olives and vines, wool production, deep sea fishing*	copper age: (Gaudo, Remedello, Fontbouisse, Los Millares)	*mixed farming augmented with small scale polyculture: water control in Almeria; first ards.*	initial bronze age (Ezeno, Baden)	*first systematic use of secondary products*
3000						
	final neolithic		middle/late neolithic (Italy), Almerian (Spain), Chassey (France)	*sedentary mixed farming now predominant*	copper age/ chalcolithic (Gumelnitsa)	*intensive mixed farming; first use of ard?*
	late neolithic	*intensification of mixed farming systems established in EN*				
4000						
	middle neolithic		early neolithic (cardinal pottery, red-painted pottery)	*mobile foraging, mobile foraging/ herding, sedentary mixed farming*	middle/late neolithic	*tell systems continue and expand; first cattle traction?*
5000					early neolithic (Starčevo, Karanovo 1)	*first tell villages and mixed farming; mixed farming/foraging in M. Danube basin*
	early neolithic	*first tell villages, sedentary mixed farming*	late mesolithic	*intensified fishing; rudimentary husbandry?*		
6000						
	late mesolithic	*intensified fishing; rudimentary husbandry?*	late mesolithic	*intensified fishing; rudimentary husbandry?*	late mesolithic	*increased sedentism, rudimentary husbandry?*
7000						
	early mesolithic	*generalised mobile foraging*	early mesolithic	*generalised mobile foraging*	early mesolithic	*mobile foraging, more sedentary foraging/fishing at Iron Gates*
8000						

UKRAINE		THE ALPINE REGION		THE CONTINENTAL LOWLANDS		ATLANTIC EUROPE	
						iron age	*oppida economies*
Scythian iron age	*steppe pastoralism*	iron age	*dichotomy increases between alpine subsistence and more specialised farming on foreland.*	iron age	*iron ploughs, scythes. largescale surplus presumed for trade*	late bronze age	*terp marsh farming climatic deterioration and settlement contraction in Holland*
bronze age	*steppe pastoralism*	bronze age	*alpine systems unchanged; dairy/wool production for exchange on foreland*	(Lausitz) bronze age	*arable-based farming on loess, stock-based farming off loess*	early bronze age	*cattle stalling and plaggen culture in Holland*
bronze age (Kurgan)	*development of mobile steppe pastoralism*	copper age late neolithic	*alpine farming continues in Switzerland; starts in northern Italy?*	late neolithic/ copper age	*horse riding, cattle traction (ard, cart)*	later neolithic (Michelsberg, Chassey)	*expansion of mixed farming to marginal soils; first systematic use of secondary products*
copper age (Tripolye)	*establishment of sedentary mixed farming*	early neolithic (Switzerland), (Cortaillod, Pfyn)	*mixed farming and foraging; dairying and cattle stalling (Switzerland)*	later neolithic (Rössen, Lengyel)	*mixed farming established off loess*	early neolithic (TRB)	*mixed farming on secondary soils; foraging/farming on coasts*
early neolithic	*mobile foraging, small scale husbandry*	?early neolithic (northern Italy) late mesolithic	*first farming in northern Italy?* *mostly foraging, but specialised fishing, and red deer foddering?*	early (LBK) neolithic	*LBK mixed farming (cattle/emmer) on loess; LBK foraging and herding off loess*	early neolithic (LBK) late mesolithic	*LBK mixed farming on primary soils; coastal/inland foraging*
late mesolithic	*foraging, some mobile, some more sedentary*	late mesolithic	*settlement expansion in central alps*	late mesolithic	*generalised mobile foraging, agglomeration at summer fishing sites?*	late mesolithic	*increased reliance on coastal resources*
early mesolithic	*generalised mobile foraging*	early mesolithic	*generalised mobile foraging*	early mesolithic	*generalised mobile foraging*	early mesolithic	*generalised mobile foraging*
early mesolithic	*generalised mobile foraging*	early mesolithic	*generalised mobile foraging*	early mesolithic	*generalised mobile foraging*	early mesolithic	*generalised mobile foraging*

Table 1 (*cont.*)

BRITAIN AND IRELAND		SOUTH SCANDINAVIA		NORTH SCANDINAVIA		b.c.
iron age	complex redistributive systems	iron age	iron scythes, rakes	iron age / neolithic	final development of sedentary mixed farming	0
late bronze age	climatic deterioration and settlement contraction	late bronze age	climatic deterioration and settlement contraction		abandonment of farming in the far north	1000
early bronze age (Wessex)	development of field systems and land boundaries	early/middle bronze age		neolithic	foraging	
		later neolithic	emmer replaced by barley expansion of mixed farming, first systematic use of secondary products	neolithic	settlement expansion to the far north foraging	2000
late neolithic	expansion of mixed farming to marginal soils; first systematic use of secondary products					3000
early neolithic	mixed farming on primary soils; mixed foraging/herding	early neolithic (TRB)	small scale mixed farming, mainly foraging	neolithic	possible farming (swidden) in the far north	
		later mesolithic (Erteból̀le)	high populations, some all-year settlements, intensive foraging			4000
late mesolithic	foraging intensification? red deer foddering?			later mesolithic	mobile foraging throughout	
						5000
late mesolithic	increased reliance on coastal resources	later mesolithic	increased sedentism, increased reliance on coastal resources	later mesolithic	sledge and ski technology	6000
early mesolithic	generalised mobile foraging	early mesolithic	generalised mobile foraging		foraging, especially sea mammal and elk hunting	
				early mesolithic (Kunda, Fosna)	first colonisation as ice caps retreat	7000
early mesolithic	generalised mobile foraging	early mesolithic (Maglemosian)	generalised mobile foraging			
						8000

Approaches to prehistoric farming

The development of economic prehistory

The Roman poet Lucretius, speculating in the first century B.C. about the origins of mankind, envisaged an age before iron when men knew only bronze, and an age of remotest time when 'the earliest weapons were the hands, nails and teeth, as well as stones, pieces of wood, flames and fire as soon as they were known' (*De Rerum Natura* V, 1283–7). The same sort of sequence of development was discussed by several philosophers and scientists after the Renaissance. As antiquarian speculation gave way to the first systematic archaeology in the second half of the nineteenth century, the same Three Age system of stone, bronze and iron was explicitly defined as the major classificatory framework for European prehistory, with the Stone Age further subdivided into old, middle and new (or palaeolithic, mesolithic and neolithic) phases (Daniel, 1964, 1967). At the same time, the sequence of technological development was also correlated with stages of economic and social progress. Three typical syntheses were Nilsson's *Primitive Inhabitants of Scandinavia* (1868), Westropp's *Prehistoric Phases* (1872) and Figuier's *Primitive Man* (1876), all of which argued that (in Westropp's words) 'there were but one history for every separate people, one uniform process of development for every race' and divided the evolution of prehistoric society into four stages of development: hunting, pastoralism or nomadism, farming and state (Table 2). Nilsson's description of the hunting, herding and farming lifestyles is quoted here in some detail, and illustrated with Figuier's charming reconstructions, because such men helped mould the intellectual framework for ensuing research on the origins and development of prehistoric farming.

1. The *savage* has few other than material wants, and these he endeavours to satisfy only for the moment. To appease hunger for the day; when requisite, to protect his body against heat or cold; to prepare his lair for the night; to follow the instinct of propagation, and instinctively to guard and tend his offspring – this constitutes all his care, all his enjoyment. He thinks and acts only for the day which *is*, not for the day which is *coming* . . . he is compelled to fish and to hunt, or he must perish . . . (Fig. 2). [Eventually he becomes]

2. A *herdsman* (nomad), subsisting chiefly on the produce of his herds; the flesh of domestic animals his food, milk his beverage, skins his clothes. The chase and fishing, formerly his *chief*, now become his *occasional* occupations . . . (Fig. 3). At last he tires of his wandering life . . . Thus the nomad gradually becomes

Table 2 *Westropp's 'Tabulation of the Stages of Development of Man and Implements', from his* Prehistoric Phases *(1872)*

Stages of the development of Man	Stages of the development of Implements		Contemporaneous Animals	Contemporaneous Trees in Denmark	Contemporaneous Burials
Barbarous	Palaeolithic	Rough Flints	Mammoth Rhinoceros Tichorinus Cave Bear, Hyena Reindeer		
Hunting	Mesolithic	{ Flint Flakes Flints chipped into shape	Red Deer Wild Boar Wild Ox	Fir	Tumuli Stone circles Body in a sitting posture
Pastoral	Neolithic	{ Stone implements ground at edge Stone implements all ground and polished	Sheep Ox Goat		Cromlechs Stone circles Body in a contracted posture
Agricultural	Bronze	{ Arrow-heads Spear-heads Swords Flat celts Palstaves Socketed celts	Sheep Ox Horse Pig } Domesticated	Oak	Tumuli Cremation
State	Iron	{ Celts Spears, swords Arrow-heads	Cereals { Wheat Barley	Beech	Tumuli Cremation Inhumation

Fig. 2. 'Man in the Great Bear and Mammoth Epoch'. (After Figuier, 1876: fig. 16)

3. An *agriculturalist*, and takes a more stable social position. The movable tent gives place to a permanently fixed dwelling; the tilled cornfields yield a richer harvest the more they are cultivated; the forests surrounding his home give him fuel and building materials; the fields provide him with grass and winter fodder for his cattle, and even the waters yield him their tribute. (Nilsson, 1868: lvii–lxx) (Fig. 4)

Although the role of herding as the necessary intermediate stage between hunting and farming was gradually discounted, the major dichotomy between the nomadic and uncertain lifestyle of the hunter and the sedentary and reliable lifestyle of the farmer remained a fundamental precept of most prehistoric research in Europe for almost a century. One practical result of this concept of a great social divide, compounded by the differences in the archaeological record, was the separation of research activity in the first half of this century on either side of the accepted boundary between hunters and farmers marked by the beginning of the Neolithic. On one side of the boundary stone tools were the principal focus of activity, whereas on the other side was a wider array of artifacts, dominated by pottery. The regional distributions observed in such material from the Neolithic onwards formed the basis of Childe's concept of the prehistoric culture: 'we find certain types of remains – pots, implements, ornaments, burial rites, house forms – constantly recurring together. Such a complex of regularly associated traits we shall term a "cultural group" or just a "culture". We assume that such a complex is the material expression of what would today be called a "people" ' (Childe, 1929: v). The principal thrust of research on the neolithic and later periods of European prehistory from the publication of the first edition of Childe's *Dawn of European Civilisation* until

Fig. 3. 'The art of bread making in the Stone Age'. (After Figuier, 1876: fig. 125)

his death in 1957 was the investigation of the chronological and spatial relationships of prehistoric cultures. The chronology had to be almost entirely relative, with the whole scheme pegged by a few absolute dates established by tenuous cross-dating with the historic and protohistoric civilisations of the eastern Mediterranean.

This kind of cultural archaeology had three important implications for the development of ideas about prehistoric farming. First, the establishment of relative chronologies using typological comparisons between different regions inevitably created a 'chest of drawers' sequence of synchronous cultural stages – a series of 'horizons', each characterised by a particular cultural repertoire, type of society and way of life. Second, the typological method had to concentrate on inter-regional similarities in the archaeological record (however isolated these sometimes now seem compared with the rest of the material), and so when archaeologists sought explanations for the change from one horizon to the other, the answers had invariably been provided already by the chronological work in terms of cultural contact: the results of either the *diffusion* of ideas or (as more commonly thought) the *migration* of people introducing new ideas, either peacefully or by force. Third, because chronological issues had to take priority – as Wheeler (1954: 245) remarked, the timetables rather than the trains – the recovery of food refuse (the animal bones and plants remains which are the best direct evidence for prehistoric farming) tended to be an incidental rather than a primary goal of excavation in most cases, and a synthesis like the *Dawn* had to throw a very wide net in order to make often the most general comments about the subsistence base of particular cultures or horizons of cultures.

In the most extreme examples of 'ethno-historical' prehistory, the archaeological cultures seemed to take on a life of their own, with the bearers of Culture A introducing one

Fig. 4. 'The cultivation of gardens during the Bronze Age'. (After Figuier, 1876: fig. 207)

way of life to an area only to be swept aside by the Culture B people, their movements being charted on maps increasingly resembling the campaign maps of Europe in the last war. Sir Mortimer Wheeler castigated this approach for its 'tendency to devolve archaeology into a sort of dehydrated humanism . . . to transform our predecessors into "battle axe folk" or "beaker folk" until . . . we begin almost to personify battle axes or beakers with a sort of hungry latter-day animism' (Wheeler, 1954: 229). Grahame Clark's *Prehistoric Europe – The Economic Basis*, a masterly synthesis which squeezed an impressive amount of subsistence information from artifacts, settlement forms, food debris, environmental evidence and rock art, was all the more remarkable because it deliberately cut right across the chronological and cultural boundaries of contemporary research (Clark, 1952). Through such a perspective he was able to show that it was impossible to divide prehistoric Europe into the series of neat subsistence stages commonly proposed (pre-neolithic hunting, fishing and gathering; neolithic primitive farming; late neolithic and early bronze age pastoralism; late bronze age and iron age mixed farming) – there was clear evidence for far more complexity in subsistence development, both chronological and geographical, than hitherto imagined.

The radiocarbon method of dating first developed in the 1950s transformed the study of European prehistory in the 1960s and 1970s (Renfrew, 1973a). In the first place, the long chronologies indicated by the first radiocarbon dates (the beginning of the European Neolithic, for example, was dated to *c.* 6000 b.c. in southeast Europe and *c.* 4500 b.c. in temperate Europe, rather than to *c.* 3000 B.C. as Childe had originally argued) tended to place an entirely new emphasis on long-term stability rather than sudden change in the archaeological record, and many narrow 'horizons' were found to span considerable periods of time. Secondly, the regional chronologies which could now be considered independently of their neighbours revealed in several instances that synchronised horizons inferred from typological studies were in fact illusory. In short, the new timetables frequently demanded some entirely new trains. Clark's reappraisal of British prehistory emphasising cultural continuity and rejecting the succession of folk movements favoured previously is a typical example of the fresh analyses precipitated by the new chronologies (Clark, 1966). Although some archaeologists continued to favour population movement as the major explanation for changes in material culture (e.g. Gimbutas, 1965; Hawkes, 1968), the growing consensus was that the new regional prehistories were poorly served by such models. The principal remaining folk movement accepted by most prehistorians was the colonisation of Europe by neolithic farmers: the early radiocarbon dates indicated a movement west and northwest from Greece between *c.* 6000 b.c. and *c.* 4000 b.c., with a secondary colonisation of the alps, western France, Britain, the Low Countries and Scandinavia after *c.* 3500 b.c. (Clark, 1965; Fig. 5). Clark's thesis was restated later, with the greater precision allowed by increased numbers of radiocarbon dates, by Ammerman and Cavalli-Sforza (1971). As I shall be arguing in the following chapters, however, the evidence for this invasion or colonisation movement is far more equivocal than commonly supposed.

Alongside the construction of the first radiocarbon chronologies in the 1960s were major developments in archaeological theory, characterised in the United States as the New Archaeology or processual archaeology, epitomised then by the writings of Binford

(1962, 1964, 1965) and resoundingly thrust upon British archaeology in 1968 by Clarke's *Analytical Archaeology*. In essence clear scientific thinking was advocated, as well as techniques of systematic analysis appropriate to such an approach, to develop an explicit theory for archaeological investigation – that is, what should be the legitimate

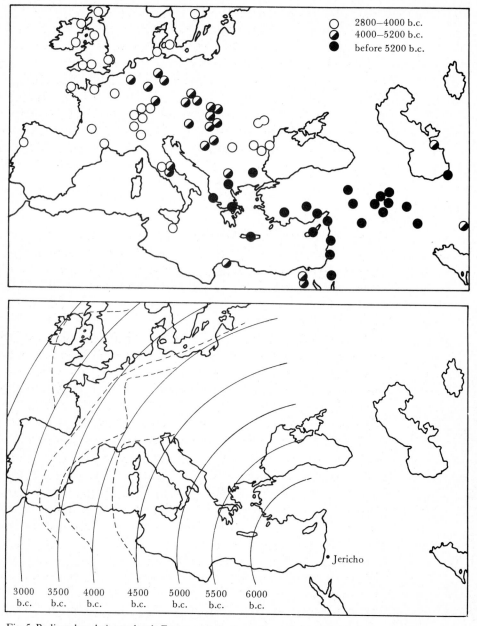

Fig. 5. Radiocarbon dating and early European agriculture: above, the spread of agriculture into Europe from southwest Asia according to the first series of radiocarbon dates, after Clark, 1965: fig. 2; and below, the 'wave of advance' of early farming (the arcs indicating the predicted position of the spread, the broken curved lines denoting regional variation), according to Ammerman and Cavalli-Sforza's model (1971: fig. 6).

questions we should ask the data, and how best should they be tackled? The traditional narrative prehistory appeared increasingly suspect in the face of such questioning: archaeological data seemed far more capable of answering questions of how prehistoric communities functioned as social and economic systems than quasi-historical questions about the origins of the Magdalenian culture or the Beaker folk. It is no coincidence that the period has also witnessed major improvements in the range of archaeological techniques available for investigating social and economic processes in prehistory: for example, in surface surveys and regional settlement studies; in recovery and sampling procedures on excavations; in the techniques of subsistence analysis and environmental reconstruction discussed later in this chapter; in physical and chemical techniques of artifact analysis to study technology and trade; in social reconstruction using settlement and cemetery studies; and in the application of quantitative approaches to all these fields of study. The account in this book of how the development of prehistoric farming in Europe appears to us today rests almost entirely on the results of the revolution in chronologies, theories and methodologies in the thirty years following *Prehistoric Europe – The Economic Basis*.

The origins of agriculture

The principal question that has dominated the study of economic prehistory during the last thirty years has been the problem of the origins of agriculture. As far as Europe was concerned, the baseline for research has always been the assumption that farming did not begin as an indigenous process but was introduced by neolithic colonists from the 'hearth of domestication' in the Near East, so the focus of work on agricultural origins has been there.

Fundamental to much research was the belief in an enormous disparity between the hunting and farming lifestyles. Childe originally proposed that farming probably began in the Near East as a result of postglacial desiccation, with men, plants and animals being compelled to concentrate together in oases (1953, 1954). He characterised the process in the memorable phrase 'the Neolithic Revolution', a great leap forward in human progress on a scale commensurate with the Agricultural and Industrial Revolutions of recent history: 'throughout the several hundred millennia of the Old Stone Age all human societies remained parasitic, depending entirely for their food on what natural processes happened to supply. Neolithic societies began deliberately cooperating with nature to increase the productivity of edible plants and to protect and foster the multiplication of animals' (Childe, 1958: 34). Braidwood, one of the main researchers on agricultural origins in the Near East, likewise argued early in his work that 'the appearance of the village farming community marked a transition . . . of great import for what was to follow. Before it were some half a million years of savagery during which small wandering groups of people . . . led an essentially "natural" catch-as-catch-can existence' (1960: 130).

In the 1950s and 1960s, intensive research took place in the hills of Palestine, Turkey, Iraq and Iran, the so-called 'hilly flanks of the Fertile Crescent', regarded as the primary habitats of the wild progenitors of domesticated cereals, sheep and goats (Helbaek, 1959). This research (summarised by Clark, 1978) demonstrated that village communities practising mixed farming (using wheat, barley, cattle, pigs, sheep, goats and dogs) were widely established here by *c*. 6000 b.c. and probably earlier. The transition from late glacial and early postglacial hunting and foraging to these systems of farming was not very clear, but the complexities of the material certainly destroyed the idea of a sharp boundary between two sets of technology, economy and society (palaeolithic/ mesolithic hunters with chipped stone tools on the one hand, and neolithic farmers on the other with pottery, polished axes and grinding stones). Research in Mesoamerica and Peru over the same period indicated rather similar shifts from foraging to farming during the opening millennia of the Postglacial or Holocene (from *c*. 10,000 b.c.), although the resources exploited were quite different from those of the Old World – domestic animals were not very important and the agricultural staples were plant foods such as maize, squashes, beans and chili peppers (MacNeish, 1964, 1965). Clearly these events had to be explained as independent processes, and a variety of cultural, ecological and demographic models was put forward in the 1960s to account for the origins of agriculture in the Old and New Worlds, notably by Binford (1968), Braidwood (1960), Flannery (1965, 1969), Flannery *et al.* (1967), MacNeish (1965), and Patterson (1971).

One study with a major impact on agricultural research at this time was *Man the Hunter* (Lee and DeVore, 1968), a collection of studies of modern hunting and gathering peoples. This destroyed once and for all the long-lived archaeological tenet that the hunting way of life was a desperate, uncertain and laborious quest for food, compared with the ordered ease of the agricultural economy. As this and related research showed, the subsistence base of most modern hunting peoples was in fact characterised by the systematic exploitation of a series of resources, normally on a seasonal basis, requiring regular movement from one resource to another, with secondary foods available if the primary resource failed. Furthermore, the time and energy requirements for obtaining food were conspicuously low compared with the demands of primitive husbandry. Moreover, as Boserup had argued in 1965 (in a study of modern farming in Africa that has had a major impact on archaeological thinking about subsistence intensification), increasingly productive methods of agriculture demand increasingly more time and effort from the farmer, and (in her case study) were adopted only in response to population pressure. Clearly, there were some uncomfortable implications for the traditional archaeological concepts of pre-agricultural savagery on the one hand (Braidwood's 'essentially natural catch-as-catch-can existence'), and the neolithic Garden of Eden on the other – and for many of the models previously used to explain the shift from the one to the other (Fig. 6).

The most direct and cogent criticisms of previous research on the origins of agriculture stemmed from the British Academy Major Research Project at Cambridge University investigating the early history of agriculture in the Near East and Europe, directed by Eric Higgs from 1967 until his death in 1976 (Higgs, 1972, 1975; M. R. Jarman *et al.*, 1982). The argument was summarised in two review papers by Higgs and Jarman (1969, 1972). First, zoological and botanical evidence indicated the possibility of early postglacial farming in the Old World outside the traditionally supposed core area. Second, the accepted dates for the domestication of a variety of plants and animals throughout the world demonstrated the continuous development of the process from the early

Postglacial to the present day, not a single sudden event. Third, the origins of agriculture probably had to be sought much further back in time than hitherto suggested if domestication was, as seemed likely, some kind of process of natural selection on the human population and not, as so often argued in the past, the result of 'cultural opportunism' (with innovative hunters 'inventing' agriculture by recognising and learning to exploit quickly some chance combination of relationships with plants or animals).

Fig. 6. A trial run for the Neolithic Revolution? – the adventures of Stanley, the Great Palaeolithic Hero. (Cartoon by Murray Ball, redrawn from *Punch*, 1973, reproduced here by kind permission of the editors of *Punch*)

'Domestication can be regarded as a long-term process whose limit at one end is defined by the present day, and at the other only by the earliest date that anyone has yet had the temerity to propose' (Higgs and Jarman, 1972: 13).

Two other papers in the first major volume of the project, by H. N. Jarman (1972), and M. R. Jarman and Wilkinson (1972), pointed to the logical and practical inadequacies of the botanical and zoological criteria proposed in the 1950s and early 1960s for detecting domestication on the assumption that it must have been a relatively rapid and measurable event in the early Postglacial. Furthermore, other studies by members of the project indicated the intensive exploitation during the last glaciation of a number of species now considered wild: for example, gazelle in the Near East (Legge, 1972), red deer in southern Europe (Barker, 1973, 1975a; M. R. Jarman, 1972), and reindeer in northern Europe (Sturdy, 1975). The exact nature of this exploitation was not clear, and various forms of selective hunting, loose herding or driving, and closer manipulation were proposed, but the evidence certainly suggested a wider spectrum of man–animal relationships than formerly envisaged separating the hunting systems which prevailed earlier in the Pleistocene from the husbandry systems of the postglacial villages. Higgs' arguments about the nature of domestication were frequently mis-understood – after a visit to Italy, for example, he was forever known there as the mad Englishman who thought that Neanderthal man had domesticated the cave bear. His project certainly prompted a long overdue reappraisal of palaeolithic subsistence, even though with hindsight some of the arguments put forward for the intensive exploitation of a single species in the last glaciation were undoubtedly oversimplified. Yet in general, there seems little doubt that foraging systems in the latter part of the last glaciation were far more sophisticated than previously supposed: in northern Europe, for example, there is quite persuasive evidence that horses were ridden (Bahn, 1978, 1980), and by the end of the Pleistocene in the Near East there is increasing evidence to suggest that there was selective hunting (perhaps involving capturing and confining animals), and that einkorn and perhaps other cereals and legumes were being deliberately cultivated (Moore, 1982).

However, whatever the nature of late Pleistocene subsistence and the roots of the domestication process, it seems to be true for most parts of the world that the irreversible transformation in subsistence represented by farming did not crystallise until the mil-lennia immediately following the end of the last glaciation c. 10,000 b.c. The range of husbandry systems practised in several parts of the world between c. 10,000 and 6,000 b.c. was sufficiently well founded to be clearly recognised as agriculture in the archaeological record. The mix of crops and animals varied from region to region: maize and other crops in different parts of the Americas; wheat, barley, sheep and goats in the Old World, probably from the Mediterranean basin right across to India; millet and pigs and then rice in China; various squashes and gourds and then rice, taro and yams in southeast Asia; but the fundamental process of domestication, and the timescale, were essentially the same (Bender, 1975; Cohen, 1977). Childe's concept of a revolution in human behaviour is supported and indeed greatly enhanced by the world perspective now available to us, and the models proposed to explain that global revolution must surely be on a commensurate scale. In this respect I find Cohen's thesis that agriculture

was primarily a necessary response to postglacial overpopulation particularly convincing:

> the record appears to show that the human populations on each continent
> first concentrated fairly heavily on the exploitation of large mammalian
> fauna . . . and then shifted gradually towards broader spectrum economies
> geared to more plentiful but less palatable resources. In each case, domesti-
> cation techniques were then focused on plant species chosen not for their
> palatability but for their ability to provide large quantities of storable
> calories or storable protein in close proximity to human settlements.
> (Cohen, 1977: 279–80)

However, it must also be said that the social context of the change to farming (the implications for sex and labour divisions, for family organisation, for concepts of resource
ownership, inheritance and so on) must surely be an essential part of the equation as
well, but it is still only being modelled very tentatively, let alone being investigated systematically in the archaeological record (Bender, 1978, 1981; Ingold, 1980, 1981).

   The study of agricultural origins in Europe has remained steadfastly in the shadow
of the Near East, little affected by this changing world perspective (Clutton-Brock,
1981). However, recent developments in subsistence studies in Europe have thrown
considerable doubt on the idea of a simple dichotomy between mesolithic hunters and
neolithic farmers, and on the assumption that the natural habitats of the principal
domesticates (cereals, sheep and goats), unlike those of pigs and cattle, did not extend
from the Near East into Europe. It is now quite clear that the transition from foraging
to farming in prehistoric Europe was far more complex than ever envisaged in the
colonisation model, and it is for this reason that the regional studies of prehistoric farming in the following chapters of necessity begin with a consideration of the nature of
settlement in the early Holocene as well as in the millennia conventionally regarded as
the period of the first farmers.

Reconstructing prehistoric farming: the sources

Potential evidence for prehistoric farming can be divided into six categories: (1) agricultural tools; (2) settlement archaeology (occupation sites, constructional features within
them, and off-site remains such as field systems); (3) pictorial evidence, in particular the
'rock art' of Scandinavia and the alpine region; (4) environmental archaeology – studies
of data primarily recording ancient ecologies but sometimes also reflecting ancient land
use (pollen, molluscs, microfauna, sediments); (5) food refuse, the primary data for diet
– particularly fragments of animal bone and collections of seeds and other botanical
residues, but also (in exceptional conditions of preservation) coprolites or fecal remains;
and (6) site location studies. These classes of data are discussed in turn below. Very
often the study of one class of data is inextricably linked to the study of other classes; at
the same time, of course, the most effective and convincing reconstructions discussed in
the later chapters inevitably derive from regions of Europe where several of these classes
of data have been well studied and their results correlated or contrasted.

Artifacts

The archaeological record surviving from prehistoric Europe consists primarily of artifacts: most commonly of stone, fired clay and metal, but also of bone and antler and, in conditions of exceptional preservation, of more fragile organic materials such as wood, leather, wool, plant fibres and the like. It is commonly assumed that artifacts provide us with easy insights into prehistoric technology, much of it of critical relevance for subsistence reconstruction, but in fact precise information about artifact function is much less extensive than we would wish.

The first systematic studies of stone artifacts in the last century classified them variously as weapons, tools or ornaments from comparisons with ethnographic material and common-sense observations. However, detailed ethnoarchaeological research on patterns of artifact use by modern 'primitive' peoples, coupled with microscopic studies of wear patterns on prehistoric tools (compared with those on modern replicas used for experimental work), have demonstrated very clearly that many earlier assumptions about tool function were either simplistic or entirely false (Gould, 1980; Semenov, 1964). Some modern peoples studied by ethnoarchaeologists have an unnerving habit of using some tools repeatedly for completely different tasks. In general, the life history of artifacts amongst such peoples varies considerably according to a complex range of variables: some 'curate' or preserve their equipment carefully, using tools repeatedly on different occasions; others make tools for a specific purpose and discard them immediately afterwards; many curate some parts of their technology and discard others. Thus the common descriptions of stone tools in the archaeological literature, with obvious functional implications – hand axe, knife, scraper, awl, projectile point, adze and so on – can in many cases really only be taken as convenient classifications of shape, not statements of function.

For example, the geometric microliths abundant in mesolithic Europe are normally taken to have been used as composite arrowheads, set in resin on wooden shafts; many undoubtedly were, as a few complete arrows have survived, but apart from the fact that such arrows could have been used for killing fish as well as game (and humans, of course), some may also have been mounted on wooden boards and used for processing vegetable foods (D. L. Clarke, 1976). Many 'polished axes' were undoubtedly used as axes for woodworking, but others were for ceremonial use, some changed from functional to ceremonial objects as they were exchanged further and further from their place of origin (Evett, 1975), and many crude 'axes' were in fact probably used as adzes, mattocks and hoes. Even flint 'sickle blades' and stone 'grinders', commonly cited as evidence for prehistoric farming, present difficulties in interpretation. The blades have a sheen or gloss from silica on their edge, and there are a few examples from prehistoric Europe of curved wooden or antler sickle hafts with these blades set in them (normally as a saw edge rather than a straight cutting edge). Most were probably used as sickles for harvesting cereals, but the gloss could also have been obtained from cutting other grasses and rushes rather than cereals. Grinding stones likewise were certainly everyday equipment for milling flour; but such stones are commonly used today by Australian aborigines for grinding up wild seeds, or grinding ochre for paint, and they cannot be taken in isolation as unequivocal evidence for agriculture.

A few artifacts, however, do provide more precise information about agricultural technology in prehistoric Europe. Wooden ards or simple scratch ploughs, for example, are known from the third millennium b.c. onwards (Sherratt, 1981; Fig. 47). The shape of a wooden 'rope-traction ard' identified from a Danish bog some years ago and dated to the third millennium b.c. (Steensberg, 1973; Fig. 89) suggests that wooden shovels very like the modern European shovel (with a heart-shaped blade and a long handle, as opposed to the British spade with a rectangular blade and short T handle) were widely used by prehistoric farmers. At Gwithian, a second millennium b.c. settlement in Cornwall, southern England, impressions from such an implement were found alongside ard furrows in the buried sands (Megaw, 1976). Agricultural equipment in late prehistoric Europe included metal sickles, reaping and pruning hooks, ard shares or points, and (eventually) scythes (Harding, 1976; Rees, 1981).

Settlement archaeology
Many early surveys of European prehistory implicitly or explicitly correlated settlement sites containing structural remains such as houses and storage pits with a sedentary/ agricultural way of life, and domestic sites lacking structures with the (assumed) nomadic lifestyle of the hunter or pastoralist. As with artifact studies, however, modern ethnoarchaeology reveals far more complex relationships between occupation debris and subsistence mode, and the same complexity can now be seen in the archaeological record from prehistoric Europe: foragers who have left only insubstantial remains, foragers who built houses and stored food, farmers with and without large permanent dwellings, pastoral-based communities with and without fixed settlements, and so on – leaving aside the various occupation sites of the many peoples who combined foraging with farming.

As with artifacts, prehistoric houses studied in isolation rarely provide clear indications of the subsistence activities of the inhabitants. On the other hand, house plans can provide crucial information about social organisation, the reconstruction of which is an essential part of modelling prehistoric farming: factors such as overall size and internal arrangements, size differences between houses in a village, spatial relationships between houses, and the nature and extent of any defence works, can be used to estimate aspects of social organisation such as the size of the community, the degree of stratification and inter-site competition, all of which are relevant to subsistence reconstruction (Cook, 1972; Plog, 1975). Other structural features in a settlement can be used to suggest very general aspects of subsistence, such as fenced paddocks (animal pens?) and pits (storage pits?), but the detailed function of many such features is often unclear. In British iron age settlements, for example, the square settings of four post holes, whilst generally thought of as the marks left by above-ground granaries, have also been interpreted from ethnographic analogies variously as traces of dwellings, hayricks, chicken coops, pigsties, racks for drying and smoking meat, lookout towers, and scaffolds for exposing bodies; stake rings, normally interpreted as houses, have also been seen as animal pens; and circular gullies, normally also interpreted as houses, have sometimes been identified as shrines, hayricks and granaries (Ellison and Drewett, 1971; Guilbert, 1981; Reynolds, 1979). Experimental work at the Butser ancient farm project has at least provided strong support for the hypothesis that the pits at these sites were for storing grain (Reynolds, 1974). There is also an increasing number of water-logged sites in Europe, particularly in the alpine region and the coastal margins of northern Europe, where modern excavations have allowed elegant and convincing reconstructions of farm layout, with the structures identified including dwellings, barns for fodder storage, granaries, cattle byres, milking parlours, and haystacks. Such detailed interpretation has normally been achieved by a combination of excellent structural preservation and careful analysis of associated organic residues.

In northern Europe, too, especially in Britain, Holland and Scandinavia, prehistoric settlements are sometimes associated not only with adjacent pens and paddocks but also with extensive systems of fields, marked by low banks and/or ditches, often covering many hectares. The particular function of individual fields (arable, pastoral, or a combination of both) can be established only by detailed chemical studies of the buried soils, which have rarely been undertaken on any scale. Even so, the study of the development of such field systems has provided some of our best information for regional agricultural organisation in later European prehistory, as well as for the detailed relationship of a farm to its fields.

Pictorial evidence

The art which has survived from prehistoric Europe surely offers us – potentially at least – some of the most revealing insights into what it must have been like to live in that world. The paucity of our understanding of so much of it only serves to remind us of the immensity of time and experience separating us from prehistoric men and women, and their minds. The three major groups of data from prehistoric Europe relevant to our enquiry consist of: Levantine art – painted and incised scenes in Iberian rock shelters, generally ascribed to mesolithic and neolithic populations; rock art – pecked and incised scenes on glacially smoothed boulders in the alpine region and Scandinavia, mostly dated to the later prehistoric periods (the third, second and first millennia b.c., especially the second); and Celtic art, surviving primarily as metal decoration, from temperate Europe at the close of prehistory. Subsistence information has been drawn from all three groups. In the rock art of Val Camonica in northern Italy, for example, are scenes of hunting, ploughing with a crook ard (Fig. 7), and of villages of wooden houses surrounded by small cultivated fields (Anati, 1961, 1976); they are loosely dated to the second millennium b.c., and the archaeological record from contemporary settlements in the region mirrors the art closely in terms of settlement layout, agricultural technology and subsistence data (Barfield, 1971; Chapter 5).

There are inevitably major difficulties in dating and interpreting much of this kind of pictorial evidence – most mural art consists of a palimpsest of drawings which can be disentangled only with the greatest difficulty, and cannot be dated absolutely. Much classification has been subjective, unsystematic and circular – at worst, a hunting scene is classified as mesolithic because it looks mesolithic because it is a hunting scene. Both the Levantine and alpine/Scandinavian rock art have suffered from a long history of studies which have tended to divide the material into what we can recognise as familiar and what we cannot: 'representative' art on the one hand (tools and weapons; individual humans and animals; scenes of fighting, hunting and farming) and 'symbolic' or 'ritual' art on the other (discs, 'worship' scenes, and the squiggles and doodles that make up the great majority of the data). As a result, serious prehistorians have tended to regard the first set of drawings as a source of useful insights into everyday life in prehistoric Europe; but the rest has often been the happy hunting ground of the lunatic fringe of archaeology, peopled by sun worshippers and spacemen. In reality, of course, all the drawings from any particular episode stemmed from the same culture and thought processes, and our interpretations must strive to encompass them all accordingly (Fig. 7). Systematic attempts are just beginning, offering exciting possibilities of yielding important insights into the symbolic linkage and reasoning behind the patterning. Whilst the art systems of course stemmed ultimately from the real world, and are potentially an important source book for subsistence information, in no sense can they be treated thousands of years later as mirror images of everyday life.

Environmental archaeology

The role of the natural sciences in reconstructing ancient environments is one of the most impressive aspects of modern archaeological enquiry. The study embraces a wide range of materials, including fossil pollen, microfauna (rodents, beetles), molluscs, macroflora and sediments (Butzer, 1972); the macrofauna and plant remains discussed later as subsistence data also provide information about prehistoric ecologies.

Pollen analysis has for long been the central pillar of environmental archaeology. The method was developed at the turn of the century, and a series of pollen zones or vegetational phases was first established in Sweden by Lennar van Post in 1916. By the 1930s and 1940s, palaeobotanists had extended and elaborated his scheme with parallel analyses of deep profiles from acidic bogs (the best conditions for pollen preservation) across northern Europe from Sweden to Ireland. Their sequence of pollen zones provided the main chronological framework for dating prehistoric settlement in Europe in the late glacial and earlier Holocene, as well as the primary ecological framework. The stages have been dated now by radiocarbon, and the accepted sequence for northwestern Europe is illustrated here as Table 3. Information is still far better for the parts of Europe where preservation conditions are ideal than for elsewhere, and regional differences in vegetation and in the chronology of vegetational change are only just being established in any detail. Interpretations also vary on the precise climatic implications of the pollen zones: the pollen zones may reflect rates of vegetation colonisation and human impact on vegetation as much as climatic change (Butzer, 1972; Harding, 1982; Lamb, 1966; Simmons and Tooley, 1981).

Although pollen can be transported great distances by wind and water, most of the pollen in a typical core is regarded as reflecting local vegetation, but given factors such as the differential production, dispersal patterns and resistance to decay of different pollen species, the relationship between a pollen core and the surrounding vegetation is by no means straightforward (Tauber, 1965). Nevertheless, impressively detailed reconstructions of small localities have been achieved by careful comparisons of adjacent cores, and such studies are an invaluable aid in subsistence reconstruction (Turner, 1975). One general problem is that areas of good pollen preservation (lowland bogs and upland

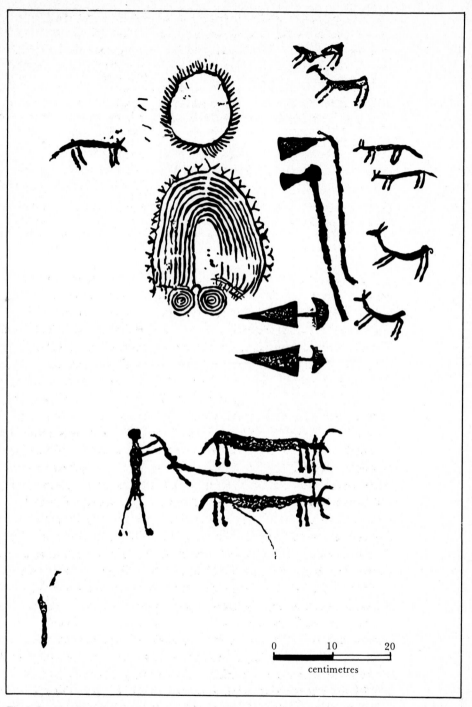

Fig. 7. Rock art from Val Camonica: a typical mixture of motifs, from Bagnolo. (After Anati, 1976: fig. 75)

Table 3 *Late glacial and Holocene/postglacial pollen zones in northwestern Europe; the division between the late glacial and the Holocene is drawn between zones III and IV.*

Zone	Approximate dates b.c.	Name	Dominant vegetation	Inferred climate
VIII	after 1000	Sub-Atlantic	beech	maritime
VII	3300–1000	Sub-Boreal	oak–beech	more continental
VI	5500–3300	Atlantic	oak–elm	warmer and maritime
V	7500–5500	Boreal	hazel–pine–oak	warmer and continental
IV	8300–7500	Pre-Boreal	birch–pine	warm continental
III	9500–8300	Younger Dryas	forest–tundra	arctic
II	10200–9500	Alleröd	birch–pine	temperate-continental
Ic	10500–10200	Older Dryas	tundra	arctic
Ib	11000–10500	Bölling	birch parkland	subarctic
Ia	before 11000	Oldest Dryas	tundra	arctic

(After Butzer, 1972; and Simmons and Tooley, 1981)

peat moors) tend to have been marginal areas of prehistoric settlement: England is typical in the wealth of pollen data from regions such as the Somerset Levels, Dartmoor, the Pennines and the Lake District, whereas the densest settlement was normally in the lowland regions with well-drained soils which are far less conducive to pollen survival.

The principal importance of pollen analysis for this study lies in its potential to record not simply prehistoric environments but also the impact of man on those environments. This phenomenon was first noted by the Danish palaeobotanist Iversen, when he found a sequence of vegetational change in a Sub-Boreal pollen core from Ordrup Møse which seemed highly suggestive of human interference (Iversen, 1941): first, levels of tree pollen fell dramatically, then levels of grass and plantain pollen rose, then tree pollen returned to dominance; he also identified cereal pollen in the phase of open vegetation, as well as charcoal (Fig. 8). Iversen argued that this sequence of events marked the arrival of the first neolithic farmers in Denmark, practising primitive swidden or slash and burn cultivation, who had cleared and burnt a small area of forest for their crops and then moved on after a few years to virgin land, allowing the forest to regenerate. He termed the phenomenon *landnam* or land clearance, and many similar episodes were then recognised by other palaeobotanists elsewhere in Europe. In addition, earlier post-glacial clearances have since been found in the pollen record and have commonly been ascribed to mesolithic foragers burning undergrowth and clearing trees to improve browse and grazing for the game they pursued (Mellars, 1976; Simmons, 1969a and b).

The evidence for both sorts of clearance is discussed in detail in later chapters. It is important to note here simply that the model of neolithic *landnam* or slash and burn farming put forward for large areas of Europe mainly on the basis of the pollen diagrams has now been criticised very effectively by Rowley-Conwy (1981b), using several lines of evidence independent of the pollen record. If his demolition of the *landnam* model (Chapter 9, pp. 234–5) is accepted (as I think it must be), it inevitably throws consider-able doubt on the ability of much palaeobotanical research in the past to distinguish natural clearings and small-scale ecological change from clearance by man, whilst the effect on woodland of animals such as the beaver has probably been underestimated in the past (Coles and Orme, 1983). The next decade should see a very welcome continuation of the reevaluation of the pollen record and the whole question of exactly how it reflects human behaviour. Certainly there has been growing concern amongst many archaeologists in the last decade that fresh pollen data were simply being interpreted within the terms of, and then used to bolster up, a model of prehistoric subsistence established forty years ago and long overdue for a drastic overhaul.

Like pollen, sediments and soils can provide both general information about past climates and environments, and specific information about human activities. Geomorphological and pedological studies have provided the primary data for the identification of glacial and periglacial phenomena, river and lake development, sea level fluctuations and so on. Apart from surface remains, most archaeological materials are found in contexts where environmental reconstruction must be an integral part of their study, such as alluvial, aeolian, lacustrine, slope and coastal sediments, or caves. In addition, physical and chemical studies of palaeosols associated with archaeological remains may give important insights into past human activities, including the intensity of cultivation and the impact of agriculture on soil structure and chemistry (Ralph, 1982). Faunas contained in palaeosols are further indicators of past environments: different species of large mammals, small mammals, birds, insects and molluscs prefer different environments today, and, assuming that preferences have not changed, fossil faunas should reflect the same range of ecological diversity as today. As with pollen, studies of all these classes of data have to deal with considerable problems in sampling, analysis and interpretation – the habitat preferences of some species have not after all remained con-

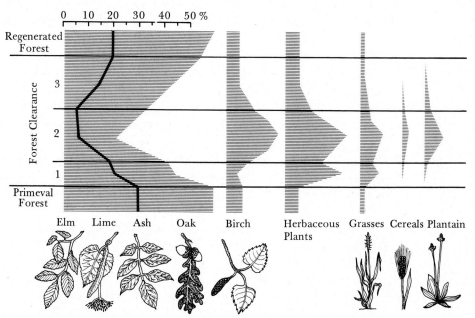

Fig. 8. Iversen's *landnam* model at Ordrup Møse: forest clearance denoted by a fall in tree pollen, a rise in grass pollen, and the appearance of cereals and weeds of cultivation, with the forest regenerating some years later. (Originally published by Iversen in 1941, but this version is after Coles, 1970: fig. 24)

stant, some species are much more tolerant of environmental, change than others, and most faunal samples are strongly biased by complex taphonomic processes. Many pioneering studies made without the present realisation of these complexities offered statements about environmental changes and the clearance activities of man in prehistoric Europe parallel to those based on pollen, often at a regional scale, which can now be seen to be unwarranted. However, all these classes of data together constitute a powerful body of evidence for palaeoenvironmental reconstruction, including the effect of man on the landscape, and environmental archaeology makes a major contribution to the models of prehistoric farming described in the later chapters.

Food refuse – animal bones and plant remains
After stone tools and pottery, animal bones are probably the most common item recovered from excavations of prehistoric sites. Complete skeletons or articulated limbs are found occasionally: they are usually regarded either as grave offerings of some sort (in funerary monuments) or (on domestic sites) as the remains of casualty animals discarded because they were not required for eating. The most common finds on domestic sites, however, are broken bones or very small splinters of bone, which are generally regarded as butchery waste.

Faunal studies in archaeology (archaeozoology) began in the last century with the pioneering studies of the animal bones from French palaeolithic caves, Danish mesolithic 'kitchen middens', and alpine lake villages. However, such detailed studies remained very much the exception rather than the rule until the last two or three decades, and earlier excavations all too frequently involved either haphazard or minimal collection of animal bones. Moreover, early studies were mainly by zoologists or veterinary surgeons, and much of their interest inevitably lay in the contribution of the animal bones they studied to the history of the modern species which were their primary concern. Even today, many faunal reports still consist of small specialist zoological appendices tucked away at the back of excavation reports, little more than a 'shopping list' of species identified and more or less completely divorced from the rest of the archaeology. At best, however, the study of animal bones from archaeological sites can provide an enormous contribution to knowledge not simply of animal development but also, more critically, of the people who exploited those animals. Faunal data therefore form an essential source for the study of prehistoric farming.

Six principal areas of investigation can be defined in modern faunal studies: (1) species identification; (2) species relative importance (whether according to numbers of identifiable fragments, minimum numbers of individuals, bone weights, or meat weights); (3) the age structure of the different species; (4) the size of the animals (the principal means of establishing sex divisions with fragmented archaeological material); (5) evidence for disease and pathological disorders; and (6) the anatomical composition of the different species samples, and the butchery and fragmentation patterns indicated by this. There are major problems inherent in each of these areas of analysis, each with a rapidly growing literature (e.g. Casteel, 1977; von den Driesch, 1976; Grayson, 1978, 1979; Silver, 1969; Wilson *et al.*, 1982).

Most faunal samples from neolithic, bronze age and iron age sites in Europe are dominated by three main domestic species: cattle, pig, and 'sheep/goat' (or caprovine or ovicaprid) – the latter often having to be treated as one species because of the difficulty of identifying many small fragments as belonging definitely to either sheep or goat (Boessneck, 1969a). It has normally been assumed that the relative frequency of the different species identified in a sample, and the age and sex groups found within each species population, can be taken as a reasonably clear guide to the relative importance and role of each species in the subsistence economy (Payne, 1972b, 1973). Thus a primitive dairy economy might be reflected in a faunal sample dominated by adult females, whereas meat production would concentrate on the fattening of animals (surplus males especially) for slaughter at a relatively early age, whilst a specialised wool economy would maintain castrated sheep (wethers) as well as ewes to maturity to provide as many fleeces as possible (Fig. 9). In reality differences are rarely as clear cut (Maltby, 1981): whilst ageing techniques are problematic enough, sexing is rarely possible for most archaeological specimens; there are interpretational problems, such as the current debate about whether or not a peak of very young deaths (as well as one of older animals) is evidence for a dairy system in which calves or lambs were removed to make their mothers' milk available for human consumption (Legge, 1981b); and in any case really specialised breeding goals tend to occur only in modern market economies, and most prehistoric farming (like most historical farming in Europe) was far less specialised (Chapter 2).

The major development in archaeozoology in recent years has been the realisation of the remoteness of the relationship between the archaeological faunal sample and the behavioural system from which it has derived (Behrensmeyer and Hill, 1979; Binford, 1981; Schiffer, 1972): a daunting series of natural and cultural processes transforms the animals exploited by a prehistoric community into the collection of bones in the laboratory (Fig. 10). First was the killing policy of the human community, selecting age and sex groups from the total population, and killing them off-site or on-site. Second, the bones would normally have been subjected to different butchery systems depending on different priorities: basic jointings, stripping meat off the bone for drying, smashing bones for marrow extraction, selecting particular bones for tool manufacture. Third, the manner of burial would have had a drastic effect on bone survival – for example, bones buried rapidly in rubbish pits would be in a far better state of preservation than those which were left lying around a site to be attacked by scavengers and the weather. Fourth, the different parts of a faunal sample would also be affected differentially by the soil environment from the time of burial to the time of excavation, with the less robust bones (those of immature animals especially) and less robust parts of bones being most vulnerable to adverse soil conditions. Fifth, an excavation procedure not involving dry or wet sieving techniques can cause huge biases in favour of the large bones of the larger animals like cow and horse and against the smaller animals such as dog, sheep and pig, and make a nonsense of the elaborate analytical procedures then applied to the material recovered (Payne, 1972a; Table 4). Finally, it is essential that a sampling strategy is used which is appropriate to the complexity of the site, to ensure that groups of material are collected from the different parts of a site which are likely to be representative of the range of activities which took place (Gamble, 1978; Meadow, 1975).

Although taphonomic studies relevant to the period discussed in this book are still very rare (Halstead *et al.*, 1978; Mounteney, 1981; Noe-Nygaard, 1977), it is quite clear that many of our assumptions about the direct relationship between faunal material and economic behaviour in prehistoric Europe have been simplistic, and that some of the

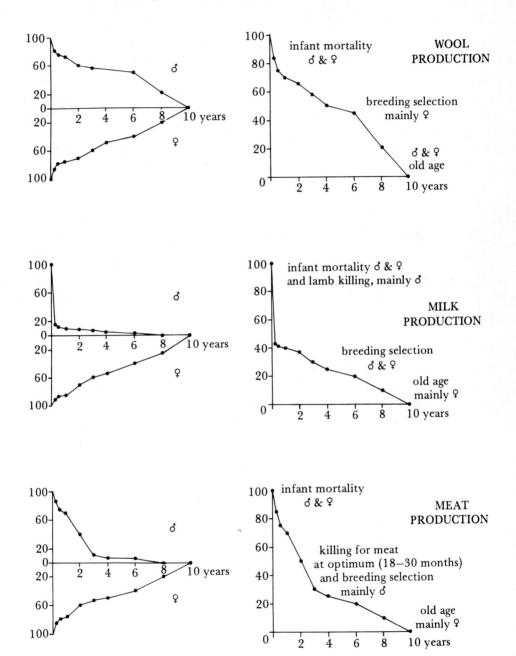

Fig. 9. Models of animal husbandry: possible kill-off patterns according to different herding strategies. (After Payne, 1973)

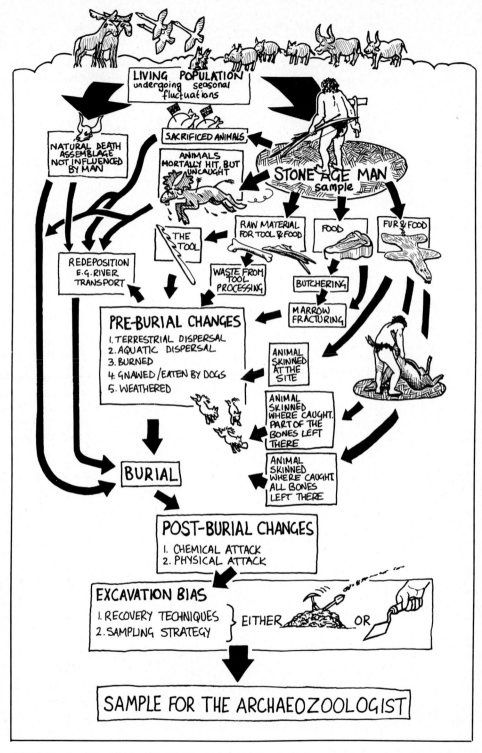

Fig. 10. The formation of the archaeological record: animal bones, from the living animals to the faunal laboratory. (By kind permission of Nana Noe-Nygaard)

Table 4 *A comparison between animal bones collected by pick and shovel excavation at a Greek prehistoric site, and those found later by sieving the discarded soil: trench recovery was efficient only for the larger animals and larger bones.*

	Cow		Pig		Sheep/Goat	
	Recovered in trench	Missed in trench, recovered in sieves	Recovered in trench	Missed in trench, recovered in sieves	Recovered in trench	Missed in trench, recovered in sieves
Single teeth	6	10	1	41	1	128
Mandible and skull fragments with teeth	2	2	5	10	1	6
Long bones and metapodia	12	7	5	21	13	73
Phalanges, carpals and tarsals	9	13	1	35	0	111

(After Payne, 1972a: 59, Table 5)

models of stock-keeping proposed in recent years are going to suffer accordingly. However, this does not mean that archaeozoologists need adopt a counsel of despair: on the contrary, the very fact that the natural and cultural factors causing bone fragmentation are being defined with better precision means that, as we understand the long journey from animal to bone sample with increasing clarity, so we can make the return journey with increasing confidence (Fig. 10).

Archaeobotany, the study of plant remains from archaeological sites, has developed along very similar lines to archaeozoology. Pioneering work began in the mid-nineteenth century with Oswald Heer's study of the plant remains from Swiss lake villages (Keller, 1878), but his work was not matched or bettered until the mid-twentieth century, with Helbaek's classic studies of prehistoric crops from Britain and Denmark (Helbaek, 1952a, 1952b, 1952c, 1954). Even more than in the case of animal bones, the excavation of plant remains has been very haphazard until the last decade or so, with most botanical material deriving either from waterlogged contexts (such as the alpine lake villages, or, most notably, Tollund man's stomach), or from accidental discoveries of large collections of carbonised seeds in ovens, hearths, storage vessels and storage pits, with additional material found as impressions in pottery and daub. The development of froth flotation machines has transformed the data base, enabling archaeologists to search systematically for carbonised plant remains from all parts of their excavation, by bulk washing the soil (H. N. Jarman *et al.*, 1972).

Early research was based on the same sort of assumption that had characterised archaeozoology – that there was a more or less direct relationship between the archaeological material from a site and the subsistence system practised by its occupants: thus if wheat was twice as common as barley in the botanical sample, there had probably been two fields or crops of wheat to every one of barley. As with animal bones, however, the relationship between modern sample and ancient behaviour is nowhere

Table 5 *Variations in sample composition (above) and grain size (below) in plant remains from different contexts at Chevdar, a neolithic settlement in Bulgaria.*

	Percentage of total sample								Total no. of seeds in sample
	Einkorn	Emmer	Bread wheat	Barley	(Cereals)	Legumes	Fruit	Others	
(a) Floors	4.4	30.9	–	13.2	(48.5)	38.5	0.8	12.5	136
	5.9	29.9	2.6	34.2	(72.5)	12.8	0.9	13.7	117
	1.3	33.9	0.4	40.6	(76.3)	11.6	–	12.1	224
	0.9	18.8	–	25.2	(44.9)	15.6	29.4	10.1	218
(b) Ovens	1.2	94.3	3.1	0.4	(99.0)	0.4	–	0.8	1000
	2.1	90.7	2.9	2.6	(98.3)	–	–	1.7	1000
	1.4	84.6	1.8	6.6	(94.4)	0.7	1.4	3.5	147
	0.7	7.2	0.8	88.6	(97.3)	0.2	0.6	1.9	1109

	Length mm		Breadth mm		Thickness mm		Volume mm^3	
	$\bar{x}$	s^2	$\bar{x}$	s^2	$\bar{x}$	s^2	$\bar{x}$	Number
(a) Floors								
Emmer	5.21	0.49	2.59	0.31	2.32	0.19	31.05	60
Einkorn	5.02	–	1.90	–	2.42	–	23.09	13
Barley	4.79	0.50	2.71	0.49	1.91	0.27	24.51	25
(b) Ovens								
Emmer	5.85	0.53	2.88	0.35	2.79	0.31	47.04	66
Einkorn	5.65	–	2.18	–	2.75	–	34.40	9
Barley	6.13	0.26	3.07	0.35	2.30	0.38	43.24	18

(After Dennell, 1972: 153, Tables 1 and 3; $\bar{x}$ = mean size; s^2 = standard deviation)

near as simple. Dennell's analysis of the plant remains from neolithic settlements in Bulgaria demonstrated that the composition of the samples varied considerably according to the contexts from which they derived: for example, samples from ovens and hearths consisted almost entirely of cereals, whereas those from floors and middens contained mixtures of cereals, legumes and weed seeds, and average sizes of grains from different contexts also varied (Dennell, 1972; Table 5).

Dennell argued in this and ensuing papers (1974a, 1974b, 1976a) that the variation in the samples was the result of crop processing activities; the details are described in Chapter 4, but the main implications for future research were that, first, plant remains would have to be analysed in terms of the context from which they came, and that, second, they would have to be studied primarily for information about the processes they had undergone on the site before archaeobotanists could expect to draw insights into the crop systems off the site. Methodology has developed considerably since Dennell's original impetus and has inevitably shown many more problems in interpretation: context identification is rarely as straightforward as in his research, mixing of different crop products commonly presents major problems, and ethnoarchaeological work has also demonstrated far more complex relationships between crop processing and crop residues than originally envisaged (Hillman, 1973, 1981; Hubbard, 1976; G. Jones,

1981). Sampling procedures both in the field and in the laboratory have become much more refined (Fasham and Monk, 1978; van der Veen and Fieller, 1982). However, as in the case of archaeozoology, the increased awareness of the complexity of the process by which growing crops became archaeological residues is enabling archaeobotanists to model prehistoric crop husbandry with increasing confidence (Dennell, 1978; Hillman, 1981; M. Jones, 1981).

One major problem which has yet to be resolved is how to develop an objective yard-stick to enable us to translate the differing abundance of plant remains and animal bones on an archaeological site into the relative importance of crops and animals in the lives of the inhabitants. Studies of the chemistry of human skeletons probably offer one of the most useful avenues for future research (Lambert *et al.*, 1979; Tauber, 1981). Site catchment analysis (discussed below) can be used to indicate the different potential of a site's locality for crops and animals, if we then assume that a bias in the catchment's resources was recognised and exploited by the community (with the dangerous presumption of an optimising strategy). We can also generate models of contrasting exploitation strategies using approaches such as optimal foraging theory (Bettinger, 1980). Our failure to resolve this problem adequately for the farming communities of later prehistory is a serious deficiency in subsistence archaeology.

Site location studies
To be successful, any subsistence system has to be adapted to the constraints and opportunities of the environment in which it is practised, and so a proper interpretation of faunal and botanical material must take account of the environment surrounding the archaeological site at the time of its occupation. Studies of the general environmental setting of a site or group of sites have a long history in archaeology, typified by Fox's classic study of the *Personality of Britain* (1932). More recently, techniques of regional analysis borrowed from modern geography have also proved successful in revealing spatial patterning in archaeological sites and sometimes also hierarchical patterning (Hodder and Orton, 1976), often with important implications for agricultural organisation.

However, the zonal or regional approach for detailed subsistence reconstruction has the major limitation that the immediate environment of an ancient settlement, critical for its location, may well be atypical of the regional environment. Hence 'site catchment analysis' was proposed by Vita-Finzi and Higgs (1970; and Higgs and Vita-Finzi, 1972) as a technique to delimit the exploitation territory of an archaeological site – the area habitually used by the inhabitants for their subsistence activities. From ethnographic data about modern hunter-gatherers and subsistence farmers, they suggested that a radius of ten kilometres (or, as a better guide, a two-hour walking limit) ought to define the area normally exploited from a hunter-gatherer site, and a five kilometre radius (or one-hour walking limit) that of an agricultural community. For the latter, Chisholm's analysis of modern peasant economies indicated that the most time-consuming and labour-intensive activities of a simple farming system usually took place much closer to home, within a kilometre of the farm or village, whereas less demanding activities such as grazing the stock could take place further afield (Chisholm, 1968).

Site catchment analysis was widely applied during the 1970s by Higgs' research team working on the early history of agriculture. Interpretation of a catchment clearly depended on detailed geomorphological fieldwork to determine the nature of any major landscape changes since the time of the occupation of the site; the best site catchment studies were based on such work (e.g. Dennell and Webley, 1975), but others could be fairly criticised for its absence. A further justifiable criticism was that the more ingenuous attempts at subsistence reconstruction using only this method tended to be self-fulfilling prophecies: the subsistence status was assumed, the appropriate catchment investigated, and the inevitable conclusion drawn about the subsistence behaviour of the inhabitants. However, if catchment analysis is applied to sites with good excavated data for subsistence and contemporary ecology, it is an invaluable tool for subsistence reconstruction, providing an essential context for the interpretation of the food refuse from an archaeological site. Examples of such work make a fundamental contribution to this book.

Many prehistorians have tended to regard not only site catchment analysis but also archaeozoology and archaeobotany as severely restricted in their relevance to late prehistoric archaeology. In this view, all three approaches were developed in the first instance to study neolithic and pre-neolithic societies, which could be assumed to be economically self-sufficient, but cannot cope with periods of social and economic complexity. In fact, the anthropological record demonstrates that virtually all primitive societies share in a network of social and economic relationships with their neighbours, which affects their subsistence behaviour to a greater or lesser extent, and the same was certainly true of prehistoric Europe (Earle and Ericson, 1977; Ericson and Earle, 1982). Moreover, whilst it is undoubtedly true that early work in all three areas of subsistence archaeology made assumptions that can now be seen to be optimistic or unwarranted, current research indicates that subsistence studies potentially can make an enormous contribution to the study of economic complexity.

At the level of the individual site, an integrated study of settlement refuse, comparing the disposal patterns for artifacts, animal bones and plant remains, can provide critical information on social differentiation and economic behaviour (Clarke, 1972, described in Chapter 8, p. 220; Halstead *et al.*, 1978). At a regional scale, subsistence data can reveal a wealth of information about production and consumption differences: in the case of iron age Wessex, for example, differences between the types of refuse at different kinds of settlements have indicated that some communities were primarily involved in the production of foodstuffs and others in their storage, redistribution and trade (Chapter 8, p. 219). In assessing land use potential around major nucleated settlements in late prehistoric Europe, site catchment analysis has clearly to take account of a range of factors including transport capabilities, defence, economic goals, access to trade routes and so on; but if the catchment study is integrated sensibly with data on the size of the population and the activities practised at the site, it remains a very useful aid to economic analysis. Bintliff (1977a), for example, found that some Mycenaean palaces had probably been sustained by their surrounding land, whereas others were only administrative centres in good strategic positions but with limited access to arable land

(Chapter 3, p. 78). Catchment studies also made a useful contribution to the analysis of town development on bronze age Melos (Renfrew and Wagstaff, 1982). A recent study of the land cultivated from three cities in the Middle East (one Hellenistic, two Islamic) found that the sherd scatters created by ancient manuring were densest between 1.5 and 2.5 kilometres from the sites, and died out between three and six kilometres from them, data which compared very favourably with Chisholm's analysis of land use around present-day agro-villages, and which led the researcher to conclude that 'the Vita-Finzi/Higgs site catchment techniques would produce acceptable data on land use within the three catchments studied' (T. J. Wilkinson, 1982: 331).

Potentially at least, therefore, the study of prehistoric farming can draw on an impressive range of techniques, and subsistence studies in general can claim to be one of the most exciting and fast developing aspects of prehistoric archaeology. In attempting to survey the development of prehistoric farming in the whole of Europe, the present study inevitably has to make use of a patchwork of data drawn from countries differing enormously in traditions of archaeological fieldwork and analysis, as well as in their archaeological remains. Of course effective models of prehistoric farming can be built only when modern analyses of subsistence data from well-excavated sites, and regional studies of such sites, are abundant throughout Europe. Yet, as I shall be arguing throughout this book, what is most striking about the evidence currently available is that it is not just a ragbag collection of facts and figures: already, coherent trends in the development of prehistoric farming can be discerned from region to region in Europe, and we are beginning to understand some of the underlying reasons for those trends, even if the more complex processes undoubtedly still elude us (Chapter 10).

2

Prehistoric farming in Europe: resources and constraints

The beginnings of modern industrial farming can be found in the eighteenth century, when major innovations took place in crop systems, animal breeding and technology, in response to the growing food requirements of the emergent industrial cities (Chambers and Mingay, 1966; Ernle, 1936; Trow-Smith, 1951). The process of intensification has been constantly accelerating since then, and the most dramatic transformations have taken place in the postwar period, in the era of cheap energy. Much European farming today is amongst the most intensive and efficient in the world, with extremely high yields and extremely low labour requirements (Grigg, 1976). Crop cultivation and animal husbandry have both become highly specialised, with large areas being given over to one or other where mixed farming formerly prevailed, and with these two types of farming further dividing into specialist systems growing standardised products for particular markets. Crop agriculture has been transformed by modern cereal strains, chemical fertilisers and pesticides, drainage technology, ever more powerful cultivation machinery and so on, to give constant high yields on an increasingly wide range of soils. Similarly there has been a veritable revolution in modern meat production (Fig. 11), with the use of elaborate housing systems, preventive drug programmes, improved green foods and fodder, and of course carefully balanced concentrated foods, resulting in dramatically more efficient rates of converting food into body growth than seemed possible even a few decades ago: 'we can look on these animals – pork and bacon pigs, veal calves, beef cattle, fat lambs and table poultry – as machines to produce meat' (Boatfield, 1980a: 90).

These colossal changes in farming efficiency seem a normal part of our rural landscape and their results make up the everyday Europeran diet rich in varied vegetable foods, meat protein and dairy produce. Farming before the agricultural revolution, however, was a very different world indeed: it is probably fair to say that prehistoric, Roman and medieval farmers would have had far more in common with each other in terms of their daily lives and the problems they faced than any of them would have had with the post-medieval farmer. The animals and crops available for husbandry in prehistoric Europe are considered in turn below, to emphasise the enormous gulf separating most of them from their counterparts on the modern farm.

Livestock

Cattle (Bos taurus) *(Fig. 12)*
Most modern cattle in the world are descended from the wild aurochs *Bos primigenius*,

Fig. 11. Problems of modern intensive stock-keeping, with high stocking rates on enclosed land: 'worm problems you never knew you had', from a Systamex advertisement in *Farmers Weekly* 1981. (1. *Trichostrongylus*; 2. *Cooperia*; 3. *Ostertagia*; 4. inhibited *Ostertagia* larvae; 5. *Dictyocaulus* (lungworm); 6. *Moniezia*; 7. *Nematodirus* (roundworms); 8. *Haemonchus*.

which was widespread over most of the northern hemisphere except north America in the late Pleistocene. It was a browsing and grazing ruminant, predominantly adapted to forest but also able to flourish in open scrub (Clutton-Brock, 1981: 63).

It has often been argued that cattle grew smaller under domestication, for cattle bones from early postglacial contexts in Europe and the Near East are as large as those of the late Pleistocene, whereas most cattle bones from neolithic and later prehistoric settlements were considerably smaller (Degerbøl, 1963). However, the primary reason for diminution was probably ecological – in general the glacial climate had favoured large body size in cattle (as in many other species), whereas the ameliorating climate of the Postglacial favoured smaller animals (Barker, 1976d; M. R. Jarman, 1969). At the same time human control could well have affected cattle size, as a result of restricted grazing and poor winter feed (rather than, as sometimes suggested, from the deliberate selection of smaller, more easily controllable, animals), and certainly by Sub-Boreal times in northern Europe there seems to have been a clear dichotomy between the very large (wild) *Bos primigenius* and the much smaller (domestic) *Bos taurus* (Smith *et al.*, 1981), as well as distinct differences in skull shape (Grigson, 1978). Domestic cattle in prehistoric Europe generally exhibit marked sexual dimorphism (bulls being large, cows small, and bullocks or castrates intermediate in size), a feature that has enabled archaeozoologists to develop some quite detailed models of husbandry (Higham, 1967a; Higham and Message, 1969; Legge, 1981a).

It is clear from both historical and archaeological evidence that cattle in Roman and medieval Europe were normally extremely small, much like the diminutive Dexter breed today. At Hamwih (Saxon Southampton), the average withers height was

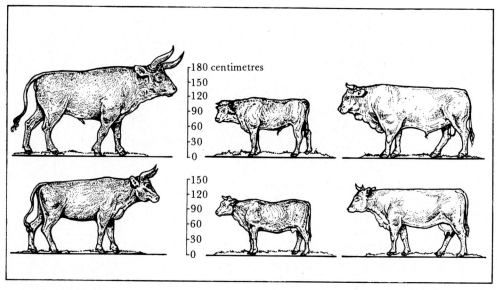

Fig. 12. Cattle in antiquity: sizes of the wild aurochs *Bos primigenius* (left) (bulls above, cows below) compared with those of iron age cattle from the Manching oppidum in southern Germany (centre) and modern European cattle (right). (After Boessneck *et al.*, 1971)

1.16 metres (Bourdillon, 1982), Roman and medieval cattle at Exeter were much the same (Maltby, 1979), and similar measurements are indicated by many other faunal samples of both periods; the average withers height of the modern dairy cow is *c.* 1.40 metres. Prehistoric cattle from neolithic, bronze age and iron age sites seem generally to have been as small (Fig. 12). The comparison with modern breeds is extraordinary: the average weight of mature cattle in the early eighteenth century has been estimated at *c.* 250 kg and *c.* 325 kg by about 1800 (Slicher Van Bath, 1963: 283–4), whereas bullocks today can be grown to 450 kg in one year and to 700 kg in two years (Boatfield, 1980a: 29–30). In Roman and medieval times there seem to have been distinct types of cattle in different parts of Europe, some of which could well be the ancestral stock of modern breeds – for example, the great white cattle bred in central Italy today are mentioned by Roman writers, and the small alpine cattle described by Pliny sound very like the brown cattle of modern Switzerland (White, 1970: 276); but breeds in the modern sense (a carefully selected group of animals with a uniform appearance that is inheritable) are essentially a feature of post-medieval husbandry.

Cattle can provide a remarkable range of products: milk, butter, cheese, cream, traction power and manure from the live animal and, from the carcass, meat and marrow for eating, fat for tallow, hooves for boiling down into gelatine and glue, and horns, bone and hide for tools and clothing. Today in much of Europe cattle husbandry divides into intensive dairy and beef systems, with specialised breeds developed for one or other purpose, but this is very much a recent phenomenon: in the case of the dairy cow, for example, the national average milk yield in Britain in 1945 (about 1200 litres a year) was only a little higher than average yields at the end of the eighteenth century, whereas good dairy cows today give some 3000 litres of milk in their annual lactation (Grigg, 1976: 200; Slicher Van Bath, 1963: 284; Trow-Smith, 1951: 215). Traction and manure were the primary products needed by most medieval and Roman farmers from their cattle, and beef and milk were luxuries. In the writings of the Roman agronomists, cattle were valued for their traction, beef was clearly a rarity, and to Pliny, for example, the drinking of cow's milk was regarded as very unusual (White, 1970: 277). Cattle husbandry in medieval Italy was very similar (P. Jones, 1966: 381–2). The principal dairy animals in Roman and medieval times, in the Mediterranean in particular, have always been the sheep and goat, and their milk was normally for cheese rather than for drinking fresh. In temperate Europe, too, cattle were few in number relative to the smaller stock, and were primarily kept as working animals (Slicher Van Bath, 1963: 67); a small quantity of milk would often have been available for the farmer and his family from a house cow, but the specialised dairy cow capable of producing milk far in excess of the natural requirements of the calf is the product of modern farming.

The principal reason for the very different role of cattle in Roman and medieval farming compared with today was the lack of good quality fodder: without it, the maintenance of cattle demanded considerable effort and sacrifice for what the modern farmer would regard as miniscule returns. However, rather than the meagre supply of meat and milk, it was the ability of the animal to work the land with its muscle and fertilise it with its dung that made it so often the cornerstone of European farming before the agricultural revolution. (The critical relationship between fodder and manure is discussed later in the chapter.) It was normally for the same reason that cattle were often a key resource for prehistoric farmers too.

Dog *(*Canis familiaris*)*

It is generally agreed that the wolf *(Canis lupus)* is the primary ancestor of the domestic dog. The criteria proposed for recognising the domestication process have included size diminution and morphological changes such as tooth crowding; on the basis of these, early domestic dogs have been identified in several parts of the world from archaeological contexts dating either to the end of the last glaciation or more commonly to the opening millennia of the Postglacial. It is quite likely, however, that wolves were tamed by many hunting peoples even earlier, given the rather similar social structures and behaviour patterns evident in the two groups of predators, and the fact that man and wolf would often have been competing for the same prey (Clutton-Brock, 1981: 34–8). Remains of dogs are present in the faunal samples from most neolithic, bronze age and iron age settlements in Europe, but by and large the bones have not been butchered into small pieces like those of cattle, pig and sheep/goat, and hence it seems likely that, although dogs were presumably eaten in times of necessity, they were not normally kept for their meat. We assume that, as today, the dog was valued by these societies primarily for its ability to hunt, herd and guard. It is of course very difficult to prove any of these activities with archaeological data, but dogs can be identified in close association with man in hunting and herding scenes in the Levantine and alpine/Scandinavian art systems. Although distinct types of dog can be recognised in the archaeological record of Roman and medieval Europe (Bökönyi, 1974; Harcourt, 1974; Maltby, 1979), the great range of highly specialised breeds today – as in the case of cattle – is a comparatively recent phenomenon. In prehistoric times the characteristic dog 'was in fact "just dog", a primitive and unspecialised animal' (Clark, 1952: 122).

The one dog that seems an essential part of modern farming in northern Europe in general and in Britain in particular is the sheepdog: breeds like the Border Collie have been developed for their remarkable skills in gathering and controlling the hill flock. Yet the kind of close working relationship between shepherd and sheepdog on these farms today was probably very much the exception rather than the rule in prehistory. Even today, this tradition of the working sheepdog is restricted to particular regions of Europe where the flock grazes in enclosed fields or loose on hill land: in the Mediterranean countries, where flocks are normally taken out to graze daily from stalls or enclosures and are under the eye of the shepherd all day, the primary duty of the dog has been to guard the flock (traditionally against wolves). The Mediterranean shepherd often controls his flock by the simple expedient of throwing stones at the stragglers and strays, while the dog looks on.

Horse *(*Equus caballus*) and donkey (*Equus asinus*)*

Large herds of the wild horse *(Equus ferus* or *Equus caballus ferus)* roamed the open plains of central and northern Europe in the late Pleistocene. Horses were also present in the Mediterranean region at that time, but the main equid was the steppe ass or steppe horse *Equus hydruntinus*, an animal about the size of a modern ass or zebra. Neither the true horse nor the steppe horse was adapted to the forests which spread across Europe in the early Holocene. *Equus hydruntinus* died out in most of southern Europe soon after the end of the last glaciation, although small herds may well have survived in isolated pockets of grassland for several millennia. The species has occasionally been identified in neolithic faunas. The horse was luckier: it could not tolerate the closed forests of temperate Europe, but was able to survive outside Europe on the vast steppes which spread eastwards across the Eurasian continent from the Ukraine to Mongolia. (The wild horse of the Mongolian steppes, *Equus ferus przewalskii*, is often regarded as a relic of these herds.)

In the Ukraine the animal remained an important food resource for the postglacial foraging population. By the fourth millennium b.c., a pastoral economy had developed in this region, the faunal record includes high frequencies of a small variety of horse, and the material culture includes items interpreted as riding equipment: the domestication of the horse by the steppe people for riding and transport seems clear (Sherratt, 1981: 272). Horse bones reappear in the European faunal record in the later third millennium b.c. Butchery evidence is rare, and the animal was clearly adopted by the peoples of temperate Europe primarily for riding and for pulling carts: harness equipment (bone and antler cheek pieces) is found in eastern Europe by *c.* 2000 b.c., together with clay models of carts with four-spoke wheels (Bona, 1960; Vizdal, 1972). The adoption of the horse coincided in many parts of temperate Europe with the first clear evidence for the emergence of elites, and it is presumed that – to begin with at least – the animal was in their service alone. The horse became increasingly widespread in late prehistoric Europe (especially as a key factor in aristocratic warfare), but did not contribute significantly to farming technology – the cow or ox was invariably the primary traction animal.

The early domestication of the donkey is obscure. The wild ass was indigenous to north Africa from Algeria to Sinai, and pictographic evidence suggests that the donkey was being used as a pack animal in Egypt and the Levant by at least 4000 B.C. (Sherratt, 1983). It is documented in the Aegean faunal record by the mid-third millennium b.c. (Gejvall, 1969) – as in temperate Europe, at a time of major social and economic change (Chapter 3). The date of its adoption by the rest of southern Europe is uncertain, but was probably not very much later. By the classical period in the Mediterranean the donkey and the mule (the offspring of a male donkey with a female horse) were the principal pack animals for long-distance transport, and (as still seen today occasionally) were also used to plough very light soils (White, 1970: 299–300).

Pig (Sus scrofa) *(Fig. 13)*
Modern domestic pigs are descended from the wild boar, a remarkably successful animal: some twenty-five sub-species have been recognised, adapted to a wide range of environments across the Eurasian continent from the Atlantic to the Pacific and from Siberia to New Guinea (Clutton-Brock, 1981: 71). Pigs were native to both Europe and the Near East, and the domestic pigs of prehistoric Europe are assumed to be descended from either or both populations, depending on the extent to which colonisation or acculturation models, or combinations of both, are preferred to explain the beginnings of farming in Europe. Pigs in both the Near East and Europe diminished in size quite

drastically in the early Holocene but, as in the case of cattle, a straightforward link between size diminution and selection by man for domestication is unlikely.

Although the pig provides only one useful product for man, its carcass, it has two principal advantages over the other farmyard stock: it is a prolific breeder, and a versatile eater. Under modern intensive conditions, with only a few days allowed between weaning one litter and conceiving the next, the sow produces between 2.2 and 2.5 litters a year, an annual production of some twenty-two piglets. Modern piglets are remarkably efficient at converting food into meat: the pork pig attains its killing weight of 70 kg after just twenty weeks, and the bacon pig attains 90 kg at twenty-four weeks. The killing out percentage is also very high – 70%–75%, compared with beef cattle at 50%–60/ and fat lambs at 50% (Boatfield, 1980a). The price paid for the awesome efficiency of modern factory farming is that the animal is extremely expensive to feed and is also very vulnerable to illness, kept in a totally protected (and of course completely artificial) environment of controlled heat and light like a hospital patient.

In Roman and medieval times pig breeding systems were obviously very different from those of today, and productive capacity much less, but the animal was still highly valued for its ability to breed fast and eat cheaply. 'A peasant really has to be exceptionally poor not to be able to gather together the feed for at least one pig' (Delano Smith, 1979: 219–20), and the Roman agronomist Varro commented to his readers 'who of our people cultivates a farm without keeping pigs?' (II.4.3). Farmyard pigs were kept in sties or pens and fed on kitchen scraps for part of the year, being taken out to pannage in the woods when the mast was on the ground, and then finished for slaughter on beans and grain; the average sow probably raised perhaps half a dozen piglets a year (White, 1970: 317–18). The system was much the same in medieval Europe, although two litters

Fig. 13. Pigs in antiquity: urban pigs in sixteenth-century Flanders, from the engraving 'The Fair at Hoboken' by Pieter Breugel the Elder. (Reproduced in Grigson, 1982, and used here with Caroline Grigson's kind permission)

a year were regarded as normal, with seven piglets in each litter (Trow-Smith, 1951: 68). In addition to the sty pigs of Roman and medieval farmers, many swine were also kept half wild in the mountain forests for most of the year, and rounded up as necessary. From both archaeological and documentary evidence it is clear that, in the rough and ready feeding conditions of antiquity, the pigs normally took several times longer than the modern factory animal to reach a reasonable weight for slaughter and even then were likely to provide only 'flat-sided coarse-boned carcasses' (Trow-Smith, 1951: 68). The prehistoric pig was probably much the same, fending for itself around the settlements for much of the year (Fig. 13).

The various techniques of preserving pig meat (by smoking and salting) were all practised in the Roman world. Pig products of all kinds were immensely popular with Romans of all social classes – Pliny mentions fifty recipes in *haute cuisine* (using every conceivable part of the carcass) – and pigs were essential in the diet of the urban poor: in the reign of Aurelian, for example, there was a free issue in Rome each day of some 10,000 kgs of pork – veritable armies of pigs were driven overland from southern Italy or shipped across from Sardinia (Pharr, 1952; White, 1970: 321). According to the classical authors smoking and salting were also known amongst the contemporary Celtic peoples of temperate Europe, but the antiquity of these techniques (such an essential part of European eating habits ever since) is unknown. Presumably lard was another valued product of the pig for prehistoric farmers, as the only major available fat. It is worth remembering that lean bacon is very much a modern taste. Cobbett urged 'make him quite fat by all means. The last bushel, even if he sit as he eat, is the most profitable. If he can walk two hundred yards at a time, he is not well-fatted' (1823: 145). Lean meat, according to Cobbett, was fit only for wasters and drunkards. John Seymour remembers how, in his boyhood, 'bacon was nearly a hundred per cent fat. There was hardly a streak of lean in it . . . It was boiled in great chunks, and every morning the cold chunk of fat was put on the table for breakfast and we ate slices of it with dry bread and a boiled egg, and mustard' (Seymour and Seymour, 1973: 77).

Pigs penned intensively (and not ringed) can be as effective as a rotivator in destroying every weed and churning the soil over, whilst heavily manuring the soil into the bargain. They are strong, inquisitive animals, and the sty pig can be difficult to control when let loose – in northern Europe, electric fencing is commonly used to contain grazing pigs. In Mediterranean peasant farming, however, the pigs are normally allowed to roam unpenned under the eye of a swineherd, grazing the stubble after harvest, and taken to fallow land or woodland for the rest of the year. Presumably prehistoric pig keeping was normally like this, although small structures in late prehistoric settlements in northern Europe are sometimes interpreted as pig sties. Pigs are highly intelligent animals, and those used to free range grazing are normally very biddable. Varro describes how village pigs were trained to follow the swineherd's horn (II.4.17–20), and the same system was used in Balkan villages in living memory, with the pigs scattering to their separate owners when they were brought back to the village each evening. One important result of free range grazing in prehistoric times would have been less danger of a build up of the parasites and worms that are a constant threat to pigs today grazed continually on the same ground.

*Red deer (*Cervus elaphus*)*

Red deer must be included in this survey because they were certainly one of the most common large mammals of the postglacial landscape in Europe, their bones dominate many mesolithic and later faunal samples, and there is a lively debate on the possibility of their being herded rather than hunted at such sites.

The red deer of Europe today vary considerably in size, with the adult weight ranging from under 100 to almost 400 kgs (van den Brink, 1973). By and large the heaviest animals inhabit the forests of southern Europe and the lightest are found in the Scottish mainland and islands. They display a remarkable tolerance for differing vegetation conditions, from closed deciduous woodland to the bleak open moors of the Scottish 'deer forests'. Red deer are social and territorial animals: the sexes are normally separated for much of the year, with the stags in loose groups and the hinds and yearling calves in more formal herds; in the rutting season in the autumn the dominant stags collect harems of hinds in territories which they defend against rivals (Darling, 1937; Lowe, 1969). In regions of differentiated topography such as Scotland, the deer normally move up to higher ground in the summer and return to lower ground before the onset of winter; the seasonal movement to the hills not only allows them access to good summer grazing but also gives them a respite from the warble flies, mosquitoes and such like that infest the lowlands then, as well as breaking the cycle of intestinal parasites.

Red deer was frequently the main food species killed by late palaeolithic hunters in southern Europe, and was invariably the most numerous animal in postglacial faunal samples in most of temperate Europe until the end of the Atlantic period, *c.* 3500 b.c. Red deer was the most common animal in more than 95% of a sample of 165 late palaeolithic and mesolithic faunal assemblages surveyed by M. R. Jarman (1972a). Mortality data taken from red deer mandibles in late palaeolithic contexts in central Italy provided strong evidence for selective culling of the deer (Barker, 1973), and Jarman argued from rather similar evidence that the mesolithic peoples of postglacial Europe probably herded the red deer in some way: 'it seems in no way improbable that mesolithic and neolithic man . . . husbanded his herds of deer in a way not dissimilar to that in which they are now treated in deer parks, or to the way in which neolithic man treated his sheep' (M. R. Jarman, 1972a: 132). In addition to its venison, the red deer was also a particularly valuable source of antler for the manufacture of tools and weapons, and velvet antler today is regarded as one of the most powerful ingredients of traditional medicine in many parts of the world (Clutton-Brock, 1983).

The degree of management of modern red deer in fact varies considerably. In most deer parks, the deer live without interference from man (apart from being fenced in), are given hay and sometimes concentrates in winter, and salt, but are not driven or stalled. More deliberate systems of deer farming are also being practised now for the meat market in several parts of Europe (Blaxter *et al.*, 1974). However, there are considerable problems involved in these enterprises because the deer remain nervous and far more difficult to handle than ordinary stock. Chain-link fences over two metres high are necessary to contain the deer, the hinds and stags must be kept separate for most of the year, and the antlers are frequently sawn off the stags to facilitate handling. At Reedie Hill Farm in Perthshire (Scotland), probably the most intensive and successful commercial deer farm (Fig. 14), on the two occasions each year when bulk handling is necessary the red deer are driven through a succession of paddocks and pens of decreasing size until the animals finally arrive in single file in a darkened handling chamber. If an animal needs to be isolated at any other time, the only feasible technique is to stun it with a dart gun.

Whilst it may be true today that 'it is just not possible to impress upon red deer that they are a part of human society, which is in effect what has been achieved with all the species of true domestic animals' (Clutton-Brock, 1981: 165), it would surely be extremely unwise to conclude in such categorical terms that it must always have been so, and that social and territorial behaviour has been immutable. The animals in the modern deer farms belong to a breeding stock that has only been farmed for about a decade, and it is unknown whether generations or centuries of handling would result in the kind of docility manifested by the normal farmyard animals (Fig. 15). There are occasional references to red deer being used by eccentric aristocrats to pull carriages two or three centuries ago (Whitehead, 1964). As the following chapters will describe, there is overwhelming evidence that red deer played a fundamental role in prehistoric subsistence for many thousands of years, whereas for the past thousand years most red deer have been managed (more or less, and if at all) simply to provide a suitable quarry for the sport of kings, with day to day contact kept to a minimum.

Fig. 14. A modern red deer farm: Reediehill Farm, Auchtermuchty, Fife, Scotland. The stags are in the foreground, the hinds are in the paddock to the rear (together with a house cow). Note the size of the fencing. (Photograph: author)

Fig. 15. Tamed red deer: above, red deer hind with keeper, Popielno Biological Station, Poland; below, red deer stag with research scientist, island of Rhum, Scotland. (Photographs: author)

*Sheep (*Ovis aries*) and goat (*Capra hircus*) (Fig. 16)*

The origin of domestic sheep and goats is very obscure. They were certainly being herded in the Near East very early in the Holocene, if not before. The modern ranges of the wild Asiatic mouflon sheep (*Ovis orientalis*) and the wild bezoar goat (*Capra aegagrus*) both extend from Afghanistan across the Iranian plateau to the uplands of the Near East, and hence these two animals have commonly been regarded as the wild ancestral stock of most if not all modern domestic sheep and goats (Clutton-Brock,

Fig. 16. Sheep in antiquity: English longwool sheep, showing the changes in appearance from the medieval to the early modern periods: A. primitive longwool, late medieval/early Tudor; B. 'unimproved' longwool, late seventeenth/early eighteenth centuries; C. 'improved' longwool, post *c.* 1800, such as the Lincoln crossed with the new Leicester. (After Armitage, 1983: fig. 2)

1981). However, there are other races of wild sheep and goats today outside the range of these two, including the European mouflon (*Ovis musimon*) and the ibex goat (*Capra ibex*) in the Mediterranean basin, the urial sheep (*Ovis vignei*) and markhor goat (*Capra falconeri*) in the Hindu Kush and Kashmir, the argali sheep (*Ovis ammon*) in central Asia and the wild sheep of Siberia and north America. The relationship of modern domesticated sheep and goats to any or all of these wild races is problematical. Clearly it is as absurd to regard modern wild sheep and goats as fossilised remnants of pre-domesticated sheep and goats as it is to regard modern hunter-gatherers as relict palaeolithic peoples. The situation is further complicated by the fact that some modern 'wild' populations of sheep and goats may well in fact be feral – animals that have escaped from human control in the distant past. It certainly seems increasingly unlikely, as the investigation of agricultural origins has expanded from the assumed 'hearth of domestication' in the Near East, that the only region where sheep and goat herding developed at the end of the last glaciation or beginning of the Holocene must have been that delimited by the present range (or rather the western edge of the present range) of the Asiatic mouflon and bezoar goat. The wild sheep today is an animal of uplands and mountain foothills, whereas the goat prefers higher, more broken country (Geist, 1971). The ranges of modern domesticated sheep and goats embrace a remarkably wide spectrum of environments, but the sheep remains a selective grazer and the goat a far more versatile browser.

The sheep can provide the farmer with milk, wool and manure during life, as well as meat, bone and sinew after slaughter. Sheep play a far larger role in European agriculture than goats, especially in the temperate regions. Systems of sheep management here vary from hill farming, where the animals fend for themselves for most of the year, to intensive feeding of housed flocks. The primary product today is meat, with wool secondary and milk normally unimportant. As with cattle, modern taste prefers meat that is lean and young, and modern breeding systems are geared to produce lean lambs (27–40 kg liveweight at 3½–4 months old). Systems of sheep production have been much improved this century (and, as always, especially in the last four decades), but intensive feeding and housing systems are the exception rather than the rule, and many more of the traditional methods survive than in the case of cattle and pig breeding (Goodwin, 1979). Sheep are hardy animals, which can if necessary be kept on poor land and fed cheaply: they can be kept outdoors all the year round in temperate Europe, with the grass supplemented by hay in the worst of the winter. Today, of course, feeding regimes are managed carefully, with the ewes fed concentrates at key times in their breeding cycle. As a result, whereas the ewe naturally would give birth to a single lamb, the lowland British farm can expect today a lambing rate over 200% (with each ewe giving birth to twins and raising these successfully), the intermediate farm over 150% and the hill farm perhaps 125%–150‰ (Speedy, 1980). The price paid for such fecundity is that the ewes are very vulnerable to metabolic disorders caused by breeding stress (magnesium and calcium deficiency, and the aptly named 'twin lamb disease', pregnancy toxaemia) and to obstetric problems, and the lambs are vulnerable to further metabolic disorders soon after birth and at the time of rapid growth. Modern shepherding therefore has to include a series of routine injections to combat the metabolic problems, but most of the obstetric problems seem unavoidable penalties of intensification 'due primarily to lack of room (inside the ewe)' (TV Vet, anon., 1980: 108).

In antiquity most of today's obstetric difficulties would probably have been rarities, and most of the metabolic disorders would not have been encountered to such a degree because the flocks were not under the same breeding stress as today. Mineral deficiencies would have been further alleviated by the dispersed systems of grazing practised before enclosure. Regular movement would also have avoided the worst effects of the bacterial and parasitical diseases which affect flocks on enclosed land. Footrot is an ever present danger on wet pasture, for example, but moving the flock off the ground for a couple of weeks effectively kills the bacteria there. Wet pasture is also a haven for the liver fluke, which kills in acute cases: the parasites are carried by the snail *Limnaea trunculata*, which attaches itself to herbage and is eaten by sheep; the parasites then penetrate the intestinal wall and reach the liver, and in due course are excreted in the dung, whence the larvae re-enter the snail to repeat the cycle (Fig. 17). These and similar diseases such as stomach and intestinal worms are variously controlled today by injections and dosing, and careful field management. Many of the diseases were recognised in medieval times, such as the 'rot among sheep' (Thirsk, 1967: 60) and 'the little white snails from which they [the sheep] will sicken and die' (Trow-Smith, 1951: 67). Unenclosed grazing in prehistoric times, as with cattle and

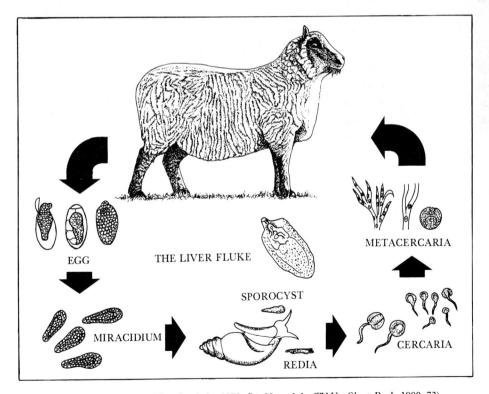

EGG

THE LIVER FLUKE

METACERCARIA

SPOROCYST

MIRACIDIUM

CERCARIA

REDIA

Fig. 17. The liver fluke cycle. (After Goodwin, 1979: fig. 80, and the *TV Vet Sheep Book*, 1980: 72)

pigs, would have effectively forestalled the worst attacks of the parasites which are the bane of enclosed grazing today (Fig. 11).

Whilst medieval shepherds did not encounter the problems of intensive management, it is clear from the documentary record that nutritional problems were severe, fertility correspondingly low, veterinary treatment extremely primitive, winter losses in the mature flock high, and lamb losses also high from sickliness, bad weather and predators. The success rate for lambing was far below 100%, and in general the sheep were slow-maturing and small (Bowden, 1967: 666–7). The faunal record confirms the poor quality and small stature of medieval sheep, and much Roman material is identical (Bourdillon, 1982; Maltby, 1979; O'Connor, 1982). The sheep bones from prehistoric sites in Europe almost invariably resemble those of the Roman and medieval collections much more than those of the domestic breeds today. (They do, however, resemble the small and slender bones of the Soay, an isolated and primitive island breed from the Outer Hebrides in Scotland.) It is assumed that sheep management and breeding success in prehistoric Europe were also much like those of shepherding before the Agricultural Revolution.

In the Mediterranean region the sheep is far better suited than the cow to cope with the heat, sparse water and poor pasture of the high summer, and has always been far easier to keep there than cattle. Moreover, it has normally been valued especially as a dairy animal, for the cheese made from its milk provided one of the few sources of storable protein before the days of refrigeration. In Roman and medieval times most peasant families kept a small flock of sheep as a multi-purpose resource: the surplus milk from the ewes provided cheese and whey, the surplus lambs (normally the wethers or castrated males) were eventually killed for meat, the entire flock provided wool, and of course the sheep were also an invaluable source of manure for the fallow land (P. Jones, 1966; White, 1970). The same policy is still widespread today despite the pressures of the modern market for specialised dairying or lamb production.

In temperate Europe the medieval peasant also kept his flock for the products of the live animal rather than for meat, but in this case wool was normally the first priority. In later medieval times the demand for wool resulted in many farmers keeping flocks of mature wethers as well as ewes for their fleeces, with elderly mutton therefore being the main meat available (Maltby, 1979: 46–9). At the same time, however, heavy use was made of the ewe's milk in temperate regions just as in the Mediterranean: 'the curds, or curdled milk, used for making cheese, and the whey, the sweet part of the milk left over, formed an important part of the peasant's diet' (Slicher Van Bath, 1963: 288). As with flock nutrition, archaeozoology supports the documentary evidence that meat was hardly ever the main reason for keeping sheep in medieval Europe. The faunal record likewise indicates that prehistoric farmers, like medieval farmers, normally kept their sheep as multi-purpose animals, although different priorities can sometimes be discerned in breeding policies.

The outer coat of modern wild sheep is stiff and hairy, covering a short woolly under-coat which grows only in winter and is shed in spring. In the domestic sheep the inner coat has been developed as an all-year-round fleece and the outer coat (the kemps) lost. The presence of woolly as well as hairy sheep can be inferred from the literary and pictorial record of urban Mesopotamia in the third millennium b.c., although the wool was probably plucked rather than shorn. The date at which woolly sheep developed in prehistoric Europe is unclear. In general, microscopic examination of fibres suggests that the wool was available for clothing by the mid-third millennium b.c., for example in the Swiss lake villages (Ryder, 1969, 1981). It may be that wool production spread across Europe at that time as part of a package of secondary products, as Sherratt (1981) has argued, but like dairying and traction, the use of wool may well have been a feature of earlier farming as well: there are very few waterlogged settlements earlier than the Alpine lake villages, so the direct record may be rather misleading, and in any case the undercoat of the hairy sheep was presumably gathered as it fell each spring, or plucked out, long before the development of the woolly sheep.

The goat offers the same range of commodities as the sheep except wool, but its hide makes excellent leather, goatskin can be used for clothing, bags and so on, and its hair is also good for rope manufacture (Thirsk, 1967: 195). Goats are not very numerous in most of temperate Europe today, and tend to be kept on a small scale for specialised dairy markets. In the medieval period their principal value was also for dairying, for kids can be born twice a year and with a good diet the goat can give three or four times as much milk as the sheep. Numbers normally seem to have been small, however: at the time of the Domesday survey, for example, the ratio of sheep to goats around Exeter was 6:1 (Welldon-Finn, 1967); in northern and central Wales c. A.D. 1600 inventories list 1767 sheep but only 29 goats, and 185 goats for the whole of Wales compared with 13,079 sheep (Emery, 1967: 126–9); and in the large faunal sample from Exeter sheep far outnumbered goats in the medieval deposits and there were no goats at all in the post-mediaeval deposits (Maltby, 1979: 42).

In the Mediterranean region, goats have traditionally played a much more important role in the agricultural system than further north, because of their ability to thrive on desiccated scrub vegetation and to produce plentiful milk into the bargain – Vergil's *largi copia lactis* (*Georgics* III.308). The Roman agronomists advised farmers to restrict goats to herds of 50–100 animals because of the difficulties of control and their depredations on vegetation. Many Mediterranean farmers today, however, will keep up to half a dozen goats with their flock of 50–100 sheep not simply for their milk but also because of their ability on the walk to and from the day's feeding area to lead the way for the sheep to follow. This sort of proportion of goats to sheep is suggested by faunal collections I have studied from several Roman and medieval sites in Italy, and from many prehistoric sites in the Mediterranean as well.

Plants

Cereals
Cereals are an extremely efficient plant food because of the amount of energy and protein provided by their large seeds. Unlike animals, they do not move, they have to be harvested rapidly in one season, and the considerable bulk of the crop requires an organised workforce to harvest, transport and process the grain and straw, as well as facilities to store them – all factors favouring sedentism for cereal farmers. The wild

cereals of the Near East are winter grains adapted to a climatic regime with well marked wet and dry seasons, and an annual rainfall over 200 mm; the seeds germinate in the spring rains, ripen rapidly, and disperse the new crop of seeds at maturity. The domesticated cereals have a tough rachis, so that the seeds are retained in the ear until harvested. Other than in this respect, the early cultivation of cereals in the Near East and in Mediterranean Europe was probably very similar to the natural regime of the modern wild cereals. North of the Mediterranean, however, the cereals had to adapt to the very different environments of temperate Europe. Different combinations of crops and different cultivation systems were developed as a result; the rapid expansion of the cereals to become the staple foods for prehistoric people across the length and breadth of Europe must rank as one of the most successful plant colonisations ever.

By far the most important crops grown in prehistoric Europe were the wheats and barleys. Of the two primitive wheats einkorn (*Triticum monococcum*) and emmer (*Triticum dicoccum*), einkorn was mainly grown in the earlier phases of cereal cultivation in southern regions, but emmer was a staple in many regions throughout the prehistoric period. Bread wheat (*Triticum aestivum*) and club wheat (*Triticum compactum*) were present from the outset, but gained in importance over time, particularly as heavier soils were taken into cultivation. Spelt wheat (*Triticum spelta*) tended to replace emmer as the major wheat in the later prehistoric period. Einkorn, emmer and spelt are all bearded wheats, much more difficult to thresh than bread wheat or club wheat. However, these primitive wheats had several advantages over the others (Percival, 1921; Reynolds, 1981). Spelt and einkorn need less nitrogen than modern crops and are very resistant to weed competition. Spelt became popular in northern Europe in late prehistory as cereal farming intensified to include autumn as well as the traditional spring sown crops as a norm – spelt resists fungus and damp, cold weather, and requires only a short growing season, so was ideal for autumn sowing in the northern climate. The importance of emmer lay principally in its ability to tolerate (and indeed thrive in) a wide variety of soil and climatic conditions; it also makes fewer demands on the mineral and chemical properties of the soil than some of the other cereals. Emmer was the traditional bread wheat for the Roman army (Reynolds, 1981: 64). The climatic limit for wheat today extends north as far as northern Scotland, and the southern parts of Norway, Sweden and Finland (Fig. 18). In Britain it can be grown as far west as Wales and Ireland, but the primary zone of wheat cultivation consists of the southern, eastern and midland counties of England. It is assumed that wheat was almost invariably grown for human consumption in prehistoric Europe. Wheat straw can be used for thatching, and for littering livestock, but is never used today for feeding livestock.

The other main cereal crop in prehistoric Europe was barley. Barley divided into two-row and six-row forms, respectively *Hordeum distichum* and *Hordeum vulgare*, both of which could be hulled (with the husks attached to the grains) or naked. The early history of these different types of barley is rather obscure, but by and large the naked and hulled barleys both seem to have been important in the earlier phases of cereal cultivation in Europe, whereas the hulled varieties were increasingly preferred in later phases as threshing technology improved. The naked barleys were easier to process, whereas the tough spikelets of the hulled varieties had to be parched to make them dry and brittle, when they could be crushed easily to release the grains from the husks. The reason for the change to the hulled barleys is therefore difficult to comprehend: one suggestion is that the hulled barleys were better adapted to the wetter climates of later prehistory, another is that this cereal was used increasingly for animal feed (so the grains could be left in the husks). Barley is a shallow-rooted crop and is best suited to light loams (rather than the heavier loams preferred by wheat), but is less tolerant of excessive moisture than wheat. In general it can tolerate a wider range of lighter soils and can ripen in a colder climate than wheat, so can be cultivated much further north (Fig. 18). Six-row barley was the main food crop grown by the crofters of northern Scotland. It is primarily grown now in the drier parts of eastern Ireland and eastern Britain; here it is either grown for animal feed, or (in the best conditions) for malting. Barley straw is also used as winter feed for cattle, and for bedding as it is more absorbent than wheat straw (Boatfield, 1980b: 78–80). There are both autumn-sown and spring-sown varieties of barley today. The former ('winter barley') yields more, but spring varieties are much more common. In prehistoric Europe both wheat and barley were probably (in the main, at least) autumn-sown in the Mediterranean and Balkans, but spring-sown in temperate regions. (This thesis is not universally held, however, and cropping systems are discussed in greater detail in later chapters.)

Millet (*Panicum miliaceum*) is best suited to cultivation in dry, sandy soils. It has a short growing season, and was especially important in central and southern Europe as a crop that could be sown in the spring and would ripen in time for the summer harvest.

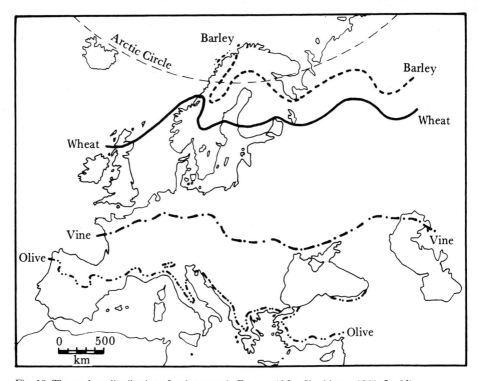

Fig. 18. The modern distribution of major crops in Europe. (After Shackleton, 1964: fig. 12)

In prehistoric Europe it may well have been taken into cultivation first in the Balkans. Oats (*Avena secale*) and rye (*Secale cereale*) are thought to have accompanied wheat and barley into Europe as weeds. They began to be cultivated on any significant scale at the very end of the prehistoric period, and then only in the most northerly regions. Optimum conditions for oats resemble those of wheat, but oats can ripen under wetter conditions and on more acid soils, and so can be grown successfully where wheat cannot thrive – for example, in western Britain and western Ireland. Both grain and straw are normally grown for feeding to stock. Rye is normally restricted to light acid soils, such as the poor glacial soils of Scotland and central Ireland. It is extremely hardy, and can stand cold hard winters better than any other cereal. Rye straw is useless for feeding stock, but can be used for thatching; it is useful particularly as a green crop, sown in the autumn to provide early spring grazing for cattle.

Legumes, fodder crops, pasture and fallow
For healthy growth, plants require three main nutrients in the soil – nitrogen, phosphorus and potassium – as well as moderate amounts of calcium, magnesium and sulphur, and minute quantities of trace elements such as iron, manganese, copper and zinc (Russell, 1961). Most soils normally contain adequate amounts of the minor chemicals and trace elements, but the cereals make great demands on the three main nutrients; without nutrient renewal, continuous cereal growth will rapidly exhaust most soils.

The primary importance of the legumes for the farmer is that these crops take nitrogen from the air and, through the bacteria in their roots, feed both themselves and the soil. Legumes are of two kinds: the pulse crops which are sown annually, such as peas (*Pisum*), beans and vetches (*Faba*) and lupins (*Lupinus*); and the grasses which stand for several seasons, such as lucerns (*Medicago*) and clover (*Trifolium*) (Percival, 1936). Nowadays nitrogen can be replaced in the soil by a chemical dressing, and peas and beans are grown as a highly specialised crop for the freezer market, but traditionally peas and beans have been grown as 'break crops' after cereals to put nitrogen back into the soil, as well as to produce protein-rich grains which could be mixed with barley for animal feed. Peas prefer light soil and warm sunny conditions, whereas beans grow best on the heavier soils used for wheat – indeed, this type of soil in Britain was often known as 'wheat and bean land' (Boatfield, 1980b: 81). Some legumes such as vetches and lupins were traditionally ploughed in as 'green manure' to increase the nitrogen content of the soil, a practice recorded since the Roman period (White, 1970: 190). Pulses were grown in Europe by most prehistoric farmers, and from Dennell's palaeobotanical research in the Balkans (Chapter 4), it seems very likely that they were being grown in rotation with cereals from the outset. The Romans certainly understood the value of alternating cereals with legumes, and from the prehistoric botanical record it is difficult to avoid the conclusion that the value of legumes as a break crop was realised very early in the history of cereal farming.

Many of the pulses grown in Roman and medieval Europe were for animal feed; the same may have been true of prehistoric farming, but the fact that many have been found carbonised in ovens on settlement sites indicates that they were also a normal food for the human population. Three varieties of vetch are mentioned by the Roman agronomists for cattle feed, either grown as separate crops or in combination with barley, oats, and emmer. The Romans also cultivated the herbage crops like lucerne for grazing, or for mowing for hay, but there is little clear evidence for the cultivation of herbage crops in prehistoric Europe. The main forage crops (those grown for their leaves and stems) and root crops grown today include the beets (sugar beet, mangels, fodder beet), brassicas (turnips, swedes, kale, cabbage, rape, mustard), and other vegetables such as potatoes, carrots and parsnips; some of these of course are comparatively recent introductions. Some are now grown as cash crops, others for animal feed, but all of them serve as 'cleaning crops' to clear the ground of weeds in a rotation system. Before the Agricultural Revolution, forage and root crops were important as a source of animal feed, and there are references from the fifteenth century onwards to the cultivation of turnips and other brassicas for green fodder for livestock (Slicher Van Bath, 1963: 179). Columella included rape and turnip on his list of foodstuffs for human consumption, but also commented that these roots were used for cattle feed outside Italy (White, 1970: 191). Suitable roots and vegetables were probably collected for animal feed by prehistoric farmers, but as with the herbage crops there is little evidence to suggest systematic cultivation on any scale, although seeds of turnip, rape and carrot have all been found recently in plant residues from iron age farms in southern England (Lambrick and Robinson, 1979; Parrington, 1978).

Grass is temperate Europe's biggest crop. Grass can be sown today as a catch crop between two other crops, or as a short ley (1–3 years), or as a long ley (4–12 years). Most grassland, however, is permanent pasture, a mixture of grasses and clovers which has grown naturally for a long time, or land sown as a long ley and allowed to remain under grass. A large proportion of Europe's permanent pasture consists of rough grazing in the uplands. There are hundreds of different grasses, and old permanent pasture normally has a rich variety, whereas only half a dozen or so are sown for leys. Leys can greatly improve the fertility and structure of an arable soil (Cooper and Morris, 1973). Re-seeding is mentioned by Columella, but White concludes that the use of leys must have been very restricted in Roman farming (1970: 211–12), and the assumption must be that the same was at least as true of prehistoric Europe, and that pasture was invariably permanent. The grazing preferences of European stock differ markedly: cattle prefer longer grass, for they put their tongue round a clump and crop it off with their teeth; sheep prefer much shorter grass, and can nibble it right down to the ground; pigs are selective in their grazing, avoiding grasses for clover and other plants; horses graze in small patches and leave clumps of grass untouched. All these animals avoid grass where dung of their own kind has been dropped. For these reasons pasture is best managed if it is grazed with different types of livestock (particularly with sheep following cattle). In temperate regions the grass grows fastest in the spring and early summer, when it produces a high yield of good quality leafy material (the 'spring flush'), rests for a time in the summer, and produces another, smaller, surge of growth in the late summer and autumn if it is prevented from flowering and seeding. Pasture must be rested from stock for several weeks for it to recoup sufficiently for cutting as hay or to be re-grazed. The location of many of the prehistoric sites described in the following chapters implies very strongly that prehistoric farmers clearly understood the qualities and constraints of the different kinds of pasture available to them around their settlements and adapted their systems of animal husbandry accordingly.

Silage – in effect preserving grass by a kind of pickling process – is a modern invention, but the cutting of grass for drying as hay is a traditional part of animal husbandry in temperate Europe. Good haymaking is still very difficult even with the aid of modern machinery, which makes the process far quicker and less vulnerable to disastrous changes in the weather. With the traditional technology (and in marginal areas still today), the grass has to be scythed laboriously, turned repeatedly, and then gathered in small cocks or put on wooden tripods or frames to complete the drying process. The Roman agronomists say little of haymaking, and most of their comments refer to temperate regions – fodder crops like the pulses seem to have been more important than hay in the Mediterranean. Clear evidence for haymaking in the form of metal scythes and settings of post-holes suggesting wooden drying racks is in fact known only from late prehistoric contexts. Deliberate hay production is probably of greater antiquity, but before the development of the scythe in the late first millennium b.c., the grass would have had to be cut with a sickle of bronze (available from the late second millennium b.c.) or, prior to that, of flint blades inset in a bone or wooden handle. Given the technology, therefore, it is no surprise that the dumps of fodder found preserved in barns at several alpine lake villages are composed mainly of coarser material such as foliage (Chapter 5). Presumably a wide range of vegetable matter was collected by most prehistoric farmers for overwintering their stock, gathered from woodland, fallow land, marsh and waste ground round the settlements.

These same areas were also important sources of food for the human population. Hunting, fowling and fishing differed considerably in importance from region to region and from period to period, but were always practised to some extent by prehistoric farmers. The gathering of plant food was also an enduring part of prehistoric subsistence, as it has been for European peasants throughout recorded history. Food remains from waterlogged prehistoric villages invariably include a long list of berries, nuts and wild fruits which must have added very welcome variety to the agricultural diet. In addition, there is strong evidence that the seeds or leaves of many plants now considered weeds were collected by prehistoric farmers. Some were probably medicinal, others for use in various crafts (treating leather and wood, dyeing textiles and such like), but most were for food or beverages. At one typical waterlogged settlement in southern Germany, 'of the 193 species . . . , 29 were more or less domesticated, including 17 which have dropped out of cultivation during the comparatively recent past; 22 were weeds and 25 meadow plants; 37 were forest species and 67 water plants; and 13 cannot be readily assigned to any single group' (Clark, 1952: 58). Peasant communities in many parts of Europe have in living memory made various more or less edible flours as substitutes for cereal flour in times of famine from pine bark, acorns, chestnuts, water chestnuts, chess seeds, dried rhizomes of the common reed and bog bean, and several others. It is a common sight in Europe outside the wealthy industrialised countries to see roadside plants being gathered for food. Plants of fallow land and wasteland, and weeds amongst the main crops, such as fat hen (*Chenopodium album*), chess (*Bromus secalinus*), chickweed (*Stellaria media*), ribwort plantain (*Plantago lanceolata*), gold-of-pleasure (*Camelina sativa*), dock and sorrel (*Rumex* sp.), rape (*Brassica* sp.), nettles (*Urtica* sp.), and black bindweed (*Polygonum convulvulus*) were almost certainly collected for food, though few if any would have been cultivated deliberately. A weed is simply a plant in the wrong place at the wrong time, and it is obvious that the hard and fast division in the modern agricultural landscape between domestic and wild, field and wasteland, meant little to our forefathers. Tollund Man's last meal, 'a gruel prepared from barley, linseed, gold-of-pleasure and knotweed, with many different sorts of weeds that grow in ploughed land' (Glob, 1971: 30), was probably not a prisoner's 'half rations' but a typical healthy breakfast for the condemned man.

One other important subsidiary crop which can also be mentioned here is linseed (*Linum usitatissimum*): the plant could be grown for the oil in its seeds, and for the fibre of the stem used in the manufacture of flax for linen. In traditional flax-making, the stalks are 'rippled' through a heavy comb, retted for several days in water, then dried and beaten, with the wooden parts of the stalks beaten out and the fibres prepared for spinning. Identical tools to those used in Europe (for example in Ireland) in recent times for preparing flax have been found in the Swiss lake villages (Clark, 1952: 232–3).

Mediterranean tree crops

The distribution of the olive forms a useful guide to the northern limits of the Mediterranean climate (Fig. 18), although the mountains of the region are too cold for its cultivation. The vine can also be grown in temperate as well as Mediterranean Europe, but is essentially a Mediterranean tree, and the olive and vine together can be regarded as the primary crops of the Mediterranean after cereals. The three traditional staples throughout the Mediterranean zone are bread, wine and olive oil, the last being extremely nutritious and virtually a food in itself.

The major advantage of the olive tree (*Olea europaea*) over cereals in the Mediterranean is its tolerance of steep slopes and rocky terrain. It survives the summer drought not by a very deep root (like the vine), but by an extensive surface system of roots. Today olive cultivation varies from carefully maintained groves on moderate slopes or flat ground with reasonably deep soils, to the rockiest hillslopes where the trees cling to the rocks and more or less fend for themselves, with husbandry being limited to picking up the fallen fruit. The tree flowers in early spring and the fruit reaches maturity in the autumn. The olives are picked unripe if required for bottling, but ripe for pressing for oil. They are traditionally picked by hand or knocked from the tree with poles (as depicted on a famous vase from classical Greece); nowadays mechanical grabs are also used that tend to bruise the fruit less. The olives are crushed first to a paste, then subjected to the main pressing which produces the best oil; two more pressings normally follow.

The olive grows wild in the Mediterranean, and its fruits were probably picked from earliest times, but the cultivation of the tree only began late in the prehistory of Mediterranean farming, thousands of years after the inception of cereal husbandry, always associated with the emergence of complex economic structures (Chapter 3). The principal reason was the slow growth of the olive, which is proverbial. The olive represents a heavy investment in time and labour for many years before anything can be recouped.

Although Columella commented that 'the olive, the queen of trees, requires the least expense of all' (*De Re Rustica* V.7.1), and according to Vergil (*Georgics* II.420) 'olives need no cultivation', in fact the Romans recognised that the trees needed very careful tending when young – the seedlings had to be protected from the summer drought, cultivated in nurseries for several years before transplanting, then pruned regularly to bear the fullest fruit. Olive cultivation, whilst important for peasant subsistence ever since it was adopted, seems to have required a level of economic organisation beyond subsistence for its inception.

The vine (*Vitis vinifera*) is adapted to the Mediterranean drought principally by its very deep root, but needs very careful husbandry for successful wine production. The art of viticulture is described in considerable detail by the Roman agronomists: the importance of soil and aspect; tending the young vines in nurseries and planting them out in deep trenches; different methods of training the vine (unsupported, staked, trellised, supported by a living tree such as an elm or ash); the complicated skills of pruning – cutting, paring, gouging, chopping – with a specialised vine-dresser's knife, the design of which remained virtually unchanged until recently; and then the harvest, the grape pressing and the production of the wine (White, 1970: 229–46). The vine grew wild in the Mediterranean and its fruits were probably picked throughout prehistory, but given the husbandry described above, it is no surprise that systematic viticulture began only late in prehistory, at the same time and in the same circumstances of economic change as olive cultivation.

The third member of the Mediterranean triad was the fig tree (*Ficus* sp.). Figs can be eaten fresh, but have also been valued at least as much in Mediterranean diet as a dried fruit of great nutritional value. The tree is clearly adapted to the Mediterranean environment: it prefers a thin dry soil on a well-drained hillside, the spreading root system takes moisture from a wide area, and comparatively little moisture is lost by evaporation because of the small leaf area. The fig has a tendency to drop its fruit unripe. One traditional method to avoid this is to plant the cultivated trees in proximity to wild fig trees, to encourage cross fertilisation by insects. A more direct remedy is caprification: branches of the wild fig are attached to the cultivated tree to ensure cross fertilisation by the fig wasps which breed in the flowers of the wild trees. The latter method was known in the classical period, and is described by Theophrastus (White, 1970: 228). The Romans recognised the importance of the fig tree in their diet when they included one in a symbolic grove in the forum, alongside an olive and a vine (Delano-Smith, 1979: 209). In traditional Mediterranean farming, certainly ever since the classical period, the three have been grown intermixed with cereals in systems of interculture, but with modern farming methods the latter sadly are a diminishing part of the Mediterranean landscape.

The agricultural circle: crops, manure and fodder

The ratio of harvested grain to sown grain in Roman and medieval times was often as low as three to one, compared with 25–30 to one today. Wheat and barley yields in medieval Europe often averaged about 500 kg/ha (Titow, 1972), a figure not much lower than yields in subsistence economies in Mediterranean and Middle Eastern countries earlier this century (Dennell, 1978: 220–1). It has commonly been assumed that cereal yields in prehistoric Europe were much the same. Yet spelt and emmer grown in experimental plots at the Butser ancient farm project in Hampshire (southern England) between 1973 and 1980, without any periods of fallow and without any nutrients being added, achieved yield ratios often higher than modern yields (2500/3000 kg/ha) and, even in years of very poor weather, never below 7:1 (400 kg/ha) (Reynolds, 1981: 109). However, the land used for the experiments had previously been permanent pasture, so levels of organic matter were very high, and it is extremely unlikely that very high yields will be maintained in years to come if the original fertility is not replaced. At the Rothamsted experimental research station, for example, where wheat and barley have been grown continuously on untreated and manured plots since the middle of the last century, wheat yields have averaged about 800 kg/ha on the untreated plots but over twice that figure on the manured plots, and barley yields have averages about 1200 kg/ha on untreated land and again over twice as much on manured land (Rothamsted Experimental Station, 1970). At Woburn in the same region of England a fifty-year experiment between 1877 and 1927 revealed the same disparity (Russell and Voelcker, 1936; Fig. 19). Continuous cereal cropping in the long term drains the soil of nutrients, has a deleterious effect on crumb structure, and builds up weeds and parasites. Prehistoric

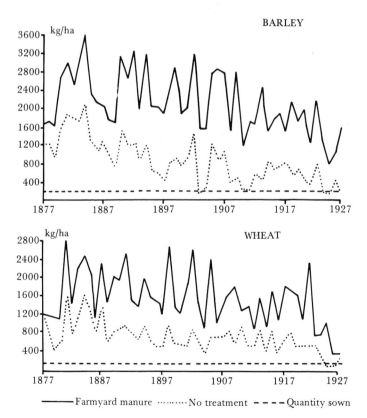

Fig. 19. Cereal yields at Woburn with and without manuring. (After Rowley-Conwy, 1981b: fig. 4, based on figures from Russell and Voelcker, 1936)

farmers cultivating cereals in permanent fields for several decades could renew soil fertility by introducing crops like legumes, by fallowing, by manuring, or – as seems most likely – by various combinations of these methods.

Legumes were clearly grown by many prehistoric farmers, but were only a partial remedy for the renewal of soil fertility. Fallowing – resting the land – was also widespread in prehistoric Europe according to pollen and macrobotanical data. In historical times fallowing was a fundamental part of agricultural strategy until the development of modern break crops and tillage methods in the eighteenth century (Slicher Van Bath, 1963: 59, 178–9). In two-course rotation, land was cultivated for one year and then left fallow for one or two years; in three-course rotation, winter wheat was sown in the first year, spring barley in the second, and the land left fallow in the third; other systems were also developed. At Rothamsted, wheat has been grown in a cycle of four years interspersed with a fallow year in two plots, one untreated and the other manured: yields were always higher in the manured plot and were best in the year after the fallow, but the effect of fallowing was clearer still in the first-year yields from the untreated plot (Fig. 20).

Human excrement and household refuse are commonly distributed by modern primitive communities in the garden plots around their settlements, and the distribution of such 'night soil' was the normal practice in medieval Europe. Spreads of potsherds and other domestic refuse around many prehistoric sites, particularly in the field systems adjacent to many late prehistoric farmsteads in northern Europe, surely indicate such manuring. Sheep are an important source of manure in European farming. (One sheep produces about 14.5 kg of nitrogen a year, compared with just over 5 kg a year from a well fed human.) They produce far less dung than cattle, but have the advantage of rarely needing stalling and so can be kept on pasture through the winter (when they will manure it directly), whereas cattle normally have to be housed in this period and their dung (rotted down with their straw bedding) then carted to the fields. Most animals void most of their dung at night, so a common practice in medieval times was to fold sheep on arable land at night; they could also be grazed on growing crops in some circumstances, and on the stubble after harvest. Particularly in temperate regions, cattle were the major source of manure. In Britain early this century a 450 kg bullock stalled for six months in winter was estimated to produce about seven tons of farmyard manure; the average from a herd of younger and older animals over the same period was about 3–4 tons per beast (Board of Agriculture and Fisheries, 1918). The nitrogen content is about 5–6 kg per ton. In the last century the rough calculation was one beast's manure per acre (McConnell, 1883), but given that many prehistoric cattle were probably nearer 200/250 kg in weight, like many medieval cattle, than the 450 kg of the bullock cited above, the likelihood is that the supply of manure was normally much less than this.

To provide the manure, the animal had to be fed fodder, and this too was almost certainly in short supply in prehistoric Europe, as it was in the Roman and medieval periods. In the Mediterranean region, pasture is minimal outside the mountains during the summer months, and until the development of modern feeds, there was hardly any fodder available for cattle. The Roman agronomists could only advise the farmer to feed his oxen team on 'whatever leaves are available' from March to September; if necessary, the family should be starved to feed grain to the oxen in the weeks before ploughing (White, 1970: 283–4). The plight of the medieval farmer in the Mediterranean was exactly the same – virtually anything edible would be fed to the plough oxen to keep them alive through the summer. In temperate Europe of course the worst time of year is the winter, and the medieval literature is full of references to the difficulties of keeping cattle adequately nourished at this time (Pounds, 1974). In the late medieval period we are told that a cow needed about a ton of fodder during the winter and a plough team of two oxen needed some three tons, as well as perhaps a kilogram of grain a day. A ton of hay was the product of about half a hectare of pasture. Given that the hayfield ideally needed manuring, and the arable certainly did, but the single animal could at best yield

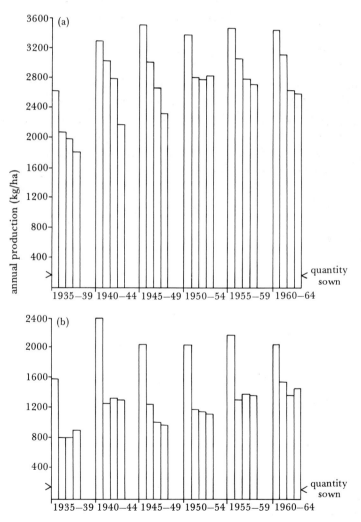

Fig. 20. The effect of fallowing on cereal yields at Rothamsted: wheat for four years followed by a fallow year, receiving (a) farmyard manure and (b) no treatment. (After Rowley-Conwy, 1981b: fig. 6, based on figures from Rothamsted Experimental Station, 1970)

sufficient manure for only about half a hectare, the chronic shortage of manure in medieval Europe is evident.

There was thus a vicious circle inherent in pre-industrial farming in Europe, of low yields and low manure: 'the evil of small harvests due to insufficient manuring, the lack of manure being in turn the result of small agricultural production making it impossible to keep more cattle' (Slicher Van Bath, 1963: 10). Exactly the same constraints charac-terised prehistoric farming. The conservatism of farmers is notorious throughout the world: particularly in peasant systems where technology is low, capital minimal, and farming a daily struggle to make ends meet, it is easy to understand why most farmers are deeply distrustful of change – there may be no margin for experiment. Crops, animals and people were bound together in complex interdependence: 'how narrow were the boundaries that restricted the practice of farming. The opportunities in ancient farming were very limited' (Slicher Van Bath, 1963: 23).

Yet the history of European farming is one of a succession of major changes in technology, productivity and organisation: the circle could be broken, for example by keeping more livestock if extra pasture was available, or by combining the various sys-tems of nutrient renewal, or by new technologies which enabled the cultivation of more land. The prehistory of European farming described here reveals transformations on an even greater scale, with self-sufficient farmers or farmer/foragers at one end of the sequence and state or quasi-state systems of agricultural organisation at the other. Chap-ters 3–9 describe the different sequences of agricultural change which can be recon-structed for each major region of prehistoric Europe, and the final chapter attempts to assess the relative importance of the various stimuli (technological, social, demo-graphic, ecological) which could have precipitated such change.

3

The Mediterranean basin

Geographical introduction

Topography and climate are the two fundamental determinants of the Mediterranean environment, and thus of the agricultural systems developed in historical times to exploit it.

The Mediterranean sea is surrounded by young folded mountains, fragments of which form the central islands (Fig. 21). In the Iberian peninsula the main mountains in the northeastern part of the region reach to c. 2500 metres above sea level, and the central plateau or *meseta* averages c. 700 metres above sea level. In the main region of southern France considered in this chapter (eastern Languedoc and western Provence), the land rises sharply to heights of c. 1000–1500 metres on either side of the Rhone valley. In Italy the Apennine chain stretches for some 1000 kilometres down the peninsula from the Apuan Alps in Liguria to the toe of Italy, Calabria; the central mountains are commonly above 2000 metres, with the highest peak (Gran Sasso) reaching to nearly 3000 metres. The mainland of Greece, too, is a rugged land dominated by the Pindhos range, the southern part of the great Dinaric system which stretches from the eastern alps down through Yugoslavia, Albania and northwest Greece (Epirus) into the Peloponnese, with the single transverse break of the Gulf of Corinth. The southern part of the Greek mainland and the Aegean islands have been aptly described as 'a drowned mountainous area, with little more than the tops of the mountains standing above sea level' (Shackleton, 1964: 121). In all these regions the upland geology is dominated by limestones. Another unifying feature is the contrast everywhere between plain and mountain – the junction is often very abrupt, resulting in considerable topographical changes in short distances, with major implications for climatic variation.

The Mediterranean climate is characterised by hot dry summers, warm wet winters, frequent clear skies and strong winds. The summer drought is the dominant feature: the region lies outside the cyclonic belt in summer, whereas the oceanic and continental regions of Europe have precipitation all the year round. Average temperatures at sea level vary between c. 70°–80°F in summer and c. 45°–55°F in winter. The mountains are much cooler in summer; in the high interiors of Greece, Italy and Iberia, the average January temperatures are below freezing. Deep snow covers the highest regions from late autumn to spring. Annual rainfall varies enormously from region to region, from c. 400–500 mm on the southern coasts to c. 900–1000 mm in the uplands, with well over 4500 mm of rain falling in the mountains of Dalmatia.

The natural vegetation of the coastal region is inevitably dominated by plants that can

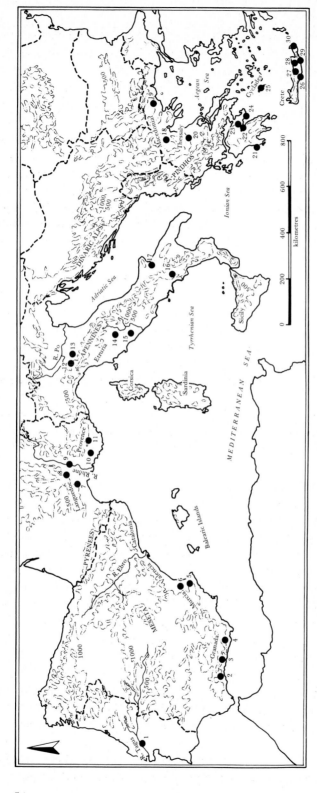

Fig. 21. The Mediterranean basin (contours in metres): principal sites and regions mentioned in the text. 1. Moita do Sebastião; 2. Hoyo de la Mina; 3. Herja; 4. Los Millares; 5. Parpalló; 6. Coveta de l'Or; 7. Vaunage basin; 8. Montclus; 9. Le Baratin; 10. Trets basin; 11. Fontbregoua; 12. Monte Leoni; 13. Sant'Ilario d'Enza; 14. Belverde; 15. Narce; 16. Tufariello and Buccino; 17. Tavoliere plain; 18. Nea Nikomedeia; 19. Sitagroi; 20. Argissa; 21. Pylos; 22. Lerna; 23. Mycenae; 24. Franchthi cave; 25. Melos; 26. Phaistos; 27. Knossos; 28. Mallia; 29. Myrtos; 30. Zakro.

would have supported communities of some fifty people (Jarman and Webley, 1975: 189). The density of settlement on the Tavoliere was probably not unique: recent intensive survey in Calabria located numerous scatters of early neolithic material every few hundred metres apart, and further investigations have indicated that each scatter probably consisted of a dozen or so huts (Ammerman and Bonardi, 1981; Fig. 25).

There were comparable societies practising mixed farming in central Italy and in northern Italy south of the Po river by c. 4500 b.c. (Subalpine Italy north of the Po is dealt with in Chapter 5.) These people grew emmer, barley and legumes; had stock systems concentrating on sheep and goats; used lithic assemblages composed mainly of long parallel-sided blades, some with traces of silica or 'sickle gloss'; and invariably selected narrow ridges of light and well drained soil for their settlements (Barker, 1975a, 1981; Calvi Rezia, 1969, 1972; Castelletti, 1974–5; Cremonesi, 1966; Evett and Renfrew, 1971; Tozzi, 1978). At the same time, however, there were also communities at the limit of the main arable soils who seem to have relied more on stock-keeping (Cremonesi, 1976), and others who lived more or less entirely by foraging, equipped with stone tools more or less identical to those of the early postglacial foragers (Acanfora, 1962–3; Bonuccelli and Faedo, 1968; Cazzella et al., 1976; Whitehouse, 1971). In the forests and marshes of the Po plain, for example, was a series of small sites used almost exclusively for hunting red deer, roe deer, cattle and pig, and for fishing and shellfish collection (Bagolini and Biagi, 1975b; Barker, 1976a, 1977; Biagi, 1980; Castelletti, 1975; Cattani, 1975). Some of the foraging sites were probably seasonal camps used by people from adjacent farming settlements, but most were not. Furthermore, there were all these different sorts of subsistence activities within each of the two main cultural groups which have ben defined south of the Po by early neolithic pottery in the fifth and mid-fourth millennia b.c.: impressed and red painted wares in southern and east central Italy, and Sasso-Fiorano incised and pitted wares in west central Italy and northern Italy south of the Po; and there was exactly the same range of subsistence practised by the contemporary people north of the Po with square-mouthed pottery (*bocca quadrata*) (Chapter 5).

By the late fourth millennium b.c., however, separate foraging sites are no longer found, and there is evidence for the gradual expansion of agricultural settlement throughout the peninsula. In southern Italy stock-keeping replaced foraging entirely in the coastal caves (Whitehouse, 1971), and in central Italy settlement expanded from ridge locations to the margins of alluvial valleys on the lowlands, and into the intermontane basins of the Apennines (Calzoni, 1939; Cremonesi, 1965).

Southern France

The first pottery in the western Mediterranean was cardial impressed ware, so called because the principal decorative motifs were made with cockle (*Cardium edule*) shells. In southern France this pottery is first dated at Cap Ragnon c. 6000 b.c. (Courtin et al., 1970–2); the same wares then appeared in Provence and Languedoc during the fifth millennium. In general, the lithic industries associated with this pottery were identical to those of the pre-pottery foragers, augmented by polished implements and grinding stones (Courtin, 1974a, 1974b; Escalon de Fonton, 1966, 1968, 1970; Guilaine, 1976a).

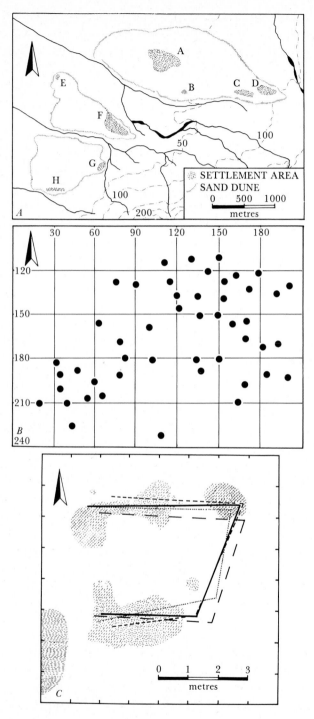

Fig. 25. Neolithic settlement in Calabria. A. settlement areas found on sand dunes by intensive survey (contours in metres); B. series of habitation areas located at one of the settlement areas by coring and resistivity survey (on a 30 metre grid); C. multi-phased rectangular structure, presumably a dwelling, found by excavating one of the habitation areas in B. (Information kindly provided by Albert Ammerman)

Most of the cardial sites known are caves or shelters (Mills, 1983; Phillips, 1982). At the open site of Le Baratin, however, Courtin found subcircular hut floors of river pebbles with post holes in the centre and round the periphery, indicating simple tent or shelter-like structures (Courtin, 1976). Grains of wheat and barley have been recovered from several fifth millennium sites, together with remains of chick pea, vetch, acorns and juniper (Courtin and Erroux, 1974; Erroux, 1976). However, the integration of all the artifactual, organic and locational data from southern France suggests very strongly that subsistence at this time was based on a broad spectrum of animal herding (particularly sheep and goats), hunting (red deer, cattle, pig), plant gathering, and the exploitation of marine food, but that cereal cultivation was of very little importance (Guilaine, 1977; Mills, 1976).

The fourth millennium then witnessed major changes in settlement, population, technology and subsistence. It seems clear that the period was marked by a substantial rise in population: for example, there are some 180 cave and 130 open sites of the Chassey culture in Provence and eastern Languedoc, compared with about 55 cave and 25 open sites for the two millennia of cardial settlement (Arnal, 1976; Costantini, 1978; Courtin, 1974a, 1974b). Excavations at the open sites have found substantial habitations of cobble hut floors, pits and ditches (Guilaine and Vaquer, 1973; Meroc, 1967; Meroc and Simmonet, 1970; Phillips, 1975: 88–90). The abundance of cereal remains and grindstones, of agricultural tools, of bladelets with sickle gloss and of faunal samples dominated by stock (especially sheep/goat) suggests very clearly that most Chasseen societies depended primarily on cereal and livestock farming for their subsistence (Barral, 1960; Courtin, 1967, 1974a; Ducos, 1957; Gagnière, 1967; Phillips, 1972; Poulain, 1966).

Mills (1981) has investigated Chassey and later prehistoric settlement in selected zones of Provence and Languedoc, interpreting the settlement archaeology especially in terms of detailed geomorphological analysis. In the Trets basin in western Provence, for example, the Chassey sites (small but dense collections of artifacts often only a few hundred metres apart) were invariably situated on low interfluves of deep calcareous soils which would have been an ideal arable resource in the fourth millennium – of deep texture, good drainage and high fertility; but their one-kilometre catchments also enclosed substantial areas of what would have been marsh, a critical grazing resource in the summer months (Fig. 26). In eastern Languedoc, too, Chassey settlements were positioned by the primary arable soils of the coastal plain or Tertiary basins such as the Vaunage, invariably near springs and streams.

Spain

Events in Spain followed a similar pattern to those of southern France. Cardial pottery was manufactured in the coastal region in the fifth millennium, but in this case accompanied by red slipped pottery (Fernández-Miranda and Moure, 1974; Vicent and Muñoz, 1973). Again, it was associated with a lithic industry almost identical to that of the pre-pottery foragers. Einkorn, emmer, bread wheat and naked barley have all been identified at the cave of Coveta de l'Or in Valencia (Hopf, 1964), but in general the subsistence data and site catchments suggest very much the same range of activities as in southern France at this time. Then, in the fourth millennium, similar industries to those of the Chassey sites were developed in eastern Spain, together with broadly comparable pottery (Muñoz, 1965). Information about settlement and subsistence is not nearly so precise as in southern France, but the impression is that agricultural systems based on wheat, barley, legumes, sheep and goats were firmly established during the fourth millennium b.c. (Arribas, 1968; Vicent and Muñoz, 1973). The period also witnessed the agricultural colonisation of Almeria, the most arid and inhospitable part of Spain. The people who established themselves here had to be much more organised than the small farming communities elsewhere: they were characterised by large permanent settlements, developed exchange networks, and the investment in corporate authority and status represented by megalithic tombs and their gravegoods; moreover, it is possible that their agriculture also involved the cultivation of the olive and the use of simple irrigation systems, key factors in the transformation of subsistence in Spain in the third millennium (Hopf and Pellicer, 1970).

So who were the first farmers?

Clearly, there is no simple equation between impressed ware and farming: there were several distinct styles of early pottery across the Mediterranean prior to 4000 b.c. (not all of them including impressed ware, and the regional styles of impressed ware in any

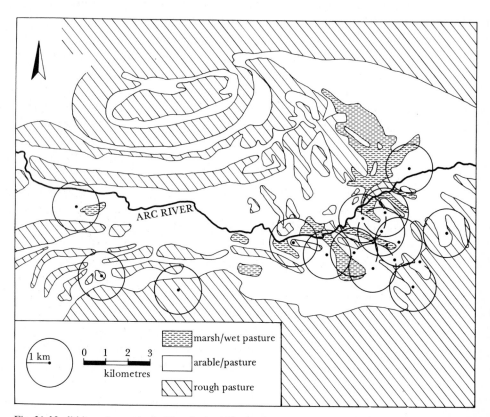

Fig. 26. Neolithic settlement in the Trets basin. (After Mills, 1981)

case being very different from each other), there is no simple trend from east to west in the first use of pottery, and each regional pottery style was shared by farmers, herders and foragers. An integrated agricultural system was established in restricted parts of Greece by *c.* 6000 b.c. but was not widespread there for another thousand years. In Italy a rather different system of mixed farming began early in the fifth millennium, but was the dominant mode of subsistence only in the latter half of the fourth millennium. In southern France sheep and goat herding was integrated into existing systems of foraging in the sixth millennium (at least), but mixed farming did not develop on a large scale until the fourth millennium; much the same process is probably true of Spain.

Four alternative models can be put forward for the beginnings of farming in the Mediterranean basin. The first is the traditional model: that farming was introduced and was practised entirely by maritime colonists; this now seems impossible to sustain, given the complexities of the data described above. The second, that farming was introduced by a small scale colonist movement, and then adopted by the indigenous foragers, is widely accepted today. However, this model would surely predict the existence of a pioneering people with a coherent material culture and way of life, and evidence for their movement from east to west; but there is no evidence at all in the archaeological record for such a pioneering group expanding westwards, and a great deal of evidence otherwise in the enormous amount of regional variation. In the third model, the domestic plants and animals would have been dispersed from east to west by exchange amongst the indigenous foragers. On the evidence of the spread of Melian obsidian to the Greek mainland, and the occurrence of deep-water fish at several coastal sites prior to 6000 b.c., it is clear that the necessary boat technology for voyages of *c.* 20–30 kilometres was available to Mediterranean foragers (van Andel and Shackleton, 1982), and the complexity of the process by which farming replaced foraging could also support this model. The final model would regard the beginnings of farming in the Mediterranean as entirely an indigenous process using domesticates that were already present. The balance of probability favours a combination of the third and fourth processes (Dennell, 1983; and see Chapter 10): local domestication in the early Holocene of indigenous resources in the Mediterranean (einkorn, barley, sheep) by people who retained foraging and fishing as the mainstay of their subsistence; and then, after *c.* 6000 b.c., the dispersal of emmer and bread wheat from the Near East (probably by exchange) and, as a result of their adoption, the establishment of integrated systems of mixed farming (Fig. 97, p. 254).

The appearance of these farming systems (but not the universal replacement of foraging by farming) coincides very approximately with the first half of the Atlantic phase of pollen zonation, but it is extremely difficult to assess the precise ecological effect in the Mediterranean beyond the fact that there was probably more rainfall. However, one significant feature of the first evidence for systematic farming *c.* 6000 b.c. is that it coincided with a marked sea level rise in the Mediterranean that flooded many marsh and estuarine areas which were a key resource for postglacial foragers (van Andel and Shackleton, 1982; Bertrand and l'Homer, 1975). In the case of southern France, Mills (1976) has pointed out that this sea level rise would also have flooded lowland grassland areas such as the Carmargue which would have been the natural habitat of the sheep if it was indigenous, so that the beginnings of sheep-herding in southern France could well have been in the context of environmental pressure on sheep and subsistence pressure on man. The same arguments can be applied to the contemporary subsistence changes at the Franchthi cave. However, the most interesting feature of the beginning of Mediterranean farming is its very incoherence compared with the rest of Europe, with farming communities representing a dramatic change in settlement and subsistence in some areas like the Greek plains and the Tavoliere, adjacent to others more or less unaffected by the new resources. It is noteworthy that the areas used for early farming also happened to be some of the least attractive for the existing subsistence system, previously utilised on a seasonal basis by low density populations, whereas the areas where farming took many hundreds of years to be adopted tended to be those which could sustain substantial populations of foragers.

Whatever the origins of the first farming, its ensuing development was certainly associated with population increase on the Mediterranean mainland, followed by the colonisation of most of the main islands by farmers during the fifth and fourth millennia b.c. (Cherry, 1981). On the Balaeric islands, colonised in the fifth millennium, the subsistence system of the first inhabitants consisted of fishing and gathering, together with the exploitation of the endemic *Myotragus balearicus*, an animal resembling in build and probably in behaviour the chamois or mountain goat; deposits of dung and trimmed horn cores (perhaps to prevent damage from butting during coralling) suggest some form of husbandry (Waldren, 1982).

Agricultural change in the third millennium b.c.

There were widespread and dramatic cultural changes throughout the Mediterranean basin during the third millennium b.c., which coincided often with critical developments in farming.

In the Aegean, this period (the Early Bronze Age) witnessed the key transition from the neolithic societies described earlier to the Minoan and Mycenaean state societies of the second millennium b.c. (C. Renfrew, 1972). Numbers and sizes of settlements increased; major settlements now not only were fortified but also contained large central buildings and smaller residential units. Gravegoods imply great disparities in wealth, metallurgy developed rapidly (especially for the production of what seem to be status objects in gold, silver, copper and lead), and craft specialists worked in pottery, stone, cosmetics, textiles, leather and wood. Renfrew concluded that 'we see in the third millennium chiefdoms, the obvious and logical predecessors of the second millennium principality or state' (1972: 403).

Fundamental changes in Aegean agriculture coincided with these events (Fig. 27). The most important was the development of olive and vine cultivation on a systematic basis. Separating vats are known at several Aegean settlements including Myrtos (Warren, 1972), and clay lamps are also common and were probably designed for olive oil; olive oil was found in a sediment in a jug from Naxos (C. Renfrew, 1972: 285), olive stones at Knossos, and olive stones and prunings at Myrtos (Rackham, 1972; J. Renfrew, 1972). Grape pips have been found at several settlements including Lerna, Myrtos and Sitagroi (Hopf, 1962b; J. Renfrew, 1972), and wine production is also indicated by spouted storage jars and a series of drinking and pouring vessels first made at this time. The fact that such vessels were sometimes made of precious metals indicates the importance of wine drinking amongst the new elites of Aegean society. Increasingly pure crop residues probably imply greater segregation of cereal and pulse fields, with the labour intensive pulses being grown near the settlements and the cereals further afield as more land was taken into cultivation to feed the increased population (rather than simply more efficient grain cleaning) (Halstead, 1981: 327). These changes favoured more specialisation in stock-keeping. In particular, the increase in numbers of sheep and goats at many sites (for example Argissa, Knossos, Lerna, Pefkakia, and Sitagroi), a rise in the ratio of male to female sheep, higher proportions of adult animals and an overall increase in sheep size have all been taken to indicate that wool production was a priority (Boessneck, 1962; Gejvall, 1969; M. R. Jarman, 1972b; Jordan, 1975). Several upland sites have been identified as seasonal encampments of specialised transhumant shepherds (Warren and Tzedhakis, 1974; Watrous, 1977). Bintliff (1977a: 540) has also suggested that more efficient deep sea fishing, especially for tunny, may have developed at this time.

It seems evident that Aegean agriculture was moving beyond subsistence and self-sufficiency in this period. At Lerna, for example, the sealings in the largest building imply a new element of food storage and control by central authority, and large central buildings at other sites have been identified as granaries (Heath, 1958; C. Renfrew, 1972: 288). On the island of Melos, settlement nucleation coincided with a greater

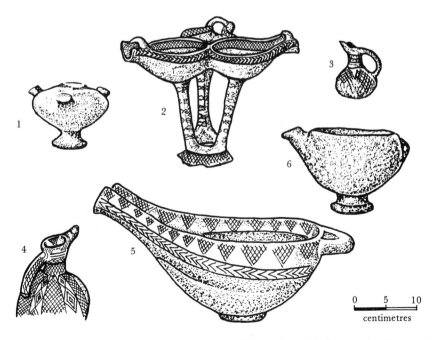

Fig. 27. Early bronze age polyculture in the Aegean: oil lamps (1. marble; 2. pottery) and jug containing olive oil (3) from a grave on the Cycladic island of Naxos. 4–6 may have been used for the service of wine. (After C. Renfrew, 1972: fig. 15.7)

dependance on cattle, the introduction of the donkey to make the transport of foodstuffs into the town (Phylakopi) more efficient, and the production of a wool surplus for exchange (Gamble, 1979; Renfrew and Wagstaff, 1982).

The third millennium in Italy was also marked by the development of copper metallurgy, the production of status equipment by specialist craftsmen, and the burial of high ranking individuals with such equipment. When the cemeteries were first excavated a century ago, the graves were thought to belong to immigrant 'warrior-pastoralists' from the eastern Mediterranean (Colini, 1898; Peet, 1909), but modern research has shown that the emergence of ranked societies in Italy must be understood primarily as a process of internal social evolution (Barfield *et al.*, 1975–6; Barker, 1971, 1981; Whitehouse and Renfrew, 1974). Certainly, however, there was a degree of maritime contact between Italy and the Aegean, and there are isolated but notable similarities in aspects of burial rite and equipment (Holloway, 1976). The most striking similarities are found in the Gaudo group of cemeteries in southern Italy, and significantly it was only in this region of Italy that there were changes in settlement and subsistence at all comparable with those of the Aegean. The Tufariello village, for example, consisted of a cluster of square or rectangular houses built on stone footings, surrounded by an impressive rubble wall – unique for Italy in this period (Holloway, 1975). The analysis of the large skeletal sample and associated gravegoods from the nearby cemetery of Buccino revealed horizontal differentiation as well as vertical stratification, with leadership shared between different kin or clan groups, and ascribed by birth rather than being achieved in life as seems likely amongst the other chalcolithic societies in Italy (Corrain and Capitanio, 1974). Plant remains from Tufariello included wheat seeds, olive stones and grape pips (Phippen, 1975); the stock economy was heavily dependent on sheep, bred for their wool and milk rather than for meat, and probably involved short distance transhumance (Barker, 1975b). Elsewhere in Italy, agriculture was based on the traditional mix of cereals, legumes and stock; grape seeds at Sant' Ilario d'Enza in northern Italy belonged to the wild vine (Barfield *et al.*, 1975). However, the process of settlement expansion noted in the fourth millennium continued in the third, and there are occasional signs of increasing competition for land as populations increased, with some settlements in key arable areas being fortified (Barker, 1975a, 1981).

In southern France at this time there was a major increase in settlement on the coastal plain and adjacent basins: in the Vaunage basin, for example, intensive survey has found almost ten times as many chalcolithic as Chassey sites (Fig. 28); they were agricultural settlements, integrating cereal cultivation with cattle, sheep and goat herding (Coste and Maurel, 1975; Poulain, 1974). On the adjacent Garrigues plateau, formerly used for seasonal grazing and hunting, pockets of cultivable soil were now farmed by communities living in small villages (Bailloud, 1973), and new sites with enclosure walls were established away from these pockets very like the shepherds' shielings of the historical period (Arnal, 1973; Poulain, 1973). On the Grands Causses, at higher elevations still, groups of megalithic tombs were built as territorial markers beside the best pastures of the karst depressions and marly soils (Costantini, 1978). Integrating this evidence, Mills (1981) argues that transhumant systems of sheep grazing developed between the Garrigues and Grands Causses, at a time when population expansion on the lowlands had caused the establishment of permanent settlement on the Garrigues (where arable land was scarce but pasture abundant). Similar expansions of settlement from the lowlands onto the Garrigues have taken place on three occasions in the historical period (Le Roy Ladurie, 1966).

In Almeria in Spain, the major bastioned settlements and corbelled passage graves of the Millaran culture indicate a major transformation in social and economic complexity during the third millennium (Almagro and Arribas, 1963; Savory, 1968). The graves mark a crucial change from communal to individualised burial, with status institutionalised and restricted; gravegoods include copper tools and weapons, elaborate funerary pottery and lithics, and objects made of exotic raw materials including amber, ivory and ostrich shell (Leisner and Leisner, 1943). In the past these developments were interpreted in terms of diffusion or colonisation from the Aegean (Blance, 1961), but internal processes are now preferred (Chapman, 1977; C. Renfrew, 1967). There were also substantial changes in agriculture. First, olives and vines were probably now cultivated by some Millaran communities (Almagro and Arribas, 1963: 263; Paco, 1954). Second, there were important developments in the pastoral economy:

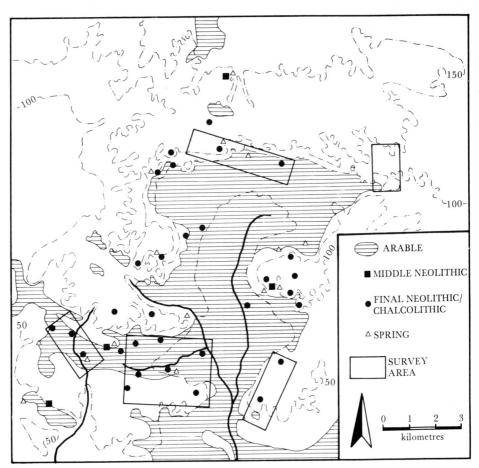

Fig. 28. Neolithic and chalcolithic settlement in the Vaunage basin (contours in metres). (After Mills, 1981)

sheep became the dominant stock, kept particularly for milk and wool, and probably managed in short distance transhumance systems; cattle were kept mainly for their traction (presumably for pulling the ard, though there is no direct evidence for this), and donkeys also became important for transport (Boessneck, 1969b; Chapman, 1978; von den Driesch, 1972; von den Driesch and Morales, 1977). Third, new methods of water control were developed: drinking water was conserved in rock cut cisterns, and settlements were positioned at stream junctions where winter/spring floodwaters were most prolific, with the water being diverted onto the fields by a simple system of dams and ditches much as in medieval farming in Almeria (Chapman, 1978; Glick, 1970; Schüle, 1967). The combination of new crops, specialised stock-keeping and water control was clearly able to sustain a substantial population in this, the most arid region of Spain, although the development of Millaran fortification presumably reflects in part at least the capital investment and social tension implicit in the new system in such a marginal environment.

Throughout the northern Mediterranean, therefore, the third millennium was a period of profound social change, agricultural intensification or expansion, and population increase. It thus presents a classic problem in archaeological explanation. On the one hand, the clear correlation between agricultural and demographic change could be taken as a typical example of Boserup's thesis (1965), that population pressure forces agricultural intensification (with the social changes being seen as an inevitable response). For the Aegean, Renfrew explicitly rejected this hypothesis, giving primacy to social factors: 'The innovations in the developing agriculture were . . . largely cultural, with human control of these species the deciding factor . . . The subsistence system developed along with the other social and technical elements: it did not lead the way' (1972: 304). It could be argued along these lines that the emergence of elites was the key factor, which stimulated agricultural production and thus population increase. However, another factor which must be added to the equation is the climatic evidence: the cooler and more humid conditions of the third millennium in the Mediterranean would have encouraged more reliable harvests in the more marginal environments (Lamb, 1977; Triat, 1978). Certainly the similarities in the processes of change across the northern Mediterranean (including many of the major islands) at this time are more remarkable than the differences, implying the need for models of general applicability, even if we cannot yet evaluate the precise relationships between technology, subsistence, social organisation, demography and climate.

The palace economies of the Aegean bronze age
Following the cultural changes of the third millennium, the Minoan civilisation emerged on the island of Crete c. 2000 b.c.; the Mycenaean states, fundamentally the same as the Minoan, developed on the Greek mainland some three centuries later, and there were comparable societies by then too on the Aegean islands. In the second half of the second millennium Mycenaean culture embraced Crete and the other islands as well as the mainland, but collapsed dramatically at the end of the twelfth century b.c. (Vermeule, 1972; Warren, 1975).

On Crete there were four great palaces at Knossos, Phaistos, Mallia and Zakro, as well as coastal towns, country mansions, villas and farms. The palace complexes included majestic residential apartments, cult rooms, shrines, workshops and storage chambers, built round a central courtyard (Fig. 29). Minoan society was elaborately hierarchical, with powerful leaders, bureaucratic officials, craftsmen, traders or merchants, scribes, priests or priestesses and agricultural workers. The craftsmen achieved

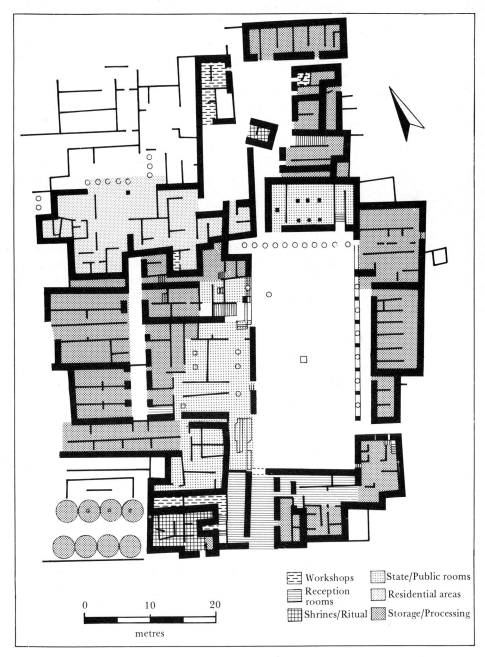

Workshops State/Public rooms
Reception rooms Residential areas
Shrines/Ritual Storage/Processing

0   10   20

metres

Fig. 29. The Minoan palace of Mallia, Crete. (After van Effenterre, 1980)

remarkable skills in the production of sophisticated wheel-made pottery, metalwork, stone vases and jewellery, with a level of sensibility that produced some of the most attractive artwork in early European culture. The same cultural achievements characterised the Mycenaean states, with a critical difference being the fact that many Mycenaean palaces and towns were strongly fortified.

Direct evidence for the nature of Minoan/Mycenaean farming includes seeds of wheat, barley, pulses and fruits, and grape pips and olive stones; faunal evidence is very limited, but all the major stock are represented and sheep and goats are invariably more numerous than the rest. Locational studies have shown that most settlements were adjacent to pockets of flysch (sandstone/shale) soil, which would have been fertile, well drained and easy to cultivate; Mycenae and Pylos were exceptions to this rule, but were ideally placed at the regional scale in the midst of the arable cells within their kingdoms (Bintliff, 1977a, 1977b). In addition, the Linear B tablets (developed as an essential part of the bureaucratic apparatus) have provided us with the most detailed information anywhere in late prehistoric Europe for the organisation of a complex agricultural system (Chadwick, 1976; Ventris and Chadwick, 1956). There are many references to the issue of foodstuffs as rations: mainly cereals, but supplemented frequently by olive oil, olives and figs, and occasionally by wine (Palmer, 1963). The tablets also indicate the existence of very large flocks of sheep, kept mainly for their wool: Knossos controlled some 100,000 sheep in central Crete (Killen, 1964), and the 10,000 sheep recorded in the Pylos archive were 'only a small percentage of the total flocks' of the palace (Ventris and Chadwick, 1956: 198). This archive also lists 1825 goats, 540 pigs and 8 oxen; at Knossos the very few oxen are recorded individually by name. Possibly the plough oxen were maintained only by the palace authorities, like the chariot horses that were a source of considerable prestige (Halstead, 1981: 332).

All of the palaces were provided with extensive magazines, including areas clearly designed for the storage of oil and wine: at Mycenae, for example, one store contained jars impregnated with olive oil, and another at Pylos contained 33 tablets dealing with olive oil as well as storage *pithoi*. Given such evidence, and the archives documenting the disbursement and receipt of goods, Finley (1957) and C. Renfrew (1972) have argued that the palaces were at the centre of a massive redistribution operation, with workers being required to reach production targets (so many fleeces of wool or litres of oil, for example) in return for their rations, and with the agricultural surplus feeding the non-producers in the social hierarchy and providing goods for overseas commerce. However, the extent and nature of the redistributive economy are somewhat open to debate. A critical problem is the scale of production outside the remit of the palace bureaucracy and its archive. The wool from the palace flocks at Knossos could have clothed 20–30,000 people, but the Minoan population of central Crete is estimated to have been twice this; pulses are not mentioned in any tablets, but have been found preserved at several sites; wool was clearly a priority of the palace economy at Pylos, but faunal evidence from the settlement of Nichoria in its territory showed that the flocks here were mainly kept for milk and meat in the traditional subsistence system (Chadwick, 1972, 1977; Sloan and Duncan, 1978). Halstead (1981) argues for a dichotomy between extensive/large scale farming on royal estates on the one hand (arable production using plough oxen; large transhumant flocks), and, on the other, intensive/small scale farming elsewhere in the palace territories (cultivation with the hoe; subsistence shepherding).

However, even allowing for a distinction between the official and unofficial economies, the degree of intensity in the system and the nature of elite power remain problematical. Halstead, for example, has suggested that the power of the leadership lay in its ability not to create wealth and redistribute it, but to guard and manipulate the stored foods in times of poor harvest. In contrast to Renfrew's arguments for the beneficial effects of the emergence of the Aegean elites for the system as a whole, Bintliff (1980) has likened land tenure to that of feudal Europe, with peasant villages tied to a local nobility, the best land farmed by tied labour as the lord's demesne, and an elite hostile to the peasantry trying to extract the maximum agricultural surplus by fair means or foul. Another view is that communities were integrated in the palace kingdoms as much by religious controls and charismatic leadership as by coercion (Gamble, 1981). Whatever the nature of the leadership and the scale of the surplus, however, it is clear that the Minoan–Mycenaean state system involved economic intensification to some degree as political leadership increasingly controlled agricultural production.

Second millennium farming in the central and western Mediterranean

In northern Italy, mixed farming continued throughout the second millennium in the traditional zone of settlement on the southern margins of the Po plain (Barfield, 1971). A good example of a typical small farmstead here was excavated at Monte Leoni near Parma (Ammerman *et al.*, 1976, 1978). Pollen studies indicated a very limited area of arable round the farm, where soils are rather clayey, and the community had developed a system of spring sowing (first millet, then wheat and barley) as the soils dried out; they also cultivated figs, grapes and pulses, and perhaps purslane and sheep's sorrel (weeds of cultivation today). The main stock were sheep/goat and pig; spindle whorls and loom weights were also common at the site. In the latter half of the second millennium, when a warmer and drier oscillation is recorded in southern Europe (Frenzel, 1966), agricultural settlement finally expanded onto the Po plain itself, hitherto used for hunting and pastoralism. The new settlements were substantial villages of one or more hectares, exceptionally rich in material including metallurgy – moulds, slag and crucibles are common at all of them (Säflund, 1939). These *terramare* villages were artificial mounds of clay, organic matter and household refuse, raised three or four metres above the plain presumably as a protection against flooding. Whereas the barley/sheep/goat mix had been the basis of farming on the foothills since the late fifth millennium, cattle and pig were now kept as better suited to the forests and damp pastures of the plain, and likewise wheat was preferred to barley because of the predominance of heavy soils. Horse bones and bridle gear show that horse riding was common.

The people of the Italian peninsula shared in a uniform material culture during the second millennium, termed the Apennine Bronze Age, characterised especially by fine dark burnished pottery (Cremonesi, 1978; Rellini, 1931). There is little evidence for ranking beyond simple 'big man' systems or perhaps chiefdoms, and metal was almost entirely reserved for the display equipment and weaponry of these leaders; most communities were basically neolithic in their technology until the end of the millennium.

Subsistence data are quite prolific, and indicate a spectrum of activities from sedentary mixed farming to specialised transhumant pastoralism (Barker, 1976b, 1976c, 1981). Apennine pottery included vessels interpreted as milk-boilers, very similar to metal vessels used for cheese-making by transhumant shepherds in Italy today (Fig. 30). One clear trend is the expansion of mixed farming into the intermontane basins and high valleys of the Apennine mountains, where cereal cultivation would have been increasingly marginal (Barker, 1972, 1975a). However, there is little evidence for major changes in the agricultural base: the range of cereals, legumes and stock remained much as before, although grape pips have been found at several sites and, given the potters' emphasis on fine drinking cups, the likelihood is that wine drinking was now practised, at least by the leadership. Evidence for food storage and surplus production has been found only at one site, Belverde (Calzoni, 1954, 1962). The Mycenaeans established trading colonies in southern Italy and probably visited central and northern Italy (Barfield, 1971: 77; Östenberg, 1967; Whitehouse, 1973), but it seems that the triad of cereals, olives and vines, and certainly the complex economic system associated with it in the Aegean, were foreign to the contemporary peoples of Italy.

In southern France the period was marked by a major decline in numbers of settlements, which does not seem to be simply a factor of site survival (Mills, 1981). Although the lack of open sites was once explained as a simple shift to pastoralism (Bailloud, 1966), in fact cereals, legumes and stock are known at most sites where the data have been sought, and olives were found at the Montpezat cave (Coles and Harding, 1979: 191). The population declines in southern France during the historical period have been explained by a combination of circumstances including a decline in soil fertility, deterioration in farming techniques, disease and market fluctuations (Braudel, 1975; Le Roy Ladurie, 1966). Although we cannot detect critical short term fluctuations in climate, it does seem likely that the same drier oscillation which encouraged the settlement of the Po plain in Italy was at least partly responsible for the collapse of permanent settlement on the marginal soils of the Garrigues.

The Argaric Bronze Age of southeast Spain was characterised by the development of ever increasing stratification in society. An emphasis on portable items of prestige suggests that the elites were recognised now in the material and visual sense rather than by kin or collective associations, but the very mobility of these prestige goods (objects of gold, silver and ivory as well as clay and bone) seems to have been an important factor in the warlike aspect of the aristocracy. Some settlements were positioned like those of the Millaran period at stream junctions, but many more sacrificed easy access to water and soil in favour of extreme defensive positions on craggy outcrops. The complex social structure rested on the same agricultural system as the Millaran culture: water conservation, irrigation, polyculture, and transhumant sheep-herding for wool and milk production (Arribas, 1968, 1976; Chapman, 1978; von den Driesch, 1971; Gilman, 1976, 1981). The moister regions elsewhere in Spain, where dry farming was possible, maintained their traditional social order: thus collective burials continued to be the main form of interest in most of Andalusia and Catalonia well into the second millennium (Gilman, 1976: 317). The data are inadequate to separate cause and effect, but we can see that in southeast Spain, as in the Aegean, dramatic social development probably

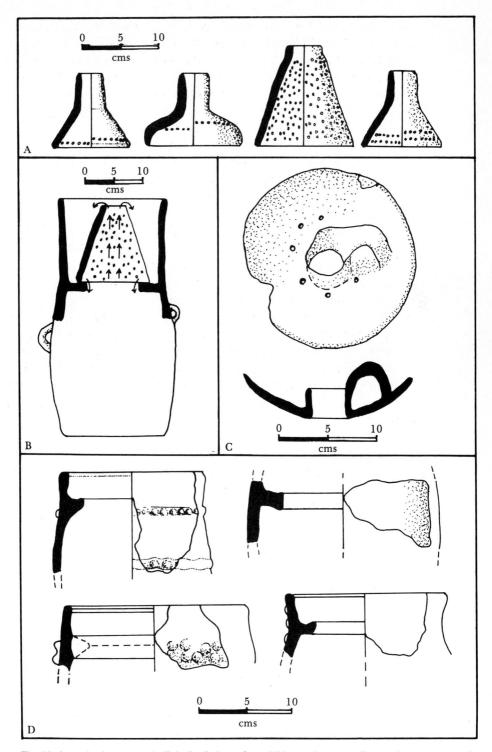

Fig. 30. Apennine bronze age 'milk boilers': A. perforated lids, northern type; B. complete equipment of boiling vessel and lid; C. perforated lid, southern type; D. boiling vessels with inner ledges. (After Barker, 1981: fig. 27)

accompanied by population increases took place where there was a significant potential for agricultural intensification, and where the emergence of an organisational capacity enabled the agricultural base to be manipulated in more productive ways.

Mediterranean farming at the end of prehistory

The collapse of Mycenaean civilisation towards the end of the second millennium was originally explained in terms of a Dorian invasion from the north, an invasion recorded in later folk memory; however, such raiding is now viewed far more as a symptom than as a cause of the end of the palace system (McNeal, 1972), which is ascribed to the internal breakdown of an overstretched power structure and economic system. Such a process may simply have been cumulative, but it is possible that a series of poor harvests in a prolonged drought exacerbated the fragile agricultural system (Bryson *et al.*, 1974). In the same period the Hittite state collapsed in Anatolia, Egypt was raided by marauders from the sea, and piracy seems to have been endemic throughout the eastern Mediterranean (Sandars, 1978). Although the transition from late Mycenaean to archaic Greece can no longer be seen as the sudden replacement of civilisation by a Dark Age, it does seem clear that olive cultivation declined with the end of Mycenaean authority and was only developed again on a large scale in the economy of classical Greece (Boardman, 1976).

The end of the second millennium in much of Italy was characterised by fundamental changes in technology and social organisation. The most spectacular developments took place in Etruria, the part of central Italy between the Arno and Tiber rivers. The Villanovan cemeteries of the tenth and ninth centuries b.c. indicate a society with at least four levels of ranking, probably headed by dynastic famiilies, a social transformation which coincided with a population explosion (Potter, 1976, 1979). Out of this society emerged the Etruscan city states in the eighth century, at a time when Etruria was exposed to the cultural and commercial impact of the Greek colonies in southern Italy. Metal production was transformed into a major industry that provided luxury goods for the Celtic market north of the Alps. The emergence of the state system here was also marked by the establishment of polyculture: perfume vases for oil were being manufactured by the end of the seventh century, olive stones and grape pips have been found in contemporary deposits in Rome, and the historical tradition also placed the beginnings of olive and vine cultivation around Rome to this period (Boardman, 1976; Gjerstad, 1966; Vallet, 1962). In the rest of peninsular Italy, however, it is very unlikely that the agricultural base changed significantly until the classical period: in the Biferno valley in Molise, for example, the 'neolithic' system of mixed farming based on cereals, legumes, sheep and goats was replaced by polyculture only in the fifth and fourth centuries B.C. (Barker, forthcoming).

From the early sixth century B.C., southern France came into the commercial and then political sphere of the Greek colony of Marseilles, and was brought under direct Roman control from the mid-first century B.C. Earlier in the first millennium the population lived in major defended villages on the basin edges, practising the cereal/legume/ sheep/goat system of farming (Aliger, 1974–6; Columeau, 1976), but Roman control led to the abandonment of the fortified sites and the establishment of an entirely new pattern of rural settlement (dispersed farmsteads, villages and villa estates) engaged in polyculture for a market economy. In Spain there was a rather similar sequence of hillfort occupation followed by major transformations in settlement with the establishment of Roman control, but agricultural data for the final prehistoric period are minimal (Savory, 1968).

Ever since the classical period, Mediterranean farming has depended on the cultivation of cereals, olives and vines, and stock-keeping concentrating on sheep and goats. It has normally been assumed that cereals, sheep and goats were carried westwards across the Mediterranean by neolithic farmers, and olives and vines by Greeks, Phoenicians and Romans; yet, as I have argued in this chapter, it is likely that most if not all the components of Mediterranean farming were indigenous to many parts of the Mediterranean region. The cereal/sheep/goat system of farming was developed at different rates and in different ways from *c*. 6000 b.c., with a rudimentary system of husbandry probably being of greater antiquity. Polyculture was established in the Aegean in the third millennium and in a restricted area of Spain (and perhaps Italy) at the same time, but was probably unimportant in most of Italy, southern France and the rest of Mediterranean Spain until the classical period. Although olives and vines were probably native to the whole region, the development of systematic polyculture took place only as part of the process when agriculture advanced beyond self-sufficiency, and society beyond egalitarianism or simple levels of ranking: the new crops supported higher populations, but became important only when there was sufficient social complexity to make their exploitation feasible, and sufficient economic complexity to make it necessary and worthwhile.

4

The Balkans, the middle Danube basin and the Ukraine

Geographical introduction

This chapter principally discusses two very diverse regions included today within the political boundaries of Bulgaria, Yugoslavia, Hungary and Rumania: the Balkans, a dissected area of upland and basin dominated by the Dinaric alps, and the middle Danube basin or Hungarian plain to the north within the ring of the Carpathian mountains (Fig. 31). In addition, reference is made to the Ukraine, the great expanse of steppeland stretching east from the Carpathians to the Caucasus (Fig.32), the homeland of nomadic peoples who on several occasions overturned the political structure of classical and medieval Europe and whose effect on prehistoric Europe, according to many archaeologists, was just as momentous (e.g. Gimbutas, 1965).

The Dinaric alps, forming the backbone of Yugoslavia, rise to over 3000 metres above sea level. There are two major eastern extensions in Bulgaria: the Stara Planina to the north (and its offshoot ridge the Sredna Gora), and the Rhodope mountains to the south forming the modern boundary with Greece. Within the Dinaric alps is a series of rift valley basins or *poljes*, and the range is also cut through by major rivers; two in particular, the Vardar flowing south to the Aegean and the Morava flowing north to the Danube, form a natural corridor linking the Mediterranean with central Europe. Drainage in southern Bulgaria is dominated by the Tundzha and Maritsa rivers; the northern part of the country consists of gently undulating plains draining north to the lower Danube.

The Carpathian range sweeps in a huge curve for almost 1000 kilometres from the Austrian alps through eastern Czechoslovakia, southern Poland and northern Hungary to Rumania, ending at the Iron Gates on the Danube, where the river cuts through the narrow gorge formed here between the Carpathians and a northern arm of the Dinaric system. On average the Carpathians are about half the height of the Swiss/Austrian alps, with comparable glacial scenery only in the Tatra mountains to the north. The southern part of the range consists of a kind of spiral which encloses the Transylvanian basin or plateau, a region of rolling hills and broad valleys. The enormous basin of the middle Danube is in fact a rather complex region of low hills and flatlands rather than an unending plain. One group of hills crosses the Danube near Budapest, trending southwest/northeast; there are other ridges between the Sava and the Danube, and between the Sava and the Drava; and the Great Alföld, the major plain between the Danube and the Carpathian foothills, also divides into a region of rolling country between the Danube and Tisza rivers, and low-lying swampier terrain east of the Tisza. These great rivers meander across wide flood plains, with much of the surrounding land only 5–10 metres above mean water level. With river maxima in late spring, large areas were liable to very serious flooding before modern flood control: the Sava, Drava and Tisza floodwaters could even hold back the flow of the Danube, and a rise of four metres in the Danube caused the Tisza to flow backwards, flooding enormous areas of adjacent farmland for some 100 kilometres of its length (Nandris, 1970: 60).

A Mediterranean climate extends into the Balkans as far as the upper Vardar and southern Bulgaria, but a continental climate predominates in the rest of the region, with cold winters, hot summers, and rainfall distributed throughout the year but heaviest in spring and summer. Violent and highly localised thunderstorms are common in the summer. Rainfall in the lowland regions averages about 600–700 mm a year, but is much higher in the mountains – for example, some 2500 mm fall in the Montenegran part of the Dinaric alps. Average summer temperatures are between 20° and 30°C, and winter temperatures little above freezing, but as with precipitation the great variations

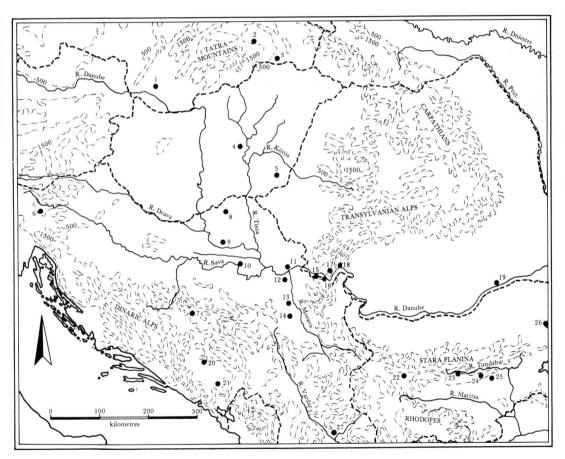

Fig. 31. The Balkans and the middle Danube basin (contours in metres): principal sites and regions mentioned in the text. 1. Sered; 2. Spišský Štvrtok; 3. Barca; 4. Toszeg; 5. Békés; 6. Ig; 7. Obre; 8. Pereš; 9. Bačka Palanka; 10. Gomolava; 11. Starčevo; 12. Vinča; 13. Selevac; 14. Divostin; 15. Padina; 16. Lepenski Vir, Vlasac; 17. Icoana; 18. Cuciulata; 19. Cascioărele; 20. Odmut; 21. Crvena Stijena; 22. Chevdar; 23. Kazanluk; 24. Karanovo; 25. Azmak, Ezero; 26. Varna; 27. Anza (begovo).

in altitude over short distances in the Balkans mean that local temperature variations can be very considerable. In the middle Danube basin, although precipitation averages 500 mm or more, the average evapotranspiration rate is equal to or greater than average annual precipitation, so much of the area suffers from aridity and is classified as moisture-deficient for agriculture (Dohrs, 1971: 275). In the worst affected areas, 'the probability is that precipitation in 75% of the years will not be enough for most plants to produce even mediocre yields' (Kosse, 1979: 31).

The most valuable agricultural soils today are the chernozems or black earths of the middle Danube basin and the comparable smolnitsas of the lower river valleys in Yugoslavia and Bulgaria. The chernozems are fertile but heavy soils rich in plant nutrients and with a stable structure. Smolnitsas, formed of lacustrine clays in conditions of impeded drainage, are also fertile, heavy and water-retentive (Dudal *et al.*, 1966; Pešić, 1967). These soils, like heavy riverine clays, are prime arable soils today because, with their gentle gradients, their fertility can be captured by large scale mechanised farming. In pre-industrial farming, however, the principal value of many of these water-retentive and heavy soils was as summer grazing. In the same way the very deep, fine textured and dry soils of the loess plateaus in the middle Danube basin

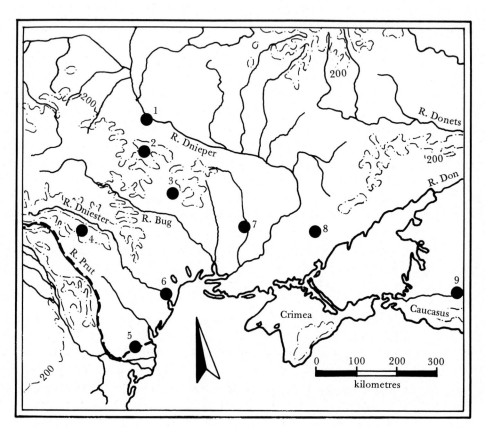

Fig. 32. The Ukraine (contours in metres): principal sites and regions mentioned in the text. 1. Tripolye; 2. Kolomiiščina; 3. Vladimirovka; 4. Soroki; 5. Mirnoye; 6. Girževo; 7. Mikhailovka; 8. Kamennaya Mogila; 9. Maikop.

are now used for intensive arable farming, but this is because modern technology has been able to develop irrigation systems tapping the deep (15–35 metres) water table (Dohrs, 1971) – until the beginning of the last century the Great Alföld was used predominantly for raising livestock (Shackleton, 1964).

There are two major soil types in the Balkan uplands. The first consists of the rendzinas of the limestone mountains – shallow and stony soils, often of low fertility because of steep gradients and excessive drainage. Brown forest soils form the second group. These soils are assumed to have developed under forest conditions, tend to be free from excessive waterlogging or aridity, but are susceptible to leaching and erosion under cultivation (Kubiena, 1953; Pešić, 1967). Erosion of the highland soils has resulted locally in the formation of diluvial soils in fans and shelves at the foot of the hills on the edge of the river valleys and *poljes*; these soils tend to be stony, well drained and moderately fertile, as plant nutrients are carried down into them by silt-laden waters from the hills, and were important arable soils for pre-industrial farmers. Small areas of arable soil are also available in the uplands, but grazing is much more abundant, including summer pastures at the highest elevations, and these have favoured a variety of transhumant systems of animal husbandry in the historical period. Widespread transhumance between the Dinaric alps and the surrounding lowlands has been postulated for the Roman period (Wilkes, 1969: 178), and is recorded throughout medieval and modern times, with stock from lowland communities being taken into the hills for the summer, and stock from upland communities such as the Vlach pastoralists being wintered on the lowlands (Matley, 1968; Popovic, 1971; Sterud, 1978; Turrill, 1929).

The Russian steppes measure some 1000 km west/east between the Carpathians and the Caucasus, and some 600–700 km north from the Crimea peninsula. The southern steppes have a climate characterised by short severe winters, intense summer heat, and low annual rainfall (*c.* 250–400 mm), most of which falls in the spring and early summer. The principal soils are black earths or chernozems on loess. The northern steppes have more rainfall (which is also better distributed through the year), longer periods of snow cover in the winter, and less extreme summer temperatures. The principal soils are degraded chernozems. Both the true and the degraded chernozems are very fertile soils with a good structure, well suited to growing cereals, but whereas the combination of soils and climate on the northern steppes is very favourable for mixed farming, farming on the southern steppes tends to be more specialised towards cereals, more precarious, and more prone to damage the soil by erosion.

Boreal foragers, *c.* 7500–5500 b.c.

Although palaeoenvironmental data for the early Holocene are still very limited for this part of Europe compared with elsewhere, we can at least characterise the broad features of the Boreal landscape from a scattered series of pollen, molluscan and sedimentary studies: steppe in the driest regions of the middle Danube basin and the southern Ukraine; steppe and mixed oak woodland in most other lowland areas (but sub-Mediterranean vegetation on the Dalmatian littoral and south of the Rhodopes); open deciduous woodland at higher elevations, up to about 100 metres above sea level; pine, birch and beech forest up to about 2000 metres; and alpine vegetation above (Beug,

1967; Bosçaiu, 1971; Bozhilova, 1975; Bozhilova and Filipova, 1975; Pop *et al.*, 1970; Protopopescu-Pake *et al.*, 1970). The climate was continental, with hot dry summers and cold dry winters.

Substantial evidence for early postglacial settlement throughout the region has been found in the last fifteen years. In the middle Danube basin, large numbers of artifact scatters have been found on small sand 'islands' in the midst of the waterlogged flood plains; most of the material consists of geometric microliths and long blades and is described as Tardenoisian (Tringham, 1968). Most of the assemblages are not accompanied by faunal or botanical data, but at Pereš and Bačka Palanka in the Vojvodina (the southern part of the middle Danube basin, in northern Yugoslavia) there were small faunal collections of red deer, pig, the steppe ass and goat (Brukner, 1966), reflecting the different resource zones in the site catchments – the waterlogged margins of the Danube, arid plains to the north and west, and low rocky hills immediately to the south. A similar industry and faunal assemblage were found at Pobiti Kamani in northeast Bulgaria (Tringham, 1971: 52). Elsewhere in the basin forest faunas (red deer, roe deer, aurochs, pig) have been recovered from similar sites associated with palaeobotanical evidence for mixed deciduous and coniferous woodland (Barta, 1973; Păunescu, 1963). In the Carpathians, a different technology was commonly used ('Epigravettian'), dominated normally by backed tools – like the geometric microliths, commonly assumed to be part of composite projectile points. At Zatyni in Czechoslovakia faunal evidence associated with this technology indicated a mixed foraging system of hunting large and small game, fowling and fishing (Prošek and Ložek, 1952). In heavily forested parts of the mountains, heavier tools were also manufactured such as flake axes, leaf-shaped points and large flake-scrapers (Mogoşanu and Bitiri, 1961; Vertes, 1960).

In the Balkans, too, the settlement evidence divides into highland assemblages characterised by backed tools and lowland assemblages with more geometric microliths. The best known highland site is Crvena Stijena, a massive rock shelter in the Montenegran alps, used in this period for hunting red deer, roe deer, pig and ibex (Benac and Brodar, 1958). Comparable occupation debris has been found in the Odmut cave in this region, at the confluence of the Piva river with one of its tributaries. Steep hills lie behind the cave, and ibex dominated the faunal sample (65%), followed by red deer (25%), roe deer, pig and bear; fish bones were also common, and several antler harpoons were discovered (Srejović, 1974). Contemporary but rather different assemblages have been found in Yugoslavia on either side of the Dinaric alps. Surface collections of geometric microliths have been reported in the north, from the terraces of the Bosna river and its tributaries (Alexander, 1972: 29). The stratigraphies of several caves on or near the Adriatic coast demonstrate the same trends in lithic technology and subsistence data as seen elsewhere in the Mediterranean basin: an earlier postglacial industry of microblades and small round scrapers associated with a large mammal fauna (red deer, roe deer, ibex), and an industry with a greater geometric component in the seventh and sixth millennia associated with a more diversified subsistence system involving hunting, fishing and shellfish collection (Cannarella and Cremonesi, 1967).

The highland Epigravettian and lowland Tardenoisian assemblages have frequently been assigned to two different cultures or peoples, but are much more likely to reflect functional differences in foraging equipment. The quality of the subsistence and arti-factual data certainly does not allow rigorous analysis, and all-year-round occupation using only one technology must have been feasible in certain favoured locations; how-ever, the increasingly dry summers on the arid lowlands and the increasingly severe winters in the mountains during the Boreal period would surely have encouraged a winter/lowland summer/upland system of foraging with a rhythm of movement much like that of the transhumant shepherds in historical times. The seasonal movements of the red deer, clearly a key resource, may well have been rather similar. Presumably the normal foraging system involved hunting the forest animals in most regions; hunting zone-specific animals in particular seasons (such as ibex in the mountains and the steppe ass on the plains); fishing, especially in the main rivers and flood channels of the low-lands but also in mountain streams; fowling, again mostly in the lowland marshes; and – as always poorly documented – gathering plant foods. The effect of such a pattern of movement would probably have been, in the middle Danube/Carpathian region, to nucleate settlement in the winter in the Alföld and disperse it in the summer into the hills, and in the Balkans, to nucleate settlement in summer in the uplands and disperse it on either side in the winter.

A third group of sites has been investigated on either side of the Iron Gates gorge, now flooded by an enormous hydroelectric scheme. The Danube here is at about 100 metres above sea level, and rugged limestone hills rise to 500 metres or more within two or three kilometres of the river; in the Boreal period they carried a vegetation of birch, juniper, pine and beech, together with many herbaceous plants and grasses (Mišić *et al.*, 1972). Subsistence strategies involved hunting red deer and pigs in these hills, together with trapping small game, fishing and collecting shellfish (Bolomey, 1973); the communities may have remained by the river throughout the year, moving from camp to camp (as Bolomey argued), or made more extensive movements into the hinterland in some seasons. She also suggested from faunal analysis that the pig popu-lation may have been managed in some way, with surplus males being culled rather than breeding females. Certainly the subsistence system seems to have encouraged an unusual degree of sedentism at the Iron Gates, in part reflected by substantial cemeteries unique in Boreal Europe: some 350 bodies have been found, including over 75 at the site of Vlasac. The analysis of this population, dated to the middle and second half of the eighth millennium b.c., indicated an average life expectancy of 30–40 years for women and 50–60 years for men and postulated a population of some 50–100 people per gener-ation at the Iron Gates, increasing at a very slow rate (Nemeskeri, 1976).

In the more forested northern zone of the Russian steppes, subsistence was broadly based and included river and lake fishing, fowling, gathering (molluscs being the prin-cipal evidence), and hunting – in particular red deer, aurochs and roe deer, as well as a variety of smaller game (Dolukhanov, 1979). Both the backed blade and geometric flint technologies were used here. Further south, where according to both pollen cores and on-site environmental data the landscape was much more open, the geometric tech-nology predominated and a more restricted group of animals was exploited, with the horse and aurochs being the principal quarries at sites such as Girževo and Mirnoye (Dolukhanov, 1979: 87).

The first farmers, *c.* 5500–4500 b.c.

The transition to the Atlantic climate in the mid-sixth millennium b.c. brought warmer and wetter winters and cooler and wetter summers, and consequent changes in vegetation. In the lower Danube region, oak and alder forest and steppe gave way to a denser vegetation of hazel, elm, lime and birch. On the evidence of over twenty pollen diagrams in the middle Danube basin, marsh and fen vegetation expanded in the major river valleys liable to seasonal inundations and deciduous woodland increased on the valley margins, but the loess interfluves still carried a mixture of forest-steppe and tree-less meadow (Kosse, 1979). The major altitudinal zonation of upland vegetation was probably not greatly changed, although deciduous oak woodland probably extended above the present limits. The steppe ass was still able to survive on the arid grasslands of the Alföld (Bökönyi, 1974), and the Atlantic was the period when the immigration of Mediterranean plant species reached its maximum in Hungary (Zolyomi, 1964). The climatic shift also coincided with the first widespread evidence for farming, associated with the introduction of new technologies and settlement forms to this part of Europe.

Five early neolithic cultures have been defined in the Balkans and the middle Danube basin from *c.* 5500 b.c. on the basis of distinct regional pottery styles: Karanovo I (the basal level of the deep stratigraphy at this site) in southern Bulgaria; Kremikovci in the highlands of the Bulgarian/Yugoslav border; Starčevo in central and southern Yugoslavia; Körös in the middle Danube basin, especially along the Tisza river and its major tributaries the Körös and Maros; and Criş (the Rumanian name for the Körös river) in Transylvania and in southern Rumania along the lower Danube. The different styles of pottery overlap considerably, and Tringham (1971) also defines a sixth group on this basis, a transitional Starčevo–Körös group in the Vojvodina. There is a notable fall-off in the ceramic range from southeast to northwest. Karanovo I fine wares have a thick red or white slip painted before firing with red, black or white patterns, a reper-toire much like that of Greek settlements such as Nea Nikomedeia; Kremikovci sites have two forms of painted decoration, white or black on a red background; Starčevo sites have only one (black on red); and Körös and Criş sites have no painted pottery. Coarse wares invariably dominate all the assemblages, mainly large storage vessels and smaller bowls, with the clay tempered with straw and chaff; they were sometimes decorated with impressed designs and rustication, especially in the northern settlements.

Stone tools consisted of trapezoidal axes and adzes of hard stone, and fairly simple blade and scraper assemblages of flint or chert. The blades were mostly unretouched, usually made from locally available stone, and wear analysis indicates that they were used for cutting, scraping, sawing and drilling (Tringham, 1971: 75). Antler sickles with flint insets showing silica gloss have been found at a few sites. Bone pins and spatulae were manufactured. Clay was also used for making small anthropomorphic figurines, spindle whorls, loom weights, weights for fish nets, ovens and perhaps lamps.

The best settlement data have been recovered from the Bulgarian settlements, which were tell villages like those of Greece (Fig. 33). Buildings were rectangular or square structures with a timber frame, walls made of clay mixed with chaff built up against a timber screen or wattle and daub, and a beaten clay floor (Georgiev, 1961, 1965). The clay was excavated from pits at the side of the houses, used later for cooking, rubbish disposal, or burying the dead. The houses were one-roomed structures, sometimes with an oven or hearth inside, but these were also built in the spaces between the houses. At Karanovo and Azmak the houses were laid out in rows, and log-paved streets are suggested at some sites. A total of sixty buildings has been estimated for the basal level at Karanovo. The differential distribution of certain artifacts in these settlements (the finest pottery, figurines, and clay 'altars', for example) and other features such as internally painted walls in some houses suggest strongly that these societies were divided into different status groups, although social organisation has never been investigated systematically.

Botanical and faunal data from the first major excavations were published by Dzambazov (1963), Hopf (1973), Mikov and Dzambazov (1960) and J. Renfrew (1969, 1973); the major corpus of data, however, consists of the samples collected under controlled conditions by Dennell during the excavations of Chevdar and Kazanluk and analysed by him in considerable detail (Dennell, 1972, 1974a, 1974b, 1974c, 1976a, 1978). Einkorn, emmer, barley, flax and pulses were identified from these two sites, and einkorn, emmer and pulses from Karanovo (J. Renfrew, 1969). At Chevdar and Kazanluk, Dennell was able to reconstruct the crop processing activities taking place at the sites from differences in sample composition, grain size and archaeological context (Table 5, p. 24; Fig. 34). In addition, the clusterings of weed species implied that emmer, barley and vetch were each cultivated as separate crops (each associated with a characteristic weed flora): 'this evidence might suggest that the inhabitants used . . . some kind of rotational cropping system' (Dennell, 1978: 122). In support of this con-

Fig. 33. An early neolithic house at Chevdar, Bulgaria: a single-roomed structure with a wall of timber uprights (marked by post-holes) plastered with clay; the entrance is to the right, and the remains of a hearth or oven are opposite at the other end of the house. (Photograph: Robin Dennell)

clusion, the carbonised grain at Chevdar was found in association with nematode cysts of *Heterodera latipons*, a species that infests wheat and causes crop failure if present in large numbers when rotations are short (Webley and Dennell, 1978).

The faunal samples from Chevdar and Kazanluk (recovered by careful dry and wet sieving) consisted primarily or sheep/goats and pigs, with fewer cattle and small numbers of red deer, roe deer, small mammals, birds and fish (Dennell, 1978). Most of the sheep and goats were between three and five years at slaughter, suggesting that the secondary products of the live animal were at least as important as meat. Pigs were killed in their second year, the normal age at which pigs seem to have reached a satisfactory killing weight in antiquity. The small cattle sample divided into two age groups, one very young, the other much older – an age structure strongly suggestive of a dairying component in the husbandry system, with the calf being taken off the mother at an early stage to release the milk for human consumption (Legge, 1981b). Chevdar is located in a small intermontane basin away from the main zone of tell settlement, surrounded by natural grazing country but with direct access to a pocket of diluvial soil. Kazanluk lies at a lower elevation, in a region of milder climate and gentler topography, with access to more abundant arable soil. In both cases, Dennell argued that the grain and pulses were grown for human consumption and the other crops as fodder, with the sheep and goats being taken into the hills in the summer whilst the cattle and pigs remained by the settlements, and with the stock being overwintered there on straw, grain husks and natural fodder.

In the primary zone of tell settlement, the Nova Zagora region (Fig. 35), the neolithic villages were placed at the junction between the limestone hills and the plain of southern Bulgaria. In their analysis of early neolithic subsistence here, Dennell and Webley (1975) argued that the heavy waterlogged smolnitsa soils of the plain and comparable riverine clays, though now the main arable soils, could not have been cultivated with the simple technology available to the first farmers, but would have provided a substantial area of grazing (as in pre-industrial farming here). The diluvial sandy soils at the foot of

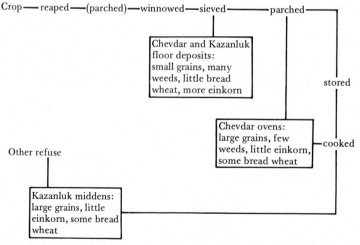

Fig. 34. Crop processing activities at Chevdar and Kazanluk (neolithic Bulgaria). (After Dennell, 1972: fig. 3)

the hills, on the same criterion, were likely to have been the most attractive arable soils, with the forest soils carrying browse and the thin stony soils of the hills providing summer grazing. The tells were located on or near the areas of diluvial soil, about five kilometres apart; the biggest tells such as Karanovo had the largest amount of diluvial soil in their catchments, suggesting very clearly that agricultural potential had a direct effect on settlement success and longevity. Although there is little detailed evidence for the nature of animal and crop husbandry in this region, the likelihood is that the farming system was much as at Chevdar and Kazanluk, involving a mobile pastoral component

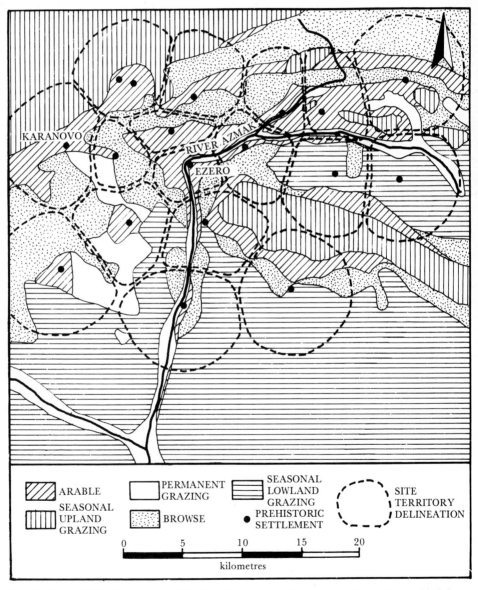

Fig. 35. The neolithic *tell* settlements of the Nova Zagora region, Bulgaria: the tells are shown with their catchments, against a background of predicted land use. (After Dennell and Webley, 1975: figs. 1 and 3)

Table 7 *Composition of the Anza faunal sample in the four main phases of settlement, according to the number of identifiable fragments (F) and the minimum number of individuals (M). (Analysed by Bökönyi, and published in Gimbutas, 1974b: 47–8)*

		1		2		3		4	
		N	%	N	%	N	%	N	%
Cattle	F	115	9.6	101	13.5	89	6.8	496	16.2
	M	12	10.6	12	15.2	10	7.6	48	17.8
Dog	F	5	.4	10	1.3	28	2.2	36	1.2
	M	2	1.8	3	3.8	5	3.8	7	2.6
Pig	F	99	8.3	74	9.9	115	8.8	351	11.4
	M	8	7.1	7	8.9	11	8.4	32	11.9
Sheep/goat	F	938	78.3	543	72.4	995	76.4	2067	67.4
	M	80	70.8	49	62.0	85	64.9	161	59.9
Game	F	41	3.4	22	2.9	75	5.8	118	3.8
	M	11	9.7	8	10.1	20	15.3	21	7.8

(principally sheep and goats) and a primary arable component, the latter based on rotational systems of cultivation. Dennell and Webley calculated from estimates of the potential productivity of the tell catchments that the larger villages could have consisted of up to 400–500 people, whilst figures for population densities in modern Near Eastern villages indicated communities of 350–400 people at the same sites. These calculations suggested a total population of 3600–4500 people for the nine largest tells, a density of 10 people/km² which compares quite favourably with densities of 25 people/km² in parts of northern Greece in 1928 (Dennell and Webley, 1975: 107), although the actual (rather than the potential) densities were probably much lower (Dennell: pers. comm.). Although limited amounts of fodder and manure were probably severe constraints on the agricultural system, the overriding impression from the structural, subsistence and site catchment data is that the first farmers in Bulgaria practised stable and well organised husbandry, much like that of their counterparts in northern Greece.

The major Starčevo settlements of southern Yugoslavia were also tells, though usually less massive than sites like Karanovo. Less is known of the buildings in them, but structural evidence at a few sites and clay house models suggest that village organisation was much as in Bulgaria. The tells were also located in similar positions, on or near patches of stony well drained soil at the junction of plain or basin and mountain (Barker, 1975c). Anza was a typical settlement, a cluster of small houses on the edge of the Ovče *polje* ('sheep basin'), which was until the last war a traditional wintering area for transhumant flocks which summered in the surrounding hills (Elster, 1976; Gimbutas, 1972, 1974b, 1976). Sheep/goat dominated the large faunal sample (some 20,000 fragments) in all phases of the occupation (Table 7); there were also small numbers of cattle and pig, and game included aurochs, badger, boar, fox, hare, red deer, roe deer and wolf. The mortality ages of the main stock closely resembled those at Chevdar and Kazanluk. The list of plant species identified was also rather similar: einkorn,

with copper being systematically mined, smelted and finished by hot and cold working into a substantial range of artifacts (tubular beads, spiral rings, pins, bracelets, and heavier tools such as chisels and perforated hammer axes). Mining developed in the same period on an extensive scale for other resources such as high quality flint and stone, graphite and vermilion, and the scale of the operations sometimes implies the emergence of specialised mining communities (Černych, 1978; Jovanovic and Ottoway, 1976; Vértes, 1964). Copper artifacts were too soft to be of any real functional use, but were highly valued as status symbols, and, like items of high quality flint, hard stone, obsidian and shell, were exchanged over very considerable distances – normally up to 200–300 kilometres from source (Sherratt, 1976).

The importance of status objects, like the development of craft specialisation and long distance exchange, reflects the fundamental change in Balkan society that can be discerned during the fourth millennium: chalcolithic communities were stratified, and probably characterised by 'big man' systems of social organisation (Sahlins, 1963). At the Varna cemetery in northeast Bulgaria, for example, the richest graves had gold diadems, ear rings and weapon shafts, as well as fine objects of copper, flint and stone (Renfrew, 1978). The richest graves were of adults, whereas child burials were rare, suggesting that rank was earned through life's achievements rather than being inherited by birth. The wealth of the Varna graves and the absence of cemeteries in the major tell areas led Renfrew to conclude that the cemetery held the elite of a large region. The evidence for pronounced ranking is as clear in the Tiszapolgar cemeteries (Bognár-Kutzián, 1972). The social transformation also coincides with the development of complex ritual or symbolic systems: clay figurines (often apparently masked) and 'shrine' models abound, and special buildings probably reserved for ritual have also been excavated (Gimbutas, 1974c). Interpretation is inevitably problematic, but it does at least seem clear that chalcolithic ideology was rooted in the natural world of birth and death, seasonal agricultural cycles, and so on.

The fourth millennium in the Balkans witnessed substantial growth in existing settlements, the development of new settlements, and major changes in their internal organisation. Chalcolithic deposits in the tells average 4–6 metres in thickness. Karanovo was a village of some fifty houses at this time, many of them large two-roomed structures and all equipped with ovens, grain bins and querns. There is consistent evidence for careful planning in settlement layout, and for specialist craft buildings (Comşa, 1976; Dumitrescu, 1965; McPherron and Srejović, 1971). The mobile-cum-sedentary system of mixed farming first established by the tell communities *c.* 5500 b.c. continued without substantial change (Dennell, 1978; Gimbutas, 1976), although larger scale wool production has been suggested from the frequencies of loom weights and spindle whorls. The principal crops recorded are einkorn, emmer and six-row barley. Millet and flax were also grown at the Gomolava tell in Yugoslavia on the Sava river (van Zeist, 1975), where high percentages of cereal and weed pollen suggested very intensive arable production around the settlement (Bottema, 1975). The development of the traction ard, first suggested by the Vădastra cattle phalanges, is further indicated by a piece of red deer antler which has been tentatively identified from traces of wear on it as an ard share, found at the Cascioărele settlement of the late fourth millennium b.c. (Dumitrescu and Bănățeanu, 1965; Fig. 38). During this period, defence increasingly became a factor in site location, with islands, promontories and finally steep-sided hills being selected, and many settlements were now surrounded by ditches, palisades or stone walls (Comşa, 1976; Sherratt, 1972: 533; Todorova, 1978). Little is known of farming in the middle Danube basin at this time, but again the first fortified hilltop settlements were established during the later fourth millennium (Kosse, 1979: 142). Correlating with this evidence for land competition, there is a consistent trend of settlement expansion to more marginal areas – for example to the marshy and forested flatlands of the lower Danube (Comşa, 1976; Dumitrescu, 1965), and further into the hills above the major Balkan rivers (Fig. 39).

In the Ukraine, the foraging-based system of subsistence probably endured more or less unaffected by contact with neighbouring agricultural systems until the early fourth millennium b.c., when there is the first unequivocal evidence for the adoption of a significant agricultural component in the form of sheep bones and emmer grains from a number of Bug-Dniester sites (Tringham, 1971: 168). Unfortunately, nothing is known of the context of this important development, but what is clear is that dramatic changes

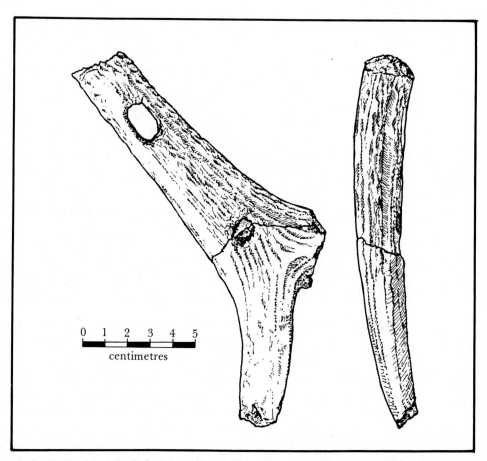

Fig. 38. The Cascioărele 'ard' of red deer antler. (After Dumitrescu and Bănățeanu, 1965: fig. 1)

followed rapidly in settlement organisation and subsistence. By the middle of the fourth millennium b.c., Tripolye communities were living in permanent villages such as Vladimirovka and Kolomiiščina of fifty or so family houses (in fact there may have been as many as 150 at Vladimirovka), the latter being substantial structures with timber

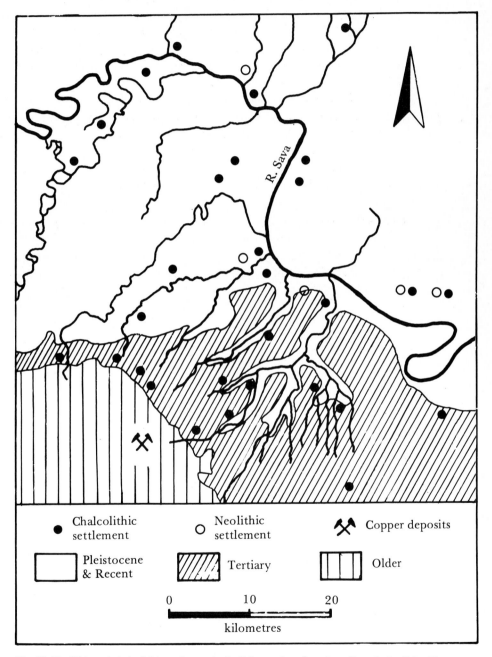

Fig. 39. Neolithic and chalcolithic settlement in the Sabac region of northern Yugoslavia. (After Sherratt, 1976: fig. 12)

frames, wattle and clay walls which were plastered and sometimes brightly painted, and equipped with clay ovens and hearths very like the houses of the Balkan tells. The communities used a technology which included flint sickles with silica gloss, stone axes and adzes, hoes and querns, grew a variety of crops including emmer, barley, millet and pulses, and kept numbers of domestic animals, particularly sheep. Although hunting and fishing remained important, it is possible that the process of domesticating the horse was also well under way by this time on the steppes (Chapter 2, p. 33; Sherratt, 1981: 272). These changes were associated with developments in crafts, ideology and social stratification as profound as those of the Balkans and the middle Danube region at this time.

The transformations in technology, social organisation, exchange and settlement during the fourth millennium were clearly interrelated. Childe once commented that 'a stone age community was, at least potentially, self-sufficing . . . the objects of stone age trade were always luxuries . . . or at least things that men could have done without' (Childe, 1951: 35). Sherratt, however, has argued that – on the analogy of exchange amongst simple farming societies today – a constant movement of subsistence products (both foodstuffs and necessary commodities such as good stone) must be envisaged amongst the Balkan chalcolithic societies, with the 'luxury' objects and raw materials being essential to mobilise demand – 'they thus act as a kind of "flywheel" for the whole system' (Sherratt, 1976: 559). The expansion of population to more marginal areas and the changes in settlement organisation related to this trend, whilst providing a favourable context for the emergence of controlling elites, also meant that exchangeable commodities were needed here to attract subsistence products from the primary centres of settlement (cereals? textiles?), with the new 'big men' providing 'nodes of concentration for circulating goods' (Sherratt, 1976: 561). Their need for status markers stimulated exchange, and the technology to mine, process and distribute the new valued commodities such as copper which, although known for some two thousand years, only now became important in the context of the social and economic transformations of the fourth millennium.

Settlement reorganisation in the third millennium b.c.

The final phase at Karanovo (Level VII, or the Ezero phase) spans the third millennium b.c., the cultural stage defined as the Initial Bronze Age in southeast Europe. Habitation at most of the Bulgarian tells ended with this phase, which was characterised by plain pottery with a very simple repertoire of shapes very different from the lavish fine wares of the Chalcolithic. On the Russian steppes, too, the settlement system of large Tripolye villages established in the fourth millennium did not endure into the third: instead, the settlement evidence is limited to a few major defended sites and the archaeological record is dominated by cemeteries of *kurgan* barrows. A number of striking similarities between Ezero material and that of contemporary sites in Anatolia (Turkey) – knobbed handles, bowls with inturned rims, two-handled 'depas' cups, clay 'anchors' (probably loom weights) – induced Mellaart (1960) to suggest an invasion from Anatolia to explain the end of the Bulgarian tells. Many Balkan scholars, on the other hand, have preferred to stress the similarities between cord-ornamented pottery in the Ezero assemblage and that of the Kurgan barrow cemeteries suggesting instead an invasion from the steppes. Gimbutas, in particular, has consistently explained the popularity of cord-ornamented pottery ('corded ware') here and in several other parts of temperate Europe in the mid-third millennium in terms of a Kurgan invasion, which she believes carried the Indo-European languages into Europe. The occurrence of corded ware has also been used by Piggott (1965: 92) to explain settlement changes in the middle Danube basin in terms of a Kurgan invasion. Today such invasion theories are viewed very sceptically, and alternative theories have been put forward citing internal developments in social and economic structure to account for the changes in the archaeological record.

In Bulgaria, for example, Dennell and Webley (1975) have argued that geomorphological change was a critical factor in the abandonment of the Nova Zagora tells. As their catchment analysis indicated, the primary cultivable soils were restricted in area, and once they were fully exploited, any further intensification had to come in the pastoral component of the economy. This situation seems to have been reached by the late fourth millennium, and further intensification in sheep pastoralism is evident at sites like Ezero in the mid-third millennium (Dennell, 1978). The formation of a massive sheet of riverine clay now around many of the tells has been dated to the third millennium, and so Dennell and Webley concluded that 'the removal of vegetational cover (by grazing) on the unstable uplands could have resulted in unforeseen erosion and consequent deposition in the valleys and lowland areas to an extent which would have impelled drastic economic and social change' (1975: 108).

Although Dennell and Webley argued for purely local factors of overexploitation and landscape change, there is some evidence that climatic change may have been a factor in the settlement reorganisation of the third millennium. In the last five hundred years of the Atlantic, glacial advance caused a sharper oscillation (the Piora oscillation) towards a colder climate than any for several thousand years previously, and the beginning of the Sub-Boreal (in the mid-third millennium in eastern Europe) then caused a return to warmer temperatures but marked rainfall fluctuations (Frenzel, 1966; Lamb, 1977: 373). In the Balkans, the effect of the change would have been late sharp frosts, which would have decreased the arable productivity of the catchments of the established settlements, and a more open landscape increasingly suited to sheep and goat pastoralism. There is consistent evidence for greater reliance on barley in the Balkans at this time (barley has a lower optimal germination rate than wheat, is less affected by rainfall variability, and is better suited to more marginal soils), although agricultural systems continued to use the same range of cereals and legumes as before – at Gomolava, for example, the third millennium farmers grew einkorn, emmer, bread wheat, barley, millet, linseed and legumes (van Zeist, 1975). Survey in the lower Morava valley has indicated that a series of large Vinča settlements was replaced in the third millennium by many much smaller sites, and Bankoff has argued that climatic change stimulated settlement dispersal here, together with increased barley cultivation and pastoralism (Bankoff *et al.*, 1980). Given that the grassland soils were more difficult to cultivate than the forest soils which were the main arable soils around the existing tells in the region, favouring pastoral rather than arable use, it was easier to disperse settlement and adapt subsistence to new areas than to attempt to intensify production at the tells by taking fresh land into cultivation by large scale ploughing, or by increasing yields from existing fields by shorter fallowing and greater manuring – both strategies which necessitated more cattle, and the fodder to feed them.

On the Drama plain (Macedonia, northern Greece) there were rather similar trends in settlement at this time, with the main tells on the floor of the basin being increasingly abandoned in favour of fortified promontories at the margins, and Sherratt (1972: 534) envisaged similar changes in subsistence. In western Yugoslavia, too, there was a proliferation of small hilltop settlements (Alexander, 1972: 57–8; Schmidt, 1945). Baden settlements in the middle Danube basin were often fortified with ditches and ramparts, and isolated hilltops in Transylvania were also fortified (Berciu, 1967: 66). Little agricultural data are available here, but there are some indications of an increase in barley cultivation and in sheep/goat and cattle herding (Bökönyi, 1968, 1974; Bökönyi and Kubasiewicz, 1961; Murray, 1970).

In the Ukraine, although settlement evidence is conspicuously lacking, it seems clear from the contents of the Kurgan barrows that the third millennium witnessed a major shift from the kind of mixed farming practised earlier by the Tripolye villages to a much more mobile and pastoral-based system of farming. Horses were ridden, cattle were used to pull carts, and sheep were the principal stock. Much wealth was now on the hoof, and social stratification and competition seem clearly reflected in the barrow inventories and fortifications of settlements such as Mikhaïlovka. Control of the Caucasus ores was probably an additional factor in the wealth of the elites adjacent to them, exemplified by the spectacular burials at Maikop (Childe, 1957: 151). As before in this region, the context of this transformation in subsistence is not clear, although it is possible that the desiccation noted in the Mediterranean in the third millennium was one factor in the abandonment of sedentary mixed farming, on the southern steppes at least. However that may be, the third millennium witnessed the establishment of the characteristic lifestyle of the steppe peoples which has endured until recent times.

In a major paper, Sherratt (1981) has argued that, after the first domestication of animals for their meat, there was then a 'Secondary Products Revolution' (animal traction, riding, plough agriculture, dairying, wool production) which, beginning in Mesopotamia, spread across temperate Europe in the third millennium b.c. The thesis is discussed again in later chapters, but as far as the Balkans and middle Danube basin are concerned, it seems clear that both milk and wool production were certainly practised well prior to the third millennium, and that cattle may have been used for their traction too (including pulling ards), albeit not on a large scale. On the other hand, it is certainly true that the third millennium marked the first systematic and widespread use of animal transport in this part of Europe: horse bones are common for the first time in Baden burials; two Baden burials also contained pairs of oxen or cattle; and several models of four wheeled carts have been found in burials and settlements in Hungary (Bökönyi, 1951, 1974; Kalicz, 1963; Korek, 1951; Fig. 40). In addition, there is clear evidence that sheep/goat pastoralism increased in significance during the third millennium, and the range of pottery produced at Baden and Ezero settlements includes new drinking and pouring vessels which – whilst some may have been for wine imported from the Mediterranean – seem as likely to have been designed for milk and milk products. 'The association of drinking and driving evidently began at an early stage in their history' (Sherratt, 1981: 282).

The cord-decorated pottery found on the Russian steppes and in the Balkans and the middle Danube basin certainly represents important contact between these regions, but almost certainly not an invasion from the steppes by Kurgan bands like indians on the warpath. The new technology became widespread at a time when pastoralism was increasingly important and when new lands were being taken into cultivation, in response in part at least to the ecological changes of the early Sub-Boreal: a social and economic context ideally suited to the wagon, the ox team, the horse and the ard. The proliferation of defended settlements during the third millennium probably reflects the mixture of uneasy dependence and hostility between sedentary farmer and transhumant shepherd of the kind that has existed in historical times, for example between the Vlach pastoralists of the Dinaric highlands and the agricultural populations of the adjacent lowlands, amongst whom the Vlachs wintered their stock and sold off their produce (Popović, 1971; Turrill, 1929).

Later prehistoric farming

Until recently, complex cultural divisions were proposed by many Balkan scholars for the bronze age (second millennium) archaeology of the region, with most of the changes in material culture being ascribed to invading peoples from central Europe and/or the steppes (Alexander, 1972; Berciu, 1967; Gimbutas, 1965). However, as Coles and

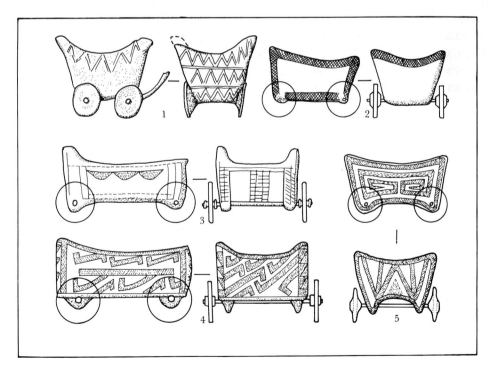

Fig. 40. Waggon models from the middle Danube basin: (wheels restored except in 1) 1. Budakalász; 2–5. Transylvania. (After Piggott, 1965: fig. 48)

Harding (1979) pointed out, the great folk movements were based on a scheme of discrete phases of pottery and metalwork (often unrelated to settlement evidence) defined by typological comparisons which has been forcefully discredited by the radio-carbon chronology. The archaeological record in fact demonstrates normal settlement continuity, and the major change in burial rite in this period (the spread of cremation) can no longer be viewed simplistically in terms of a population spread.

Life for most people for most of the Bronze Age in this region was probably neolithic in everyday technology – bronze ornaments, tools and weapons were primarily manu-factured for the upper echelons of society. At Békés, for example (a mid-second millennium settlement in Hungary), there were hundreds of polished axes, antler hoes and flint sickles, and house construction demonstrated quite sophisticated carpentry involving dowelled cross beams (Banner, 1955). At Ig, a waterlogged settlement in Slovakia, the primary technology was of clay, antler, stone, flint and wood (Alexander, 1972: 61). By the end of the second millennium metal was far more common: bronze artifacts were buried with all levels of society, buried hoards were both numerous and substantial (4000 kg in one example from Rumania), bronze working was practised on a major scale, and agricultural implements of bronze (sickles and axes especially) were probably in everyday use. Many settlements had special buildings set aside for smith-ing, and it seems likely that the late bronze age economy included more or less full time craftsmen in most settlements of any size. Although evdence for social organisation is much more detailed in central Europe (Shennan, 1975; Chapter 6), we can observe a broad trend towards the development of hereditary power groups across the region by the mid-second millennium, and the burial goods of the major cemeteries of the late sec-ond millennium imply four categories of rank: most graves are without gravegoods, many have just a pin or a razor, a small group of 'warrior burials' has fine weapons and body armour, and there are rare but elaborate 'chieftain burials' (Dumitrescu, 1961).

In the middle Danube basin the major settlements of the river valleys were tells, the best known of which is Toszeg; they were substantial villages of wattle and daub or plank houses, protected by various combinations of ramparts, ditches and palisades (Kalicz, 1968). Villages were often established on defensible promontories formed by river bends. Variations in house size in the settlements correlate with the cemetery evi-dence for marked ranking in second millennium society. Hillfort villages were particu-larly common in the upland margins of the basin. One of the most impressive of these, Spišský Štvrtok in Slovakia, was enclosed by a ditch and rampart, both faced with stone, ending in bastion towers at the main entrance; twenty-six houses were found inside, those in the central acropolis being of stronger construction than the others (Vladar, 1972). Here and at Barca, a comparable defended settlement, gold and bronze objects were found hidden under the floors of some of the houses, with a distribution that indicates considerable wealth differentiation within the communities. Contemporary settlements in the Balkans included tells like Gomolava and fortified hilltops enclosing small hamlets or single farmsteads. Lowland waterlogged villages, substantial com-munities in palisaded enclosures, have also been excavated in the lower Danube region.

The economy of the region in the second millennium also included exchange systems on an ever increasing scale. For bronze age societies in general, Rowlands (1973: 596) has argued that 'Europe was connected by a number of inter-locking regional exchange networks, in which goods moved internally by such mechanisms as gift exchange or redistribution, and in the peripheral areas and between networks by barter and trade'. Unfortunately we know almost nothing about the scale and nature of local exchange systems in most regions, presumably concerned primarily with subsistence commodities. On the other hand, although the amount of Mycenaean commerce through the Balkans to central Europe has probably been exaggerated in the past, it remains clear that inter-regional exchange of high value commodities amongst the ruling elites was current here throughout the second millennium (Harding, 1975; Harding and Warren, 1973; Rowlands, 1973).

Technology, craft specialisation, social stratification, settlement organisation and trade – all these facets of bronze age life obviously imply that most agricultural communities in this region during the second millennium were geared to surplus production. That being said, however, it is very difficult to characterise farming systems in any detail. At several middle Danube sites and at Gomolava a very wide range of cereals and legumes was cultivated (Hajnalova, 1972; Tempir, 1964; van Zeist, 1975); the presence of new crops such as rye and spelt at the end of the second millennium could have been in response to the trend towards the cooler and wetter conditions of the Sub-Atlantic, as in northern Europe at this time. Cattle, pigs, sheep and goats were all important, and horse bones are present at most sites (Bökönyi, 1959, 1968, 1974). Model carts and miniature wheels have been found at several settlements, and horse harness is also common. It is presumed that cattle were used for traction and horses for riding. At Cuciulata the maturity of the cattle may imply an important role for dairy cows. Loom weights and spindle whorls found in very great quantities at all sites indicate the importance of textile products in the middle Danube basin. The period was also marked by a major expansion of settlement onto the driest plateau areas between the Danube and Tisza rivers, presumably in response to population increase in the main valleys, the improved pastoral technology and transport facilities, and the wetter conditions. However, it is impossible to measure the extent to which a surplus of foodstuffs was produced by these agricultural systems to maintain non-agricultural workers and the aristocracies, or to determine the role of foodstuffs in systems of local and inter-regional exchange.

The archaeology of the first millennium b.c. has suffered like that of the second from a concentration on culture history, and again, invasion models abound. In the eighth and seventh centuries b.c., for example, the occurrence in eastern and central Europe of horse riding equipment, weaponry and wagon burials similar to those of the steppe people has been taken to indicate raids by 'Thraco-Cimmerians' (Bandi, 1963) – 'the evidence . . . shows the arrival of mounted and probably cart-driving peoples from southern Russia' (Alexander, 1972: 92). The impact of Scythian art styles on European crafts in the sixth and fifth centuries has been regarded as further evidence of steppe incursions. Like the erstwhile bronze age 'migrations', however, such changes in material culture and burial fashions can now be seen to represent internal developments in European society: apart from the settlement evidence in support of this view, skeletal studies have revealed the same broad differences in the populations of the steppes and central/eastern Europe as today, with no evidence for intermixing in the first millennium (Schwidetzky, 1972). Significantly, too, the major cremation groups ('urnfields') of the late second millennium correlate roughly with the main European peoples described by classical writers at the end of the first millennium: the western urnfields and the Celts; the northern Lausitz group and the Slavs; the southern group with the Italic peoples; the Dinaric urnfields with the Illyrians; and the Bulgarian and Rumanian cemeteries with the Dacians (Clarke, 1968: 391).

Iron working was developed in the Balkans and middle Danube basin in the first two or three centuries of the first millennium, although for a long period it was on a small scale relative to the well established bronze industry. By the end of the first millennium such crafts were on a highly organised scale, with centralised production at major nucleated settlements or specialised industrial sites, and highly professional schools of craftsmen, almost certainly full time specialists. Other crafts included working in gold, silver, lead, tin, pottery, leather, glass, bone and wood. Wine, luxury ceramics and metalwork were traded from the classical world to the aristocracies of the region: Etruscan bronze vessels, for example, were traded across the alps from Italy to the middle Danube basin (Frey, 1966) and the Greek colonies established *c.* 600 B.C. on the Black Sea coast were also trading emporia for the lower and middle Danube regions and the Crimea, exporting high quality pottery, metalwork and textiles. Ranking systems were elaborate, and in the regions adjacent to the classical world, state or quasi-state societies may have developed by the end of the first millennium. For example, Ptolemy's description of the Dacian state in the lower Danube region indicates a society almost urban in character: major settlements acted as economic, political, military and religious centres, local coinages were produced, and craftsmen manufactured lavish items of weaponry and display (the gold helmet from Cotofăneşti being the best known example). According to Homer, Rhesus the king of the Thracians (in Bulgaria) kept a lavish court with magnificent horses and armour and chariot trappings of gold and silver. Despite the exaggerations of poetic licence, it looks as if great wealth did indeed exist in these regions: the magnificent Vratsa treasure, of the mid-fourth century B.C., included armour and horse trappings in gold and silver, and an enormous range of other artifacts in precious metals.

The agricultural basis for these remarkable societies remains almost entirely unstudied by archaeologists. Cattle and sheep seem to have been the principal stock for many communities, maintained for their secondary products as much as for their meat; animals on the hoof were probably a major source of wealth (Vörös, 1982). Probably the most critical developments took place in the closing stages of pre-Roman tribal life, when there were massive increases in settlement densities, the major nucleated settlements ('oppida') were established, metal at last dominated agricultural technology (and now included iron plough shares) and, as a result, heavier soils hitherto reserved primarily for animal husbandry were at last taken into cultivation – giving the basic pattern of farming which survived here to the recent period. The poverty of the archaeological evidence for the nature and scale of these agricultural systems is all the more notable given the comments in the classical sources that the aristocracies of the lower and middle Danube regions brought grain, honey, wax, salt fish and slaves to the

Black Sea emporia (Berciu, 1967), whilst the Illyrians of Dalmatia exported salt, cattle, horses and slaves to pay for the excessive wine drinking for which they were notorious (Wilkes, 1969: 187).

5

The alpine region

Geographical introduction

The alpine region consists of a great arc of mountains, stretching from the eastern borders of France through Switzerland, northern Italy and Austria to northwestern Yugoslavia, with an east/west length of some 800 kilometres and a north/south depth of 150–250 kilometres (Fig. 41). The arc contains hundreds of peaks over 3000 metres high and many peaks in the central range over 4000 metres high. Glaciation in the Pleistocene shaped the distinctive alpine topography of today, gouging out the flat-bottomed and steep-sided valleys and carving the magnificent skyline of craggy ridges and pyramid peaks. In the same period, the great lakes were formed on the fringes of the mountains in deep valleys blocked at the outward end by morainic debris. The central spine of the region is formed of crystalline rocks, bending round to form the barrier at the western end of the Po plain in northern Italy. Limestone formations dominate the northern and southern margins of the range.

Lying as the great barrier between Mediterranean and temperate Europe, the alpine region shares in the climatic regimes of both. As in all mountainous areas, climate at the local scale varies considerably according to height, slope and exposure: north-facing slopes are colder than those facing south, whilst the widest valleys are colder in winter from temperature inversion than the slopes above (and often filled with mist), and are extremely hot in summer. Most of the range is under snow for at least three months in the winter and snow above 2000 metres often lies for six months. Although rainfall is heavier than in the surrounding lowlands, it is in fact both variable and in many areas quite limited. There is a summer rainfall maximum in the northern Alps and an autumn maximum in the south. Although rainfall is heavier than in the surrounding lowlands, it varies considerably from region to region, averaging from 750 mm a year in the central interior to 2000 mm in the eastern Alps and 4000 mm in the Veneto on the borders of Italy and Yugoslavia. Thus many farmers in the interior valleys in fact suffer from water shortage rather than surfeit, and irrigation systems are necessary for the arable and hay fields (Netting, 1972, 1976). The foothill zone and foreland valleys of northern Italy have relatively mild winters (milder than those of the Po plain, for example), because of the shelter provided by the alpine range: in fact the olive can be grown successfully on the southern foreland but not on the Po plain.

Vegetation in the Alps correlates closely with climatic variations. In the northern Alps, there are four altitudinal zones of vegetation today: (1) beech and hornbeam deciduous forest up to 1500 m; (2) fir, pine and spruce coniferous forest between 1500 m and 2000 m; (3) sparser coniferous forest and dwarf pines and juniper up to about

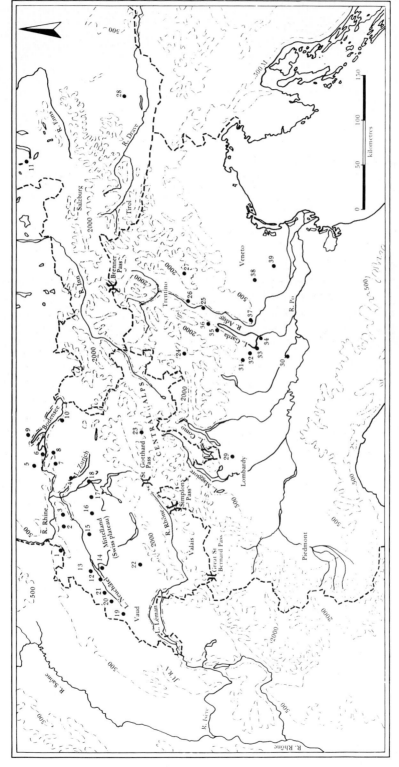

Fig. 41. The Alpine region (contours in metres): principal sites and regions mentioned in the text. 1. Birsmatten; 2. Sissach; 3. Wittnauer Horn; 4. Zurich Alpenquai; 5. Thayngen Weier; 6. Wangen; 7. Niederwil; 8. Pfyn; 9. Sipplingen; 10. Arbon Bleiche; 11. Mondsee; 12. La Tène; 13. Twann; 14. Lüscherz; 15. Burgäschisee; 16. Egolzwil; 17. Baldegg; 18. Zug Sumpf; 19. Abri de la Cure; 20. St. Aubin; 21. Cortaillod; 22. Ranggiloch; 23. Crestaulta; 24. Val Camonica; 25. Romagnano; 26. Gaban; 27. Colbricon; 28. Magdalensberg; 29. Lagozza; 30. Vhò; 31. Monte Covolo; 32. Barche; 33. Lavagnone; 34. Polada; 35. Ledro; 36. Fiave; 37. Quinzano; 38. Molino Casarotto; 39. Este.

3000 m; and (4) the true *alp* or summer pastures above the tree line. In the drier and warmer southern Alps, the prevailing vegetation consists of Mediterranean shrubs resistant to the summer drought, and both forests and pastures are sparser than on the temperate side of the mountains.

Alpine farming in historical times

The major constraints on farming in the alpine region are of course topography and climate. Arable land is limited to the lowest elevations, and even here much of the land is poorly drained and very marginal for crop cultivation; the growing seasons for cereals are also short. On the other hand, the valley floors can support major stands of deciduous forest and wetland grazing suitable particularly for cattle and pigs, and the cultivable soils and climate are adequate for good hay production. Further grazing is available in spring and autumn on the mountain slopes, and there are extensive pastures on the *alp* amongst the high peaks during the summer.

In such conditions, animal-based economies have predominated in most areas in the historical period. The classic alpine economy of the central mountains has been dominated by cattle keeping, because of the suitability of cattle to the seasonal grazing and the type of pasture, and systems of crop husbandry have been organised particularly to meet the fodder requirements of the stock. The majority of each community remained in the main settlements on the valley floor throughout the year, farming the surrounding arable land for cereals, fodder crops and hay. In the spring herdsmen took most of the stock (cattle, pigs, sheep and goats) up to the middle pastures on the mountain slopes. The pigs remained here, whilst the rest of the stock were taken up to the *alp* for the summer. At the end of September the stock were brought down to the village, with the cattle being stalled soon afterwards (late October or early November) and the sheep and goats being stalled in December, although the latter were sometimes taken up to the middle pastures (like the pigs) during the winter if weather permitted (Cole and Wolf, 1974; Dumont, 1957; Lurati, 1969; Fig. 42).

Market forces and modern communications have of course encouraged specialised dairying systems in most alpine valleys today, whereas alpine villages in the medieval period were more or less self-sufficient in food, raising enough oats, rye and (where possible) vines to feed the community (Duerst, 1923; Pounds, 1974). At the same time, flocks of sheep and goats were extremely important: sheep in particular were bred for their milk and their wool, and most communities produced their own woollen clothing. Sheep were often far more numerous than cattle – their numbers were double those of today even a century ago (Gubler-Gross, 1962). Pigs were also normally kept by most communities in some numbers. The traditional *alp* system of grazing is recorded throughout the medieval and post-medieval period essentially as today (Carrier, 1932), and there is a document as early as A.D. 1204 referring to summer alpine transhumance in Switzerland (Gubler-Gross, 1962: 10). Records of small scale irrigation works of the kind still constructed today go back to the fourteenth century (Carrier, 1932: 26).

Agricultural systems in the alpine foreland regions have been rather different. In Switzerland the central plateau or Mittelland between the Alps and the Jura mountains is the main arable zone today, especially the western part in the Jura rain shadow, and arable systems also prevailed here in the medieval period (Duerst, 1923). In northern Italy olive and vine cultivation is possible in parts of the alpine foreland, and the other major difference between here and the temperate side of the Alps is that the slope and summit pastures have for the most part been better suited to sheep and goats than to cattle. The Jura range, forming an outer rim to the Swiss plateau, has a dissected topography of parallel valleys and ridges; poor soils of the podsolised forest type like those of the Alps are common and arable land is sparse, but cereals and fodder crops can be grown up to 1000/1300 metres above sea level.

An important element in the historical agricultural systems of the alpine region has been long distance transhumance, in addition to the short distance vertical movements described earlier. Very large flocks of sheep and to a lesser extent herds of cattle were pastured in the central mountains during the summer and wintered in the lower Rhone valley and Po plain, systems of movement recorded from the twelfth century onwards (Carrier, 1932; Gubler-Gross, 1962). As in the Mediterranean, however, such systems normally required both heavy investment by the state, or the church, or private individuals, and regulated political conditions.

Perhaps the most characteristic feature of traditional alpine farming is the amount of labour required. Feeding and mucking out the stock every day for six months has to be combined with manuring, ploughing and planting the fields. The labour required for animal husbandry is far less in the summer months, but haymaking then around the settlements and in the higher pastures is a long and back-breaking task, reaching a crescendo of activity from dawn to dusk at the peak. Furthermore, the small fields and rugged terrain mean that a great deal of work is required for small yields: Dumont's

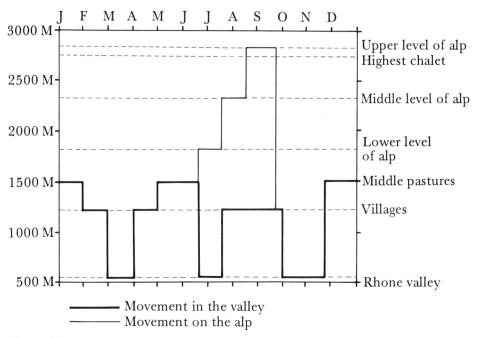

Fig. 42. Alpine grazing systems. (From information in Brunhes and Girardin, 1906: 349)

analysis of a farmer's labour in the Val d'Anniviers found that he spent 65 hours a year on the management of a half-acre hay field (22 hours irrigating, 8 hours manuring, 32 hours haymaking, 3 hours in maintenance work), and the harvesting rate (averaging accessible and inaccessible fields) was about a tenth of the rate with the same technology on a lowland farm (Dumont, 1957). Cereal yields on the alpine foreland are also much lower than those of southern Germany.

Early postglacial foraging economies

Hundreds of postglacial pollen diagrams have been constructed for the alpine region, and although the data are far more detailed for the Swiss and Italian forelands than for the central mountains and intermontane valleys, we can reconstruct the broad vegetational differences across the region as a whole (Cattani, 1977; Horowitz, 1975; Kral, 1979; Sala, 1977). With the postglacial warming, pine forests with smaller stands of birch rapidly colonised the Jura, the Swiss plateau, the alpine valleys and the Italian foreland, although the glaciers in the mountains still reached down to about 1700 m above sea level in the late eighth millennium. In the Boreal, the alpine climate seems to have been less continental and rather wetter than before, with warmer summers but with winter temperatures still colder than today (Markgraf, 1969). Pine and birch remained in parts of the Swiss plateau and in the alpine valleys, but hazel and oak forest spread over the Jura, much of the plateau and the northern margins of the Alps; on the Italian side, alder and spruce were the dominant trees of the upland forests in the Boreal, and hazel and oak at lower elevations, but open vegetation was still common in major valleys such as the Adige (Cattani, 1977). In the Atlantic period, pine forest dominated the highest parts of the Jura and the higher slopes of the northern Alps, whereas spruce remained more common in the southern Alps; fairly dense mixed oak forest covered the lower Jura slopes and the Swiss plateau, but again the valleys on the Mediterranean side of the Alps were less forested except perhaps at the climax of the Atlantic. There was pasture on the *alp* above the treeline throughout the Boreal and Atlantic periods. The glacial lakes on either side of the Alps were at their maximum early in the Postglacial, but with the decreased precipitation, less glacial meltwater and higher temperatures, most shrank by several metres in the Boreal and Atlantic (Joos, 1976; Schindler, 1971; Schwab and Müller, 1973).

The Jura mountains and Swiss plateau were colonised early in the Holocene by foraging peoples equipped like those of southern France and southern Germany with a lithic technology dominated by backed tools. In the Atlantic period industries of geometric microliths were developed, together with small round scrapers and transverse arrowheads, and it was in this period too that the central Alps were inhabited (Wyss, 1968). On the Italian side of the Alps, the same lithic sequence has been established (Broglio, 1969, 1971; Perini, 1971), and here also settlement concentrated on the main foreland, with the Dolomites being utilised systematically only in the Atlantic (Bagolini *et al.*, 1975).

Large numbers of Pre-Boreal and Boreal sites have been found around the small morainic lakes of the Swiss plateau, particularly Burgäschisee and Wauwilermoos (Wyss, 1968). The sites tend to occupy small sandy outcrops, especially by the lake outflows, which were islands of drier ground in a very marshy terrain. Reinerth's pioneering fieldwork in the 1930s identified about thirty sites around the Wauwilermoos, marked by clusters of flint tools in areas averaging 50 × 80 m (Reinerth, 1936). Early excavations suggested small family camps, perhaps reed huts or windbreaks (Bodmer-Gessner, 1949–50). Further excavations by Wyss (1979) of another of the lakeside camps found rubbish pits containing a fauna dominated by the bones of red deer – 58% according to the minimum number of individuals and almost 95% when all the 'probable but not definite' red deer-sized fragments of bone were included (Stampfli, 1979). Roe deer, aurochs and elk were also identified from the pits, and one of them contained an antler harpoon. A number of lines of evidence suggested winter/spring occupation at these sites. Caves on the edge of the plateau at the foot of the Jura have evidence for short but repeated occupations by people with similar lithic technologies; faunal samples are invariably dominated by red deer, and caches of hazelnuts suggest that the caves were at least used in the autumn. Other caves high in the Jura were used for hunting both forest animals (red deer, roe deer, cattle, pig) and mountain species such as ibex, chamois and marmot (Bandi, 1964; Piningre and Vuaillat, 1976). From such variations in subsistence data, site catchments and (such as it is) evidence for seasonality, as well as variations in lithic assemblages, Sakellaridis (1979) has argued that – whilst some communities may have remained on the plateau throughout the year – early postglacial foraging in Switzerland normally involved considerable mobility: annual territories stretched from the lowland marshes and lakes to the Jura mountain pastures, with winter settlement mainly on the plateau and summer settlement in the hills. In northern Italy contemporary subsistence also involved base camps on the valley floors and summer camps at higher elevations (Broglio, 1971).

Much the same range of settlement and subsistence data has been recovered from sites in the plateau lake basins and in the Jura caves dating to the Atlantic period. Settlement also extended further into the central mountains as the glaciers retreated and game colonised the mountain heights. Shelters in the upper Rhine valley south of Bodensee were now used for fishing and for hunting red deer, cattle, elk, ibex and chamois (Vonbank, 1952). In the Simmental, sites were now used above 1000 m on the slopes of the Jungfrau (at 1850 m in the case of Ranggiloch, just below the modern tree line) as summer hunting stands for the pursuit of ibex and chamois (Andrist *et al.*, 1964). In the Adige valley in northern Italy, base camps were still in the lower valley, but high altitude camps have also been found in the mountains at the head of the valley: at Colbricon, for example, at about 2000 m above sea level (entirely snow-covered today from autumn to spring), hunters brought prepared toolkits with them from the lower valley in order to hunt ibex and chamois (Bagolini *et al.*, 1975). West of the Adige, too, contemporary foraging extended from the marshy edges of the foreland up to summer lakeside camps above 2000 m (Biagi, 1976a, 1976b).

Although the main subsistence data document large mammal hunting and to a lesser extent fowling, and fish bones are rather uncommon in the archaeological record, the occurrence of harpoons and other fishing equipment indicates that fishing is substantially under-represented. Gathering, as so often in mesolithic Europe, is also assumed to have been extremely important despite the poverty of the data. However, whilst mixed foraging systems are likely, it seems clear that red deer in particular was an essential resource given its dominance in nearly all except the high altitude faunal samples. It is noteworthy that small scale clearances have been detected by pollen analysis in several Atlantic contexts on the Swiss plateau, and in the Abri de la Cure on the edge of the Jura one of these was associated with a major increase in ivy pollen (to values of 40%) suggesting that ivy was collected as fodder or bait to attract the deer (Simmons and Dimbleby, 1974).

The first farmers in Switzerland, *c*. 3500–2500 b.c.

Although agricultural communities had been living on the northern edge of the Swiss plateau at sites like Bottmingen and Gachlingen from the late fifth millennium b.c. (LBK farmers, discussed primarily in the next chapter), and cereal pollen has been found associated with a late Atlantic clearance episode in one of the Burgäschisee diagrams (Welten, 1955: 62), the first systematic evidence for farming in Switzerland correlates with the transition to the Sub-Boreal climate in the second half of the fourth millennium b.c. Pollen and dendrochronological data indicate that the climate became significantly more continental, with cooler winters and less precipitation but warm summers (Frenzel, 1966). Beech and fir colonised the lower Jura and the plateau, mixing with the oak forests, and spruce increased at the expense of fir at higher elevations (Tauber, 1965). There was a general lowering of lake levels, although there is also consistent evidence for quite dramatic short term fluctuations as well, some of which may have been related to the new systems of plant and animal husbandry (Kaenel, 1976; Winiger, 1976; Zimmerman, 1966). The new agricultural settlements divide into four regional groups according to their material culture: Cortaillod on the western plateau and in the Jura; Pfyn on the northern plateau, particularly around Zurichsee and Bodensee; Egolzwil in the central plateau region of Burgäschisee and Wauwilermoos; and St Leonard in the upper Rhine and Rhone valleys.

The lakeside Cortaillod settlements are part of the complex of neolithic and bronze age 'lake villages' in Switzerland which caused such a sensation on their discovery in the last century (Keller, 1854; Munro, 1890). Cortaillod pottery consisted mainly of simple curved and round-based vessels, but at a later stage carinated vessels were made of a handsome burnished fabric, sometimes decorated with strips of birch bark, an assemblage which has many similarities with that of the contemporary Chassey sites in southern France and Lagozza sites in northern Italy (von Gonzenbach, 1949). The stone industry included new elements such as polished axes and occasional perforated hammer axes, as well as a blade assemblage larger than but similar to the preceding technologies of the Atlantic (including backed blades and geometric microliths, for example). The waterlogged conditions have also resulted in the survival of a marvellous range of organic material: bone and antler axe and mattock sleeves, combs, harpoons, fish hooks; wooden hoes and hand-held ards or furrowing sticks; wooden and birch bark cups, boxes, ladles, trays; textiles, basketwork, rope, fishing nets and so on (Fig. 43). 'We have from some of these lacustrine dwellings materials for reconstructing the entire life history of their inhabitants, giving, as it were, a complete picture of their arts, industries, luxuries and amusements' (Munro, 1890: 496). The analyses of animal

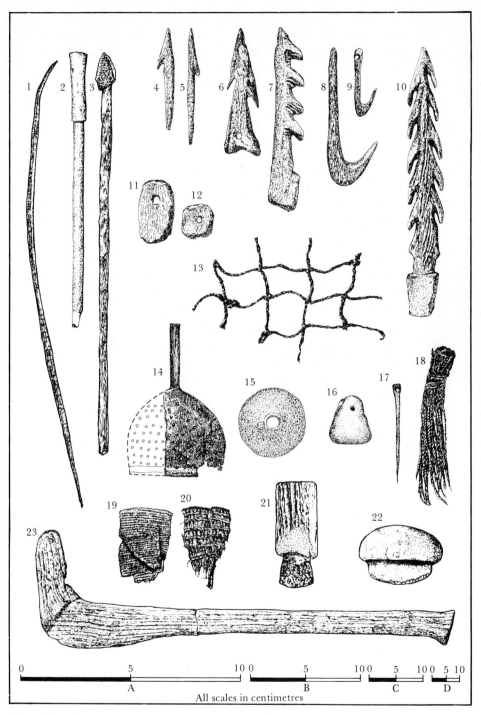

Fig. 43. Cortaillod subsistence technology: 1. wooden bow; 2. wooden fowling arrow; 3. wooden arrow with flint point; 4, 5. bone harpoons; 6, 7. antler harpoons; 8, 9. bone fish hooks; 10. antler harpoon; 11, 12. wooden floats; 13. fish net; 14. wooden carding board for flax; 15. bone spindle whorl; 16. clay loom weight; 17. bone needle; 18. skein of thread; 19, 20. textile fragments; 21. stone axe in antler sleeve; 22. flint knife or scraper in wooden sleeve; 23. wooden handle for axe or adze. All at scale B except 13 (A), 14 and 23 (C), and 1 (D). (After Wyss, 1969: figs. 6, 8, 11 and 15)

bones from these sites by Rütimeyer (1862) and of the plant remains by Heer (1866) are some of the most impressive pioneering studies in European subsistence archaeology.

Over 120 neolithic sites are known around the Jura lakes of Neuchâtel, Bielersee and Murtensee, and at least half of these were occupied in this period. For over a century archaeologists have debated the *Pfahlbauproblem* (Guyan, 1955), the problem of lake settlement construction: were the villages built on stilts in shallow water, or were the piles and horizontal timbers found at the sites designed simply as stable platforms on the marshy banks? For most of the Swiss sites the second system seems to have been the case. What is also clear is that most Cortaillod 'lake villages' were in fact extremely small hamlets and sometimes even single farms. Most of them consist of between three and eight buildings (usually simple one or two roomed cabins); if all of them were used for people (rather than some for storage and stock), with an extended family in each house, maximum populations of about fifty people are indicated (Sakellaridis, 1979). The hamlets were usually surrounded by a palisade or fence. A very wide range of plant remains has been recovered from many of these sites: cereals and legumes; nuts, berries and wild fruits; and many seeds of wasteland plants (including large caches) gathered for their edible, herbal or poisonous qualities, as well as plants collected for bedding and thatching (Table 8).

Site catchment analysis at several of these sites indicated that, although a small area of well drained arable soil was invariably near to hand, the greater part of the five kilometre catchments would have consisted of browse and grazing (Sakellaridis, 1979). Furthermore, grazing resources differed on different sides of the lakes: wetland pasture and forest were plentiful on the flatter eastern side, whereas the thin soils of the Jura slopes on the western side would have carried scrub grazing and light woodland. Faunal samples from a dozen Cortaillod sites showed subsistence adaptations to these differences: there was a consistent preference for cattle on the eastern side, pigs were not very important, and red deer and roe deer were not hunted on a large scale; on the western side, cattle, pigs, sheep and goats were kept in roughly equal numbers and deposits in caves high in the Jura suggested that summer herding and hunting trips were made from the lakeside hamlets (Sakellaridis, 1979: 346–53). At St Aubin IV and Twann-Bahnhofes, cattle were killed either in the first six months or as mature animals, and the same mortality structure was found in the sheep/goat material (Higham, 1967a), strongly suggestive of a dairying system in which calves and lambs were killed and their mothers milked; some males of these species were also raised to young maturity for their meat. Cortaillod subsistence thus involved, on the one hand, the continuation of the mobile foraging systems practised in the Atlantic and, on the other, an agricultural system that bears all the hallmarks from the outset of the classic alpine economy – mixed farming, mobile stock keeping, and dairying.

Pfyn communities used flat-based jars and jugs, often decorated with a thick uneven slip, but their flint industry was much the same as the Cortaillod (save for an absence of microliths), as was the bone and antler repertoire (Wyss, 1970). One important difference in technologies was that copper was smelted at several Pfyn settlements, with beads being manufactured as exchange items with high scarcity value (Ottoway and Strahm, 1975). The Zurichsee has a higher summer rainfall today than the Jura lakes, and most

Table 8 *Principal plant remains from some Cortaillod neolithic sites:* x = *present;* X = *frequent; X = storage context. (After Sakellaridis, 1979: 344–5, 358–9)*

	Chavannes	Cortaillod	Lüscherz	Neuenstadt	Port	St Blaise	Thun	Wangen
Cultivated plants								
barley, 2 row								X
barley, 6 row		x	x		X	x	x	X
bread wheat	x		x	x				X
club wheat	x		X		X	x	X	x
einkorn							x	x
emmer							x	x
flax			X	x	x	x	X	X
lentil						x		
millet			x					x
pea			x		X	x	x	x
poppy			X		x	x	x	
Nuts, berries, wild fruits								
acorn	x	x	X	x				
apple	x		x	x			X	X
beechnut		x					x	X
blackberry			x	x	X	x	X	X
cherry	x	x	X			x		x
elderberry				x			X	X
hazelnut	x	X	X	x			x	X
pear					x	x		X
plum			x		x	x		x
raspberry			x	x	X	x	X	X
rosehip			X				X	x
strawberry					x		x	x
water chestnut								x
Wasteland plants								
black bindweed					x	x	x	
buttercup			X	x		x	x	
chickweed						x	x	
dogwood			x				x	x
elders			X	x		x	x	
fat hen			X		x	x	x	x
mustard			X					
plantains			X					
sedges			X			x	x	

Pfyn settlements were on the eastern bank, the sunnier and drier side with lighter soils. The main group of Pfyn sites was on the western side of Bodensee and by the lakes and in the river valleys further west, again cooler and wetter than the western plateau. Two sites in particular, Niederwil and Thayngen Weier, have been particularly informative about settlement history and layout. Dendrochronological analysis indicated that Niederwil was occupied for about fifty years, during which period the site developed from a collection of small cabins to substantial longhouses, internally subdivided and enclosed with a palisade (Fig. 44). If the houses were used at the same time, Niederwil would have contained a population of some 100–150 people (Ferguson *et al.*, 1966; Waterbolk and van Zeist, 1966, 1978). Thayngen Weier began on much the same scale, with between eight and ten one-family cabins; settlement was not continuous, but after two hundred years there were about thirty houses and perhaps 150–180 people.

Pfyn subsistence systems were much like those of the Cortaillod settlements apart from less of an emphasis on sheep and goats because of the wetter and more forested landscape. The range of crops and wild fruits was very similar (Jørgensen, 1975; van Zeist and Casperie, 1974), the site catchments have pockets of good cultivable soil near the settlements with grazing and browse further afield (Sakellaridis, 1979), and pollen analysis also indicates cultivated and fallow fields and a certain amount of pasture in the midst of a forested landscape (Troels-Smith, 1956, 1960; van Zeist and Casperie, 1974). There was a possible threshing floor at Thayngen Weier. Adult cows were bred for dairying and young males were killed for their meat; sheep and goat husbandry was similar (Clason, 1966; Kuhn, 1932; Soergel, 1969). Significantly, the pottery assemblage from Thayngen Weier included a bowl very like the *satte* vessel still used in traditional dairy farming in Switzerland (Guyan, 1966). Hunting and fishing were also important, and satellite camps were used as well as the main settlements; there were wooden bows at both Thayngen Weier and Niederwil, and evidence for fishing at Niederwil included antler harpoons, pike bones and a net.

Several waterlogged sites have provided remarkable evidence for the organisation of animal husbandry. Apart from the stockades surrounding the sites, there was an area of straw and dung at Pfyn and a stalling area for sheep and goats at Niederwil. At Thayngen Weier one building had a deposit with a large number of puparia of the common house fly, which overwinter especially in warm cow houses (Guyan, 1955). There were also

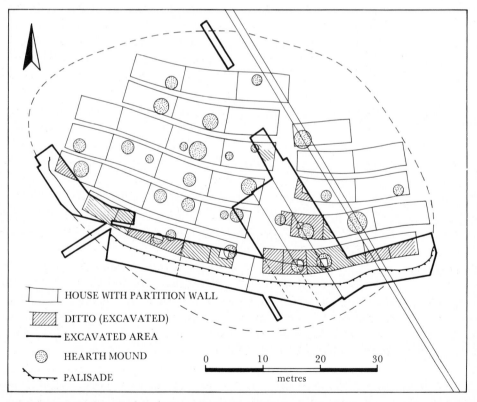

HOUSE WITH PARTITION WALL

DITTO (EXCAVATED)

EXCAVATED AREA

HEARTH MOUND

PALISADE

0   10   20   30

metres

Fig. 44. The settlement at Niederwil. (After Waterbolk and van Zeist, 1966: fig. 2)

storage barns here containing animal fodder – ivy, ash, twigs, clematis, elm shoots and so on; and pollen from one floor included about 40% ivy pollen, compared with 1.5% in the normal occupation layers. Such facilities are strongly reminiscent of the byre-barn system of stock overwintering in traditional Swiss husbandry.

The Egolzwil group of sites by the morainic lakes and marshes of Burgäschisee and Wauwilermoos has pottery which is essentially a variant of Cortaillod styles (Bandi and Müller-Beck, 1963–74). The new settlements were small palisaded hamlets of up to fifty inhabitants. Light dry loams suitable for cultivation lie at some distance to most of the sites, suggesting that crops were not of prime importance, although a light wooden ard was found at Burgäschisee. Pollen analysis also indicated small scale cultivation at some distance from the settlements, and few cereals have been recovered – poppy seems to have been the most common crop, followed by club wheat, barley and flax; but wild fruits, berries and nuts were gathered intensively (Villaret-von Rochow, 1967). At the earliest site, Egolzwil 3, the main stock in a sample dominated otherwise by game were sheep and goats, and mortality data suggested that they were kept for their meat, but the Cortaillod/Pfyn system of mixed dairying and meat production using cattle, sheep and goats soon prevailed. However, all the faunal samples here are dominated by the forest game – red deer, roe deer, and aurochs; adult males predominated in the case of the first three species, suggesting that breeding females were husbanded or at least protected (Hescheler and Rüeger, 1942; Higham, 1967a, 1967b; Stampfli, 1976). Fishing and fowling were also important activities: there are antler harpoons, net weights, fish scales, fish bones, wooden fowling arrows and bird bones. Layers of sheep and goat dung at Egolzwil 3 showed that the animals were stalled at the site, and the pollen in the dung indicated that this was for most of the year (Vogt, 1951). At Egolzwil 4 two areas were identified as possible stalls from fly puparia (Vogt, 1969), and several sites have provided evidence for fodder storage.

In the alpine valleys of the Rhone and the Rhine, stock-keeping was probably the main means of subsistence, with meat and dairy production evident in both cattle and sheep/goat husbandry (Chaix, 1976a, 1976–7; Hartmann-Frick, 1960). Pollen analysis indicates cereal cultivation on a very small scale (Markgraf, 1969; Welten, 1977). Chamois and ibex were the principal game pursued on the mountain slopes above the settlements (Andrist *et al.*, 1964). In the upper Rhone valley spring and summer occupation is inferred from the altitude of the sites, and as burial cists here are identical to those down-valley round Lac Léman, Sakellaridis (1979: 139) argues reasonably for a transhumant system up and down the valley.

The subsistence systems practised in Switzerland in the early Sub-Boreal differed markedly in the respective roles of foraging, crop cultivation and animal husbandry, but were clearly adapted to local ecology. At the same time, the most striking feature of the evidence is that the two fundamental elements of traditional alpine farming in historical times – dairying and winter stalling – can be observed in the earliest prehistoric farming in Switzerland. Why did such farming begin so rapidly and on such an organised scale? The traditional hypothesis has been that neolithic colonists pushed into Switzerland from the north European plain, where farming had been established more than a millennium earlier (Troels-Smith, 1956). The hypothesis has had to be adapted substantially to new data, with sites like Burgäschisee-Sud having to be regarded as the settlements of 'lapsed neolithic farmers' who reverted to the hunting systems of their forefathers (although where did those forefathers hunt, given that Swiss farmers were assumed to derive ultimately from LBK farmers, in turn assumed to be colonists from southeast Europe?). In fact the Swiss evidence – the underlying continuum in technology and subsistence between Atlantic and Sub-Boreal populations, and the distinct regional pottery styles correlating roughly with the regional groups of material culture recognised in the Atlantic – can surely be interpreted far more realistically in terms of internal subsistence change, with an existing population adapting new resources to local conditions.

The system of forest foraging had endured without major change in Switzerland throughout the Holocene until the end of the Atlantic. The climate then became significantly colder and drier. The 'elm decline', a dramatic and widespread fall in elm pollen in the late fourth millennium across western Europe, was once taken to indicate the arrival of the first farmers, collecting elm leaves for their cattle (Troels-Smith, 1956, 1960); but although early farmers certainly collected a wide variety of vegetation (including elm leaves and shoots) as winter fodder – like many stock farmers in temperate Europe until quite recently – the elm decline is now recognised to mark one of the critical natural changes in the temperate deciduous forests at the beginning of the Sub-Boreal, like the falls in ivy and mistletoe pollen and the greater variation in the widths of tree rings. The impact of these changes on plant gathering is unclear, but the increasing frequency of natural clearings began to favour cereal/stock systems as much as hunting forest game, and the drop in lake levels must also have put pressure on fishing. Although we have no data at all on the demographic state of Atlantic and Sub-Boreal populations in Switzerland (their relationships to real or perceived carrying capacities, for example), it seems more reasonable to propose that landscape changes precipitated by the Sub-Boreal climate finally made the new resources and technologies (used by adjacent LBK farmers for some 1500 years previously) a useful or necessary supplement for the indigenous foragers despite the labour and organisation required to house and feed the stock, than that neolithic colonists moved into Switzerland from the existing agricultural areas, developed new systems of farming and new styles of pottery unrelated to their homeland, organised themselves into regional groups which mirrored those of the Atlantic foragers (and what became of them?) and happened to develop rather similar technologies and foraging systems into the bargain. Compromise models integrating complex processes of colonisation and acculturation seem to me to demand as much distortion of the data as the colonisation model on its own.

The first farmers in sub-alpine Italy, ?4500–2500 b.c.

Although the impressed ware found in coastal caves such as Arene Candide in Liguria (on the border between Italy and France) was once thought to define early neolithic settlement across the whole of northern Italy (Brea, 1946, 1956), there were in fact three major regional groups of pottery: impressed ware in Liguria, Fiorano pottery south of the Po, and square-mouthed pottery (*bocca quadrata*) north of the Po (Barfield and Broglio, 1965). Fiorano pottery was also used by a few communities north of the Po before *bocca quadrata* (Perini, 1971). The earliest radiocarbon dates for square mouthed pottery are *c.* 4500 b.c. at Molino Casarotto, but a later series of samples processed by the same laboratory yielded dates a millennium later (Barfield and Broglio, 1971), and early dates from other sites are *c.* 4000 b.c. The *bocca quadrata* tradition was extremely long lasting in parts of northern Italy – Barfield has defined three stages of stylistic development, the last of which ended in the mid-third millennium (Barfield, 1971; Barfield and Broglio, 1966). In the western half of sub-alpine Italy, however, Lagozza pottery was developed in the first half of the third millennium.

The Romagnano and Gaban shelters in the Adige valley were two sites with Fiorano pottery stratified below *bocca quadrata*. The Fiorano pottery was associated with classic mesolithic trapeze industries of the kind found in the pre-pottery Atlantic levels at Romagnano (Bagolini, 1971a, 1971b). At both sites the people using this pottery were foragers hunting large mammals (red deer, roe deer, pig, ibex, chamois), fowling, fishing, and gathering shellfish (Bagolini, 1976): it seems clear that the indigenous foraging population of this region adopted Fiorano pottery at some time in the middle of the fifth millennium, but made no other changes in their technology or lifestyle. Small scale farming was practised at Molino Casarotto, probably in the late fifth millennium, by people who were primarily foragers. The site consisted of a series of small wooden platforms constructed along the edge of a lake in the Berici hills, an offshoot of the foreland hills projecting into the Po plain (Barfield and Broglio, 1971). Simple huts or shelters are suggested, with perhaps one family group to each platform area. At the main platform excavated there was a massive stone hearth; scattered around this were dumps of pottery, animal bones, fish bones and freshwater mollusc shells, whilst the hearth itself contained layers of pure shell alternating with layers of carbonised water chestnut husks (Fig. 45). The main animals represented in the faunal sample were red deer and boar, the red deer being mainly young males (M. R. Jarman, 1971, 1976) – a cropping policy which would have maintained a productive breeding herd (Darling, 1937). Cattle, sheep and goats made up only 3% of the total sample. Similarly, cereals formed only a minute percentage of the plant remains, most of which were the husks of water chestnut (a starvation food in this area during the last war). The resources of the site catchment – the lake, its surrounding marshes, and steep wooded hills above – were clearly marginal for an agricultural system. Jarman argued from aspects of the catchment and subsistence data that the lakeside camps were probably inhabited between spring and early autumn, with the communities moving short distances into the hills for the rest of the year (M. R. Jarman, 1976).

It is difficult to gauge whether Molino Casarotto was typical or atypical of sub-alpine subsistence at this time, as there is little reliable data from contemporary *bocca quadrata* settlements on the foreland. It is possible that sheep and goat herding had assumed some importance here by about 4000 b.c. at sites like Romagnano, Quinzano and Garniga (Bagolini and Biagi, 1975a). Certainly mixed cereal and stock farming was firmly established by the middle of the fourth millennium b.c., with emmer and barley the principal crops and sheep/goats and cattle the principal stock (kept mainly for meat rather than their secondary products), although venison remained important in the diet (Bagolini and Biagi, 1976; Fedele, 1973; M. R. Jarman, 1970, 1971).

The alpine dairying system can first be discerned in northern Italy in the first half of the third millennium. Lagozza itself was a pile village in a peat basin, excavated in the last century. The waterlogged conditions here and at contemporary lakeside settlements have provided detailed botanical evidence, as in Switzerland: cultivated plants included einkorn, emmer, club wheat, barley, lentils and flax, and a similarly wide range of fruits, nuts and edible plants was harvested. Animal bones were not collected at Lagozza, but the material culture includes large numbers of straining vessels, loom weights, spindle whorls, bone combs and so on that are strongly indicative of a wool/ dairy system of husbandry (Barfield, 1971). The Lagozza settlements tend to be much like the Cortaillod settlements in their location, with small areas of arable soil in the vicinity and large areas of different kinds of pasture and woodland at the lakeside and on adjacent mountain slopes. Cattle and sheep dairying and wool production are clearly

Fig. 45. One of the open air hearths at Molino Casarotto. Left – seen from above, the hearth is a roughly circular mass of boulders and clay, lying on criss-cross timbers laid at the lake edge; right – section through the hearth, showing the dumps of food refuse lying against it (the white layers are snail shells, the black layers are carbonised plant remains); both scales are a metre long. (Photographs kindly supplied by the excavator, Lawrence Barfield)

implied by the age structure of the faunal material from the Monte Covolo shelter (Barker, 1977–9), which was associated with carbonised seeds of emmer, barley, einkorn and millet as well as a range of fruits and berries (Pals, 1977–9).

On the basis of the subsistence data from Molino Casarotto and later prehistoric sites in sub-alpine Italy, Jarman argued that a gradual transition from foraging to farming could be observed here, with the red deer/pig/wild plant system of subsistence being replaced over a thousand years (4500–3500 b.c.) by the cattle/sheep/goat/pig/cereal system, in a context of population pressure and associated woodland clearance (M. R. Jarman, 1971). The model is no longer so attractive given the uncertainties over the date of Molino Casarotto and the evidence (albeit limited) for at least stock-keeping elsewhere in sub-alpine Italy by the early fourth millennium, but clearly the develop-

ment of farming here still seems to have been rather protracted compared with Switzerland. In either case, the archaeological record surely indicates that local foraging communities adopted the new agricultural resources (from south of the Po?), rather than that these people were mysteriously displaced by neolithic colonists who then adopted existing technologies and foraging systems, and invented entirely new local pottery styles (unrelated to any possible homeland), once they had arrived. At the outset, the agricultural system practised was a version of Mediterranean farming, relying principally on emmer, barley, sheep and goats, but within a few centuries a system better adapted to the ecology of the sub-alpine foreland had been developed.

Later prehistoric farming

There were widespread changes in the neolithic pottery of Switzerland in the second half of the third millennium, with the development of the thick-walled and crudely decorated Horgen styles rather like contemporary ceramics in southern Germany (Michelsberg) and central and eastern France (Seine–Oise–Marne). This material was formerly taken to indicate various invasions into Switzerland, but modern studies have demonstrated its evolution from earlier ceramics, and its division into similar regional groups (Furger et al., 1977; Itten, 1970). Other new items in the material culture included drinking beakers in the corded ware and bell beaker styles, perforated stone 'battle axes' and 'maces', fine daggers of imported flint, and copper tools and weapons, once regarded as clear evidence of incursions by warlike pastoralists but now recognised as the status markers or ceremonial repertoire worn by the emergent elites of an increasingly stratified society. Arguments for a reversal to hunting or pastoralism at this time, pursuits expected of warlike newcomers, are quite unfounded; if anything, agricultural intensification was the case. Around the Jura lakes, for example, the system of mixed farming established by the Cortaillod settlements continued, with hunting less important; there is clear evidence for cattle dairying (Chaix, 1976b; Josien, 1955), and increases in the proportion of female to male sheep suggest more systematic wool production (Sakellaridis, 1979: 80). Exactly the same processes can be discerned elsewhere on the Swiss plateau (Higham, 1967a; Vogel, 1933). In the alpine valleys, the systems of stock-keeping were as before (Hartmann-Frick, 1960), and similar systems have been found at contemporary settlements in the Austrian Alps (Wolff, 1977a). There is consistent evidence in the pollen record for increased clearance throughout the region.

The settlement record for the second millennium (the Bronze Age) demonstrates the continuity of regional agricultural systems within the overall alpine strategy and, in places, further evidence for intensification in husbandry. On the Swiss plateau in the first half of the millennium, the commonest settlements were still hamlets of ten or a dozen simple cabins surrounded by a palisade, but some were also protected by rather substantial defence works at their entrances (Coles and Harding, 1979; Fig. 46). Many were built on massive understructures of piles and horizontal timbers. The scale of clearance continues to increase in the pollen record and, whereas the pollen of domestic grasses had earlier been more common than that of wild grasses, the abundance of plantain and other pasture species at sites like Arbon Bleiche suggests that open pasture was now much more abundant (Lüdi, 1954). Animal husbandry responded to these

Fig. 46. The settlement at Baldegg, showing the major wooden uprights and the reconstruction of house plans set inside a palisade. (After Coles and Harding, 1979: fig. 65)

changes: increases in young mature cattle in the faunal samples imply that there were now significant numbers of beef cattle as well as the dairy/breeding cows, a strategy better suited to the more open landscape, as milking cattle had to be kept in the vicinity of the settlements whereas bullocks could be grazed further afield (Higham, 1967a).

The plateau settlements of the second half of the millennium were much more substantial, with two hundred inhabitants or more. The abundance of ordinary metal tools – axes, chisels, gouges, hammers, anvils, saws, sickles – indicates that, by the late second millennium at least, bronze finally played a significant role in everyday (including agricultural) technology. Furthermore, many villages contained pottery, metal and textile workshops, with craftsmen presumably maintained by an agricultural surplus, and one site contained a butcher's store, implying that meat was carefully processed in the village for distribution to the community (Drack, 1971; Sauter, 1976: 105). At Zug Sumpf, fields and pasture were much more extensive than they had been at Arbon Bleiche, and animal husbandry turned increasingly to sheep and goats and particularly to wether sheep – wool was clearly now an increasingly important goal in agricultural production, presumably as a valuable commodity of exchange; exactly the same trends were noted at Zurich Alpenquai (Higham, 1967a). For the first time, too, Higham found evidence for working oxen at these sites.

In sub-alpine Italy, as in Switzerland, the second half of the third millennium was a period of major social change, with new elites being buried in special cemeteries accompanied by status markers of pottery, copper and imported flint. There are, however, little agricultural data to set alongside these developments. At Monte Covolo, the system of plant and animal husbandry established at the beginning of the third millennium continued unchanged (Barker, 1977–9; Pals, 1977–9). At Le Colombare in the Adige valley, although poor recovery and survival conditions had almost certainly biased the faunal sample against juveniles, nevertheless the data indicated that the secondary products of cattle and sheep must have been as important as their meat (Riedel, 1976a).

Evidence for dairying and wool production is far clearer in the second millennium. The Polada lake settlements consist both of *palafitte* (sites with vertical beams driven into the lake bed) and *bonifiche* (timber platforms), with tightly packed wooden houses surrounded by palisades (Peroni, 1971). Like the Swiss villages they contained craft workshops for pottery, metal and textiles. Equipment for dairying includes conical ceramic sieves at Ledro and a wooden whisk at Barche probably for cheese making, and, at Ledro, long wooden churns of hollowed out logs with a short handle at the rim, like the wooden stave churns used in the region today (Barfield, 1971; Battaglia, 1943). All the sites have yielded large numbers of bone combs, loom weights and spindle whorls, and linen textiles and balls of flax thread were preserved at Ledro. Agricultural implements include wooden sickle handles, hoes, and light wooden ards for yoked oxen (Fig. 47), the latter very similar to those depicted in the rock art of Val Camonica (Fig. 7).

Crop systems have not been studied in great detail, and much of the material was collected in the last century, but the principal crops seem to have been emmer, six-row barley, flax and pulses (Battaglia, 1943; H. N. Jarman and Gamble, 1975). Fruits, berries and nuts were all collected systematically – all the villages have produced such material, and at Ledro there were thick layers of cornelian cherries across the settlement, and huge caches of acorns. At Fiave the community collected apples, blackberries, cornelian cherries, hazel nuts and raspberries, as well as a variety of other plants from aquatic, pastoral and woodland locations (H. N. Jarman and Gamble, 1975).

Faunal studies have been more detailed. All the main stock were kept, but sheep and goats were normally the most frequent; game (especially red deer) normally comprises between 5% and 15% of the total material. At Ledro, sheep were twice as numerous as goats; there were two main peaks in the mortality data of young lambs and adult animals, but 25% of the sheep died in their second and third years; and of 180 sheep pelves, 50% were certainly female, 10% male, and the rest had the thick wall and shape characteristic of castrates or wethers (Riedel, 1976c, 1977). Clearly, the ewes were kept for dairying once they had lambed, and castrates were kept to provide at least two or three fleeces before slaughter. Rather similar systems of mixed dairy, wool and meat production were practised elsewhere on the alpine foreland at Barche (Riedel, 1976b) and Fiave (M. R. Jarman, 1975; Perini, 1975), and at a series of small settlements on the

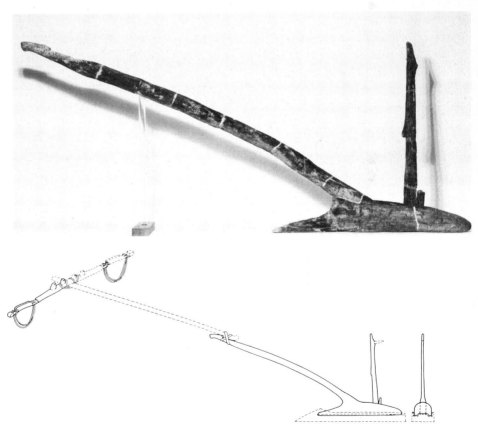

Fig. 47. The Lavagnone ard: above, photograph of the main shaft, share and steering mechanism; below, drawing of the complete find, with the assumed position of the yoke. The main timber is 1.8 m long. (Photograph and drawing kindly provided by the excavator, Renato Perini; published by Perini, 1983: fig. 1 and plate 12)

northern margins of the Po plain (Clark, 1984). From site catchment analysis at Fiave, Jarman argued that, whilst the settlement was permanent, some of the cattle and sheep were probably driven up to *alp* pasture in the summer, much as happens today (M. R. Jarman, 1976: 546).

The last stages of the second millennium in northern Italy were characterised by settlement nucleation on the southern foreland, and the development of major settlements here incorporating specialist craftsmen working in old and new materials (the latter including glass) on an altogether more industrial scale (Bietti Sestieri, 1981). Subsistence data are rather limited. By and large mixed farming much as before is indicated (Riedel, 1977), but studies of several faunal samples from sites in the Berici hills and northern Po plain have suggested more complex agricultural organisation, with some small communities supplying meat on the hoof and wool to the major settlements (Clark, 1984; M. R. Jarman, 1976). As Barfield (1971) pointed out, textile production in this region, as on the Swiss plateau, would have provided an obvious portable commodity to trade with the celtral alpine communities for metal ore.

Thus far I have discussed the alpine economy in terms of alpine subsistence, but the passes through the Alps have always been crucial routes for commerce and trade since the Roman period, and their role in the prehistoric economy was also considerable. Prior to the second millennium, there seems to have been a steady but limited movement of artifacts across the mountains (Barfield, 1981): Mediterranean shells reached Atlantic foragers in the Dolomites and Switzerland, and neolithic communities practised gift exchange in fine pottery, jadeite axes and shells, whilst identical stelae on the two sides suggest shared ritual. The sulphide copper ores of the central mountains (the Austrian Tyrol and upper Adige in particular) were one of the principal sources of raw material for European bronze smiths in the third and second millennia. Much of the mining was probably small scale and on a part time basis (Primas, 1976), but by the late second millennium some specialist communities were processing several tons of ore a day (Pittioni, 1954; Preuschen, 1973). Another critical resource in the mountains was salt. Evidence for a level of trading standardisation across the region in the later second millennium consists of a group of clay plaques stamped with quite similar geometric symbols, found on Polada settlements in the Lake Garda area and in Hungary, Slovakia and Yugoslavia: 'the rather abacus-like appearance of the general design and the numerical character of the stamps suggest that they might have been used as a sort of counting device – trading tallies, in fact' (Barfield, 1971: 77).

Clearly transalpine trade was an important element in the economy of second millennium Europe, and most of the major passes were probably in use. New settlements were established on the trade routes, such as Crestaulta at the foot of the Little St Bernard pass (Rüeger, 1942), presumably to exploit the traffic in some way, although we know nothing of the scale and organisation of the trade in general, or the role of such sites in particular. Moreover, the majority of the settlement data in the central Alps – which shared in a uniform material culture at this time (the Melauer group) – suggests that, except for a few communities on the key routes or by the key resources, the traditional way of life was largely unaffected by the new commerce of bronze age Europe. There is hardly any evidence for social stratification in the mountains on a scale at all comparable with that of lowland societies to the north or south, or even for the common use of bronze tools or weapons by the end of the second millennium. Sheep/goat transhumance continued as the primary mode of subsistence in the upper Rhone valley (Chaix, 1976–7), and cattle/sheep dairying in the central mountains (Amschler, 1939; Würgler, 1962). Most of the settlements were small undefended hamlets: the terraced barns and houses of Sissach, for example, could be part of the alpine landscape today (Wyss, 1971; Fig. 48).

The same dichotomy between foreland settlement and mountain communities can be observed in the first millennium b.c. On the Swiss plateau, the lake villages were replaced by open farms and nucleated fortified sites. The earlier hillforts like the Wittnauer Horn were often quite substantial, with populations of several hundred people (Sauter, 1976). Contemporary cemeteries include *Fürstengräber* or 'princely burials': barrows with rich gravegoods including carts, horse trappings, bronze vessels and gold jewellery, with many of the finest objects obtained by trade with Greeks and Etruscans. In the latter part of the first millennium, sites such as La Tène were massive nucleated settlements and industrial centres. The Magdalensberg oppidum in Austria was a comparable factory site covering some 350 hectares and producing iron and bronze objects for export, particularly to Roman Italy (Alföldy, 1974; Vetters and Piccotini, 1969). Epigraphic evidence has shown that a colony of Italian traders lived at the site and indicates the sophistication of the transactions, mentioning business deals with credit, loans, and payment in gold; Roman coinage, fine wares and bronzes have also been found. There were comparable cemeteries and huge industrial settlements on the Italian foreland (Barfield, 1971; Frey, 1966; Kossack, 1956–7). The Este sites in particular produced a magnificent series of sheet bronze buckets (situlae) decorated with figurative art, which were traded across the Alps probably as wine containers (Frey, 1969). The art portrays a warrior aristocracy involved in martial arts and sports (raiding,

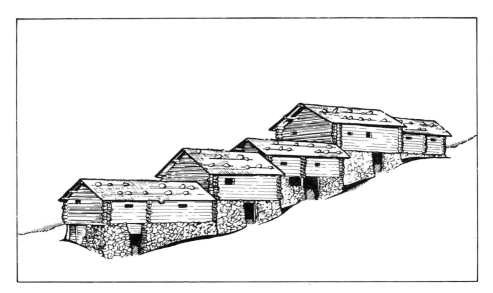

Fig. 48. A reconstruction of the Sissach hamlet. (After Wyss, 1971: fig. 8)

taking prisoners, hunting, boxing, chariot-racing, banqueting to the sound of the lyre and pipe), as well as scenes of ordinary rural life – a man snaring rabbits, another shouldering his plough home after the day's work in the fields. Polybius, writing in the second century B.C., described the life of the north Italian Celts as one of war and pastoralism, with wealth measured in gold and flocks. According to Caesar, the population of the Swiss plateau was huge, with land hunger in 58 B.C. forcing a migration of 350,000 men, women and children of the Helvetii from here into southern France (where he slaughtered most of them). Even allowing for the exaggerations of literary licence, it is clear from the archaeological evidence that the lowland margins of the alpine region at the end of the prehistoric period were characterised by very dense settlement, highly organised tribal societies, craft production on a large scale and luxury trade between the ruling aristocracies. A coordinated agricultural economy producing a substantial surplus can probably also be assumed – but we know nothing of it.

It was a very different story in the central mountains: there was still a unified material culture, with little evidence for social stratification or for metal as an everyday commodity. The Swiss communities lived in small hamlets as before. In sub-alpine Italy, fortified farms (*castellieri*) were more common; the inhabitants made simple crude pottery, still used flint arrowheads, and the little available faunal data suggest they practised the traditional sheep/cattle dairy system. The Romans established control of the western passes in 143 B.C., but the main alpine population was left alone in its mountain fastness for another century before final subjugation.

6

The continental lowlands

Geographical introduction

The continental lowlands stretch eastwards from the Rhine across the two Germanies and Poland into European Russia, bounded on the south by the Alps and Carpathians and on the north by the Baltic littoral; the Bohemian plateau in Czechoslovakia, separated from the north European plain by the Sudeten and Erzgebirge hills, is considered as a southerly extension (Fig. 49). Continental Europe has generally cooler summers than the Balkans or the middle Danube basin, and heavier precipitation. Winters are colder, with mean January temperatures below freezing. Rainfall is well distributed throughout the year, with summer maxima.

The dominant physical features of the Germano-Polish lowlands are the result of Pleistocene glaciations or their aftermath. The retreat of the ice sheets left a mantle of boulder clay, morainic material, gravel, sand and wind-blown loess, often of very great thickness, across the lowlands. West of the Elbe, the northern plain consists mainly of moors or bogs separated by higher sandy areas of heath (*Geest* or 'infertile land'), cut by marshy river valleys. East of the Elbe the plain divides into three sub-regions. Immediately south of the Baltic coast is a zone of ground moraines, heavy but fertile soils with a climax vegetation of deciduous forest, mainly beech. Adjacent to this is the end moraine zone, a lakeland region of sand and gravel hummocks, unsuitable for cultivation today and covered in coniferous forest. The main part of the lowlands, however, consists of alternating depressions and sandy interfluves. These depressions (German: *Urstromtäler*; Polish: *Pradoliny*) run east–west, and were formed by meltwaters running along the edge of the glaciers (Fig. 50). They have poorly drained floors, often choked in part with coarse sand dunes carrying pine forest and heathland. Great marshlands dominated the waterlogged floors for most of the historical period. The land between the depressions is also poorly suited to agriculture, consisting mainly of outwash sands and end moraines, an infertile *Geest* zone. Only in the eighteenth and nineteenth centuries were these regions turned into major arable resources when the depressions were reclaimed by drainage and the *Geest* improved with fertilisers such as potash salts (Shackleton, 1964: 248–50).

The most promising agricultural soils were at the junction of these lowlands with the Hercynian highlands of central Germany and southern Poland. Here, on the southern edge of the glaciated plains, a mantle of wind-blown loess soils was laid down, which has resulted in degraded chernozems and brown forest soils of good drainage and great fertility (Fig. 50). The principal belt of loess runs from the Rhine valley at Aachen across central Germany into southern Poland and Bohemia. The medieval cities on the loess

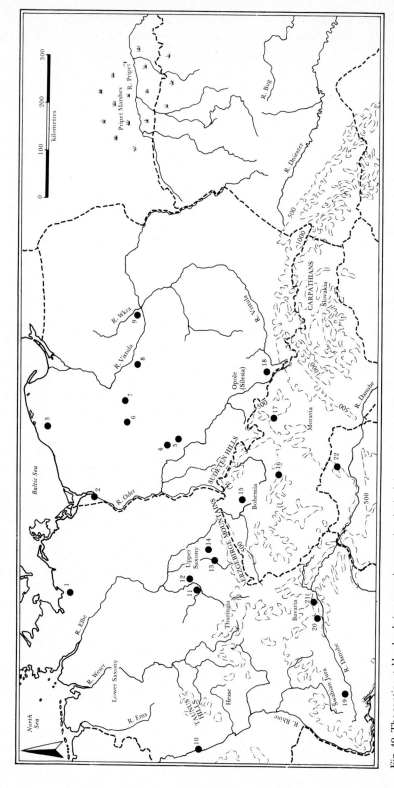

Fig. 49. The continental lowlands (contours in metres): principal sites and regions mentioned in the text. 1. Höhen Viecheln; 2. Szczecin; 3. Słupca; 4. Łęki Małe; 5. Bruszczewo; 6. Smuszewo; 7. Biskupin; 8. Brześć Kujawski; 9. Kołozab, Poświetne; 10. Köln Lindenthal; 11. Leubingen; 12. Dieskau; 13. Helmsdorf; 14. Döbeln; 15. Zatyni; 16. Bylany; 17. Blučina; 18. Olszanica; 19. Heuneburg; 20. Manching; 21. Hienheim; 22. Frauenhofen, Poigen.

were centres of agriculture, crafts and commerce, often too the administrative centres of political and ecclesiastical authority: their catalogue is eloquent testimony to the enormous natural wealth of the region (with arable wealth further augmented in recent times by coal and lignite mining) – Aachen, Köln, Essen, Dortmund, Hannover, Brunswick, Halberstadt, Magdeburg, Halle, Leipzig, Chemnitz and Dresden. The zone is still the best agricultural land, with cereals and stall-fed cattle dominating the farming systems, and rural densities are generally very high.

The central Hercynian uplands of Germany (the Mittelgebirge, from the Taunus hills by the Rhine to the Erzgebirge separating Germany and Czechoslovakia) consist of rounded forested hills with thin soils, enclosing narrow plains or basins some of which are filled with degraded chernozems of considerable fertility. Between these hills and the Danube valley are the scarplands of southern Germany, dominated by the sandstone and granite hills of the Black Forest and the Swabian/Franconian hills (limestone plateau or *alb*), but separated by attractive cultivated valleys with old river alluvium over marls and limestone resembling loess in its structure and fertility. In Bohemia fertile chernozem soils on loess are frequent in the north, but further south there are marshy clay basins and poor thin upland soils.

Postglacial foragers prior to *c.* 4500 b.c.

By the Pre-Boreal, birch woodland had developed across the continental lowlands, and pine and birch forests covered most of southern Germany, with heavier stands of birch by lakes and at higher elevations (Firbas, 1949). The upper forest limit was much as today. In the Boreal, mixed pine and birch forests spread across the north European plain, especially on sandier soils, whilst spruce colonised wetter soils (Borówko-

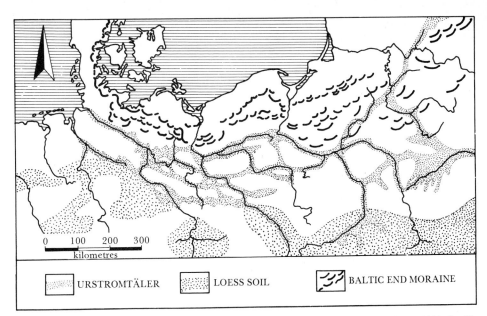

Fig. 50. The continental lowlands: *Urstomtäler* and loess. (Generalised map, after Shackleton, 1964; fig. 77 and additional information)

Dłuzakowa, 1969); in the major valleys such as the upper Danube mixed oak forest grew very thickly, and mixed deciduous and coniferous forests covered the highlands, but there was probably a mixture of open woodland and grassland on the loess (Ložek, 1966). With the development of the Atlantic climate after *c.* 5500 b.c., mixed oak forest colonised the northern plains and the Danube valley, and pine and birch forest covered the highlands; there was closed deciduous woodland on moister loess soils and open parkland in the drier loess basins, with birch and willow around lake margins and pine forests on poorer podsolised soils (Butzer, 1972: 446; Firbas, 1949). The forests, marshes, lakes and rivers offered a wide variety of animals, birds and fish for the post-glacial foraging population. In southern Germany, for example, von Koenigswald (1972) has shown that over a dozen species over 1 kg in weight were killed by Boreal and Atlantic hunters: aurochs, badger, beaver, brown bear, chamois, elk, fox, hare, lynx, otter, red deer, roe deer, stone marten, wild boar, wild cat, wolf and wood marten. Birds included duck and grouse, and fish included carp, grayling, perch, and pike.

Large numbers of Boreal and Atlantic occupation sites have been found across the northern lowlands from the Elbe to the Pripet marshes. Most of the sites have been found on the sands edging the *Urstromtäler*, or by moraine lakes (Dolukhanov, 1979; Gramsch, 1973, 1976; Isaenko, 1970; Prinke, 1973). Excavated open sites consist of deep and quite substantial pits containing hearths. In Bohemia the location of sites varied from sand and gravel terraces in the river valleys to the adjacent uplands; variations in assemblages are taken to reflect variations in the subsistence activities practised in the different locations, and there is evidence for a mixture of hunting, fowling and fishing (Prošek and Ložek, 1952; Vencl, 1971). At Höhen Viecheln on Lake Schwerin in East Germany, the main mammals killed (aurochs, red deer, wild boar, elk and reindeer) represented over 4000 kg of meat, whereas the remains of a wide range of water fowl and fish represented 150 kg of meat (Gramsch, 1976). Blunt headed wooden arrows were used for fowling, and wooden spears for hunting or fishing; microlithic composite tools were also used. Although plant gathering is hardly represented at all, the impression from each region of the lowlands is of mobile foraging systems exploiting the full range of forest, marsh and aquatic resources. In the Oder/Elbe area, Gramsch (1973) argued that some fifteen bands could be distinguished in the archaeological record, each with an annual territory of *c.* 3500 km^2.

A particularly detailed model of Boreal/Atlantic foraging has been put forward by Jochim (1976) for southwestern Germany. On the basis of the list of species recorded in the faunal samples and the modern behaviour of these species, Jochim predicted the amount of food and other products provided by them, and their seasonal abundance, and from these calculations the probable importance of the different resources during the year (Fig. 51). Ethnographic data predicted seasonal variations in band size, and there was a general correlation between these estimates and population numbers suggested by the sizes of the different sites in the study area containing different seasonal occupations. Jochim concluded that two bands of *c.* 20–30 people each spent the autumn, winter and spring in the Danube valley or the Swabian *alb* to its north, moving south to the alpine foreland to link up during the summer at the Federsee, where raised ridges have been identified as barriers of birch poles constructed by foragers of this period to block off shallow bays as fish traps (Fig. 52). The annual subsistence round for each band would have covered a range some 50 km long; plant foods are assumed to have been important from spring to autumn, fish in spring, summer and autumn, small game in winter, and large game throughout the year.

Such a strategy would have been specifically adapted to local topography, vegetation and seasonal abundance, and different strategies should be expected where these variables differed. Thus, atlantic salmon and migratory waterfowl would probably have been key resources in the Rhine valley, whereas salmon but not waterfowl would have been plentiful in the limestone country of northern Bavaria. Presumably resource variation must have caused variations in the size of territories and aggregations, but if similar groups of about seventy people occupied territories of similar size to those predicted by Jochim for his study area, a dozen such areas would have encompassed the whole of southern Germany as far north as Frankfurt, with a total population approaching a thousand people – the kind of population indicated by ethnographic and simulation studies as necessary to provide a self-sustaining mating network for groups of hunter-gatherers (Damas, 1972; Wobst, 1974).

Linearbandkeramik farming, *c.* 4500–3000 b.c.

In the middle of the fifth millennium b.c., an entirely new settlement phenomenon was superimposed on the Atlantic foraging systems of temperate Europe. The sites were characterised by simple pottery of organic tempered fabric, decorated with curvilinear and rectilinear designs. The German term for the pottery, *Linearbandkeramik* (commonly shortened to LBK), is normally used to describe the new settlements, although Childe (1929) originally defined them as the first in his Danubian sequence of neolithic

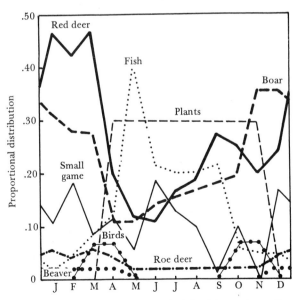

Fig. 51. Predicted annual resource schedule of the southwest German Mesolithic. (After Jochim, 1976: fig. 25)

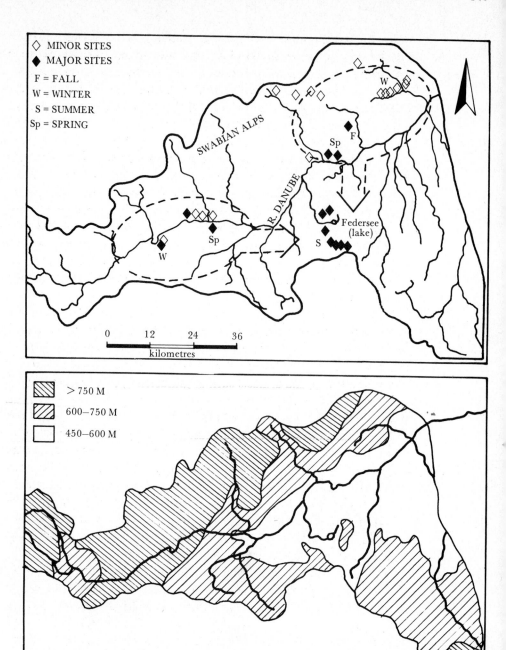

Fig. 52. Mesolithic sites in southwest Germany: above, Jochim's model of mesolithic subsistence for the upper Danube, with two bands spending most of the year in the main valley and its tributaries or adjacent uplands, and coming together for summer fishing at Federsee; below, simplified topographical map of the region. (After Jochim, 1976: figs. 12 and 38)

cultures. The distribution of LBK pottery is enormous: from eastern France, Belgium and the Netherlands down the Rhine valley to northern Switzerland, across Germany and Poland, into lower Austria, western Czechoslovakia and northwest Hungary, and down the outer rim of the Carpathians into Moldavia and the Dniester valley. Early excavations at sites such as Köln Lindenthal found large pits which were interpreted as dwelling pits (Buttler and Haberey, 1936), but large scale excavations after the last war in Holland (Fig. 63) and Czechoslovakia discovered traces of massive timber houses amongst such 'dwelling pits': the houses were built of heavy posts, with wattle and daub walls, the daub being quarried from pits around the buildings (Modderman, 1958–9a, 1958–9b, 1958–9c; Soudsky, 1962). The most impressive structures were aisled long-houses, 7–45 m long and 5–6 m wide; some had much heavier construction at one end (perhaps with a raised platform), others had a Y-shaped setting of posts in the centre making a more open living space, some had room divisions and several hearths: combinations of human habitation, with or without animal stalling and grain storage, have been proposed. Most settlements also had at least as many short structures, which may be barns, byres or single family units.

From their first discovery, it became clear that most LBK sites were agricultural settlements. Whenever faunal material was recovered, bones of domestic animals outnumbered those of game. Evidence for cultivation survived in the form of ovens for drying grain, storage pots and pits containing carbonised grain, cereal impressions in pottery and daub, and artifacts such as grindstones, sickles and narrow high backed 'shoe last' adzes interpreted as shares for wooden ards. In 1938 Buttler demonstrated that the LBK settlements of central Europe were predominantly on loess soils (Fig. 53). At first it was thought that the loess must have offered an open corridor through hostile forests, but in the 1930s and 1940s palaeobotanists argued that forested conditions probably prevailed here and Iversen's *landnam* model of slash and burn farming (Fig. 8) was universally applied. 'The best known exponents of the extensive, shifting agriculture of neolithic times were the Danubian peasants who colonised the loess of central Europe . . . clearing small patches of forest, taking a few easy crops, and passing on to fresh ground' (Clark, 1952: 95–6). At the local scale, Soudsky proposed a model of cyclical swidden farming at Bylany, whereby the community moved round a series of sites in the locality as soils were exhausted, returning to Bylany after a generation or more (Soudsky, 1962; Soudsky and Pavlů, 1972). Similar systems of shifting cultivation were envisaged for later LBK (Rössen) farmers in the fourth millennium. Radiocarbon dates in the mid-fifth millennium b.c. were obtained in the 1960s from early LBK sites as far apart as Hungary, Bohemia and Holland, suggesting a very rapid process of colonisation (Clark, 1965; Fig. 5), and the radiocarbon chronology was used by Ammerman and Cavalli-Sforza (1971) to compute the 'wave of advance' of the first LBK farmers as 1.08 km per year.

However, recent investigations afford a very different perception of LBK subsistence. On the loesslands of southern Poland, Bohemia, lower Austria and the two Germanies, there were highly organised systems of sedentary mixed farming from the outset. Emmer, einkorn, barley and legumes have been found at most sites on the loess where plant remains have been collected, and millet and flax at several, but emmer is invariably the principal crop (Hopf, 1977; Knörzer, 1972; Modderman, 1977; Murray, 1970; Tempir, 1971; Willerding, 1980). Emmer does not extract nutrients from the soil to the same extent as some other cereals, and could have been grown on loess soils for indefinite periods with simple systems of manuring and crop rotation; rotation systems have in fact been inferred from the composition of the plant residues from Hienheim in southern Germany and the Langweiler sites on the Aldenhoven plateau west of Köln (Knörzer, 1972; Modderman, 1977). Modern swidden systems in the tropics make little use of stock, but LBK farmers kept cattle, sheep and pigs; and cattle – better adapted than sheep to the temperate forests, and the prime source of manure – were the principal stock right across the loesslands (Clason, 1967a, 1968; Kratochvil, 1972; Kulczycka-Leciejewiczowa, 1970; Müller, 1964; Stampfli, 1965; Wolff, 1977b). Mortality data from the Bylany material suggest that cattle were kept primarily for their meat (Clason, 1968), and horn core and long bone measurements from sites near Leipzig further suggest the practice of castration for efficient meat production (Müller, 1964). Cattle could supply manure in bulk, sheep could be penned on the arable (providing the manure and treading the ground into a good tilth), and pigs could strip fallow land of weeds as well as manuring it heavily: 'each of the domestic animals thus has a definite role in an economy based on permanent fields' (Rowley-Conwy, 1981b: 95). Rowley-Conwy's further arguments against the ethnographic and palaeobotanical components of the swidden model are described in Chapter 9 (p. 234), but it seems very clear from

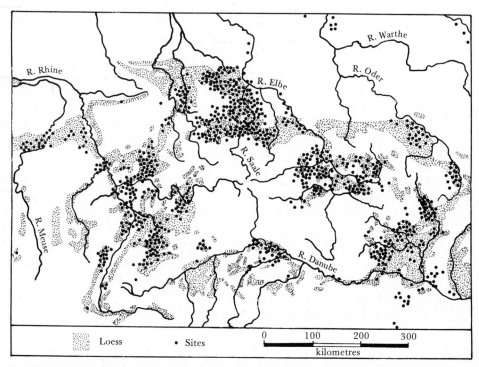

Fig. 53. *Linearbandkeramik* settlement and loess soils: a relationship first noted by Buttler and Haberey, 1936, and here after Clark, 1952: fig. 45.

Table 9 *Game habitats at Heinheim.*
(After Clason, in Modderman, 1977)

Species	Habitat preference
aurochs	deciduous forest and clearings
badger	deciduous forest and clearings
beaver	light woods alongside river
bear	deciduous forest
elk	open woods, much undergrowth, marsh
fox	dry terrain
red deer	deciduous forest and grassland
roe deer	young woodland, much undergrowth
squirrel	young dark forest
wild boar	deciduous forest

the subsistence data recovered at these LBK sites that 'shifting cultivation would not have been necessary and would probably have been wasteful of resources' (Jarman and Bay-Petersen, 1976: 181) – and indeed that it was not practised by LBK farmers.

Furthermore, the evidence of detailed regional surveys and site catchment studies makes far better sense in terms of settled farming than of shifting cultivation. In southern Poland, Kruk's survey near Krakow demonstrated that both earlier and later LBK settlement consisted of enclaves of 8–10 sites (both large villages and satellite camps) at the junction of the loess plateau and river flood plain (Kruk, 1973, 1980). The continuity, density and patterning of the settlement data were such that 'the regular use of the burning economy seems virtually impossible' (Kruk, 1973: 255), and he concluded that LBK farming here consisted of the intensive garden cultivation of prime arable soils (light and well drained loess-based chernozems) at the junction between slope and flood plain, integrated with stock-keeping using both the plateaus above the sites and the main valley floors. Similar locations were selected by LBK farmers elsewhere in southern Poland (Jarman and Bay-Petersen, 1976), lower Austria (Ruttkay *et al.*, 1976), southern Germany (Modderman, 1977; Sielmann, 1971; Fig. 54), the middle Elbe and Elster valleys (Baumann and Quietzsch, 1969; Lies, 1974; Quitta, 1970) and the Aldenhoven plateau (Farrugia *et al.*, 1973; Lüning, 1976), and similar systems of farming seem likely given the subsistence data. The range of weed species associated with the crops at the Aldenhoven plateau sites suggests that fields were small and overshadowed by higher vegetation (many species are shade loving), and that the grain was harvested by cutting off the ears high up on the stalk, with weeds of similar height being reaped in the process (Knörzer, 1972). There is little evidence for the collection of wild plants, apart from those of the fallow land, but game (particularly red deer, roe deer, and pig) contributed up to a third of the meat at several sites. The habitats of the game killed at Hienheim demonstrate the mosaic of open country, closed and open woodland typical of the environs of the loessland LBK settlements (Table 9).

LBK subsistence beyond the loess was very different. In the *Urstromtäler* zone of central Poland, for example, sites consist primarily of spreads of debris without the substantial structures, storage pits and ovens of the loessland villages; grindstones and

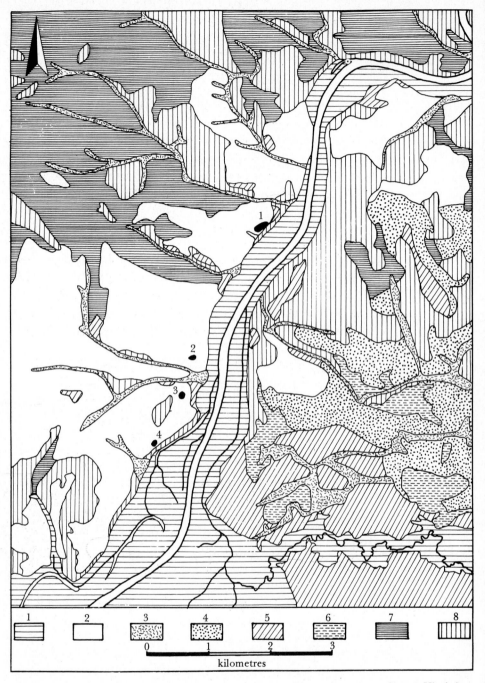

Fig. 54. *Linearbandkeramik* settlement at Hienheim on the Danube in southern Germany. Sites: 1. Hienheim 'am Weinberg'; 2. Hienheim-Fuchsloch; 3. Irnsing-Schanze; 4. Irnsing-1. Geology and soils: 1. younger alluvial loams; 2. loess; 3. colluvial material; 4. sands; 5. gravels; 6. shallow stony soils on sandstone; 7. fine sandy to silty loams on limestone; 8. shallow stony soils on limestone. (After Bakels, 1978: fig. 17)

sickle flints are also very rare, all the environmental evidence (pollen, large and small mammal bones, bird bones, molluscs) suggests a heavily forested landscape with small clearings, and cereal cultivation was practised only on a very small scale (Bogucki, 1981, 1982). Cattle were the key resource, and mortality data at the best investigated site, Brześć-Kujawski, imply that they were kept for both meat and dairy produce – pottery strainers assumed to be cheese-making equipment are in fact common at these sites but are not found in the loess settlements to the south. Foraging was also important. At Brześć-Kujawski fish, molluscs and turtles were collected from a nearby lake and stored alive in bell-shaped pits (Bogucki and Grygiel, 1981; Grygiel and Bogucki, 1979), game was hunted (principally red deer and roe deer), and the natural harvest of plant foods was far richer in these lowland forests than on the dry loesslands – there were between 250 and 450 species of edible plants in this environment (D. L. Clarke, 1976: 454): perennials, roots, tubers, rhizomes, shoots, buds, flowers, leaves, fruits and nuts.

The notable absence of pig bones at the lowland sites, despite the suitability of the pig to the forests, suggests that LBK subsistence here placed a premium on mobility. From the nature and distribution of habitation debris in the Brześć-Kujawski area, Bogucki (1982) concluded that LBK herders (with perhaps 30–50 cattle: cows, their followers, and bullocks) used major residential bases for a month or more and smaller camps around them for a few days or a week or so (Fig. 55). There is little evidence for winter

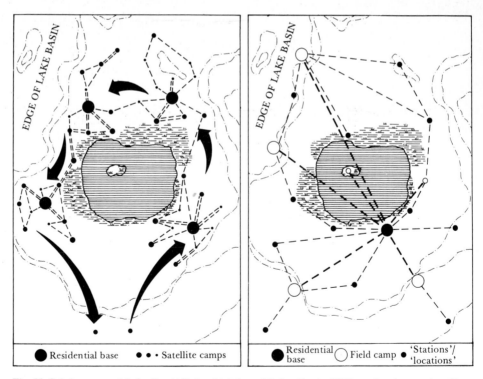

Fig. 55. Subsistence models for Brześć Kujawski: left, mobile herding by LBK people using a series of base camps and satellite camps, moving away from the area in the winter; right, the all-year-round village of multiple longhouses established in the third millennium, sustained by mixed farming and foraging. (After Bogucki, 1982: figs. 33 and 40)

occupation at these sites, and Bogucki suggested that they might be herding camps to which the main loessland villages sent their stock in a system of inverse transhumance, but it is equally possible that the population remained in the area all year, dispersing to outlying camps in the winter when food and fodder were in shortest supply. (Recent analysis of LBK pottery from the two areas indicates two quite separate production zones, in support of the second hypothesis: see Cowie, 1985.) Stock-based farming has also been argued for other sites in this region from their subsistence data and catchments (H. N. Jarman and Bay-Petersen, 1976; M. R. Jarman *et al.*, 1982). In the highlands of central Germany, some sites seem to have been primarily hunting stations, others have faunal samples composed principally of sheep and goats (Sielmann, 1971). Further north in the morainic regions and east in the Pripet marshes were hunter-fisher-gatherers with predominantly microlithic flint technologies and simple pointed-based pottery, often decorated with comb impressions; there are occasional sherds at some of these sites of what is assumed to be imported LBK pottery (Dolukhanov, 1979; Gramsch, 1973; Kowalezyk, 1969).

The enormous variation in subsistence practised by people with LBK pottery correlates with other evidence for differences in social complexity. On the loesslands were the most substantial and numerous villages, as well as a hierarchy of smaller villages, hamlets and farmsteads, whereas the settlements of the lowland forests were clearly much more ephemeral. On the loesslands, too, everyday necessities such as stone for agricultural implements were normally obtained from the locality (up to 20/30 km from the site), but many communities were also linked in systems of longer distance exchange of status products such as fine pottery, high quality flint, shell and obsidian(Buttler and Haberey, 1936; Schietzel, 1965; Schwabedissen, 1966). At Olszanica, moreover, the clustering of obsidian around selected longhouses suggested that 'probably the obsidian exchange occurred between more prominent families or individuals' (Milisauskas, 1978: 88), and there is in fact consistent evidence for status differentiation and 'big man' systems of achieved ranking in LBK cemeteries (Gabołowna, 1966; Kahlke, 1954; Pavuk, 1972). One longhouse at Olszanica with many polished axes in the vicinity was interpreted as the men's house, or the house of the community leader (Milisauskas, 1976). The settlement organisation, exchange networks and ranking systems of the prime arable areas (the loesslands) contrast markedly with the pastoral and foraging societies with LBK pottery of the mountains and lowland forests. The same dichotomy persisted through the fourth millennium, without significant changes in settlement or subsistence (Knörzer, 1971a; Kruk, 1973; Lies, 1974; Quitta, 1970).

Sherratt (1980) has argued that the first farmers in both the Balkans and temperate Europe, as in the Mediterranean, used spring-sown crops. I have not accepted his thesis in the Mediterranean and Balkan studies previously, and now again I follow Butzer's argument (1972: 580) that the key change in LBK farming north of the Carpathians was the development of spring sowing as an adaptation to the temperate climate: spring sowing eliminated the problem of winter cold and took advantage of the higher spring rainfall, and the selection of the dry loess avoided the worst effects of the wetter summers. At the same time the new arable system involved an entirely different form of stock-keeping: whereas in the Mediterranean and the Balkans sheep and goats were the easiest stock to keep and were well adapted to autumn sowing (manuring the stubble fields over the winter, and able to nibble the green shoots without damage), the climate and vegetation of temperate Europe clearly favoured cattle and pigs rather than sheep and goats, cattle were the key source of manure, and the fields were best manured in the autumn after the harvest, with the muck rotting down over the winter before the spring sowing. In short, LBK mixed farming on the loess was an efficient adaptation to temperate conditions in terms of crops, animals, soil selection and techniques.

The traditional model for the LBK phenomenon has been that of a rapid migration of swidden farmers from the Balkans across the continental lowlands. Although swiddening must be discounted, many archaeologists still hold to the model, with the variations in LBK subsistence and society *c.* 4500 b.c. (like those in the Balkans *c.* 5500 b.c.) having to be explained in terms of cultural adaptation as the pioneers moved deeper into frontier country, or in terms of a primary migration across the loess and acculturation with indigenous foragers on the margins. However, radiocarbon dating has now shown that LBK settlement did not in fact spread across Europe with a clear chronological fall-off from Hungary to Holland: after the rapid expansion of Mediterranean farming into southeast Europe *c.* 5500 b.c., the cereal/stock system did not cross the Carpathian barrier for a thousand years – and then expanded with quite remarkable speed over a huge area. There seems every reason to view LBK farming as fundamentally a temperate European invention, in the one optimal arable region which was (as the Atlantic climate deteriorated) also the most marginal region for the existing foraging economy. What is also clear, as in the alpine region, is that an internal change in subsistence on the loesslands had to be sudden, from one 'package' to another: cereals were an efficient and productive use of open country or clearings on dry soils in temperate Europe, but had to be integrated with cattle husbandry for manure, just as penned cattle needed the cereal straw for fodder and bedding.

Agricultural expansion and intensification, *c.* 3000–2000 b.c.
In the late fourth millennium b.c. over much of continental Europe the evolved LBK pottery styles were replaced by new traditions which can be clustered into three main groups: Lengyel in the south, Funnel Beaker (*Trichterbecher*, usually abbreviated to TRB) in the centre, and Michelsberg in the west. The different styles overlap, and tended to be interpreted once in terms of ethnic groups struggling for supremacy, but modern ceramic and settlement studies have discounted such notions.

The second half of the third millennium b.c. was characterised by the widespread appearance of barrow cemeteries across continental Europe. The barrows contain single burials, with the dead often accompanied by cord-ornamented pottery, ranging from beakers in the western region to large amphorae in Poland, as well as perforated stone 'battle axes' and copper ornaments and weapons. As I described in Chapter 4, general similarities with contemporary burial practices in southern Russia have traditionally been regarded as evidence for a major incursion of a warrior people from the steppes (Gimbutas, 1965): 'the general opinion is that in essentials they [the burials] seem to represent a diffuse and perhaps rapid movement of inter-related peoples from the south Russian steppe, northwestwards at least to the Rhine or the Low Countries' (Piggott,

1965: 85) . . . 'violent clashes no doubt occurred in that melting pot of population' (Briard, 1976: 13). Again, however, the modern view of the corded ware burials is that they reflect important internal social changes, with the emergence of elite leadership whose status was affirmed by distinct styles of dress and equipment (Phillips, 1980: 187). High status individuals in most TRB and corded ware graves were normally adult males, but the occurrence of a few juveniles with high status gravegoods implies the beginning of inherited rather than achieved rank (Milisauskas, 1978: 167–72). Commodities such as obsidian, high quality flint and copper were exchanged amongst the new elites in some bulk, sometimes over hundreds of kilometres (Ottoway, 1973; Sherratt, 1976; Sulimirski, 1960); as an example of the scale of production generated by these exchange systems, Krzemionki flint in Poland was mined on an intensive scale (there are about 1000 shafts over some four kilometres) by more or less specialist mining communities (Tabaczynski, 1970).

The third millennium also witnessed a considerable expansion of settlement, particularly on the loesslands. In the Krakow survey of southern Poland, the enclaves of LBK sites were replaced by regularly spaced sites along the plateau edges, and the period also marked the first large scale colonisation of the dry plateaus; there are some indications of a hierarchy of central places and satellite communities (Kruk, 1973). Exactly the same trends have been found in Germany in the Magdeburg region (Lies, 1974), the Aldenhoven plateau (Kuper et al., 1974) and the upper Rhine valley (Sielmann, 1971). The largest settlements were increasingly protected by substantial palisades and ditches (Behrens, 1973; Ehrich, 1956; Kuper and Piepers, 1966; Lüning, 1967). Emmer continued to be the main crop, integrated with cattle and pig keeping in the traditional zone of settlement (Klichowska, 1970; Kulczycka-Leciejewiczowa, 1969), although sheep and goats steadily increased in importance (Beyer, 1972; Poulain, 1975).

In the *Urstromtäler* zone of central Poland, pollen diagrams indicate a major increase in the amount of clearance, correlating with the establishment of permanent villages practising mixed farming instead of the mobile herding and foraging of the LBK communities here (Bogucki, 1981; Fig. 55). Brześć-Kujawski was now an all-year-round village of multiple longhouses, with a population of perhaps 70–120 people; crafts practised here included potting, smelting, working in flint, antler and bone, and the preparation of hides. Permanent occupation was possible because the preceding system of cattle herding and foraging was augmented with pig keeping and grain cultivation, yielding two key resources for the hungry months of winter and spring (Fig. 56). Red deer were killed in increasing numbers, especially in spring when they would have been attracted to the growing crops. Agricultural settlement in central Germany and Poland also extended at this time to sandy soils which, whilst light and tillable, were prone to aridity, cold and leaching. There is a marked increase in the frequency of barley and einkorn, both crops better suited than emmer to poorer soils, in the new settlements (Matthias and Schultze-Motel, 1971).

There were also major changes in agricultural technology during the third millennium in temperate Europe (Sherratt, 1981). Lightweight wooden ards dating to the middle of the millennium or later have been found in Germany and Poland, and scoring caused by cross-ploughing with such ards has been found under many barrows in these countries (Fowler, 1971; Glob, 1951). Over a dozen burials of oxen pairs are known from Poland and central Germany, models of yoked oxen have been found as well as actual wooden yokes, and castration has been noted in some collections of cattle bones. The light ard is efficient only when the soil has already been disturbed, or where there is little thickness of roots to cut through as in the Mediterranean, but in temperate Europe high rainfall and cool temperatures tend to result in a thick mat of roots on many soils. The sandy soils may initially have been broken up with hand tools, but the ard would have been well suited to them. The efficient use of the ard in appropriate soil conditions can increase the cultivable area by a factor of three compared with hand cultivation (Clark and Haswell, 1964), although some of the resultant produce needs to be set aside to maintain the plough team. The introduction of the ard clearly facilitated the expansion of cultivation to the sandier soils in the third millennium. The use of horses for riding and pulling carts also developed across the continental lowlands at this time: horse bones occur frequently in the faunal record and although carts have not survived, there are convincing representations of four wheeled carts on some TRB pottery (Milisauskas, 1978: 126), and wooden wheels found in Danish bogs date to this period (van der Waals, 1963).

Although dairying and wool production were practised prior to the third millennium on the continental lowlands, there is certainly clear evidence that the other components of Sherratt's Secondary Products Revolution – horse riding, and cattle traction for the ard and the cart – were developed at this time. Just as the ard correlates with agricultural expansion, so horse riding correlates with the emergence of clearly defined elites for whom (as today) equestrianism was as much a desirable symbol of prestige as particular

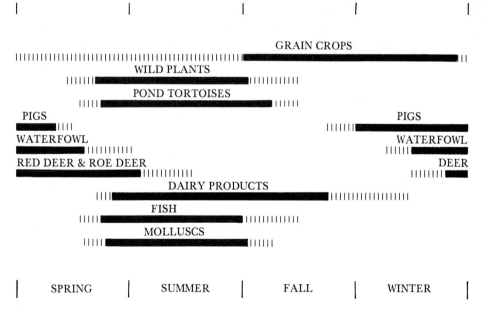

Fig. 56. Brześć Kujawski: predicted annual resource schedule of mixed farming and foraging for the third millennium village. Solid lines = periods of peak utilisation; broken lines = periods of intermittent use. (After Bogucki, 1982: fig. 35)

styles of dress and equipment. Furthermore, as Sherratt points out (1981: 297–9), the adoption of the ard almost certainly had major implications for social relationships: amongst hoe agriculturalists today, female labour is normally dominant in sowing, weeding and harvesting, and systems of matrilineal inheritance are common; plough agriculturalists, on the other hand (like specialised pastoralists), tend to be characterised by the dominance of male labour and by patrilineal descent (Keesing, 1975). In addition, land tends to be a major inheritable commodity for plough agriculturalists, whereas property amongst many African hoe agriculturalists today belongs to a lineage and not to individuals to pass on to their offspring (Goody, 1976). The scene was set in temperate Europe during the third millennium for the development of increasing competition for land (once cultivable land came into short supply as populations grew) and 'the development of relationships such as lord and serf, landlord and tenant, which exist [today] in Eurasia but not in Africa' (Goody, 1976: 25) – the kind of relationships strongly implied for many parts of Europe by the first millennium b.c.

Related to the other social and economic changes of the third millennium, stock were probably becoming symbols of status and wealth valued beyond the basic requirements of subsistence. At Grosshoften Föllik in Austria, one extraordinary grave contained the burials of a cow and calf, ewe and lamb, goat and kid, and mare and foal (Amschler, 1949). What seem to be animal enclosures are common at third millennium settlements, and big palisaded sites like Dölauer Heide enclosing a large area but only a few houses must also have had an important function as stock enclosures (Behrens, 1973). Given the emergence of elite groups marked by warlike status kits, it would be very surprising if competition and wealth accumulation did not extend to land and to the crops and stock it supported: the substantial palisades around the major settlements presumably served to keep both the stock inside and the raiding party outside.

Two further elements must be added to the complex equation of social and economic change in the third millennium. The first was population increase, which has been inferred in all the settlement surveys discussed earlier documenting the colonisation of secondary soils. The second was climatic instability. The main phase of agricultural expansion in the first half of the millennium coincided with a wetter oscillation (Frenzel, 1966), which favoured the development of arable systems on the arid soils of the loess plateaus and the unstable forest soils and sands of the *Urstromtäler* interfluves. The trend to colder and drier conditions in the second half of the millennium noted by Frenzel for temperate Europe could well have placed considerable strain on subsistence systems in the colonised areas, particularly if podsolisation had started to develop. It is impossible to separate out one factor as a 'prime mover', but probably both internal (demographic) and external (ecological) pressures provided a critical context for the agricultural transformations of the third millennium, and the social transformations to which they were married.

Farming in the second millennium b.c.

Bronze age studies in central Europe have traditionally focused primarily on burial evidence: this has been used to characterise society as divided in earlier phases between warrior-chieftains, craftsmen and commoners, and in later phases between chieftains (or kings), warriors, craftsmen and commoners. Undoubtedly such a view is greatly oversimplified: for example, Shennan's elegant analysis of some 300 graves in the early bronze age cemetery of Branc in Slovakia revealed distinct age and sex groups with well defined dress and ornamentation to show social status and an emphasis on rich female graves that could mean either that descent was through the female line or that society was patrilineal with women being used as vehicles of display for their husbands' wealth (Shennan, 1975). As she pointed out, bronze age stratification was unlikely to be uniform, although the cemetery evidence in general suggests that dynastic families or clans held hereditary power across much of the continental lowlands by the early second millennium b.c. The best known burials of the middle of the millennium are the Únětice barrows (such as Helmsdorf and Leubingen in Germany and Lęki Małe in Poland) containing high status individuals buried in timber mortuary houses with bronze weapons and gold and silver ornaments (Piggott, 1965: 127–9). In the latter part of the millennium cremation became the dominant mode of burial. Gravegoods became in general much poorer and, instead, wealth was often discarded lavishly (for example into rivers), bringing to mind the potlatch system of some recent societies in which competing elites indulged in the conspicuous consumption of wealth: 'social status may have depended less on access to prestige items than on the capacity to discard them in quantity on public occasions' (Bradley, 1980: 4). As in the Balkans and the middle Danube basin, these regional elites supported several craft industries and traded widely in metal (both ore and finished objects), and luxury commodities such as amber and faience, but nothing is known of the role of foodstuffs and animal by-products in such trade (Coles and Harding, 1979).

Settlement data in general and agricultural data in particular are still extremely poor for this part of Europe in the second millennium, but two major systems of land use can at least be discerned, one in the traditional primary areas of settlement, the other on the secondary soils of the German and Polish lowlands. The loesslands of southern Poland, Bohemia and Germany were still key agricultural regions, supporting dense settlement. In the earlier part of the second millennium, villages consisted of 20–30 houses with populations of perhaps 100–200 inhabitants, settlement was densest at the junction of the loess plateaus and river floodplains, and the arable/cattle system of farming first established by LBK communities was still practised, with emmer the primary crop (Baumann and Quietzch, 1969; Coblenz, 1973; Hnízdóva, 1953; Lies, 1974; Wojciechowski, 1966). It was precisely in these regions that the most lavish burials (such as Helmsdorf and Leubingen) and the richest hoards (such as Dieskau) occur. The main phase of barrow building tends to coincide generally with a decline in settlement numbers on the loesslands and in comparable parts of western Germany, and a significant increase in pastoralism has often been inferred (Balkwill, 1976; Bouzek *et al.*, 1976; Bradley, 1982; Hundt, 1958, 1964). In northwest Bohemia this was correlated with climatic trends less favourable to crop systems, for an integrated analysis of pollen, molluscan and sedimentary data indicated a climatic oscillation in the middle of the millennium characterised by more oceanic weather – mild winters, cool summers, and high rainfall (Bouzek *et al.*, 1976). Unfortunately the available subsistence data are quite inadequate to test the pastoralist model. However that may be, the late second millennium certainly witnessed an enormous expansion of settlement. In Bohemia and Silesia villages were spaced at kilometre intervals (Bouzek *et al.*, 1976; Bukowski, 1974), and light scatters of pottery stretching two or three kilometres from the largest settlements suggest intensive manuring systems to sustain them (Gedl, 1962). Bradley (1980) argues that the late bronze age elites of central Europe reorganised agriculture to produce a surplus of crops, animals, textiles and so on with which to engage more fully in the consumption of prestigious metalwork, but the argument – whilst plausible – is entirely indirect, based on changes in burial rite and the treatment of wealth. In the face of high population densities and a 'war-structured hierarchy' (Balkwill, 1976: 208), fortified hilltop settlements were increasingly preferred; at one of these sites, Blucina in Moravia, there were two hundred mutilated skeletons in the outer ditch (Neustupny and Neustupny, 1961: 118).

The distribution of wealthy graves and metalwork shows that the lowlands of Germany and Poland were probably also characterised by the surplus production of subsistence commodities to sustain the ruling elites and their craftsmen. Thus Bruszczewo, a typical settlement of the first half of the millennium (a collection of small wattle and daub houses inside a large stock enclosure), produced abundant evidence for metallurgy and other craft activities at the site (Coles and Harding, 1979: 37). In the *Urstromtäler* region, settlements were often on headlands jutting into lakes, backed by low sandy hills. No detailed faunal studies have been published, but cattle are invariably reported dominant, followed by sheep/goats and pigs, and horses are also usually identified; emmer, bread wheat and barley were the principal crops, along with millet, which was well suited to the light sandy soils (Rajewski, 1970).

By the latter part of the second millennium, most Lausitz settlements in this region were defended by banks, ditches and stockades, with complex entrances of gate towers and causeways at the major sites (Coblenz, 1974). This system of settlement endured into the late first millennium b.c. The best known site, Biskupin, has been marvellously reconstructed: inside the massive stockade were rows of log-built cabins, probably divided into residential and stalling areas, with an estimated population of several hundred people (Fig. 57). The subsistence data have been analysed in detail by Ostoja-Zagorski (1974). Botanical samples run into hundreds of thousands of seeds at several sites. The most frequent cereals reported were emmer, spelt, club wheat, bread wheat, barley and millet; peas, beans and lentils were also grown (Table 10). Emmer and barley had been the most common cereals earlier in the second millennium, but spelt and to a lesser extent oats and rye increased in importance as colder and wetter conditions developed at the end of the millennium. Weed seeds have been found in huge numbers – half a million seeds of gold of pleasure (*Camelia sativa*), for example, at Smuszewo. Faunal material has not been studied in detail, and recovery methods have often been inadequate, but large samples are available from several sites (Table 11). Cattle predominated at most of them (40–65%), usually followed by sheep and goats in the sandy areas and by pigs in the northernmost region; horses were present but not common at most sites, being abundant only at Jeziorko to the northeast of the main settlement zone. Pollen analyses consistently indicate a widespread increase in pasture plants on the German and Polish lowlands in the late second millennium, and Ostoja-Zagorski con-

Table 10 *Plant remains from Lausitz settlements: numbers of identified seeds. (After Ostoja-Zagorski, 1974: 126)*

	wheat	barley	millet	oats	rye	pea	bean	lentil
Szczecin-Wal	4	4	–	–	–	–	17	4
Wolin-Młynówska	–	7	–	2	1	–	–	–
Wolin-Wzgórze Wisielców	3	831	3	–	–	1743	539	–
Biskupin	6865	733	514	–	–	234	83	209
Kotlin	1	30	1	–	–	–	–	–
Słupca 1	43	18	–	–	10	57	–	–
Słupca 2	1	1	–	–	–	131	1	–
Smuszewo	101616	28025	76460	71	–	8885	13762	9648
Sobiejuchy	3	31	–	–	–	–	1	–
Kamieniec	140	15	10	–	–	25	20	1
Wrocław-Osobowice	1	8	3	40	1	–	–	–

Table 11 *Animal bones from Lausitz settlements: frequency of main stock. (After Ostoja-Zagorski, 1974: 127)*

	cattle	dog	horse	pig	sheep/goat	stock as % of total fauna
Szczecin-Grodzka	32.0	+	6.6	39.0	22.4	94.7
Szczecin-Zamek	31.9	+	–	49.4	18.7	100.0
Tolkmicko	47.0	–	–	26.5	26.5	100.0
Jeziorko	17.3	+	39.3	12.8	30.3	88.3
Biskupin	54.8	+	+	23.4	21.4	76.6
Jankowo	63.2	+	8.2	16.3	9.4	91.9
Kotlin	52.3	+	6.6	24.1	8.3	91.4
Smuszewo	41.7	+	8.3	34.8	8.3	95.6
Słupca 1	65.8	+	+	14.3	20.4	92.6
Sobiejuchy	49.9	+	5.8	14.8	24.6	98.0
Gzin	56.4	+	14.4	1.3	25.5	99.2
Niemcza	45.0	–	12.0	22.0	21.0	100.0
Wrocław-Osobowice	57.0	+	10.0	17.0	15.0	98.0

cluded that agriculture here was stock-based, augmented by extensive cultivation systems on the sandy soils which perhaps involved forest burning but which were also organised systematically using ard technology and crop rotation.

The quality of the grazing in this region during the medieval period was such that milk yields were very low– 720 litres per lactation compared with 1000/1500 litres or more in the most favoured regions of Germany (Slicher Van Bath, 1963: 284). Ostoja-Zagorski cited other medieval analogies to argue that there must have been considerable problems here in overwintering stock, and that very large grazing areas would have been necessary as well as foddering – perhaps much of the plant growth was primarily intended for this purpose. He suggested that the Lausitz herds were ranched for beef on a large scale, as well as for dairy products. Wild animals – red and roe deer, boar, bison and elk – were an important meat resource at many sites, and fishing was well organised – fish bones and scales have been recovered in great quantities, along with net sinkers, bark floats, and fish hooks of bone, antler and bronze; plant foods were also collected intensively. The big fortified enclosures were normally some ten or twenty kilometres apart, on or near the morainic lakes, with many small settlements clustered in enclaves around them (Fig. 58). None of these sites has been excavated: they could be satellite camps used by herdsmen or foragers from the main villages, or small farming communities either operating at a subsistence level or producing a surplus for the main villages. Whilst settlement here was certainly less populous than on the loesslands, and subsistence much more broadly based, the proliferation of massive defences suggests a comparable world of competing elites, with agricultural produce a major prize.

Late prehistoric farming

The archaeology of the first millennium in central Europe has frequently been interpreted in terms of invasions and counter-invasions (with Hallstatt people spreading out from a central homeland, in turn replaced by La Tène people from the west), but most workers now see a broad development of Celtic society in western Europe out of the preceding bronze age societies (Hatt, 1970), and such continuity is even clearer in the Teutonic/Slav region, where Lausitz culture and settlement forms developed more or less uninterrupted from the mid-second well into the first millennium (Ostoja-Zagorski, 1974).

Field investigations have concentrated on major defended sites and on cemeteries. In the first part of the millennium some defended sites were clearly occasional refuges or small agricultural communities, but many were centres of nucleated settlement housing

Fig. 57. The modern reconstruction of Biskupin, a Lausitz fortified settlement in Poland of the late second and first millennia b.c. The photograph shows the reconstruction of the main gateway, with the timbers of the ancient ramparts running from it. (Photograph: author)

elite groups and craftsmen as well as agricultural workers. One of the best known Hallstatt forts was the Heuneburg in southern Germany, a roughly triangular hill about five hectares in extent enclosed by a massive timber-reinforced rampart (Kimmig, 1975). In one phase part of this was replaced by a wall of sun-dried mudbrick on lime-stone foundations, strengthened by a series of square turrets; the design and execution of this construction were quite foreign to Celtic Europe, but were widespread at this time in the Mediterranean, suggesting direct knowledge on the part of the local Celtic chieftain or perhaps assistance from a (say) Greek engineer. Celtic Europe was in fact in regular commercial contact with the Mediterranean (Wells, 1980), and there is evidence at the Heuneburg both for luxury Greek drinking vessels and for the wine they accompanied. Crafts at the Heuneburg included bronze and iron metallurgy, glass making, potting, bone working, and textile production.

The societies living in and around these hillforts were highly stratified. Spectacular graves of high ranking individuals buried with wagons, weaponry and luxury goods (textiles, glass, metal, amber, coral) cluster around the hillforts in a broad band north of the Alps from France to Bohemia. Frankenstein and Rowlands (1978) concluded from an assessment of the burials and the craft and trade evidence in the hillforts that a complex hierarchy of leadership can be observed, with paramount chiefs at the top in each sub-region, surrounded by vassal chiefs, sub-chiefs, lesser chiefs and minor chiefs, with differing degrees of wealth in their burials depending on their position in the

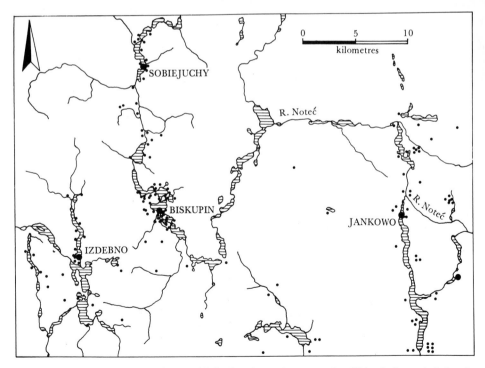

Fig. 58. Lausitz settlement in north central Poland: major settlements such as Biskupin (large circles) each with a cluster of smaller satellite sites (small circles). (After Ostoja-Zagorski, 1974: fig. 7)

hierarchy. In their view, power rested especially in control over prestige items, with the paramounts linked in exchange systems with each other and through this network indirectly with the Mediterranean trading posts such as Massilia.

In the last two or three centuries of the first millennium there was a considerable acceleration in craft production and its organisation and control, marked above all by the emergence of major industrial centres – 'oppida'. (*Oppidum*, literally 'town', was the term used by Caesar to distinguish major tribal centres in Gaul from smaller hillforts and refuges.) About fifty are known in central Europe, distributed across central and southern Germany, southern Poland and Bohemia (Collis, 1975a). One of the most impressive was Manching, in the Danube valley near Ingolstadt (Jacobi, 1974; Krämer, 1960; Krämer and Schübert, 1970): within the huge enclosure (some 350 ha) were extensive occupation areas with separate living quarters for different social classes, and workshops for a large number of crafts including potting, bronze and iron smithing, weaving, bone and antler working, glass making, leather and wood working, and even coin minting. The oppida were also centres of long distance trade: Manching, for example, was a distribution centre for graphite pottery to the Rhine valley and central Germany, and wine amphorae and fine bronze and ceramic tableware all reached the site from the Mediterranean. The scale of production, trade and class differentiation is such as to persuade some scholars that parts of temperate Europe had achieved a degree of urbanism in the last two or three centuries before the Roman conquest (Collis, 1979a), although others prefer to see a transitional stage towards state formation rather than state formation itself (Crumley, 1974). Either way, however, the earlier hillforts and (still more so) the later oppida represent a most complex economic system characterised by centralised wealth and power and by the regional control of production, both of which have clear implications for agricultural organisation.

Subsistence reconstruction has lagged far behind the development of other studies, and direct evidence for the agricultural base of the economic pyramid is desperately limited. Nevertheless, the division between 'primarily arable' and 'primarily stock' systems of farming established by the first neolithic farmers can still be discerned in the first millennium b.c. Although mineral resources and trade routes clearly affected the location of major sites, the main series of hillforts and oppida is distributed across the primary regions of agricultural settlement, on the loesslands and related soils. Manching, for example, controlled a territory of prime loess soils which supported a dense agricultural population, but the oppidum itself was adjacent to an area of bog and marsh rich in iron ore, as well as in a key position in the Danube valley for both north/south and east/west trade. In Bohemia the distribution of cemeteries indicates extremely dense settlement on the loess in the first half of the millennium (Collis, 1975a: fig. 29), and towards the end of the millennium the major oppida were established about thirty kilometres apart, at the junction between the loess and the hills of southern Bohemia rich in iron and graphite (Kruta, 1975). The integration of arable and mineral exploitation is as clear in the functioning of the oppida in Hesse (Jorns, 1960; Werner, 1953).

Cultivation systems in this region for most of the first millennium relied on the traditional range of cereals (emmer, bread wheat, club wheat and barley) and legumes, but the two millets (*Panicum* and *Setaria*), oats and rye all became more important in the later phase (Hajnalova, 1973; Knörzer, 1971b, 1972). The climate of the later first millennium in central Europe was markedly cooler and wetter than before, with temperatures a degree or so lower, rainfall higher by as much as 5%, and humidity up by as much as 15%. Rye and oats, both winter sown crops, were well adapted to these conditions, whilst the millets were ideal crops for spring sowing to complement them. Hence two course rotation systems were practised, with alternate winter sown crops (such as oats, rye and winter wheats) and fallow. Probably the fallow plants were also harvested systematically (Knörzer, 1971b). The introduction of the new system coincided with the production of iron ploughshares, spades, sickles and scythes on a major scale. The iron ploughs meant that heavier soils could be cultivated, and that ploughing could be deeper (particularly important for the root system of rye). At the same time, increased arable production also demanded larger cattle herds for manuring, and hence increased hay production, and the replacement of the sickle by the much more efficient scythe was clearly an integral part of the process of intensification. It is notable that iron technology, available in this part of Europe throughout the greater part of the first millennium b.c., was used to transform agricultural technology only in the period of the oppida to meet the requirements of increased agricultural production. Pieces of wagons and horse trappings also attest to the widespread availability of efficient transportation in this period.

Something of the regional support systems serving the nucleated centres in the primary arable zone can be discerned from Frankenstein and Rowlands' model of the settlement system around the Heuneberg, which suggests that the production of an agricultural surplus was organised at a regional scale by the hierarchy of paramount and vassal chiefs. Some of the vassal domains straddled the Danube valley (like the Heuneberg itself), others lay on the edge of the Swabian limestone uplands (Fig. 59). There is hardly any direct evidence for agricultural organisation, or the use of foodstuffs as tribute, but the paramount household was several times larger than those of the other chiefs in the area, and the Heuneberg also had considerable facilities for grain storage. Hence Frankenstein and Rowlands concluded that the Swabian sites may have engaged in specialised iron and lignite exploitation, and perhaps grazing systems as well, to provide the hides and fleeces which were buried in the rich graves of the paramount's household. 'It would be those commodities (such as iron, lignite, wool, (?) slaves, etc.) which a paramount would use to exchange with his external trading partners, whilst being saved himself the direct labour of their extraction, exploitation, refining etc. Instead, the labour of a paramount's immediate dependent group can be used to produce the domestic prestige items to be redistributed, the production of foodstuffs, and the organisation . . . of external trade' (Frankenstein and Rowlands, 1978: 93).

It is likewise assumed that the oppida controlled both industrial and agricultural production in their territories, redistributing goods and services and living off the agricultural surplus, but again agricultural data are very limited. At Manching barrel shaped pits were used for food storage, and large four-post structures may also have been granaries. An enormous faunal sample was recovered, but the analysis provides few insights into the role of animal husbandry in the complex economy envisaged for the site (Boessneck *et al.*, 1971). There was no information about lateral variation in the faunal material from different parts of the site, although dietary variation according to status is quite likely. The sample consisted almost entirely of stock: cattle, pigs, sheep and goats were killed in roughly equal proportions, but cattle provided half of the meat eaten, pigs a quarter, and sheep and goats together only an eighth. Half of the cattle survived to their third year and over 70% of the sheep were older than two years, and it is therefore thought that secondary products must have been a major element in the stock economy. Moreover, Collis (1973) has pointed out that the very wide range of metric data obtained from the faunal material could be a result of Manching's role as a central place, supplied by herds from different parts of a large territory.

Agricultural settlement on the northern lowlands was entirely different. In Poland, the system of stock-based farming at the Lausitz settlements survived well into the middle of the first millennium. The effects of the Sub-Atlantic climatic deterioration were particularly marked in the *Urstromtäler* region, where flooding and swamp growth were considerable. The fortified centres were largely abandoned, and settlement continued in small farmsteads and hamlets. At the confluence of the Vistula and Wkra rivers northwest of Warsaw, intensive survey has discovered a series of small settlements situated on outcrops of dry sandy soil every few hundred metres along the valleys; pollen analyses and sedimentary studies indicate that the settlements were located in the midst of small enclaves of arable and pasture, in an otherwise forested landscape

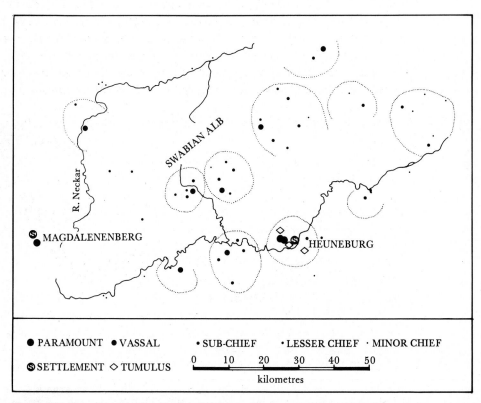

Fig. 59. The Heuneburg domain: a model of social stratification and territoriality with predictions for economic integration. (After Frankenstein and Rowlands, 1978: fig. 1)

(Pyrgala, 1970; Fig. 60). Grain and chaff were found in daub from the sites, and cereal samples were also recovered from the excavations: main crops seem to have been barley and millet, followed by wheat and rye. At Poswietne, traces of a shed designed for drying sheaves of corn round a hearth were found, and traces of wooden frames for drying hay were also discovered, much like the traditional equipment of the region. A two course rotation system is reconstructed by Pyrgala. Faunal samples were dominated by cattle and pig bones, and a variety of bowls and sieves indicated the importance of dairying; weaving equipment was also found in most dwellings. Fish and game made up a small proportion of the diet, but one main purpose of hunting was probably for furs: at Kołozab, for example, half of the bones were of beaver, and limekilns (necessary for tanning hides and treating furs) were common at most sites. The picture emerges from this impressive investigation of small self-sufficient communities, with a subsistence system depending on stock for meat and secondary products, a crop system adapted to the damp forested conditions, and with hunting and trapping providing furs – perhaps for exchange.

At the end of the first millennium, iron ploughs were adopted in this region and the heavier wetlands were taken into cultivation to a limited extent. Increases in cereal pollen in the palynological record, and in the numbers of corn driers found at the excavated sites, support an argument for the development of intensified agricultural systems using both wetlands and sandy interfluves (Pyrgala, 1970). However, whilst agricultural intensification and surplus production can be seen in the *Urstromtäler* region, the disparity between these systems and the complex oppida economies of the primary arable zone is very striking.

The dichotomy between the two regions continued into the medieval period. Pounds, for example, draws a clear distinction between the two regions in terms of

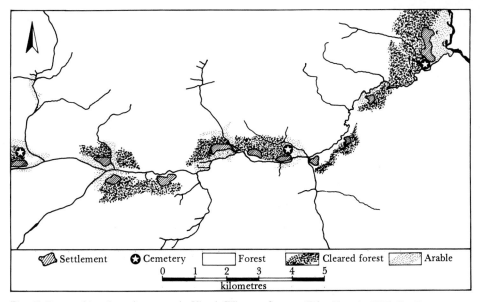

Fig. 60. Late prehistoric settlement at the Vistula/Wkra confluence. (After Pyrgala, 1970: fig. 1)

agricultural efficiency, market development and population densities (Pounds, 1974). Settlement densities were highest in the loesslands of southern Poland, Silesia, Saxony and Bohemia, and farming systems the most developed. The Polish lowlands were characterised by 'a high degree of local isolation and economic self-sufficiency, with the local economy responding only to external factors like the weather and other such influences on crop yields . . . population was relatively sparse and agricultural techniques primitive' (Pounds, 1974: 113). Most farmers still used a light wooden hooked plough which was essentially the same as the iron-tipped ard of the first millennium b.c., and it was only in the fourteenth century that rising populations finally led to the large scale cultivation of the Polish clays and, for this, the adoption of the heavy plough with coulter and mouldboard (Pounds, 1974: 195–6). Meanwhile, the prime arable zones of central Europe provided the essential agricultural base for the flowering of the medieval city north of the Alps, the culmination of a sequence of agricultural wealth reaching back through prehistory to the first LBK farmers.

7

Atlantic Europe

Geographical introduction

The British Isles (dealt with separately in Chapter 8), northern France, Belgium and Holland form a unified region in their exposure to the oceanic climatic regime. This region is characterised by much milder but wetter winters than those of continental Europe, as westerly winds sweep warm water from the Gulf Stream onto the Atlantic coasts. Summer temperatures are more or less comparable with those of central Europe, but the critical feature of the oceanic climate is its instability or fickleness, and its capacity for abrupt fluctuations.

Northern France divides principally into the Armorican peninsula (Brittany) and the Paris basin (Fig. 61). Brittany, like southwest England, has a very high number of days with rainfall and extremely mild winters, resulting in lush pasture for stock and an early growing season for fruit and vegetables. The interior is a mosaic of meadows, orchards and woodland at lower elevations (*bocage*) and moorland on the upland granite (*landes*). Rocky coasts and natural harbours abound, and there is a strong maritime tradition. The Paris basin forms the principal agricultural lowland of western Europe, measuring almost 500 km from west to east (from Brittany to the Ardennes and Vosges hills) and some 300 km from north to south (from the English Channel to the Massif Central); most of it is under 250 m above sea level. The core area, in the region of Paris, divides into three main units: dry limestone plateaus mantled by finely grained *limon* soils, in fertility and structure like loess – a prime arable resource today; river valleys filled with moist alluvium, used today especially for market gardening; and heavier, wetter, soils on impermeable clay-with-flints, predominantly used for pasture. There is much the same variety in topography and land use north of the core area in Normandy and Picardy, apart from *bocage* country west of the Seine. East and southeast, the country varies from the dry chalklands of Champagne, with thin soils like the southern English downs (mainly used for sheep grazing in the past), to the wetter higher scarplands of Lorraine. Southwest of the core area, the Loire region divides into fertile valley soils used for mixed farming, separated by dry sandy interfluves like the Champagne chalklands.

The *limon* soils extend northeast into Belgium, particularly into the provinces of Brabant, Hainaut and Hesbaye, and form a final outcrop further east at the southern tip of Holland where they cover the dissected plateau of southern Limburg around Maastricht. The borderlands of Holland and Belgium are dominated by the waterway complex formed by the lower reaches of three great rivers (the Schelde, Maas and Rhine) and their tributaries, which flow into the North Sea as an enormous delta system

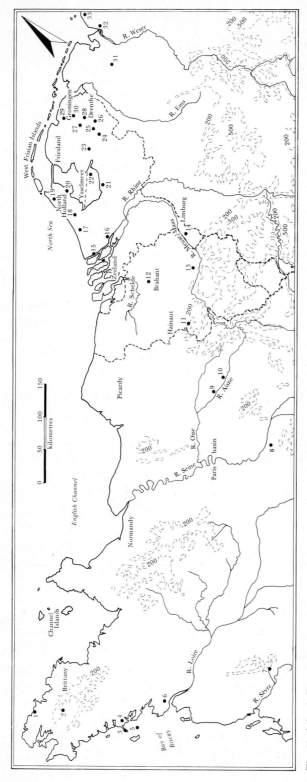

Fig. 61. Atlantic Europe (contours in metres): principal sites and regions mentioned in the text. 1. Le Lividic, Porsguen; 2. Camp d'Artus; 3. Carnac, Lizo; 4. Teviec; 5. Houat; 6. Dissignac; 7. Camp Durand; 8. Misy-sur-Yonne; 9. Chassemy; 10. Cuiry-les-Chaudardes; 11. Spiennes; 12. Nekkerspiel; 13. Remouchamps; 14. Valkenburg; 15. Vlaardingen; 16. Hazendonk; 17. Valkenburg; 18. Assendelft; 19. Schagen; 20. Bovenkarspel, Hoogkarspel, Zwaagdijk; 21. Vaassen; 22. Swifterbant; 23. Havelte; 24. Wijster; 25. Elp; 26. Eeserveld; 27. Vries, Zeijen; 28. Anlo; 29. Ezinge; 30. Paddepoel; 31. Dümmerlohausen; 32. Feddersen Wierde; 33. Fochteloo.

in southern Holland (Zeeland). Glacial ice sheets spread south across Holland almost as far as these rivers; as a result, the area south of the rivers in southern Holland and north-ern Belgium is covered by huge sheets of outwash sands, and the provinces of northern Holland east of the Ysselmeer (the freshwater lake formed by sealing the Zuider Zee inlet before the last war) consist of a mixture of outwash sands, clay ground moraines and morainic ridges. The sands form barely perceptible ridges and islands of higher ground amongst the peat bogs created by the poor drainage of the region, most of which is only a few metres above sea level.

The sands and peats together were very well suited to mixed farming in the medieval period: the settlements were built on the sands, surrounded by the arable fields; the stock (mainly cattle) were taken onto the peat in the summer and housed around the settlements in the winter (often in byres integral to the domestic dwellings) and fed on natural hay cut from the drier margins of the peat. This system is attested both histori-cally and archaeologically (Waterbolk and Harsema, 1979). The sandy soils are naturally poor in plant foods, and the traditional solution was *plaggen* cultivation, the use of dung mixed with sods (*plaggen*) carried onto the fields to fertilise them. Many areas of eastern Holland and northern Belgium have degenerated into heaths and dunelands at some time in the past (a process discussed further in this chapter), although in the last two or three centuries some of the Dutch heathlands have been reclaimed by manuring and irrigation, just as the Flemings reclaimed the sands of Flanders in the medieval period, and many peat bogs have also been reclaimed by cutting drainage canals and mixing the peat with sand and manure. Today these reclaimed wetlands are some of the richest agricultural soils in Europe.

The last major structural unit consists of coastal sediments stretching in a wide band from the Flanders coast across the Rhine delta and around the Ysselmeer to Groningen province in northern Holland. The rise in sea level at the end of the last glaciation led to the formation of a sand bar along the present coast line; later, small changes in the relative heights of land and sea changed the salt marshes to freshwater lagoons, and eventually to peat. However, this general sequence masks a complex pattern of land-scape change: the slightest rise in sea level or high water in the river estuaries meant flooding on a large scale, with obvious implications for coastal settlement. The remark-able system of protective dyking and windmill pumping which protects all of Holland west and north of the glacial sands was begun in the early medieval period.

Postglacial foraging prior to *c.* 4500 b.c.

Surface 'Tardenoisian' flint assemblages dating to the Boreal period have long been known in the sandy regions of Holland, Belgium and northern France, but the absence of associated structural evidence and organic material has meant that in most areas very little was known of the lifestyles they represented (Clark, 1936; Newell, 1973; Rozoy, 1973). However, a recent programme of excavation and artifact analysis in the Drenthe province of northern Holland has generated an imaginative model of Boreal society in Atlantic Europe (Price, 1975, 1978; Whallon, 1978). Spatial analysis of six artifact scatters excavated on the Havelte ridge, integrated with comparisons of artifact scatters elsewhere in Holland, indicated five categories of occupation site, and Price (1978) was

Table 12 *Classification of Boreal mesolithic sites in Holland*

	Site composition	Functional interpretation	Social interpretation
Group 1	Small artifact concentrations ($c.$ 25 m^2); limited range of artifacts; one type predominant	Extraction camp, brief occupation, task specific (chipping, butchering, etc.)	Task group
Group 2	As for 1, but with low numbers of several tool types	Small base camp, general purpose maintenance	Nuclear family
Group 3	Medium artifact concentrations (75 m^2); full range of artifact types; 1500–2500 artifacts	Medium, short term base camp	2 to 4 nuclear families
Group 4	As for 3, but 2500–10,000 artifacts	medium, long term base camp	2 to 4 nuclear families
Group 5	Single large concentration, $c.$ 300 m^2	Large aggregation camp	$c.$ 30 individuals

(After Price, 1978)

able to interpret the variations in the size and composition of these five categories in terms of functional and social differences, given such variations today in the ethnographic record (Table 12).

The surface sites entirely lack subsistence data. However, pollen analyses suggest that, with summer temperatures some 2–4° centigrade higher than today, the Boreal landscape of Atlantic Europe was a mosaic of pine forests, oak woodland, marshes, shallow lakes and streams (van Zeist and van der Spoel-Walvius, 1982); the latter were rich in fish and waterfowl, and terrestrial conditions were favourable for an abundant range of large game (aurochs, elk, red deer, roe deer, pig) and small game (badger, beaver, hare, otter, pine marten, squirrel, wild cat, wolf). These species are all represented at Boreal sites with better preservation in Britain, Belgium, northern Germany and Denmark – at the Belgian cave of Remouchamps, for example, was a typical selection of large and small game (De Laet, 1962). From such data Price developed a model of optimal resource utilisation in Holland rather like Jochim's study of southern Germany (Jochim, 1976), calculating the seasonal changes in the productivity and availability of the different resources according to such factors as weight, aggregation size and mobility. Cluster analysis indicated a system of hunting, fishing and gathering based on five major seasons (Table 13). Aurochs, red deer and roe deer emerged as the primary game, heavily exploited for most of the year; small game were the main contingency resource in the late autumn and winter; plant foods were important from spring to autumn. Correlations between the site types in Table 12 and the subsistence activities in Table 13 can only be very speculative, but the primary spring and autumn resources (fish and nuts respectively) could have supported aggregation camps (Group 5); the late autumn would be the period of maximum dispersal (Group 2); restricted activity in winter would favour Group 4 sites; and the mobility and multiple resource base of the summer would favour Group 3 sites (Price, 1978: 107–8).

Table 13 *Model of Boreal foraging in Holland*

Winter	Spring transition	Summer	Autumn transition	Late autumn
January to March	April to May	June, July and August	September and October	November and December
red deer	fish	plants	plants	small game
small game	plants	small game	aurochs	wild boar
wild boar	aurochs	fish	red deer	aurochs
aurochs	red deer	aurochs	wild boar	red deer

(After Price, 1978)

The Atlantic phase in these latitudes was characterised by warmer winters than today (with temperatures some 2° centigrade higher), by increased precipitation, and by extended spring and summer seasons (Lamb, 1977; Simmons *et al.*, 1981: 89). Mixed deciduous forest dominated the vegetation, probably with a dense canopy. The evidence for the rate and scale of sea level change is complex, but it seems clear that there was a rapid rise of the order of ten metres in the first half of the sixth millennium b.c., slowing down in the second half, and reaching present levels by *c.* 5000 b.c. (Tooley, 1974). Barbed points dredged from the North Sea provide evidence of the earlier mesolithic utilisation of this region, and a new group of sites in the tidal flats and reed swamps of western Holland known as the De Leien–Wartena complex is thought to mark the movement inland of foragers from the North Sea basin at the beginning of the Atlantic (Newell, 1973: 409; Louwe Kooijmans, 1980: 116).

There is consistent evidence for an increased emphasis on coastal resources as the land available for settlement shrank and territorial ranges contracted accordingly, a process as clear in Britain and Scandinavia. At Swifterbant in the southeastern part of the Ysselmeer, work on a new polder discovered a submerged tidal delta system dating to the Calais II phase of clay deposition, which began soon after 4500 b.c. (Ente, 1976; van der Waals and Waterbolk, 1976). The landscape at this time consisted of narrow clay levees covered with a deciduous forest of oak, elm and lime, with alder brushwood at the margins and willow reed marshes beyond (Casparie *et al.*, 1977; Fig. 62). Scatters of settlement debris were found along the levees (Roever, 1976; Whallon and Price, 1976). As well as the typical lithic industry of Atlantic foragers, sherds of crude pottery were found from vessels with round or pointed bases, sometimes decorated with impressions at the rim, very similar to the pottery manufactured by the contemporary coastal foragers of Denmark (Ertebølle) and northern Germany (Ellerbek). The subsistence base of these communities has not yet been established in detail, but is thought to have consisted of a broad spectrum of hunting, fishing, fowling and gathering – all activities documented at the later settlements of the fourth millennium in the rich deltaic environment of Swifterbant. The same sort of subsistence was practised by late Atlantic foragers on the coasts of Brittany, where middens contain a very wide range of shellfish, birds, fish, and mammals such as red deer, roe deer and pig (Pequart *et al.*, 1937). Moreover, as in Britain and Scandinavia, there is some evidence that the coastal economies of northern France and Holland sustained more sedentary and more numer-

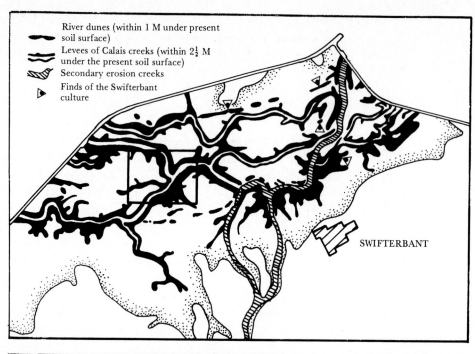

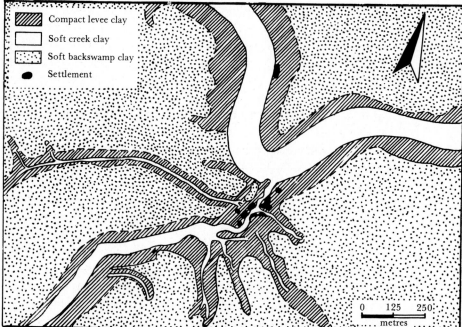

Fig. 62. The environment of Swifterbant in the fourth millennium b.c.: above, the submerged tidal delta system, and below, detail of Swifterbant area. (After Ente, 1976, and van der Waals and Waterbolk, 1976)

ous populations in the late Atlantic than before – the sites are uniformly larger, with far denser concentrations of artifacts, and small cemeteries were often interspersed amongst them (Duday, 1976; Roever, 1976).

The first agricultural settlements, *c.* 4500–3500 b.c.

Agricultural settlement in Atlantic Europe begins with the LBK complex, termed Omalian in Belgium and Danubian in France. The earliest sites date from the mid-fifth millennium b.c., and are found at the eastern end of the region in southern Limburg, some 50 km west of the Aldenhoven plateau sites discussed in the previous chapter. Excavations began here soon after the last war and have continued to the present day, with settlements such as Elsloo, Geleen, Sittard and Stein being regarded as type sites for the LBK complex generally, like Bylany in Czechoslovakia (Modderman, 1959a, 1959b, 1959c, 1970; Fig. 63).

Elsloo was occupied for some four centuries; almost one third of the settlement has been excavated, yielding almost one hundred structures. The first settlement probably extended over 2–3 ha, consisting of a dozen buildings grouped around a single long-house, with a community of perhaps ninety people (van de Velde, 1979: 137). Although LBK society has traditionally been regarded as egalitarian and unstratified, ceramic and structural analysis in fact suggested that there were clear status differences between households and that the community was probably headed by some kind of council of elders led by an elected *primus inter pares* or 'big man' (van de Velde, 1979: 171). Animal bones have not survived at these sites (the Elsloo faunal sample consisted of a single bovine radius), but cattle are assumed to have been the main stock by analogy with the nearest sites in Germany. Modderman (1970: 110) suggested that one end of the Elsloo longhouses, built with solid wooden walls rather than (as elsewhere) wattle and daub, housed the cattle; if so, the cattle must have been tied, as no partitions have been found. However, such reinforced areas are very limited, with the settlement's total stabling suitable only for a handful of animals – stabling does not seem to have been a regular feature of Dutch cattle husbandry until later in prehistory (Waterbolk, 1975: 393).

The location of the Dutch LBK sites was very similar to that of the loessland LBK sites discussed in the previous chapter: on the edge of the loess plateau, immediately above the river valley (Bakels, 1978; Fig. 64). Different woodland associations have been defined: on the loess, open woodland of oak and lime with hazel thickets and brambles and a variety of herbs, grasses, ferns and mosses; mixed deciduous forest (alder, ash, sycamore, elm, oak) and thick shrubs in strips along the rivers and on the alluvium of the lower terrace; and alder carr with dense undergrowth in the wettest areas (Janssen, 1960; van Zeist, 1958–9). The principal cereals grown were emmer and einkorn, probably as a single crop, together with barley; the composition of the weed species implies successional cropping on the loess, and Groenman-van Waateringe (1970–1) has argued that the fields were used so long that a hedge-like vegetation of thorny scrubs developed around them. Presumably the edge of the loess plateau was selected because of the abundance of browse and grazing on the valley alluvium. In short, as in central Europe, a model of small scale intensive mixed farming involving successional cropping on the loess is far more likely than the traditional model of shifting

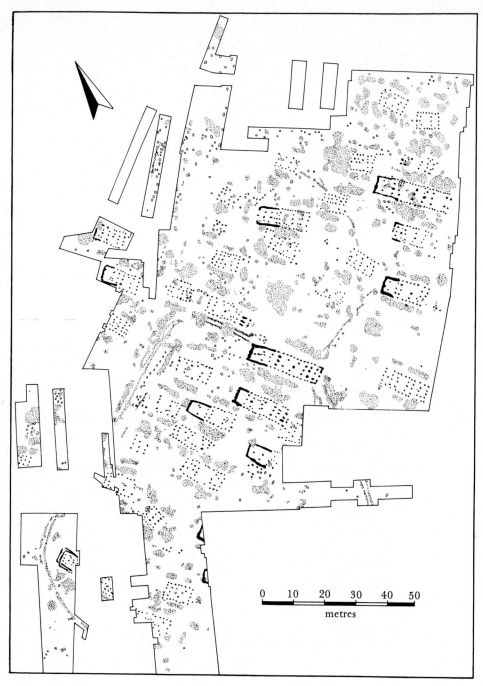

Fig. 63. The *Linearbandkeramik* settlement of Sittard in the Dutch Limburg: post-holes and bedding trenches in black, pits and other excavated features stippled. (After Piggott, 1965: fig. 21)

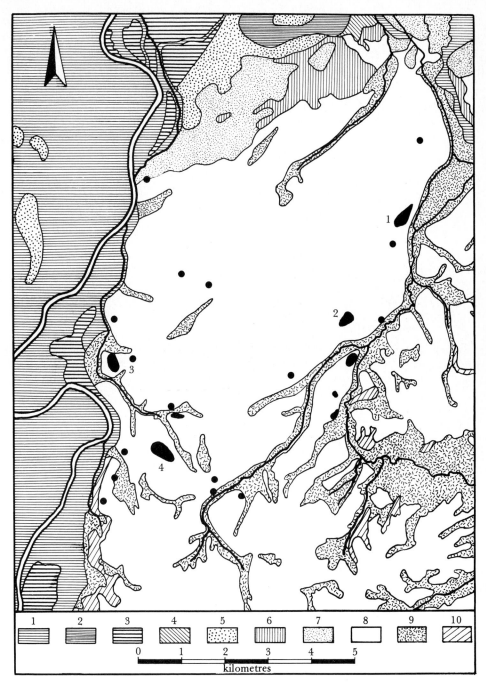

Fig. 64. *Linearbandkeramik* settlement in southern Limburg. Sites: 1. Sittard; 2. Geleen; 3. Stein; 4. Elsloo. Geology and soils: 1. younger alluvial clays, mostly wet; 2. older alluvial clays, wet; 3. older alluvial clays, dry; 4. sands, wet; 5. sands, dry; 6. sandy loess, wet; 7. sandy loess, dry; 8. loess plateau; 9. valleys and valley slopes within the loess landscape; 10. sands and gravels exposed in slopes. (After Bakels, 1978: fig. 16)

cultivation and slash and burn. *Chenopodium album* was eaten as a leaf vegetable, and the seeds of chess (*Bromus secalinus*) – always found separated from their glumes like the cereals – were also consumed. Bakels concluded that the territory of each settlement would have allowed self sufficiency in food and most raw materials, with very few essential resources needing to be brought in from outside (Bakels, 1978: 146–7).

The structures, burials and artifacts of the LBK sites in Belgium and France were very similar to those of the Dutch settlements, although chronologically they are somewhat later (Ilett, 1983; Phillips, 1980: 170). Subsistence data are generally rather limited, but the main crops reported are again emmer, einkorn and barley (particularly the latter), and the faunal record is usually dominated by cattle, with sheep secondary (Bailloud, 1974; Poplin, 1975; Poulain, 1977). At Reichstett in Bas Rhin pollen evidence indicated cereal cultivation in small permanent fields on the *limon* soils around the settlement (Heim, 1978). In the Aisne valley, sites have been found about ten kilometres apart, normally on the floodplain alluvium of the lower gravel terrace below the *limon* soils of the plateau (Boureux and Coudart, 1978). Like LBK farmers elsewhere, the French communities seem to have selected limited areas of high productivity for their crops: for example, the lower terraces of the Aisne at the time of LBK settlement offered light and well watered soils covered by an open meadow vegetation, regularly fertilised by flooding (Howell, 1983a).

As in Germany, the later (Rössen) phase of LBK settlement in Holland during the first half of the fourth millennium b.c. was marked by an expansion of settlement away from the prime locations, in this case especially north down the Maas valley onto the lower terraces and alluvium (Bloemers, 1972). Pollen diagrams from the lower Rhine show increased clearances (de Jong, 1970–1). The increasing aridity of the last stages of the Atlantic is suggested very reasonably by Dohrn-Ihmig (1976) as the main reason to account for the cultivation of moister soils and the use of a wider range of crops (such as club wheat, spelt, and, especially, barley) at this time. In France the LBK pottery style divided into several regional groups such as Aisne, Cerny and Beaurieux (Scarre, 1983a). Subsistence data are minimal, but settlement trends seem to have been similar to those in Holland: the continuation of existing methods of farming, but the small scale expansion of settlement away from prime locations and an increase in the size and complexity of individual settlements (Burkhill, 1983). Pontavert in the Aisne valley, for example, consisted of several trapezoidal longhouses surrounded by a substantial palisade (Soudsky, 1975), and Barbuise (Aude) also seems to have been a major enclosed settlement (Joffroy, 1972).

Agricultural expansion, *c*. 3500–2500 b.c.

Five main cultural groups are recognised in western Europe during this period: TRB in northern Holland (the westernmost extension of this complex); Swifterbant on the Dutch littoral; Michelsberg in the lower Rhine region of Belgium and Holland (as higher up the Rhine); the northern Chassey group in the Paris basin; and the Breton Neolithic. These groups share many similarities in their ceramic assemblages, with plain globular and carinated bowls predominating, although each also has characteristic forms of more restricted distributions.

The majority of TRB material in Holland has been recovered from *Hunebedden* megalithic tombs on the glacial sands (De Laet, 1962). The beakers are associated with a simple flint industry of flakes and blades, transverse arrowheads and polished axes; there are also occasional perforated stone axes and ornaments of amber, bone, jet and copper, all assumed to be items of display worn by an emergent leadership. There is hardly any direct information about TRB farming in this region. Cattle, sheep/goat and pig are reported from the settlement at Heemse-Hardenberg (Clason and Brinkhuizen, 1978: 73); the TRB community at Dümmerlohausen in north Germany grew einkorn, spelt and barley, herded the three main stock, and augmented their subsistence by gathering fruits and nuts, fishing, and hunting a range of forest fauna (aurochs, beaver, elk, red deer, roe deer, wild boar) (De Laet, 1962: 88). Clearances noted in the pollen diagrams of Drenthe are invariably very small, and cereal and plantain pollen are very rare (van Zeist, 1955). From the frequency of heather and bracken pollen in buried soils under TRB monuments, Waterbolk (1956) argued that heathlands had started to form on the sands by this period as a response to soil exhaustion caused by early farming, but it is clear that TRB farming was on a very small scale, and the formation of heathland seems to have been going on to a limited extent from earlier in the Holocene (Groenman-van Waateringe, 1978).

Most of the *Hunebedden* in Drenthe clustered along a narrow ridge of sand at the eastern edge of the plateau, normally only one or two kilometres apart, and most traces of domestic occupation have been found in the same localities (Bakker, 1980; Fig. 65). Catchments with a radius of five kilometres, the maximum area normally exploited by farmers according to site catchment analysis (Chapter 1, p. 25), would thus extend from the sand ridges across the wetter sands at the margins onto the adjacent bogs and marshes, just like the territories exploited by the medieval villages of Drenthe. The inference is that TRB farmers, like medieval farmers, needed the wet soils just as much as the sands: grazing stock on the bogs in the summer and keeping them near the settlements on the sand ridges in the winter. If the cattle were stalled or simply penned in the open, their manure would have been close to hand for the arable fields.

Western Holland at this time consisted of an expanse of tidal flats edged on their landward side by fen peat. At Swifterbant (Fig. 62) the clay levees were relatively stable for most of the fourth millennium (thereafter they were drowned completely), but they only just reached above mean high water, and winter flooding was a regular occurrence (van der Waals, 1977). The neolithic encampments consisted of spreads of occupation debris, hearths and stakes along the levees. The wet and restricted levee soils were hardly ideal places for arable farming, but the presence of threshing remains as well as carbonised seeds (mainly naked six-row barley and emmer) indicated that the crops were indeed grown here, rather than being grown further inland and brought to Swifterbant as prepared food (Casparie *et al.*, 1977: 51). The range of plant species suggests that the communities arrived at Swifterbant in March or April in time for planting, and left in late September at the end of the crab apple and hazelnut harvest. Other fruits

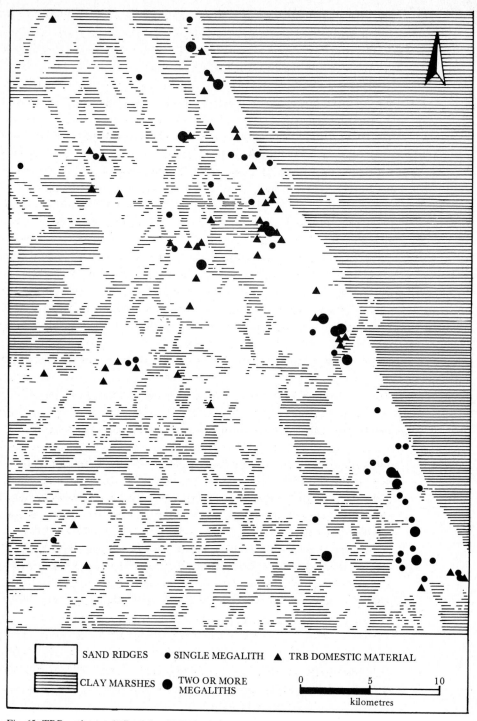

Fig. 65. TRB settlement in Drenthe, Holland. (After Bakker, 1980: fig. 4)

collected included blackberries and rose hips, and weeds such as fat hen and knotgrass were also gathered systematically. Cattle and pigs were brought to the site, and the cattle which died there included both very young and old animals – conceivably evidence for dairying (Clason and Brinkhuizen, 1978).

However, the main subsistence activities at Swifterbant were fishing, fowling and hunting. The levees were probably selected each summer primarily as a crucial place in the creek system for fishing. Fish were by far the most abundant part of the food refuse and included both marine species that move into fresh water for short periods (catfish, sturgeon, grey mullet) and the freshwater species of the creeks (eel, perch, carp); sturgeon and grey mullet could have been caught only in the spring or early summer. Birds such as cormorants, mallards, swans, cranes and eagles were killed; game included red deer, horse and aurochs, but the main animals killed were beaver and otter, probably for both food and fur (many of the beavers were large adult specimens). An identical system of summer fishing, fowling, hunting and gathering augmented by small scale farming was practised at the Hazendonk, a sandy knoll in the Rhine estuary occupied in the late fourth and early third millennia b.c. (Brinkhuizen, 1979; Louwe Kooijmans, 1974, 1980). Although nothing is known of the winter subsistence activities of the people who came to these summer camps in the tidal flats, presumably they moved away from the floodwaters with their stock and seedcorn, to the higher ground 20–30 km inland (Fig. 66). Pollen analysis shows that the mixed oak forests here were still very extensive, and probably these communities continued to augment farming with foraging – in Price's model of Boreal foraging, red deer, wild boar, aurochs and small game were the key autumn and winter resources (Table 13, p. 165).

The main areas of agricultural settlement in Atlantic Europe supported far denser populations and more complex societies than these coastal marshes (though the subsistence data are generally far poorer). The main Michelsberg settlements were large enclosures, protected by substantial banks and ditches (Hubert, 1971a, 1971b; Vermeersch and Walter, 1974). Fine quality flint was mined on a considerable scale – at Rijckholt in the Limburg the workings extended over 25 ha, with scores of shafts and interconnecting galleries, and daily production of axes and cores has been estimated in hundreds (Bosch, 1979), although the nature of the residues at Spiennes suggests that the people were part-time miners, who farmed the surrounding land for most of the year (Clason, 1971: 9). Cereal impressions in pottery from Spiennes include those of emmer, millet and spelt (De Laet, 1962: 79), and crops at Entzheim consisted of emmer, einkorn, naked barley and legumes (Hopf, 1975). The three main stock species were represented at the latter site, but little further information is available (Poulain, 1975; Schmitt, 1974). At Spiennes, however, the two-peak mortality structure possibly indicative of a dairy system was found in the case of both cattle and sheep/goat, whereas pigs were normally killed as mature animals (Clason, 1971). Game killed (of minor importance in the diet) included aurochs, bear, beaver, elk, fox, hare, horse, marten, red deer, wild boar and wild cat.

In the Paris basin Chasseen settlement continued to expand away from the valleys, and both valley sites and new promontory sites were now protected with ditches and palisades (Blanchet and Petit, 1972; Mordant and Mordant, 1972). The agricultural sys-

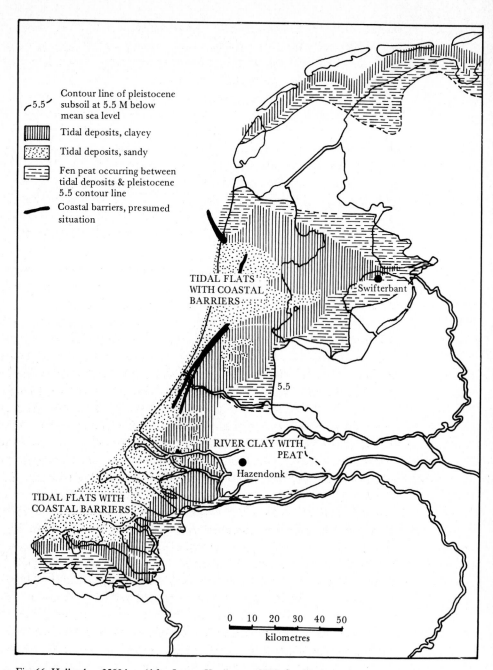

Legend:

- ⁓5.5⁓ Contour line of pleistocene subsoil at 5.5 M below mean sea level
- ▥ Tidal deposits, clayey
- ▨ Tidal deposits, sandy
- ▤ Fen peat occurring between tidal deposits & pleistocene 5.5 contour line
- ▬ Coastal barriers, presumed situation

TIDAL FLATS WITH COASTAL BARRIERS

Swifterbant

5.5

RIVER CLAY WITH PEAT

Hazendonk

TIDAL FLATS WITH COASTAL BARRIERS

0 10 20 30 40 50
kilometres

Fig. 66. Holland, *c.* 3500 b.c. (After Louwe Kooijmans, 1980: fig. 1)

tem stayed essentially the same as before (Bailloud, 1976; Planson, 1979; Poulain, 1976a), but Howell (1983a) suggests that there may have been an increased reliance on animal husbandry, with the development of the Sub-Boreal climate putting pressure on agricultural resources, and the more warlike society that emerged concentrating on mobile wealth (cattle in particular) which could be protected in the new settlements.

The best known feature of neolithic settlement in Brittany is the remarkable group of megalithic tombs, which includes passage graves, long cairns, transepted chambered graves and trapezoidal mounds, though the lithic repertoire was much as in the rest of northern France (Hibbs, 1983; L'Helgouach, 1965). The construction of the tombs probably began in the earlier part of the fourth millennium b.c. (Delibrias *et al.*, 1976: 871–3). The only evidence for cereal cultivation consists of a few grains of cereal pollen found in the buried soil underneath the Dissignac passage grave on the south coast (L'Helgouach, 1976: 366); the other pollen diagrams available from Brittany show only small episodes of pasture and grazing in a predominantly forested landscape (Morzadec-Kerfourn, 1969, 1974; Visset, 1973; van Zeist, 1964). It is presumed from the concentration of neolithic monuments on the coast and on the offshore islands that fishing was an important part of subsistence. Unfortunately many habitation sites were probably inundated by sea level rises in the mid-fourth millennium (Ters, 1976: 28), and the few sites known are insubstantial collections of hearths and domestic debric producing hardly any organic material. However, later prehistoric subsistence in Brittany certainly included both maritime exploitation and pastoralism, and it is likely that fourth millennium subsistence here also entailed a mixture of herding, hunting and fishing with little or no cereal cultivation, with most communities settled on the coast but foraging and grazing their stock in the interior.

Although Breton megalithic culture has traditionally been regarded as an implantation by neolithic colonists from the Mediterranean (Daniel, 1958), radiocarbon dating showed that the Breton graves were considerably earlier than their supposed predecessors, and Case has argued that the tradition could well have stemmed from the burial customs of the local foraging population practised in the sixth and fifth millennia (Case, 1976); a microlithic industry was in fact found in possible association with the construction of the Dissignac passage grave (L'Helgouach, 1976). Perhaps, therefore, the Breton communities of the late fourth millennium can be compared with the contemporary peoples of the Dutch littoral, in their successful integration of new resources into an existing system of subsistence. Conceivably the rise in sea level in the mid-fourth millennium had a detrimental effect on the marine economy and helped precipitate the adoption of the new resources. The passage graves are distributed around the coast in about a dozen distinct clusters; perhaps their construction was in part a response to the need to reaffirm territorial divisions and ancestral rights to land and sea.

Transformations in society and subsistence, *c.* 2500–1500 b.c.

Traditionally this period in Atlantic Europe has been divided into the Late Neolithic and, after *c.* 1800 b.c., the Early Bronze Age, but as in Britain in recent years, the two phases are now seen to form a cultural continuum. The period began with the appearance of new burial rites in most areas (single rather than collective burial) and new funerary material: tanged copper daggers, stone 'wristguards', V-perforated buttons, pressure flaked arrowheads, and finely decorated beakers. Like the corded ware assemblage of continental Europe, the beaker assemblage is now taken to be the death equipment not of warlike invaders (in this case metal prospectors from the Mediterranean) but of high status individuals in the indigenous societies, marking the emergence of more clearly defined leadership across western Europe (Shennan, 1976).

The millennium between 2500 and 1500 b.c. was characterised by the warm and dry climate of the Sub-Boreal, interspersed with at least one main cooler and wetter oscillation in the middle. Very few settlements of the period have been preserved in the sandy regions of eastern Holland, but the distribution of barrows is assumed to represent a significant expansion of agricultural settlement related to population increase. Whereas earlier TRB settlement had concentrated on the driest parts of the sands such as the narrow ridges, settlement now expanded onto the moister soils on the margins of the sand outcrops, particularly west of the Drenthe plateau and south to Veluwe. As elsewhere in temperate Europe, this process, presumably facilitated by the drier conditions of the period, coincided with changes in agricultural technology: solid wooden wheels recovered from peat bogs indicate the development of carting (van der Waals, 1964), and scratch marks under barrows are presumably from the ox-pulled ard (De Laet, 1962: 98). Carbonised seeds from the fill of a barrow ditch at Eeserveld in Drenthe consisted mainly of naked barley, a crop well suited to the drier climate, and emmer (van Zeist, 1968: 60–1). However, pollen preserved in the beaker barrows indicates very high values for plantains and grasses and very low values for cereals compared with those from TRB barrows (Casparie and Groenman-van Waateringe, 1982), and Louwe Kooijmans (1974: 376) earlier argued that, whilst large areas of forest were being cleared, land use in eastern Holland was predominantly pastoral. The well known enclosure at Anlo in Drenthe is also taken to indicate an expanded pastoral economy (Waterbolk, 1960). There are no detailed faunal studies to document the nature of the stock systems, but it is quite likely that cattle were kept not only for traction, meat and milk, but also for prestige: complete cattle carcasses accompanied the dead in a few barrows (Louwe Kooijmans, 1974: 322–3). The trackways built at this period across the marshes in Drenthe must also have facilitated more extensive systems of summer grazing than hitherto possible (De Laet, 1962: 106).

In western Holland a series of new coastal barriers was established outside the older dunes during the third millennium, and many of the tidal flats behind them changed into salt marsh connected to the sandy hinterland by narrow creek levees which meandered across the intervening peat bogs and marshes (Louwe Kooijmans, 1980). The communities of this region shared in a cultural assemblage named after the site of Vlaardingen in the Rhine estuary (van Regteren Altena *et al.*, 1962, 1963), and practised a system of subsistence integrating mixed farming with fishing and foraging. Like the farmers of eastern Holland, the coastal communities now used ox traction for ploughing and horses for riding (Louwe Kooijmans, 1974: 331). Settlements have been found on the coastal barriers, in the estuarine marshes and salt flats, and on the stream ridges further inland.

Some of our best information has come from one of the inland levee systems (Louwe

Kooijmans, 1974; Fig. 67). On the Schoonrewoerd stream ridge, survey located a series of small occupation sites every few hundred metres. The ridge was a narrow strip of sandy soil about 100 m wide, covered in deciduous forest before the settlements were established; on either side, extending out for up to a kilometre, were clay wedges carrying pasture and alder carr, with swampy marsh beyond. There were very high values for cereal and associated weed pollen immediately by the settlements: the arable land, limited to about 5–8 ha per site, was clearly on the sand ridge, suggesting that the sites were individual family farms. Cattle were the main stock, followed by pigs, with sheep and goats kept only on a small scale; hunting and fishing supplemented the diet. Similarly mixed strategies of farming, foraging and fishing were practised in northern Holland on either side of the Ysselmeer (Brinkhuizen, 1979; Clason, 1967b; van Zeist, 1968). Fishing and foraging were particularly important for the farmers living on the coastal barriers, who were able to fish pike and sturgeon and butcher stranded sea mammals such as sperm whales and grey seals (Louwe Kooijmans, 1974: 327). At a few sites known, fishing and foraging were probably the dominant activities. At Vlaardingen itself, for example, carbonised plant remains included emmer, bread wheat, club wheat and naked six-row barley (van Zeist, 1968: 55–8), but levels of cereal pollen were far lower here than at other sites; and although cattle were the main stock, followed by pigs, some two thirds of the faunal sample consisted of red deer, wild boar and beaver (Clason, 1967b). No sieving was carried out at the excavation, but three large species of fish were certainly exploited (grey mullet, sturgeon and pike), and a fish weir suggests that many other smaller species were also caught (Brinkhuizen, 1979; van Iterson Scholten, 1977).

In this phase, as before, the subsistence data from northern France are extremely poor, yet the settlement record indicates a far more complex social and economic struc-

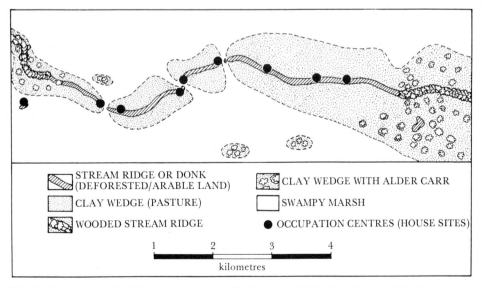

STREAM RIDGE OR DONK (DEFORESTED/ARABLE LAND) CLAY WEDGE WITH ALDER CARR
CLAY WEDGE (PASTURE) SWAMPY MARSH
WOODED STREAM RIDGE ● OCCUPATION CENTRES (HOUSE SITES)

1   2   3   4
kilometres

Fig. 67. Settlement on the Schoonrewoerd stream ridge in the late third millennium b.c. (After Louwe Kooijmans, 1974: fig. 29)

ture than in the Dutch littoral (Thévenot and Carré, 1976; Verron, 1976).In the lower Sèvre valley in the Vendée, for example, air photography has revealed over a dozen major ditched camps of this period constructed every five kilometres or so along the edge of the limestone uplands which surround the Marais marshes (Scarre, 1980, 1982, 1983b). Excavations at one of the sites, Camp Durand, found substantial dry stone ramparts and major defensive gatetowers as well as the ditches, with evidence for houses, craft areas and stock enclosures inside, and a population is estimated of several hundred people. The subsistence data from the sites have yet to be analysed in detail, although cattle and sheep/goat are reported as the principal stock, and at the Thiré dolmen the major species butchered in the funerary rites were cattle, sheep/goat and pig killed either as very young animals (two or three months old) or as adults (Poulain, 1976b). The camps are certainly in a classic junction position, with limited areas of good arable soil around them but with access to very large areas of seasonal grazing below them in the Marais marshes and behind them on the limestone plateau. The scale of the defensive works also implies considerable competition for grazing and stock.

In the Paris basin the dry soils of Champagne and of the central plateaus elsewhere were now colonised by very different settlement: a network of small sites with evidence for a very diversified system of subsistence (cereal cultivation, stock keeping concentrating on pigs, and often heavy reliance on hunting, fishing and gathering). Howell (1983a, 1983b) argues that the old centralised system of farming was replaced by dispersed family farms as a result of the adoption of the ard. Certainly the main phase of clearance seems to have been at this time (van Zeist and van der Spoel-Walvius, 1982).

In Brittany there is also evidence for major subsistence changes at this time correlating with an increase in population and the remarkable florescence of megalithic culture marked by the construction of the extraordinary series of standing stones (menhirs), alignments and megalithic enclosures best known at Carnac but also found elsewhere in the peninsula (Giot, 1960; Hibbs, 1983). The pollen diagrams register far more intensive clearances in the late third millennium than before, together with the first widespread presence of cereals (Morzadec Kerfourn, 1969; van Zeist, 1964). The clearances were also probably accompanied by forest burning – the pollen diagrams now include charcoal layers for the first time (Morzadec Kerfourn, 1976). A few major defended settlements may belong to this period, such as Lizo in the Gulf of Morbihan, but most habitation sites found are insubstantial collections of occupation debris; at one such site, Porsguen in Finistère, cereal and grassland values increased dramatically in the pollen record at the time of occupation, and remains of sheep/goat and cattle were found in the excavation (Briard *et al.*, 1970). The palynological evidence for the establishment of mixed farming across the interior of the Armorican peninsula coincides with the construction of a new form of community tomb, the gallery grave, which significantly has a distribution throughout the region quite unlike the coastal clusters of passage graves. Although mixed farming was clearly the dominant element in the subsistence system now, foraging and fishing persisted, rather as in the crofting economy of the poorest people in Brittany in the historical period: Le Lividic, for example, was a seasonal camp used by cattle herders who also collected shellfish (Hallegouet *et al.*,

1971), and stock keepers also crossed over to the island of Houat in the Gulf of Morbihan for collecting shellfish, hunting seals and beavers, fowling and fishing (Reverdin, 1960).

Later prehistoric farming, *c*. 1500–500 b.c.

The period between 1500 and 500 b.c. embraces the last main warm and dry phase of the Sub-Boreal and then, after about 1000 b.c., the gradual development of cooler and wetter conditions leading into the markedly wetter climate of the Sub-Atlantic. This sequence of a climatic optimum followed by deterioration inevitably had major repercussions for prehistoric settlement. Again, the evidence is far more prolific in Holland than in the rest of Atlantic Europe.

As in previous periods, there is a broad division between agricultural systems in the interior sandy regions of Holland and on the low-lying coastal margins. For the former, probably the most informative excavation has been that of the settlement at Elp, on a low sand ridge in Drenthe (Waterbolk, 1964). Some thirty main structures were built during the life of the settlement (*c*. 1300–800 b.c.), but at any one time the farmstead seems to have consisted of a longhouse on the central part of the ridge, with a smaller house or barn on one side and a large and a small shed on the other (Fig. 68). Each longhouse (25–30 m long) was three-aisled; the western half was used for habitation, but the interior posts were doubled in the eastern half to make stall partitions sufficient for 25–30 cattle. The subsidiary building was either dual purpose like the longhouse (with about a dozen stalls), or designed solely for stalling 15–20 cattle. The large shed was constructed with six very stout posts, thought to have carried a storage platform, probably for grain. The smaller shed was about the same size but built from normal timbers. The most frequent plant remains were of emmer and naked barley, but there were occasional seeds of millet, oats and various weeds (van Zeist, 1968). Animal bones did not survive, but it is presumed from the stalling that cattle were the main stock, now clearly overwintered inside; the massive construction of the granaries may have been necessary to protect the grain from pigs loose in the settlement, and U-shaped enclosures may also have protected haystacks. The only indirect evidence for sheep was a single spindle whorl.

The domestic debris at Elp was generally very poor, and it was impossible to tell whether the smaller buildings were the dwellings of people subordinate to the central family as the excavator preferred (Waterbolk, 1964: 122) or agricultural buildings such as milking parlours, calving pens and barns. Very similar farmsteads have been investigated elsewhere in eastern Holland (Modderman, 1955; van der Waals, 1967). Although the location of these settlements and the components of their farming systems were still essentially the same as those of earlier farmers in this region, land use had probably become more intensive. The numbers of weed seeds in the botanical samples are taken as clear evidence for permanent fields and intensive crop systems, and there are hints of the first development of sod manuring or *plaggen* culture (Groenman-van Waateringe, 1978). The stalling of cattle also meant that manure could be collected efficiently each winter for distribution on the arable land: on the analogy of Hoogkarspel (described below, p. 181) two clusters of irregular pits at Elp could have been

Fig. 68. The settlement at Elp, in the second millennium b.c. (After Waterbolk, 1964)

caused by covering over the muck heap at intervals during the winter to mix the manure and straw with soil.

Pollen analysis has shown that the landscape of eastern Holland was predominantly open by the early first millennium b.c., and that sand drifts covered by a heather podsol were quite widespread (Bakels, 1975; van Zeist, 1967). The very large number of urnfield cemeteries in this period is taken to indicate that settlement expanded over the entire sand region, to include both the dry ridges and the wetter marginal sands. A detailed analysis of the cemeteries has shown that most of them served single families and that a few contained the dead of two or three families (Kooi, 1979). On the assumption that the farmsteads were nearby, the family catchments would have been about 300–450 ha in extent, always centred on the sand outcrops and normally bounded by stream valleys and marshlands. Roadways have been found running through several cemeteries, and Kooi argued that a simple network of such tracks linked the settled areas. Systems of 'Celtic fields' are also found on the sands in many of the territories; although some certainly date to the later first millennium, the origins of the system are thought to correlate with the settlement expansion of the urnfield period (Brongers, 1976; Kooi, 1979: 169). Kooi calculated that population density was probably only 3–6 per km^2, and that only about 20% of the habitable area was under cultivation, figures which do not support Waterbolk's thesis that population pressure at this time pushed the agricultural system to the limit, exhausted the soils, caused heath formation, and eventually led to the widespread abandonment of the sands (Waterbolk, 1962, 1965–6). (Heaths were undoubtedly forming on the sands in this period, but the process had been going on for millennia and was to continue afterwards, though not on any large scale until the historical period.)

Contemporary settlement in western Holland is best documented in West Friesland, west of the Ysselmeer. Salt marshes and creek deposits were formed there during transgression phases in the third and second millennia b.c., and were intensively occupied between *c.* 1200 and 700 b.c. Four sites in particular have been investigated in exemplary detail: Andijk (van Mensch and Ijzereef, 1975), Het Valkje at Bovenkarspel (Ijzereef, 1981), Hoogkarspel (Bakker *et al.*, 1977) and Zwaagdijk (Clason, 1967b; Modderman, 1964). Pollen and macrobotanical studies suggest a contemporary landscape of salt marsh and natural pasture, interspersed in some areas with isolated stands of trees and alder carr (Bakels, 1974; Pals, in Bakker *et al.*, 1977; van Zeist, 1974). The normal settlement form was the single farmstead as at Elp, with a three aisled longhouse and subsidiary barns and sheds. The farms were built on narrow sand ridges, surrounded by their arable land in small fields measuring about 50 × 50 m, marked out by low ditches (Fig. 69). The ditches were cleaned out and recut at frequent intervals, but they were so shallow that they would have been effective drains only when the water table was very high. The fields were cultivated with the ard, and tiny fragments of pot and bone in the ard channels suggest that the arable was fertilised with manure and household refuse. At some of the sites there were large pit circles some eight metres in diameter, connected to the ditches surrounding the houses: Ijzereef (1981) argues that the manure was swept out from the cattle stalls either into the ditches (which were cleared out from time to time) or into central muck heaps, where it was composted with

Table 14 *Stock frequencies at bronze age farmsteads in West Friesland, according to the number of identifiable fragments*

	Andijk		Bovenkarspel		Hoogkarspel Watertoren		Hoogkarspel c. 1000 b.c.		Hoogkarspel c. 700 b.c.		Zwaagdijk	
	N	%	N	%	N	%	N	%	N	%	N	%
Cattle	986	86.2	7885	76.2	228	75.5	846	84.6	4396	80.7	231	83.7
Dog	16	1.4	243	2.3	25	8.3	6	0.6	75	1.4	2	0.7
Horse	–	–	5	>0.1	–	–	6	0.6	13	0.2	–	–
Pig	40	3.5	668	6.5	22	7.3	41	4.1	436	8.0	11	4.0
Sheep/goat	102	8.9	1553	15.0	27	8.9	101	10.1	528	9.7	32	11.6
Total	1144		10354		302		1000		5448		276	

(After Ijzereef, 1981, and Prummel, 1979)

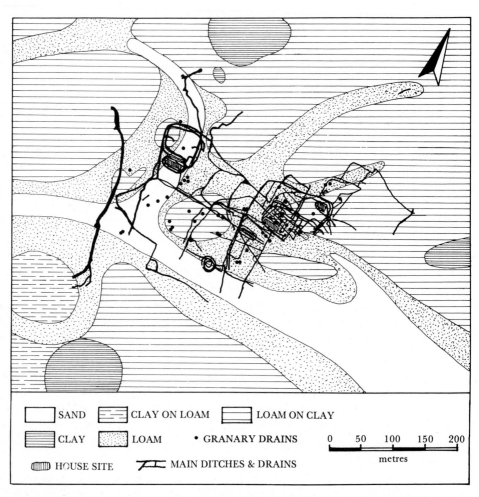

SAND CLAY ON LOAM LOAM ON CLAY

CLAY LOAM • GRANARY DRAINS 0 50 100 150 200

metres

HOUSE SITE MAIN DITCHES & DRAINS

Fig. 69. The late bronze age settlement of Hoogkarspel, West Friesland, at the end of the second millennium b.c. (After Bakker *et al.*, 1977: fig. 7)

soil from the surrounding pits – a primitive form of *plaggen* culture. At Bovenkarspel, too, were clusters of small circular trenches thought to have enclosed storage areas for hay or straw – the rodent remains from these were mostly of the house mouse and field vole (Ijzereef, 1981: 159–60).

The principal crops grown by these farmers were emmer and six-row barley, together with a little flax. Cattle were by far the most important animal in the stock system: all of the faunal samples were dominated by cattle – *c.* 75% at least. Sheep were the second stock, but far fewer, and pigs were quite rare (Table 14). Most of the Bovenkarspel cattle were slaughtered before the age of three years, and assuming that bones of juvenile and new born animals had been destroyed in the soil, only about one third of the cattle reached thirty months or more. Meat production was thought to have been the primary goal, with dairying probably being practised on a small scale as well. A complete skeleton of a cow in a pit at Bovenkarspel showed that the bronze age animals were almost as long as modern cattle, but substantially smaller, standing only just over a metre high compared with the 135 cm of the modern Dutch cow. Half of the sheep/goat population at Bovenkarspel was older than twenty-eight months at death, probably indicating a generalised system of meat, milk and wool production. Dogs may have been consumed occasionally, but the correlation between the number of sheep and dogs in the different phases at Bovenkarspel suggests that they were mainly kept as working animals (Ijzereef, 1981: 196).

Game was of little importance in the diet – there were just 62 bones of game species at Bovenkarspel compared with 11,418 identified specimens of domestic animals. Fish may have been more important – sieved examples at Bovenkarspel included bones of bream, eel, perch, pike, and roach. Presumably pigs were few because of the openness of the landscape (Prummel, 1979), and sheep would have been very susceptible to the liver fluke, which must have been prevalent in the damp pastures: shells of the host snail *Galba trunculata* were found at Hoogkarspel (Bakker *et al.*, 1977: 198–200), and seeds of water forget-me-not and marsh pennywort were also found, both plants of the damp pasture which is optimal for this snail (Pals, in Bakker *et al.*, 1977: 200–4).

Ijzereef was able to construct different models of agricultural production at Bovenkarspel from the wealth of structural and subsistence data and from the size of the holdings. As the faunal evidence for dairying is inevitably rather ambiguous, he estimated diet both with and without milk, but in any case argued that dairying would have been on a small scale for a short period, the farmers collecting surplus milk after the calves had fed. His breakdown of diet at two levels of calorific intake is shown in Table 15. (Interestingly, Brandt – in Bakker *et al.*, 1977 – reached very similar figures for Hoogkarspel.) The comparison of the amount of arable land needed at the Bovenkarspel farms (to obtain the vegetal calories in Table 15) with the amount that could be harvested by average households of six people (adults and children) indicated that a crop yield ratio of 1:5 would have been necessary for the 2000 Kcal diet and a 1:6 ratio for the 3000 Kcal diet, but if two thirds of the arable were under fallow, a ratio of 1:30 would have been needed at the phase of maximum settlement on the ridge. These yields seem extremely high given that Roman and medieval yields were often as low as 1:3 (Titow, 1972), but comparable yields have been obtained at the Butser ancient farm project in

Table 15 *Dietary models for Bovenkarspel: animal and vegetal calories in percentages*

| Phase | 2000 Kcal per person per day | | | | 3000 Kcal per person per day | | | |
| | without milk | | with milk | | without milk | | with milk | |
	animal	vegetal	animal	vegetal	animal	vegetal	animal	vegetal
1	55	45	68	32	37	63	46	54
2	39	61	49	51	24	76	33	67
3	23	77	31	69	16	84	21	79
4	26	74	33	67	18	82	22	78

(After Ijzereef, 1981)

southern England with primitive cereals (Reynolds, 1981). The impression is that the agricultural system depended on the small scale but intensive management of land, with the limited areas of arable being intensively manured to keep fallow to a minimum – hence the suitability of the small 'Celtic' fields despite their miniscule size by modern standards.

This agricultural system, however, was not static – adaptations to both demographic pressure and then ecological change can be discerned. The number of farms on the Bovenkarspel ridge doubled between *c.* 1250 and 850 b.c., and the arable component was increased at the expense of stock keeping to provide more food: a decline in cattle keeping was inferred from the decreased stalling capacity of the later longhouses, and an increase in grain production from the fact that the buildings were shifted lower down the ridges to make more land available for cultivation (Table 16). After *c.* 850 b.c. groundwater conditions worsened as sea levels rose; the diminished population retreated to the highest land, deepened the drainage ditches, and raised the field levels with the excavated soil. (The ridges became so wet that the water voles formerly found only in the ditches on the edge of the settlement colonised the habitation area as well.) As cereal cultivation became more difficult, the cattle herd was managed more intensively, with dairying almost certainly increasing in importance: changes in mortality rates in the final phase of occupation suggest this development, and whereas the respective percentages of cow, steer and bull horncores in the earlier phases were 44, 37 and 19, they altered to 75, 20 and 5 in the final phase. Fishing also assumed a critical role in subsistence at this time. Eventually the people were forced to abandon the Bovenkarspel ridge *c.* 700 b.c.

The dispersed and relatively unstratified agricultural societies so elegantly investigated in Holland contrast markedly with the rest of Atlantic Europe, where the archaeological record is dominated by major defended settlements and complex cemeteries. Again, however, it has to be said that our understanding of the social and economic organisation of Belgium and most of northern France in this period is minimal. In the lower Vendée valley, settlement shifted westwards along the northern edge of the Marais basin as the inland area became increasingly waterlogged (Scarre, 1982). A mixed stock economy was practised at Misy-sur-Yonne: the three main species were kept in roughly equal numbers, most of them being killed as adults (Poulain, 1977). There is a certain amount of evidence for a steady decrease in hunting in the late

Table 16 *Changing patterns of land use modelled for Bovenkarspel*

Phase	Date b.c.	Length of farmhouse (m)	Number of cattle	Pasture required (ha)	Total pasture available (ha)	Total arable available (ha)	Maximum number of farms
1	1250	25	30	35	860	101	24
2	1050	20	20	20	670	270	33
3	850	15	10	10	502	438	50
4	750	15	10	15	337	101	22

(After Izjereef, 1981)

second millennium (Poulain, 1976a). Sheep and goats seem to have become increasingly important in several regions such as Charentes, the Paris basin and the Massif Central during the climatic optimum (Poulain, 1970, 1976a). It can also be said that the pollen diagrams record ever more substantial clearances by the end of the second millennium (Planchais, 1976), coinciding with the impact of bronze technology on the ordinary farmer, when sickles and axes became widespread. But the real nature of the bronze age economy here eludes us completely.

In Brittany the archaeological record is again dominated by burials: there are six hundred barrows, about forty of which are known to have contained elaborate burials of high status individuals with fine pottery, metal weapons and flint arrowheads in mint condition (Briard, 1976). The great concentration of wealth represented by the Armorican barrows was clearly related to the mineral wealth of the peninsula. In the later Bronze Age, too, the metal industry here was on a very large scale, culminating in the production of thousands of square socketed axes in lead-bronze or lead which were traded widely in France and Britain, probably as currency or ingot metal (Briard, 1965) – 'the first mass production industry in western Europe' (Coles and Harding, 1979: 474). Almost all settlement traces have been found on the coasts, and subsistence data are as poor here as in the rest of northern France, but the changing distribution of barrows may bear witness to changes in settlement organisation. At first the barrows were constructed at intervals around the coast, with half a dozen scattered across the interior (Briard, 1970; Giot, 1960). The distribution suggests half a dozen or more territorial groupings, each of which controlled a river valley and which would have enabled control of the inland mineral resources as well as herding between the coastal settlements and the interior. The later barrows, however, divide into three main groups, implying a process of territorial consolidation: one in the northwest of the peninsula, one in the southwest, and the third further east from the Gulf of Morbihan to the Guerlédan heaths; empty 'cenotaph' barrows further reinforced these territorial divisions. Undoubtedly the barrow distributions tell only a very partial story, but at least they imply a broad correlation between social divisions and the control of mineral wealth, and the emergence of regional systems of agricultural organisation controlled by the ruling elites.

Farming at the close of prehistory

It is now clear that the sandy regions of northern Holland continued to be settled in the Sub-Atlantic after *c.* 500 b.c., although the climatic deterioration forced a contraction in settlement. Small farmsteads in the Elp tradition continued, with the same range of buildings; cattle remained the most important stock, and the main crops were still emmer and naked six-row barley (Waterbolk, 1977: 110; van Zeist, 1968). At the same time, cultivation technology was intensified and land divisions formalised. At Vaassen, for example, land organised in irregular plots in the early first millennium b.c. was divided up into the small regular plots of the Celtic field system in the second half of the millennium, and the ground completely cleared of all remaining tree stumps (Brongers, 1976). Pollen analysis indicated that the fields (which were divided into larger units of about two ha), were used for intensive arable systems; and humic material was delibately added to the plots to maintain soil fertility – irrefutable evidence now for *plaggen* culture. In other areas of Holland the fields were marked out by ditches but the cultivation system was much the same (Groenman-van Waateringe, 1978: 11–12); *plaggen* cultivation was also practised at this time in northern Germany at Flögeln in lower Saxony (Zimmerman, 1978: 149) and on the island of Sylt west of the Jutland peninsula (Kroll, 1975). Arable soil was in such short supply on the Dutch sands that waste land was brought into cultivation and even barrows were ploughed over.

The period was also characterised by settlement nucleation and increased social stratification in this part of Holland. In Drenthe, several settlements were transformed in the second and first centuries B.C. from single farmsteads into major enclosures defended by earthen walls with palisade revetments, ditches and outer palisades (Waterbolk, 1977; Fig. 70). The enclosures were only 3–4 kilometres apart, each controlling a block of territory much the same size as the parishes of the medieval villages. Inside the forts were granaries and large barns, but not the normal dual purpose house/barns suggesting all-year-round settlement, although quantities of domestic refuse show that the enclosures were inhabited at least for short periods. Waterbolk concluded that the forts were used as central storage places for the stock and harvest products of each community, a response to internal competition and conflict between adjacent communities at a time of population stress. There may be some evidence for regional leadership by a king or paramount chief in the concentration of cemeteries at Rolde and, 35 km away, at Havelte (Waterbolk, 1977: 170). An indication of the social organisation within individual communities was found at Fochteloo: a longhouse enclosed by wattle fences was situated five hundred metres away from a hamlet of three houses with sheds and granaries, suggesting a relationship between a local landowner or chieftain and his client tenants or adherents. The same sort of social structure, but within a nucleated farming community, is suggested for the early first millennium A.D. villages of Wijster and Flögeln (van Es, 1967; Schmid, 1978; Zimmerman, 1978).

North of the Drenthe sands in Groningen and Friesland, a stabilisation in the rise of the sea level resulted in the development of extensive salt marshes in the mid-first millennium b.c. These were colonised rapidly by farming communities, probably from the Drenthe plateau, who protected their houses from flooding by building them on *terpen* or artificial mounds of sods – the *tumuli alti* seen by the elder Pliny during his visit to northern Europe (*Natural History* 16.1.3). Many poorly situated farms such as Paddepoel and Ezinge had to be abandoned in the late third century because of an increase in flooding (van Es, 1968), but the system of settlement continued as a successful adaptation to the marshland environment right up until the eleventh century A.D., when the development of dyking finally began the process of drainage and reclamation that was to create the modern Dutch landscape (van Giffen, 1936; Waterbolk, 1965–6). Settlement was possible in the region because internally lined wells or cisterns were developed from the outset to collect freshwater (Brongers, 1976: 69), but crop cultivation was clearly hazardous because the soil was both brackish and regularly inundated, and the main crops had to be spring sown and relatively salt resistant – barley, flax, millet, beans, oats and gold of pleasure (*Camelina sativa*), but not wheat or pulses (van Zeist, 1968). Modern experiments have shown that such crops can be grown successfully on the highest parts of the unprotected salt marsh, though they are always vulnerable to sudden flooding (van Zeist *et al.*, 1976). The stock system was essentially the same as in the bronze age farms of West Friesland: cattle were the mainstay, providing milk, meat, hides and traction; sheep were kept in smaller numbers; and pigs were relatively uncommon (Louwe Kooijmans, 1980: 127). Aurochs, red deer, elk and bear were hunted, and seals were caught on the coast.

The Dutch *terpen* were poor in their material culture and appear to have been subsistence communities, but evidence for more complex social and economic organisation has been found in the adjacent coastal marshes of Germany, where the dwelling mounds are termed *wurten* or *wierden*. The site most thoroughly investigated is Feddersen Wierde near Bremerhaven, which was occupied from the first century B.C. to the fifth

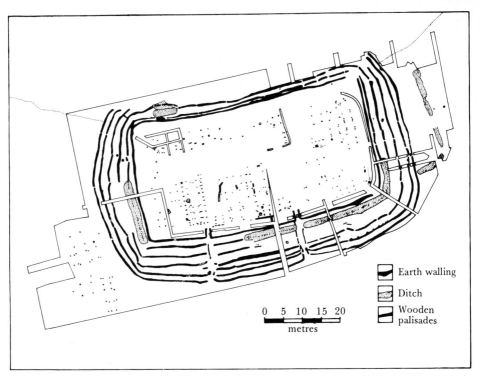

	Earth walling
	Ditch
	Wooden palisades

0 5 10 15 20
metres

Fig. 70. Zeijen, a late prehistoric fortified enclosure in Drenthe: the post-holes mark buildings which are interpreted principally as storage facilities rather than dwellings. North is at the top of the plan. (After Waterbolk, 1977: fig. 8)

century A.D. (Haarnagel, 1979). Over this period the community grew from a couple of farms to a substantial village. In the second century A.D. a large house was constructed in one part of the settlement, surrounded by a palisade and ditch, presumably for the headman or chief; adjacent buildings housed craftsmen working in wood, leather, antler and bone, and the main cattle stalls and granaries were also within this enclosure.

The establishment of the Roman frontier on the Rhine did not have a massive impact on the way of life of the agricultural population of northern Holland. There is evidence for both resistance and response to the Roman imperial economy. In western Holland the main stock kept at native settlements on both sides of the frontier were cattle and sheep, but cattle and pigs were the main stock killed at the Valkenburg fort: pork was a favourite meat of the Roman army, and Clason (1967b: 22) suggested that the pigs had to be reared by the military because the native farmers could not supply them. On the other hand, a small settlement at Assendelft near Amsterdam seems to have sent cattle and horses north to a regional centre at Schagen in West Friesland, which the tribal leadership then traded with the Roman frontier towns (Brandt, *pers. comm.*); trade in horses across the Roman frontier has been suggested from the analysis of the animal bones from Nekkerspiel south of Antwerp (Gautier, 1968: 255); and the impetus for the cultivation of rye in Drenthe in the second and first centuries B.C. may have come from the Romans (van Zeist, 1976).

Northern France in the sixth century was outside the sphere of the Greek and Etruscan trade which had helped to stimulate the extraordinary social transformations marked from Bergundy to Bavaria and beyond by the 'princely burials' and hillfort settlements (Chapter 6). In the fifth and fourth centuries, however, there were major changes in pottery, weapons and jewellery, and a dramatic shift northwards in the centres of industry, trade and wealth. One of the richest areas seems to have been the Marne and Aisne valleys in the region of Rheims, where the La Tène Marnian culture has been defined by the distribution of chariot burials: two wheeled carts, probably war chariots, were buried in trench graves, the men accompanied by ornaments and weapons, the women by jewellery, and both by pottery and food offerings. Almost nothing is known of Marnian farms or farming, apart from at Chassemy near Soissons in Aisne (Rowlett *et al.*, 1969). A substantial farmhouse with a timber framework, wattle and daub walls and a large central fireplace was excavated here; the community grew einkorn, emmer, bread wheat, barley and legumes, and kept all the main farmyard stock in a system of mixed husbandry that probably concentrated on secondary products as much as on meat. Hodson and Rowlett (1974: 182) pointed to the correlation between the increased rainfall of the Sub-Atlantic and the emergence of the Marnian societies, suggesting that the wetter conditions made settlement possible on the arid chalk plains of Champagne and Picardy at much higher densities than before. At the same time, agricultural considerations alone do not really explain the wealth of the Marnian elites and, given the evidence for contact with Brittany and Britain, Hodson and Rowlett argued that they may also have controlled trade in tin and other raw materials. A similar combination of agricultural resources and minerals (in this case iron ore) can be postulated to account for the wealth of the Hunsrück-Eifel communities to the east.

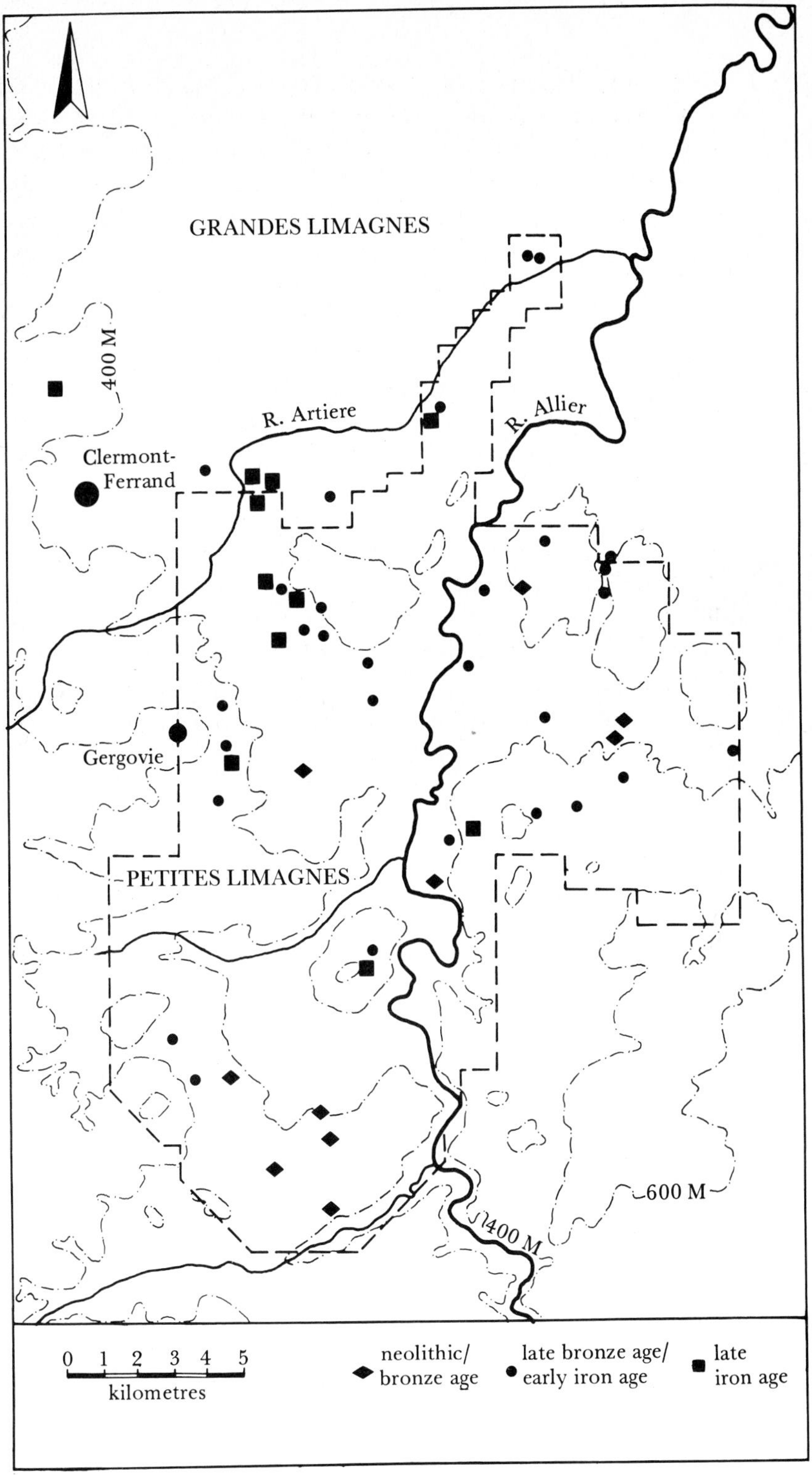

GRANDES LIMAGNES
400 M
R. Artiere
R. Allier
Clermont-
Ferrand
Gergovie
PETITES LIMAGNES
600 M
400 M
0 1 2 3 4 5
kilometres
neolithic/
bronze age
late bronze age/
early iron age
late
iron age

Fig. 71. Prehistoric settlement near Clermont Ferrand; dashed line = survey area. (After Mills, in press: fig. 6)

According to Caesar, northern France at the time of his campaigns was occupied by some thirty Gallic tribes. These societies consisted of a chief, his personal followers, artisans, peasants and herdsmen. The people lives in *aedificia* (isolated farms), *vici* (hamlets or villages) and *oppida*. The word *oppidum* seems to have been applied by Caesar to both large nucleated settlements and small hillforts, some of which may have been simply temporary refuges. In Brittany, for example, Caesar tells us that the oppida of the Veneti were small promontory forts, from which the people could escape by sea (*Gallic Wars* 3.12). Many such forts have been identified in Veneti territory, and most seem to have been small permanent settlements, but the largest in Brittany, Camp d'Artus near Huelgoat, is thought to have been an emergency refuge to meet Caesar's attack (Wheeler and Richardson, 1957: 2). On the other hand, there were also large oppida like those of central Europe which were quite clearly major tribal centres, such as Alesia, Bibracte, and Gergovia. These sites were political and military strongholds, centres of population and industry (including the minting of coins), and regional markets.

Iron age research in France has concentrated on the excavation of major settlements and cemeteries, and almost nothing is known of agricultural organisation, or the economic role of the oppida in the territories they controlled. However, a major insight into these problems has been provided by a recent programme of survey and excavation near Clermont-Ferrand. The prime arable soils of the region today are on the low ground east of the volcanic Monts Dômes hills, but they divide into two groups: the more fertile are the black silty clays (*terres noires*) of the Grandes Limagnes plain, but they are poorly drained and require extensive drainage before cultivation, whereas the soils flooring the Petites Limagnes basin and Allier valley are naturally well drained as well as being moderately fertile (Fig. 71). Intensive survey has shown that the latter soils were intensively farmed in the neolithic and bronze age periods; by the early first millennium b.c. settlement on these soils was particularly dense, and marginal arable soils at higher elevations were also taken into cultivation. The settlement pattern then changed radically in the late first millennium b.c.: there were fewer but much larger sites – villages, probably – in the Petites Limagnes and Allier valley; abundant finds in and on the edge of the Grandes Limagnes show that these heavy soils were now taken into cultivation; and the oppidum of Gergovie was established overlooking the plains (Mills, in press). Aulnat, one of the new villages established on the edge of the Grands Limagnes plain in the second and first centuries B.C., had specialised artisanal workshops for bone cutting, bronze working, iron smelting, glass making and minting, and there were numerous imports of Mediterranean wine amphorae (Collis, 1975b, 1980). (Pigs were the principal stock here, in the best traditions of Astérix the Gaul.) We know from historical sources such as Caesar that this period marked a considerable increase in the power and influence of the Arverni tribe inhabiting this part of France, probably associated with greater hierarchisation of society as a whole and with the increased control by the ruling elite over both social and economic relations. Farming the Grandes Limagnes would have required both an organised system of drainage and outlets for specialised produce – presumably the Mediterranean markets which supplied wine to the Arverni elites.

8

Britain and Ireland

Geographical introduction

For any visitor to these islands, one of the most striking discoveries is the extraordinary mosaic of diverse landscapes packed within our narrow confines. However, one simple division of the British landscape, into a northwestern Highland Zone and a southeastern Lowland Zone, has repeatedly been drawn by British geographers, on either side of a diagonal line running from the river Exe in the southwest to the river Tees in the north-east (Stamp and Beaver, 1963). In 1932 Sir Cyril Fox pointed out that this natural division correlated with broad cultural divisions in prehistoric settlement, and although the strength of this division has been exaggerated, the concept of lowland and highland environments remains a useful starting point for this discussion (Fig. 72).

The southernmost part of the Highland Zone is the peninsula of Devon and Cornwall (with Somerset as an outlier): a succession of elevated plateaus and intervening lowland areas. The whole of the Welsh massif lies in the Highland Zone; the grain of the country is from southwest to northeast, with many peaks rising almost 1000 metres above sea level. The Pennine chain forms the backbone of central and northern England, from the Derbyshire Peak in the south to the Cheviot Hills on the Scottish border, although its topography varies considerably according to major geological divisions; two upland out-liers are the Lake District or Cumbrian hills to the west and the north Yorkshire moors to the east. North of the border and south of the Clyde and Forth rivers is another major series of hills. North of these rivers the Highlands of Scotland dwarf the rest of the High-land Zone in scale and grandeur: there is a substantial area over 1000 metres above sea level, and many peaks in the Grampians rise to over 1300 metres.

South and east of the lowland/highland boundary are the broad plains or low-lying plateaus of the English Midlands, with undulating or featureless lowlands extending north on either side of the Pennines. South and east of the Midland plateaus is a line of Jurassic rocks which forms a limestone or sandstone scarpland running diagonally across England, from the Mendips and Cotswolds in the southeast to the Cleveland and Hambledon hills in north Yorkshire; on the dipslope normally are major clay valleys (such as the Upper Thames valley, the middle Ouse valley and Lincoln Vale) and then the parallel scarp of the chalklands, from the Dorset and Wiltshire downs to the Lincolnshire and Yorkshire wolds. Two other lines of chalk downs run across southeast-ern England, separated by the low-lying clays and sands of the Kent, Surrey and Sussex Weald; another major area of chalk is East Anglia, but here it is normally overlain by glacial deposits to form a low undulating plateau. Lying as a wedge between here and the uplands of Lincolnshire are the fens, deposits of peats and silts at sea level around

Fig. 72. Britain and Ireland (contours in metres): principal sites and regions mentioned in the text. 1. Dun Carloway; 2. Oronsay; 3. Knap of Howar; 4. Skara Brae; 5. Isbister; 6. Kilphedir; 7. Dalladies; 8. Morton; 9. Broxmouth; 10. Behy-Glenulra; 11. New Grange; 12. Stanwick; 13. Star Carr; 14. Thwing; 15. Mam Tor; 16. Mount Gabriel; 17. Breiddin; 18. Croft Ambrey; 19. Billingborough; 20. Fengate; 21. Grimes Graves; 22. Gwithian; 23. Trevisker; 24. Shaugh Moor; 25. Somerset Levels, Glastonbury, Meare; 26. Eldon's Seat; 27. Hambledon Hill; 28. Little Woodbury; 29. Danebury; 30. Windmill Hill, South Street barrow; 31. Old Down Farm; 32. Farmoor; 33. Ashville; 34. Rams Hill; 35. Aldermaston Wharf; 36. Black Patch.

the Wash, impassable marshes for much of the historical period, though now drained and a prime agricultural resource. In Scotland the only major lowland region, apart from the outlying islands to the north and west, is the broad corridor between the Grampians and the southern hills on either side of the Clyde and Forth rivers.

Ireland contains both highland and lowland zones, but the hills form a rim around a central basin. The basin is formed of carboniferous limestone covered by glacial and later deposits; drainage is poor, and the result is a landscape of waterlogged boulder clay, infertile glacial sands, and huge peat bogs, providing at best large areas of wet pasture – the 'beef and bog-land' (Stamp and Beaver, 1963: 730). The west and north-west of Ireland are a lonely landscape of mountains, lakes and bogs, the heartland of crofting poverty in recent times with rainfall the highest in Ireland and the potato the major crop.

The fickleness of British weather is proverbial. The climate is determined by the complex fluctuations in the three main pressure systems which surround these islands, and by their reactions to secondary cyclones and intervening ridges of high pressure. The results are highly changeable, and 'it is sometimes said that the British Isles have no climate, since climate is described as the average state of the weather' (Stamp and Beaver, 1963: 71). However, in general winter temperatures are higher in the west than in the east (mean values averaging 7°C and 4°C respectively) and summer temperatures are higher in the south (16–17°C) than in the north (13–15°C). Rainfall is well distributed throughout the year, but western regions tend to receive most rain in winter, while eastern regions have more rain in summer; the average number of days with rain increases from southeast to northwest. Average rainfall is about 500 mm, but is much higher in the uplands, and can be as high as 2500 mm in the mountains of Wales, western Scotland and western Ireland.

Despite modern market forces, factory farming, EEC subsidies and so on, there are still very marked contrasts in farming systems from region to region related to the traditional constraints of relief, soil and climate. In particular, the broad dichotomy between highland stock-based and lowland arable-based farming remains, although at the same time upland stock keeping is closely integrated with stock systems on lowland farms – traditionally the upland farms supply young strong stock for the lowlands, either for fattening for slaughter or for replenishing breeding stock. Sheep farming in the Highland Zone has normally been characterised by short distance seasonal movements between summer grazing on the moors and winter grazing at lower elevations. Cattle are also reared successfully in the uplands, but unlike sheep are normally housed in winter; the major areas for cattle rearing, however, are the damp lowland pastures of southwest and midland England, western Wales, eastern Scotland and the central plain of Ireland. Pigs are also kept primarily in the lowland counties. Cereal cultivation tends to be restricted to regions with less than 750 mm of rain, with the primary zone for wheat being the southern, eastern and midland counties of England and for barley the drier parts of eastern Ireland, eastern England and eastern Scotland.

The most marginal type of subsistence farming, now fast disappearing, has been the crofting economy of the most marginal areas of the north and west (Fig. 85, p. 222). The crofting farmer relied principally on a small flock of sheep and also kept one or two cows, some poultry, and perhaps a pig. He cultivated a few small fields for vegetables and for winter feed for his stock. On the Scottish islands the meagre diet was often supplemented by fish, sea birds and their eggs (Handley, 1953). The little manure produced by the stock had to be used for fuel because of the lack of wood, and in regions like Orkney, seaweed was the only other available manure despite the labour of getting it from the shore to the fields: 'the most ordinary mannour they have for their land is seaweed . . . methinks it is the greatest slavery in the world for the common people, as they do there in winter, to carry this wrack . . . on their backs to their land' (Wallace, 1883: 47). The lack of manure meant low crop yields, with little or nothing to spare beyond the immediate needs of the family. There was a chronic shortage of winter feed, and stock often had to be fed on seaweed (raw or par-boiled) or dried fish bones (Fenton, 1976: 141).

Postglacial foragers, *c.* 8300–3500 b.c.

The retreat of the icesheets from Britain and Ireland allowed a rapid climatic amelioration: winter temperatures in the Pre-Boreal (after *c.* 8300 b.c.) averaged 5°C below zero and summer temperatures just over 10°C, but during the Boreal (*c.* 7500–5500 b.c.) temperatures rose rapidly to winter averages a few degrees above or below freezing (for lowland and highland regions respectively) and to summer temperatures as high as or higher than today's average (Lamb, 1966); the climate was continental, with short hot summers and less precipitation (Evans, 1975; Simmons and Tooley, 1981). For most of this period Britain was part of continental Europe, with a wide plain stretching between eastern England and Denmark, and a narrower plain extending westwards as far as the Isle of Man; the land bridge to Europe was severed by *c.* 6500 b.c. (Tooley, 1974). (The rise in sea level separated Ireland from the rest of Britain very early in the Holocene.) During the Pre-Boreal and Boreal, the open landscape of the late glacial was gradually covered by birch scrub and woodland, which were then rapidly invaded by pine and hazel; as temperatures rose in the latter part of the Boreal, mixed deciduous forest developed. The fauna which colonised these forests included aurochs, brown bear, elk, red deer, roe deer, pig, fox, wolf, beaver, otter, hare, pine marten, badger, hedgehog and possibly a woodland horse (Simmons *et al.*, 1981: 115). Ireland, because it was cut off at such an early date, was not colonised by elk, aurochs, and a variety of amphibians, snakes and other reptiles (Wijngaarden-Bakker, 1974).

Mesolithic settlement in Britain divides into an earlier and a later phase, before and after the cutting of the continental land bridge. The division is clearest in the lithic technology, which is characterised as 'broad-blade' in the early phase and 'narrow-blade' in the late phase (Mellars, 1974). The early material is more or less identical to that of north Germany and the Low Countries; as the land bridge shrank, isolated similarities remained with Holland, but once it had been breached the technologies on either side of the Channel remained fundamentally distinct (Jacobi, 1976).

The wealth of organic remains preserved in the lake muds at Star Carr in Yorkshire provided remarkable insights into the way of life of a foraging community *c.* 7500 b.c. (Clark, 1954). The excavations discovered a collection of birch trees and brushwood covered with stones, clay and moss to form a rough living platform on a waterlogged lakeshore, presumably to support shelters of reeds or skins. Domestic debris lay prolifically on and around the platform, including flint axes, adzes, microliths and other small tools; hundreds of barbed points of red deer antler and blanks for these; a variety of other artifacts made of organic materials (bone tools, mattocks of elk antler, a wooden paddle, birch bark rolls); and a large sample of animal bones and plant remains. The faunal sample consisted mainly of aurochs, beaver, elk, pig, red deer and roe deer, with red deer the major source of meat. Nine species of birds were caught, mainly water birds, but no fish remains were found (and no fish hooks). Plants collected for food probably included reeds and bog beans from the lakeshore and nettles, chickweed, knotgrass and goosefoot from forest clearings.

In his major reassessment of the site, Clark (1972) argued that Star Carr was the winter base camp of a community of three or four families, who gathered there primarily to hunt red deer with bone and antler spears (the occurrence of shed antlers of red deer and elk indicated that the site was certainly occupied in the winter and early spring). Red deer tend to spend the winter on low ground, but move to higher elevations for the summer (where grazing is best and insect irritation least in that season). As small assemblages of microliths have been found in the hills adjacent to Star Carr, Clark concluded that the people followed the deer into the hills in the summer, hunting them there with bows and arrows. More recently, however, other studies have indicated that the subsistence, seasonal and artifactual data are all less precise than predicted by Clark's model of seasonal mobility and specialised deer hunting (Jacobi, 1978; Noe Nygaard, 1975, 1977; Pitts, 1979): in fact, Star Carr was probably a hunting site used on many occasions, over a considerable period of time, and at different times of the year, as an 'intercept location' where a variety of game was driven into the mud or shallows and dispatched at close range (Andresen *et al.*, 1981). Elsewhere in Britain, too, it seems likely that Boreal foraging was generalised rather than specialised. Nevertheless, whilst the model of winter/lowland and summer/upland hunting is clearly oversimplified, the frequency of high altitude sites in northern England, their composition and location (especially on ridges and at valley heads overlooking lower ground) suggest that the uplands were normally exploited by summer hunting parties of perhaps a dozen people primarily concerned with the larger species of game such as red deer (Jacobi, 1978; Spratt and Simmons, 1976).

The more oceanic climate of the Atlantic period developed in the mid-sixth millennium b.c.: winter temperatures were about 2°C above those of today, the spring and autumn seasons lengthened, and average rainfall was higher than today. Mixed deciduous forest covered much of the landscape, although the climate also encouraged the growth of alder carr and peat as lake levels increased. The later phase of mesolithic settlement was probably characterised by significant population increase, the effects of which were exacerbated by the contraction of land available for settlement as sea levels rose. Previously unoccupied parts of Britain and Ireland were colonised, and although subsistence data are generally very poor, there are several indications of diversification and intensification in subsistence techniques much as in southern Scandinavia at this time.

There are grounds for thinking that there was a distinct trend towards the increased use of coastal resources by Atlantic foragers, even though it is true that sea level rises would have flooded any coastal camps of Boreal people. Locations with access to a variety of inland, coastal and marine resources were increasingly preferred for settlement and were used for diversified foraging (Churchill and Wymer, 1965; Palmer, 1976; Rankine, 1961). For example, Morton on the coast of Fife in eastern Scotland had easy access to forests, marshes, tidal flats, rocky shores and the open sea, and a very wide range of food sources was exploited: land mammals (aurochs, pig, red deer, roe deer), sea birds (cormorant, fulmar, gannet, guillemot, puffin, razorbill, shag), shellfish (mainly cockles), crabs, fish (mainly cod, but also haddock, salmon, sturgeon, and turbot), nuts, and the same sort of plants as at Star Carr; dugout canoes were used for the sea fishing (Coles, 1971). The site was visited repeatedly, but probably on most occasions just for a couple of weeks (especially in late winter or early spring). Most of the coastal sites known were part of foraging strategies which also used hunting camps inland in adjacent hills up to 15–20 km away (Bonsall, 1978; Simmons, 1969a; Spratt and Simmons, 1976). The tiny island of Oronsay in the Inner Hebrides may well have been part of an annual foraging system which embraced not only the larger islands of Islay and Jura 12 km to the east but also the Scottish mainland 30 km to the east (Mellars, 1978; Mercer, 1971). The principal reason for using the island was probably to fish saithe in the early spring (using simple weirs or traps in the tidal waters), but it was also visited on other occasions for killing seabirds and seals and – perhaps in starvation years – for collecting the limpets which abound there (Grigson, 1981; Mellars and Wilkinson, 1980; Wilkinson, 1982).

Ireland was probably colonised early in the Holocene. Settlement evidence is most abundant in the north, although there are increasing indications of early occupation in the central and southern parts of the island (Woodman, 1978a, 1978b). As in mainland Britain, far more Atlantic than Boreal sites are known. Woodman argued that, because of its early isolation, Ireland did not have a dense population of large mammals like red deer, so that subsistence had to be based on a broad spectrum diet of fish, small game, birds, shellfish and sea mammals. In his model, the annual subsistence round in Ulster would have utilised an inland lake (Lough Neagh), the coast some 30 km away, and the intervening mountains of Antrim, but would have concentrated on the Bann river, where salmon would have been a major resource in spring and early summer during their run upstream, and eels in late summer and autumn when their shoals moved downstream to the sea.

Further insights into the possible intensity of Atlantic foraging in Britain have been provided by palaeobotanical evidence for deliberate habitat alteration (Dimbleby, 1962; Simmons, 1969b; Smith, 1970). Two phenomena have been noted: an expansion of alder and hazel; and episodes of small clearances with plantains, sometimes associated with charcoal deposits (Simmons, 1975). Mellars (1976) has summarised the considerable ethnographic data for deliberate and systematic burning by recent foragers occupying forested or shrubland environments. The principal advantages of such burning for Atlantic foragers, he argued, would have been to increase the mobility of the hunters and reduce escape cover for the game, but above all to improve the amount and quality of browse and so increase game densities. In certain types of woodland, burning could have increased the overall productivity of the environment in terms of animal protein by as much as 500%–900% (Mellars, 1976: 22–6). The animal to profit most from such browse improvement is assumed to have been red deer (Mellars, 1975). In the Pennines, the first development of the moorland peats with their characteristic heather vegetation seems to have begun in the Atlantic period, and could well be related in part to human pressure on the forest vegetation (Radley *et al.*, 1974).

The introduction of farming, *c.* 3500–2500 b.c.

Despite the demise of so many other invasion models formerly used for British prehistory (Clark, 1966), the origins of British and Irish neolithic farming have continued to be explained by colonisation, immigration or invasion from across the Channel in the mid-fourth millennium b.c. The actual practicalities of such an event were first discussed explicitly by Case (1969), who argued that large scale communal movement across the Channel must have entailed the use of skin boats like the Eskimo *umiak*, each with a cargo of about a dozen people and a few stock (say two adult cows and two calves, or six pigs, or ten sheep and goats), with the most likely period of voyage both in terms of sea conditions and agricultural seasons being between August and November. The principal monuments surviving from the period 3500–2500 b.c. consist of causewayed enclosures and earthen long barrows, found especially in central southern England and in the Yorkshire/Lincolnshire wolds. Traditionally their builders have been regarded as egalitarian communities (as their burials were collective), who practised shifting or slash and burn cultivation (as habitation sites were rare, and the British palaeobotanical data could be fitted to the *landnam* model). However, in recent years it has become clear that the main phase of monument building was in fact associated with sedentary and rather complex social and economic systems. As a result, some researchers have argued that there must have been an initial pioneering phase of agricultural settlement – low density and mobile, much as in the traditional model for the Earlier Neolithic of Europe as a whole (Mercer, 1981; Whittle, 1977a, 1977b). Arguments about the context of the first farming are discussed at the end of this section.

Some forty causewayed enclosures are known, principally across southern England; the best known were for long those of the chalk downs, typified by Windmill Hill (Smith, 1965), but aerial reconnaissance has discovered many more on river gravels. It has always been assumed that the enclosures were not defensive because of the breaks in the banks and ditches, and there has been a continual debate about other possible functions, apart from the consensus that an enclosure was probably 'the centre or rallying point for the population of a fairly wide area' (Smith, 1965: 19). The evidence of location, construction, internal organisation and refuse is very variable, and Whittle concluded that the functions 'probably included the provision of both permanent and non-permanent places to live, protection of both stock and people, and centres for exchange and distribution of imperishables and perishables' (1977b: 345). Mortuary rituals were also important, and to these functions must after all be added defence on the evidence of palisades, continuous ditches and slighted earthworks at sites excavated in recent years (Dixon, 1981; Hedges and Buckley, 1978; Mercer, 1980). Renfrew (1973b, 1976) has argued convincingly that the societies who built these substantial monuments were both populous and sedentary, and were probably organised in segmentary lineages headed by chieftains. He calculated that an average enclosure represented some 100,000 man hours of labour, and Mercer (1980) has reached rather similar figures for the Hambledon Hill complex, suggesting that a seasonal labour force of about fifty men working in the autumn and early summer (before the harvest) could have constructed the site in two or three seasons. Renfrew also pointed out that the Wessex enclosures were usually 10–30 km apart, implying a degree of regularity in the territories inhabited by the communities using these sites, and the same is true of the enclosures in Sussex (Drewett, 1977, 1978) and East Anglia (Hedges and Buckley, 1978). The burial barrows, which certainly contain only a small proportion of the population (Atkinson, 1968), also tend to cluster around the camps (Ashbee, 1970) – further support for Renfrew's model of ranking and territoriality.

In Wessex, most of the monuments of this period are concentrated on the two major areas of higher ground, the limestone Cotswold hills and the chalk downs, which are separated by the Thames and Avon valleys (Fig. 73). Evans (1971a) and Whittle (1977a) both argued that the region was heavily forested at the time of the first farming, with slash and burn cultivation the inevitable response (integrating environmental data from the neolithic monuments with palaeobotanical data for *landnam* elsewhere in Britain). However, on the basis of a reassessment of the local environmental data and correlating this with modern pedological and geomorphological studies in the region, D. P. Webley and I have argued instead for a natural mosaic of vegetation types at the time the early neolithic monuments were built rather than blanket forest, with open country and light woodland on the higher ground and closed forest and wet pasture in the river valleys (Barker and Webley, 1978). Like Rowley-Conwy (1981a), we concluded that swidden farming would have been both unsuitable and unnecessary given the soils and vegetation of this landscape. Instead, the distribution of monuments and the available subsistence data suggested a model of more or less sedentary mixed farming, with each community exploiting a transect of country from river floodplain to upland plateau (rather like many of the historical parishes in the region). The barrows of each community were on the higher ground, the causewayed enclosure either here or on the valley floor, with both areas being primarily used for grazing and the main arable soils lying in between (Fig. 74).

In our view the most attractive soils for low technology cereal cultivation would have been the light freely drained soils carrying open woodland, particularly the Cornbrash and Greensand deposits edging the plateaus, the Corallian ridge in between, and the alluvium of the upland valleys. Settlement evidence is very poor, but the distribution of storage pits, broken flint axes and other lithic debris suggests that the cultivation activities of the farming system did indeed concentrate on these soils (Bradley and Ellison, 1975: 176, 188; Field *et al.*, 1964; Shennan, 1981: 112–13; Tyler, 1976). Emmer and six-row barley were the principal cereals, together with einkorn, flax, bread wheat and spelt (Helbaek, 1952a; Smith *et al.*, 1981: 186–9); emmer was the principal crop on the loamy soils edging the Cotswolds and barley was preferred on the lighter soils on the edge of the downs and in the downland valleys (Dennell, 1976b). Faunal evidence from the camps and barrows indicates that cattle, pigs, sheep and goats were kept

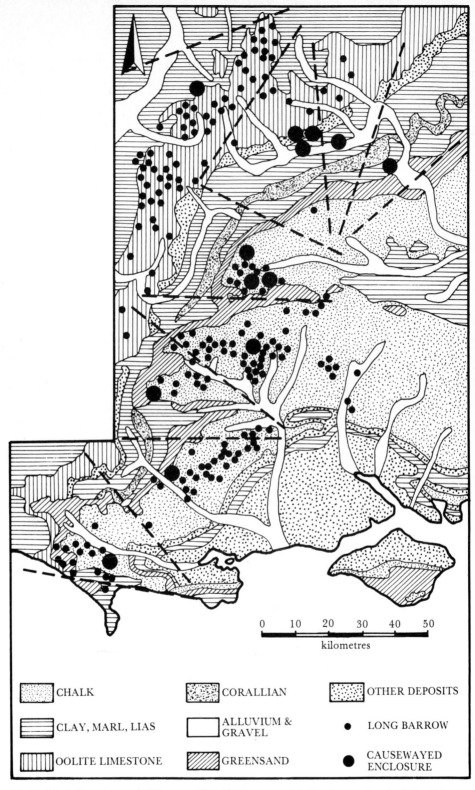

Fig. 73. Neolithic settlement in Wessex, *c.* 3500–2500 b.c.: a model of land use and territoriality. (After Barker and Webley, 1978: fig. 2)

CHALK

CORALLIAN

OTHER DEPOSITS

CLAY, MARL, LIAS

ALLUVIUM & GRAVEL

LONG BARROW

OOLITE LIMESTONE

GREENSAND

CAUSEWAYED ENCLOSURE

by these farmers, who also hunted on a small scale. In general terms the dry uplands would have suited sheep and goats and the river valleys the cattle and pigs, but in the gentle topography of this part of England animal husbandry was probably characterised by small scale movements from day to day rather than polarised systems of grazing.

Clearly the faunal samples cannot be treated as the normal food refuse of neolithic communities, for there is abundant evidence for the role of animals in complex ritual in both camps and barrows (Grigson, 1966, 1980; Smith, 1966; Smith *et al.*, 1981: 199). However, the predominance of cattle probably mirrors a real trend in animal husbandry. Articulated cattle limbs have been found in the ditches of several camps, the faunal samples in general do not show the degree of fragmentation found in normal domestic contexts in prehistoric Europe, and comparison with such faunas suggests 'periods of high meat consumption at the causewayed camps with a lower degree of bone processing in consequence' (Legge, 1981a: 174). Size differences in metapodials indicate male and female populations of domestic cattle at Windmill Hill and Hambledon Hill, with the majority being female (Fig. 75). Legge concluded that dairying must already have been a component of the agricultural system. Furthermore, mortality data show that the cattle killed at the camps were only a selected part of the breeding population, which was presumably maintained elsewhere in the territory, and in the same way the grain at Hambledon Hill consisted of a clean crop threshed and processed elsewhere (Legge, 1981a: 174–5). Some form of surplus production and redistribution seems increasingly likely. Both the networks of subsistence territories and the complex agricultural system practised within it can of course be integrated with Renfrew's model of emergent chiefdoms far more easily than the traditional subsistence model of swiddening pioneers. Very similar models of sedentary mixed farming are emerging from other regional studies in England, for example in Somerset (Coles and Hibbert,

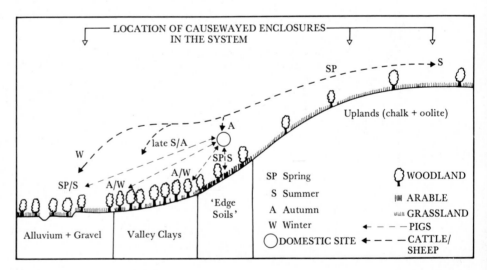

Fig. 74. Neolithic land use in Wessex, *c.* 3500–2500 b.c.: integrated stock and cereal systems exploited a range of resources from the main valleys to the central uplands; causewayed enclosures might be built in the valleys or in the uplands, but the systems around them were essentially the same. (After Barker and Webley, 1978: fig. 4)

1975), Sussex (Drewett, 1977, 1978) and East Anglia (Clough and Green, 1972; Hedges and Buckley, 1978; Wainwright, 1972).

The Somerset Levels were an expanse of fen carr and marsh at this time, and neolithic communities built wooden trackways to cross from one side to the other. Modern excavations of the trackways have transformed our knowledge of neolithic technology. Different timber was carefully selected for different parts of the trackway: hazel was used for pegs and posts, and may have been coppiced to ensure a supply of suitable lengths; substantial trees of oak, ash, and lime were split radially into planks and rails. Wooden objects found alongside the Sweet track, a plank walk dated *c.* 3200 b.c., included a spear, parts of two or three bows and arrow shafts, a mattock, possible paddles and a throwing stick, a variety of small awls and pins, toggles (for clothing or fishing floats), a pouring funnel, a dish and simple spoons (Coles *et al.*, 1973). Neolithic

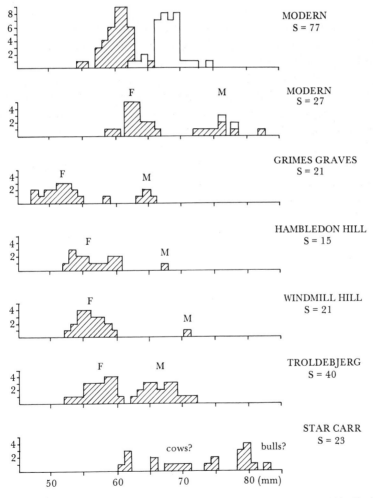

Fig. 75. Sexual dimorphism in prehistoric cattle: metacarpal dimensions (width, distal articulation) for cattle from five prehistoric sites (four British, one Danish) compared with modern samples; the open boxes in the top two histograms are castrated males. (After Legge, 1981a: fig. 4)

carpentry was clearly very skilled, for the techniques used by the people who built and used the Sweet track included chopping, splitting, planing, whittling, cutting, grinding and smoothing. It is quite possible that the ox-traction ard was also used by early farmers in Britain, although Webley and I argued that the remarkable depth of the South Street furrows (15 cm, cut into chalk subsoil: Evans, 1971b; Fowler and Evans, 1967) could not have been manufactured by any of the light wooden ards which have survived from prehistoric Europe, and are more likely to have been produced by turf-cutting operations. Mercer (1981: x) postulates the existence of a massive wooden 'rip ard' to explain the South Street furrows.

North and west of southern England, earlier neolithic material clusters in a few islands of regional settlement, but in most cases there is comparable evidence to that of Wessex for a varied natural landscape, well defined subsistence territories, and mixed farming systems linking hills and valleys but pivoting on well drained arable soils at their junction. Examples include the Lincolnshire wolds (May, 1976), the Yorkshire wolds (Manby, 1963, 1976a; Pierpoint, 1980), north Yorkshire (Spratt and Simmons, 1976), the Trent valley and the adjacent Peak District (Hawke-Smith, 1979; Hicks, 1971; Reaney, 1968), and south Wales (Moore, 1973; Webley, 1976). There is very little evidence for earlier neolithic settlement in Scotland, but a study of the location of Clyde tombs on Arran (Scott, 1970) supported Childe's original contention (Childe, 1934) that they were invariably restricted to the freshwater alluvia and higher raised beaches which provide the principal areas of light well drained soil on the island.

Irish archaeologists have traditionally viewed their prehistory in terms of cultural responses to changes in mainland Britain. Neolithic studies have thus been transformed in the past decade by the discovery that houses and megalithic tombs with early neolithic pottery were being constructed at least as early as in mainland Britain and probably earlier (ApSimon, 1976; Burenhult, 1980). Furthermore, clearance episodes have been dated to the earlier part of the fourth millennium b.c. (Lynch, 1981; Pilcher and Smith, 1979; Smith, 1975), and cereal pollen has also been identified in deposits dated to the first as well as to the second half of the fourth millennium (Teunissen and Teunissen-van Oorschot, 1980). The likelihood is that some kind of mixed farming was practised, but though the details elude us, the important point is that an agricultural system was probably able to develop in Ireland at an early date in the fourth millennium because the normally mild but wet climate of the Atlantic seaboard was further ameliorated in the late Atlantic, ensuring a limited growth of grass for most of the year and a favourable environment for cereal cultivation, whereas in the rest of Britain the cereals do not seem to have been cultivated until the trend to aridity was fully established in the Sub-Boreal at the end of the fourth millennium.

Outside the regions discussed above, the evidence for early agriculture is restricted almost entirely to clearance episodes inferred from the pollen record (Pennington, 1969; Turner, 1975). For many years these clearances were thought to follow the decline in elm pollen of the last two or three centuries of the fourth millennium, commonly ascribed to the activities of the first farmers (Troels-Smith, 1960). However, given the broad synchronism of the elm decline, but the increasing complexity of the archaeological evidence for where, when and how early farming began in Britain, the elm decline is far more likely to reflect climatic change in the early Sub-Boreal than the coordinated onslaught on the forest by neolithic colonists (Smith *et al.*, 1981: 152–83). With the recognition of clearance episodes earlier in the Atlantic, it seems increasingly difficult to correlate fourth millennium vegetation changes with a phase of pioneering agriculture – for which otherwise there is minimal evidence.

It seems to me that the beginnings of cereal and stock farming in Britain and Ireland can probably be understood just as much in terms of internal changes in the existing foraging economy as in terms of a system imposed or introduced by a new people, a thesis also put forward by Dennell (1983). Of course cereals and most if not all the domestic stock must have been transported to Britain and Ireland from mainland Europe, but sites such as Oronsay suggest that late Atlantic foragers had quite efficient maritime communications between mainland Scotland and the offshore islands, as was also the case in Brittany, Holland and Scandinavia. Whilst it is true that we know little of late mesolithic settlement in most of Britain in the thousand years before the first clear evidence for plant and animal husbandry, it is very striking that the agricultural economy began in these islands – just as in Switzerland, the Low Countries and southern Scandinavia – in the last two or three centuries before 3000 b.c., at a time when a more arid climate was probably opening up the Atlantic forests. In the Somerset Levels, the first trackways were built at this time, as the Atlantic reed swamps dried out and fen wood slowly began to develop (Coles and Hibbert, 1975). As in those other areas of temperate Europe, it seems reasonable to conclude that the climatic changes in Britain put pressure on forest foraging, and that the drier and more open landscape also provided increasing opportunities for the new resources to make an efficient replacement for or supplement to the old. In Ireland, the new economy was implemented several centuries earlier. Parts of Britain such as western Scotland maintained the foraging economy; in other regions such as Derbyshire, north Yorkshire and Somerset, farming may well have been integrated into existing systems of foraging; but in the drier regions most affected by the vegetational changes of the Sub-Boreal, highly organised systems of farming developed very rapidly, probably within the space of two or three centuries. It is true that on existing archaeological evidence we cannot really identify who the first farmers were or where they came from; however, the critical feature of the new economy in areas such as Wessex and east Yorkshire was that it was associated with a transformed world of land division, communal labour and social control, and with the substantial population levels that these promoted and maintained.

Agricultural consolidation and expansion, *c.* 2500–1500 b.c.

The archaeology of this period in Britain was conventionally divided into three distinct cultural episodes: the Late Neolithic, a development of preceding neolithic culture; the 'Beaker horizon', with graves with beaker pottery assumed to represent the immigration of a new people from mainland Europe who introduced copper metallurgy to these islands; and the Early Bronze Age, best known from the 'chieftain cemeteries' of round barrows on the southern chalklands defined as the Wessex culture. Interpretations of the archaeological record have now altered enormously, and its fundamental coherence is stressed. In particular, the beaker package of pottery, archery equipment (flint arrowheads, stone 'wrist guards') and the first copper artifacts (knives, axes and jewellery) has now been re-interpreted – as elsewhere in western Europe – as the status equipment of increasingly separate and secular (but indigenous) elites. The demise of the Beaker Folk lends further support to Renfrew's thesis of regional chiefdom development in Wessex (Renfrew, 1973a, 1973b): he pointed out that in most areas of the region an earlier neolithic causewayed enclosure (which, he calculated, served perhaps 2000 people) was replaced in the later third millennium b.c. by a henge or group of henges (serving perhaps 5000 people), and that the clusters of early bronze age barrows strongly suggested the survival of these territorial divisions into the mid-second millennium, with perhaps a paramount chief in the Stonehenge area. It is very clear that Wessex society was structured, with the rich and powerful in each chiefdom being buried in special barrows and people of lesser rank (perhaps kin or retainers) being buried in other mounds or as secondary burials in the main mounds (Burgess, 1980: 98–100). Dynastic leadership is often assumed, although the ascribed rather than achieved ranking implied by this has not been clearly shown.

Despite the wealth of ceremonial monuments, settlement evidence for this period in Wessex is again very rare, and is restricted to much the same range of enigmatic pits, hearths and surface artifact spreads as before (McInnes, 1971). Nevertheless, widespread trends in land use have been postulated. For example, the absence of cereal impressions in Grooved Ware induced Wainwright and Longworth (1971: 266) to conclude that pastoralism dominated later neolithic subsistence. Whittle (1978) linked pollen evidence for forest regeneration in various pollen diagrams in East Anglia, Cumbria, western Scotland and Ireland with molluscan evidence for 'uncultivated grassland' on the chalk, and argued for the replacement of early cultivation systems by pastoralism in these regions *c.* 2500 b.c. Bradley (1978b) and Mercer (1981) have envisaged a similar sequence of intensive arable farming *c.* 3000–2500 b.c., forest regeneration and economic decline *c.* 2500–2000 b.c., and increased pastoralism and mobility *c.* 2000–1400 b.c. However, whilst in any case the argument about overstretched cultivation systems has rested on assumptions about the dominance of forest fallow agriculture which (as the previous section described) are highly questionable, the critical evidence for soil degradation and erosion noted in previous studies of buried soils has now been effectively destroyed by a reassessment of their pedogenesis (Fisher, 1982).

Major fluctuations in third millennium farming cannot be discerned in Wessex. The distribution of henges indicates the same territorial units as before, with transects of country from the valley floors to the upland plateaus. The presumed domestic sites (the pits and hearths) were again on the lighter soils in these territories, and water flotation at three such sites with Grooved Ware has recovered grains of emmer, bread wheat, barley, legumes and fallow species, as well as crab apples and hazelnuts (Jones, 1980). The faunal material from the henges has to be treated with the same caution as that from the causewayed enclosures as a reflection of ritual activity (Harcourt, 1971, 1979a) – patterns of bone breaking and dispersal at Durrington Walls, for example, were extremely complex (J. Thomas: pers. comm.). However, mature cows again dominated the cattle sample at this site, and Legge (1981a) concluded that they were probably, as before, the surplus animals brought in from settlements elsewhere. Environmental analysis of buried soils under later neolithic monuments has repeatedly indicated open grassland on the Wessex uplands, but this was an extension rather than a transformation of the grazing conditions here *c.* 3000 b.c.

Pollen and molluscan samples indicate ever more extensive open country in Wessex during the first half of the second millennium b.c., in valleys as well as on the plateaus, as drier conditions developed (Bell, 1981; Evans, 1975). Given the dearth of settlement data to set alongside the barrow cemeteries, Fleming (1971) argued that this landscape was inhabited by transhumant pastoralists, who brought their stock up onto the higher ground around the cemeteries (where their leaders were buried) in the summer and moved them down to the coastal lowlands or major river valleys in the winter. However, although animal husbandry was undoubtedly important, there is clear evidence now for mixed farming, probably associated with much more organised systems of land ownership. Most of the 'Celtic' field systems of southern England probably date after *c.* 1500 b.c., but associations with barrows and artifact distributions suggest very strongly that some systems in Wessex were laid out in the first half of the second millennium. Ard furrows have been noted under several barrows, and cereal impressions have now been found in early bronze age pottery. Amongst the blocks of fields were small settlements of round houses, and sunken droveways led through the fields to stock pens (Coles and Harding, 1979: 246–8). Faunal samples from barrows and enclosures such as Rams Hill (Bradley and Ellison, 1975) indicate that sheep were increasing in importance alongside cattle, presumably in response to the dry and open environment. The evidence therefore suggests that the agricultural base of Wessex society by the mid-second millennium was still mixed farming, but on a much more intensive scale to support higher populations: territorial divisions were much as before, but land tenure was now formalised by field systems, the layout of which implies overall planning rather than piecemeal development and the use of organised labour in their cultivation, although little is understood of the extent to which land was managed and owned at the household level rather as in medieval peasant economies, or by larger groupings or collectives with more flexible access to land (Fleming, in press). Presumably the detailed division of the landscape was primarily in response to the competing needs of arable and pastoral farming in each territory; the range of soils encompassed by the new fields also implies an increased ability to tackle heavier land. We assume that the production and control of an agricultural surplus were at least as integral to chieftain power in Wessex as their postulated command of mineral traffic, regional ritual, astronomical observations and so on, although at present this can be no more than speculation (Burgess, 1980: 103).

Comparable evidence for landscape planning in this period, but for an entirely different agricultural system, has been found by the major investigations of the Fengate region east of Peterborough in the Midlands (Pryor, 1976, 1978, 1980). Prehistoric settlement here concentrated on the gravel terraces of the river Nene, at the point where the river entered the fens; in the second millennium b.c. there were pasture and open scrub on the marginal fens and reed and sedge marsh nearer the sea. In the first two or three centuries of the second millennium, a ring-ditch farmstead was established on the fen edge, adjoined by several small rectangular enclosures, and wells were also constructed. About the same time, a large system of similar fields was laid out along the gravel terrace to the northeast, with the axis of the fields at right angles to the fens (Fig. 76). The fields were marked out by ditches, and probably also by banks and hedges; narrow trackways led into the fields from the fens, and phosphate analysis indicated that these were in fact droveways for animals. The mainstay of the agricultural system was animal husbandry. Cattle made up some 70% of the faunal sample and most were mature, suggesting that activities such as dairying were important; in fact the very slight dental attrition of one human skeleton from the site led Dr Calvin Wells to report that 'this woman's basic diet was fairly soft: perhaps she lived largely on cheese, porridges and similar food' (Pryor, 1976: 41). In the medieval period cattle were taken out to graze on the fens in the summer and brought back to the main settlements on the margins as the fens flooded in the winter, and Pryor argued for a similar method of prehistoric husbandry. The construction of the elaborate field system and reliable water supply represented a major intensification in land use, replacing earlier extensive systems of grazing which did not require such controlled use of the winter pastures. Given the settlement pattern of small non-nucleated farmsteads spread across the enclosure system, the likelihood is that this shift from extensive to intensive cattle-keeping reflects increased pressure of people and animals on the landscape, but not the emergence of a stratified hierarchical society as in Wessex. Rather similar systems of seasonal pastoralism at this time have been proposed for the Ouse valley (Green, 1976) and the Somerset Levels (Coles and Hibbert, 1975), and may also be represented in the Vale of Belvoir (Hills and Liddon, 1981).

Subsistence intensification can also be discerned in northern England, but with

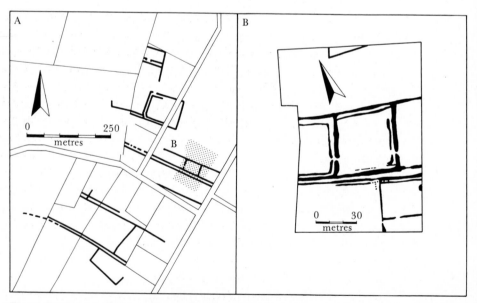

Fig. 76. Prehistoric settlement at Fengate, Peterborough, in the early second millennium b.c.: (A) general plan of the field system; (B) detail of the northern part of the system (stippled in the general plan). (After Pryor, 1976: figs. 3.2 and 3.6)

territorial divisions being marked symbolically rather than by fixed boundaries. In the Derbyshire Peak, the limestone plateau was colonised for permanent settlement in the later third millennium, probably from the Trent valley. Each community exploited a block of land which enabled the farmers to cultivate their crops on the deeper loessic soils of the plateau depressions and graze their stock variously on the surrounding plateau and in the major valleys that dissect it (Hawke-Smith, 1979, 1981). The distribution of chambered tombs suggests that the siting of community burials served to underline territorial rights. There was a major expansion of settlement onto the gritstone uplands during the first half of the second millennium, where cereal cultivation at high altitudes is indicated by pollen diagrams, clearance plots and small fields (Hart, 1981; Hicks, 1971; Machin, 1973; Fig. 77). By *c*. 1500 b.c. settlement in the Peak appears to have reached the environmental limits for cereal cultivation, stimulated by the warmer climate of the time – summer temperatures were 2–3°C higher than today and winter temperatures perhaps 1.0–1.5°C higher (Taylor, 1975). As before, barrows were used as a symbolic expression of territorial control, although the distribution of particular burial forms may indicate that certain areas were available as common grazing for different communities (Hawke-Smith, 1981). On the north Yorkshire moors, detailed fieldwork by Spratt (1981) has allowed a plausible model of contemporary land use at the head of the Rye valley. The main settlements were on the lower ground (though many have probably been obscured by soil wash), linked to satellite camps on the high ground now marked by cairn fields; deep hollow-ways led up to these from the lower ground (Fig. 78). An arable/pastoral economy was practised, with the main community working the land in the valleys and herdsmen taking the stock onto the moors as soon as there was pasture or woodland browse in the spring. Natural boundaries such as rivers and watersheds divide the region into a series of agricultural 'estates', each with valley and riverside terrain and about eight square kilometres of moorland; the watershed was marked by a series of intervisible barrows, suggesting again the 'ritualised control over land and society, maintained and regulated by the artifacts and monuments' (Pierpoint, 1981: 53).

There is little detailed information about subsistence at this time on the Scottish mainland, but on the islands to the north and west there is consistent evidence for the development of crofting systems of mixed farming and coastal foraging. In Orkney, palaeobotanical studies have demonstrated that the characteristically bleak and treeless landscape of today was fundamentally the same in the late third millennium b.c. (Davidson *et al.*, 1976; Jones, 1979). The subsistence data from both settlements and tombs indicate that all the major resources of the traditional crofting economy were already exploited by these communities (Table 17). Modern excavations at Skara Brae, the Knap of Howar and Isbister have recovered quantities of carbonised grain, principally naked six-row barley (Clarke, 1976; Ritchie, 1975; Hedges, 1983). This crop, known as *bere* in Orkney, was important in recent crofting because it withstands wet weather better, matures earlier, and thrives on poorer soils, than other cereals. In the Isbister sample the crop was heavily intermixed with the seeds of what are today regarded as undesirable weeds, but which were probably consumed in neolithic times as they were in the eighteenth century, when 'the daily fare consisted of a "morning

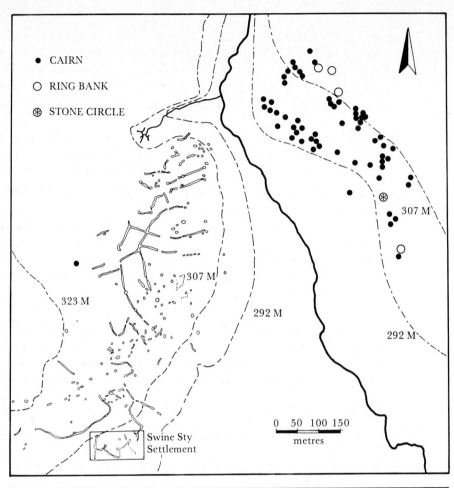

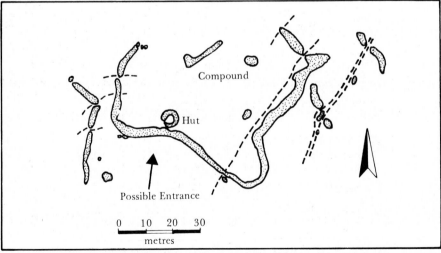

Fig. 77. Agricultural settlement at Swine Sty in the Derbyshire Peak District in the second millennium b.c.: a bronze age landscape with an upland farm, its fields, clearance cairns and ritual monuments. (After Hart, 1981: figs. 6.5 and 6.9)

piece" of half a bannock of bread made from *bere* mixed with seeds of all kinds of weeds' (Handley, 1953: 80). The sheep and cattle in the faunal samples were very small and slender; similarities between the neolithic sheep of Orkney and the modern fine-limbed Soay sheep of western Scotland have been noted by several archaeozoologists (Clutton-Brock, 1975; Platt, 1934; Watson, 1931), and in the historic period, too, the small size of Orkney sheep and cattle was a subject of comment by visitors to the islands – 'the most stunted animals in the whole of Great Britain' (Handley, 1953: 108), presumably an adaptation to the harsh environment and lack of winter fodder. The few cattle and sheep that could be kept in recent crofting systems were particularly important for their milk and, in the case of sheep, for their wool (Fenton, 1976); exactly the same herding regime seems likely from the prehistoric faunal samples.

In addition to the crops and animals, harvesting the resources of the sea was an integral part of neolithic subsistence on Orkney. The large middens of shellfish (oysters, limpets, shelks, razor fish and so on) have provided the bulk of the evidence until recently, but the modern excavations have recovered very large quantities of fish bones as well. Most of the fish could have been caught by hook or gorge line fishing or by spear from the shore, although some of the species must have been fished offshore from small boats (A. Wheeler, 1979). Fish has an overwhelming importance in the diet in historical crofting, filling the hungry gap before harvest in the days before the potato. The role of the shellfish for the prehistoric crofters is rather problematical. In recent times shellfish were normally a starvation food only, and Clarke (1976: 22) suggested that the shellfish

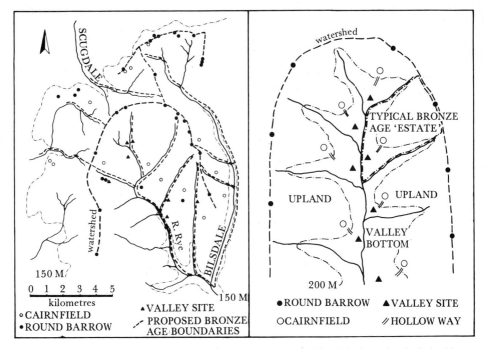

Fig. 78. Second millennium settlement in the Rye valley, north Yorkshire: left, the archaeological evidence and proposed territorial divisions; right, the model of a bronze age 'estate'. (After Spratt, 1981: figs. 7.3/5 and 7.6)

Table 17 *Fauna reported at neolithic sites in Orkney.* (x = *reported;* X = *reported as common*)

	cat	cattle	dog	fox	horse	otter	pig	rabbit	red deer	sheep	cretacean	fish	seabird	shellfish	Source
Blackhammer		x							x	X		x	x	x	Platt 1936–7a
Calf of Eday		?	x							?		?	?	?	Platt 1936–7b
Howar		X					x		x	X	x	x	x	x	Platt 1936–7c; Ritchie 1975
Isbister		X	x				x	x	x	x	X	x	x	x	x	Barker, 1983
Knowe of Ramsay		x							X	x		x	x	x	Platt 1935–6
Knowe of Yarso		x	x						X	x		x	x	x	Platt 1934–5
Midhowe		X					x		x	x		x	x	x	Platt 1934
Quanterness	x	X	x	x	x	x	x	x	x	X	x	x	x	x	Renfrew 1979
Rinyo		x							x	x	x				Childe 1938–9
Skara Brae		X					x		x	X	x	x	x	x	Watson 1931
Stones of Stenness	x	x								x					Clutton-Brock 1975

at Skara Brae were primarily collected as fish bait, but given that neolithic farmers did not have recourse to crops like the potato and oats, it is likely that harvesting the total range of marine resources was customary. In the same way sea birds and their eggs have tended to be a useful supplement rather than a staple resource in the crofting diet except in really marginal situations, but both were found in some quantities at Skara Brae. The clear impression is that neolithic subsistence on Orkney involved a very broad spectrum of plant and animal husbandry, fishing, gathering and hunting. Contemporary crofting in the western islands was very similar (Burgess, 1976; Shepherd, 1976; Simpson, 1976).

The archaeological record for Ireland between 2500 and 1500 b.c. is prolific. The burial monuments include the enormous and lavishly decorated passage graves of the Boyne valley and their satellite tombs, hilltop passage grave cemeteries to the west such as Loughcrew, isolated gallery graves in the south (more or less identical to those of northern France), and a wide variety of smaller related forms. Copper mines such as those of Mount Gabriel in the far southwest were possibly being worked at this time, and Irish craftsmen working in copper and gold were amongst the best in Europe. However, whilst some sort of stratified society and economic surplus are implied in many parts of Ireland by these artifacts and monuments, there is hardly any precise information about the agricultural system. Some of the best data derive from the Boyne valley, which today supports an agricultural population of about 1200 people, but which Mitchell (1976) calculated may have had to sustain a workforce two or three times larger to build the passage graves. An integrated system of mixed farming has been reconstructed for the beaker settlement established on the Newgrange passage grave (Groenman-van Waateringe and Pals, 1982; Wijngaarden-Bakker, 1974, 1981). Cereals and legumes (emmer, barley, vetch) were grown here probably in some sort of rotation system, with the arable land manured by the stock (principally cattle and pigs). Animal husbandry was generalised: bullocks were raised for meat, cows for breeding and perhaps dairying, pigs for meat (some of which was probably smoked), sheep for milk, wool and meat, and horses for riding and traction. Elsewhere, agricultural d largely indirect, restricted to vegetational changes in the pollen record (Lynch, 1981; Smith, 1975). However, at Behy-Glenulra in County Mayo long strip fields and associated enclosures have been interpreted in terms of a cattle-based system of husbandry, sustaining a network of dispersed families in isolated farmsteads with little evidence of social stratification – rather similar to the Fengate settlement system (Caulfield, 1978; Fig. 79). Other field systems buried under peat indicate that the traditional methods of ridged cultivation still used today to combat poor drainage ('lazy beds') had probably been developed by this period (Herity and Eogan, 1977: 50).

Climatic change and late bronze age farming, *c.* 1500–500 b.c.

In his major analysis of later prehistory in Britain, Burgess (1980) argued for a sharp break in most aspects of the archaeological record on either side of *c.* 1100/1000 b.c., with the 'Age of Stonehenge' on one side and the 'Age of Hillforts' on the other. In the uplands, many open settlements and fields were abandoned and defended settlements were established; in the lowlands hillforts were also constructed, and 'ranch boundaries' (long linear earthworks) cut across the existing agricultural landscape. The emphasis on fortifications coincided with the development of more efficient bronze weaponry. 'This was an agricultural and population crisis, building up for some time, but as long as new

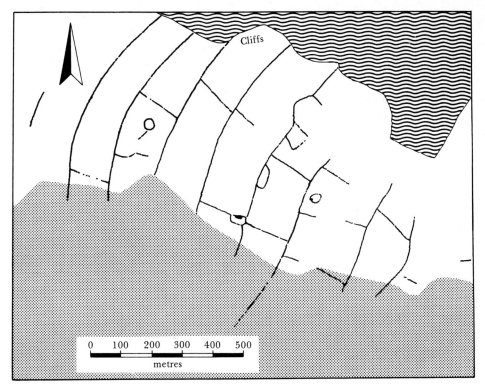

Fig. 79. Prehistoric fields and farmsteads at Behy-Glenulra, County Mayo; stippling marks the approximate limit of the cutaway peatbog. (After Caulfield, 1978: fig. 19.1)

lands could be opened up and even larger tracts enclosed by field systems it could be kept at bay. This whole complex process now collapsed over the length and breadth of the country' (Burgess, 1980: 157). He concluded that the trigger for this social and economic collapse was the sudden worsening of the climate at the end of the second millennium (the transition to the Sub-Atlantic), which forced people to abandon their upland farms in the face of the expansion of blanket bog and rough grazing, and, on the lowlands, to specialise increasingly in stock-keeping, agricultural trends which inevitably stimulated the emergence of a more warlike society. The major thrust of the argument has been repeated in several syntheses (e.g. Barrett and Bradley, 1980; Bradley, 1971, 1978b; Fowler, 1981a, 1981b; Mercer, 1981).

However, whilst the general phenomenon of climatic deterioration at around this period is undoubted, its detailed chronology, scale and impact are in fact much less clear than this model implies: whilst the major impact of the climatic deterioration in most areas was probably in the first half of the first millennium b.c., it is now clear that the suddenness and uniformity of the event have been greatly exaggerated (Dansgaard *et al.*, 1969; Moore, 1973; Mörner and Wallin, 1977; Tinsley, 1981). Radiocarbon dates of peat deposits indicate a broad trend to more oceanic conditions, developing first in western Ireland and northwest Scotland perhaps as early as the late third millennium and reaching Wales and western England by the late second millennium; the main highland areas were affected at different times and in different ways in the late second and early first millennia (Tinsley, 1981). In the fens, too, modern research indicates major differences in the extent and chronology of inundation over comparatively short distances. As Whittle (1982) has argued, not only is the chronology of landscape change much more complex than commonly envisaged, but so also was its impact on settlement: in most areas – whether moorland, down or fen – the environmental changes demanded the adjustment rather than the abandonment of the agricultural system. Responses not only varied considerably from region to region in relation to ecological change but also reflect very considerable differences in the complexity of regional economies.

In southwest England the site of Gwithian in Cornwall has provided quite detailed information about the layout of a small farmstead used for mixed farming on the coastal lowlands (Megaw, 1976; Fig. 80). At the end of the second millennium there were two or three main buildings here set amongst a cluster of very small fields. Preserved in the sand within the fields were the criss-cross furrows left by ard cultivation; a fragment of greenstone in one of the furrows was probably part of the stone tip of a light wooden ard and domestic rubbish scattered across the fields indicates that the land was almost certainly manured. The edges of the fields could not be cultivated effectively with the ard, and were dug by hand – marks were preserved here of a heart-shaped implement very similar to the wooden 'rope traction ard' of Satrup Moor (Steensberg, 1973; Fig. 89) or the modern continental (and Cornish) shovel. No evidence was found for cattle stalling here, but at the contemporary and similar Cornish farmstead of Trevisker, the worn floor of one building was thought to have resulted from mucking-out operations (ApSimon and Greenfield, 1972).

Dartmoor has long been recognised as one of the best preserved areas of later bronze age settlement in Britain (Fox, 1973), and recent investigations of the land boundaries ('reaves') there have revealed a remarkable and hitherto unsuspected system of agricultural planning and territorial organisation (Fleming, 1978, 1979; Fleming and Collis, 1973). The upper part of the moor was enclosed by a contour reave; the river valleys radiating out from the centre were further divided from each other by boundary reaves; and within each territory so defined was a portion of land carefully divided up by adjacent parallel reaves (Fig. 81). Each territory contained a major settlement complex, but other domestic sites were located elsewhere in the enclosed transect and on the moor above the contour reave. Fleming (1978) concluded that Dartmoor was divided up into half a dozen territorial units, with each group of communities ('sociopolitical groups whose activities transcended those of the individual farm or hamlet', p. 103) controlling their enclosed valley and the parallel reave system within it, and having access to common grazing on the high moor. Subsistence data are very poorly preserved in the acidic soils, but pollen, soil and macrobotanical studies of the settlement and reave excavations on Shaugh Moor suggest mixed farming with a heavy dependence on stock-keeping; the excavations here even found the stock routes around the farm, where animal footprints had been preserved in the trampled ground (Balaam *et al.*, 1982; K. Smith *et al.*, 1981). A rather similar system of land use may have operated earlier in the second millennium, but with land divisions marked by ceremonial monuments rather than fixed boundaries; there then seems to have been a preliminary system of wooden hurdles before the earth and stone reaves were constructed. Perhaps fixed boundaries became necessary as population increase put pressure on the land, with the major contour reave being constructed

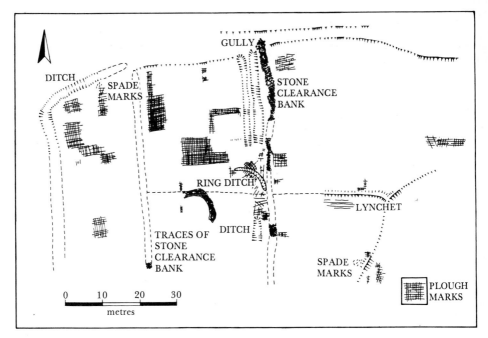

Fig. 80. The Gwithian (Cornwall) farm and its fields in the late second millennium b.c. (After Megaw, 1976: fig. 4.1)

late in the history of the system as the spread of blanket bog on the upper moor demanded an increased control of private and common grazing.

On the Sussex downs the main agricultural unit was the single family farm, consisting of three main structural components: a large circular living hut; ancillary huts used variously for food preparation, weaving, fodder storage and perhaps cattle stalling; and

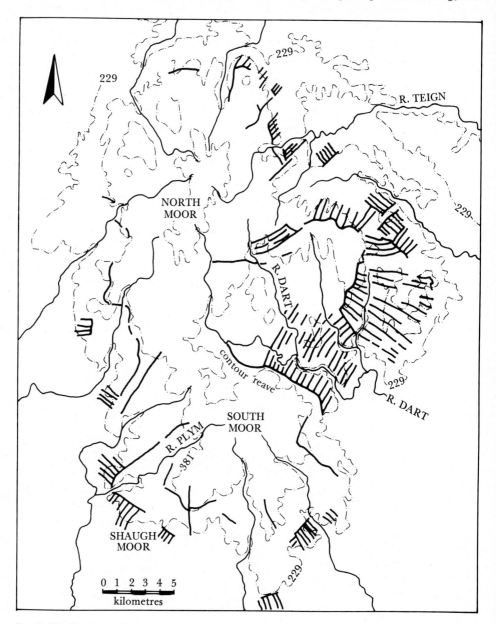

Fig. 81. The Dartmoor reave system: the area is divided by the reaves (low banks) into a series of territorial units based on the rivers which radiate from the central upland; each unit has a parallel reave system assumed to be the main agricultural land, with access to common grazing on the high moor. (After Fleming, 1978: fig. 2, with additional information kindly provided by Andrew Fleming; contours in metres)

further storage facilities nearby in the form of small pits cut into the chalk or four or six post timber structures most commonly assumed to be platform granaries (Drewett, 1980, 1982; Ellison, 1978). The major and ancillary huts were probably for males and females respectively. The compounds of these farms were defined by low banks, ditches, hedges or palisades, and connected to a cluster of small rectangular fields (Fig. 82). The farms were located on the edge of the chalk, where they had easy access to light arable soils nearby, dry pasture on the downland above, and wet pasture in the lower valleys, with parallel strip transects rather than the radial transects of Dartmoor (Ellison and Harriss, 1972). Most of the settlements have produced evidence for mixed farming: cattle and sheep were the main stock, loom weights and spindle whorls are common, and emmer, spelt, barley and legumes were the main crops (Burstow and Holleyman, 1957; Drewett, 1982; Table 18). The indications are that rotational systems of cultivation were practised, and spreads of household rubbish in the fields are almost certainly the result of manuring. The subsistence data are not precise enough to investigate whether the farms were self-sufficient units, but there are some indications otherwise. Apart from the burial and artifactual evidence for ranking, there is a major enclosure in their midst (Highdown Hill) where the concentration of bronze and gold suggests 'a higher-ranking function, possibly linked to a developing system of redistribution' (Ellison, 1978: 36). As all the farms would have had the same range of surplus, redistribution on the downs was probably for social reasons (for bride wealth, gift exchange and so on), although these communities were also linked in exchange systems beyond the downs to the major river valleys, the coastal plain and the Weald (Drewett, 1982: 398–9).

In southern England generally there is increasing evidence for surplus production, the exchange of foodstuffs and differentiation and specialisation at the regional scale. At

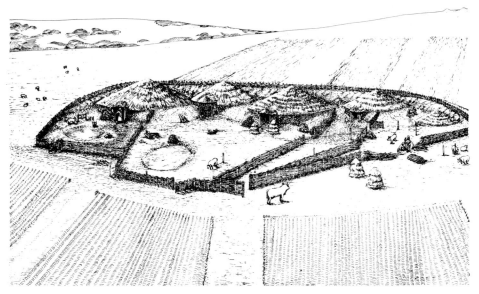

Fig. 82. A reconstruction of one of the Black Patch farmsteads, Sussex. (Published by Drewett, 1982: plate 30; original kindly provided by the artist, Lysbeth Drewett)

Table 18 *Evidence for food production at the Black Patch settlement, Sussex*

	Surviving elements of the tool kit	Surviving features	Surviving waste products
1. *Growing crops*		lynchets	carbonised seeds (barley, beans, cabbage, emmer, spelt)
2. *Collecting wild food*			carbonised seeds (blackberry, chickweed, goosegrass, hazel nut, orache, sloe)
			marine molluscs (cockle, limpet, mussel, periwinkle)
3. *Animal husbandry*		trackways, enclosures, pounds; calf/lambing huts?; fence lines?	animal bones (cattle, sheep, pig)
4. *Hunting*			animal bones (bird, red deer)
5. *Storing food*	pottery	pits	
6. *Food preparation*	flint scrapers flint flakes for cutting? quernstones hammerstones for crushing food?		
7. *Water storage*	pottery	ponds	
8. *Making fires*	fabricators ('strike-a-light' flints) iron pyrite nodules		fire-cracked flints charcoal

(After Drewett, 1982: table 1)

Rams Hill in Berkshire, for example, a ditch and palisade enclosure protected a typical farmstead with male and female residential units (Bradley and Ellison, 1975); the dominance of the main meat-bearing bones over cranial and extremity bones indicated that the cattle and sheep consumed at the site had been butchered elsewhere, a bias also found in the Eldon's Seat farmstead in Dorset (Carter, 1975; Cunliffe and Phillipson, 1968). In the Kennet valley near Reading there were arable-based settlements on or near what are today the best cereal soils in the district, and stock-based settlements on low islands of dry soil surrounded by seasonally waterlogged pasture. At Aldermaston Wharf, one of the arable-based farms, the pits around a lower status building had only the capacity for storing the grain needed for the single family, but a considerable surplus above the family's needs could be stored around the higher status building (Bradley *et al.*, 1980). Rowlands (1980) has argued that the location of high ranking sites in this period was increasingly determined by access to prestige trade, and the most abundant and richest metalwork has been found in the Thames valley, the major communication route of the region. Metal is far more common in the Kennet valley than on the downs, and Bradley concluded that the Kennet sites, whilst not of the highest status, were clearly producing a surplus for exchange, and were 'probably engaged in intensive production both to produce tribute for an elite living in the Thames valley and as part of a wider attempt to convert surplus into social prestige' (Bradley *et al.*, 1980: 293).

In East Anglia and the Midlands there are similar indications of increasing differentiation in agricultural organisation alongside social status. At one end of the economic spectrum, perhaps, was the settlement at Grimes Graves in the Breckland heaths, which seems to have been a more or less self-sufficient farming community in a rather marginal environment, where the arable soils are easily worked but tend to be somewhat infertile and prone to drought; calculations of the productivity of the agricultural system suggested a likely community of about fifty people and a cattle herd including a dozen or so cows, with dairy products being an important part of the diet (Legge, 1981b). At Fengate the linear field systems seem to have been abandoned early in the first millennium b.c. as the summer fenland grazing was inundated (Pryor, 1980), but settlement continued elsewhere in the wetlands: at Billingborough in Lincolnshire, for example, a very similar system of land use survived well into the first millennium b.c. (Chowne, 1978, 1980). Although nothing in the subsistence data from these sites indicates anything other than self-sufficiency, the fenland communities were now probably part of a wider regional economy and social hierarchy: the marked distribution of bronze weaponry along the major rivers of Lincolnshire, rather than (as before) in the regions of greatest agricultural productivity, has been taken to indicate the existence of an elite group controlling trade and supported by agricultural produce from the hinterland (Gardiner, 1980).

Northern England also witnessed important changes in settlement and society at this time. In the Peak District there is widespread palaeoenvironmental evidence for land deterioration – heath formation, podsolisation, erosion and so on – related to climatic deterioration but also perhaps precipitated by overexploitation (deforestation, overgrazing, overcultivation) earlier in the second millennium in the phase of maximum agricultural colonisation (Hawke-Smith, 1979: 184–5). The farms on the impoverished soils of the gritstone uplands and on the less resilient soils of the limestone plateau were abandoned; much of the high ground developed into pasture or rough grazing best suited to sheep farming; and defensive enclosures such as Mam Tor (if the defences there are as old as the dated house platforms) were established, each of which controlled blocks of such grazing – territories were now visibly defended on the ground and perhaps defended by force of arms. On the Yorkshire wolds, Hambledon Hills and north Yorkshire moors there were not dissimilar developments: the territorial boundaries once marked symbolically by barrow lines were formalised by systems of linear ditches and dykes, and major defended settlements were established to protect the centralised power structure (Pierpoint, 1981; Spratt, 1981). At one such site, Thwing, detailed faunal analysis has indicated a fundamental shift in agricultural organisation when the site was fortified, 'from a more or less self-sufficient village slaughtering animals as and when required for domestic needs, to a more complex economy in which Thwing became the centre of some kind of regional redistribution or tribute system, with groups of selected animals being brought to the site for slaughter in quite substantial numbers on separate occasions' (Mounteney, 1981: 83).

Evidence for broadly contemporary settlement in the form of hut circles, clearance cairns and field systems is prolific in many other parts of upland Britain, and there is increasing evidence for the construction of defended enclosures in the first half of the first millennium b.c. (Challis and Harding, 1975; Feachem, 1973; Ritchie, 1970). Whilst the detailed chronology and character of the settlement and environmental changes are still very ambiguous, broadly similar trends in land use have been postulated: the abandonment of marginal land for cultivation, a concomitant increase in pastoralism, and the use of defended enclosures to protect grazing territories, perhaps in the context of landscape degradation. In coastal Scotland the crofting economy continued unchanged (Tinsley, 1981: 224). The nature of the agricultural economy in Ireland eludes us completely, despite the importance of the island for other aspects of bronze age studies.

Late prehistoric farming: the foundations of the British agricultural landscape

British iron age society is normally characterised as hierarchical, tribal and warlike, but there were probably distinct regional differences in this pattern, with the widest social spectrum in the lowland areas of greatest agricultural wealth and population density. In southern England in particular, the acceleration in cultural complexity in the last century or so before Caesar was enormous: massive nucleated settlements (oppida) were seats of tribal government and centres of both regional and long distance trade, and the economic structure included the centralised production and marketing of wheel-made pottery, querns and salt on an industrial scale, the use of standardised units of measure for trade, and the development of superb craftsmanship in metals and glass. In fact these may have been state societies, with the oppida fulfilling most if not all of the functions of the Roman towns which were to replace them (Collis, 1971, 1979b; Cunliffe, 1974, 1976; Haselgrove, 1976).

Bog stratigraphies indicate that the climatic deterioration of the early first millennium b.c. was replaced by warmer drier conditions after about 400 b.c., and pollen diagrams in many parts of Britain show deforestation on a far greater scale than before (Turner, 1981). Both trends in many regions tended to favour sheep rather than cattle in husbandry systems, although increased reliance on sheep was also related to other factors. The classic investigation of iron age farming was Bersu's excavation of Little Woodbury in Wiltshire, where structural and subsistence data indicated a system of mixed farming, with grain cultivation playing a major role (Bersu, 1940; Helbaek, 1953). Piggott (1958) argued for a dichotomy between an arable-based 'Little Woodbury economy' in the lowland zone and a pastoral-based 'Stanwick economy' in the highland zone (named after Stanwick in Yorkshire where contemporary excavations by Mortimer Wheeler had revealed a possible stock corral). Whilst there is still some truth in the lowland arable/highland pastoral dichotomy, the major disparity was in the scale and organisation of agricultural production in the two zones.

The settlement record in Wessex is extremely complex, with both enclosed settlements and hillforts varying enormously in size, defences, and internal organisation; furthermore, interpretation of many of the structures within these sites is often problematical (Chapter 1, p. 13). However, the agricultural system of several individual farms can be reconstructed in reasonable detail. The principal crops were normally spring-sown hulled barley and autumn-sown spelt wheat, with emmer and perhaps other cereals as subsidiaries as well as legumes; rotation cropping was practised, and both cattle and sheep were used to manure the arable. Of course cropping systems varied according to the soils cultivated: in Hampshire, for example, wheat tends to be more common at sites on clay loams and barley at sites on the dry light chalk soils (Monk and Fasham, 1980; Murphy, 1977). The cereals were cut with iron reaping hooks and perhaps dried on racks; the main crop was then stored in pits, probably sealed with clay (Reynolds, 1974), and (perhaps) the seed corn stored in platform granaries. Fields were ploughed with light wooden ards, although these could now be tipped with iron shares; they were probably pulled by one or two oxen. The faunal samples normally consist of cattle, sheep/goat (primarily sheep), pigs, horses, and dogs; all of these were eaten, but cattle and sheep were the main stock. All the stock were extremely small by modern standards. A bias towards mature cattle and sheep has often been noted and taken to indicate the importance of secondary products as well as meat (Carter and Phillipson, 1965; Cunliffe and Phillipson, 1968; Hamilton, in Parrington, 1978; Harcourt, 1979b; Wilson, in Parrington, 1978), a conclusion supported by the artifactual evidence in the settlements for dairying, weaving and hide processing. Subsistence data have not been published in similar detail for many of the hillforts, but there are consistent indications of mixed farming in the form of storage pits, ancillary pens and carefully divided grazing and arable areas in the vicinity (Fig. 83).

Moreover, agricultural organisation at a regional scale integrating a hierarchy of different types of settlement has become increasingly clear from recent subsistence studies in Wessex. At Old Down Farm in Hampshire, for example, the quantities of meat represented in some of the one-off faunal dumps were too large for immediate consumption by the community: either surplus meat was cured for later consumption at the site or, more likely, it left the site in some kind of exchange or tribute system (Maltby, in Davies, 1981). In the Thames valley there were major villages such as Ashville practising intensive crop cultivation on the upper terraces (Parrington, 1978) and small pastoral camps on the floodplain such as Farmoor (Lambrick and Robinson, 1979). Plant remains were abundant at the arable sites and included both processed debris and waste crops, whereas they were sparse at the pastoral sites and consisted of only weeds and chaff. Hence Jones (in press) argues that the latter were cereal consumers, not producers, who relied on communities such as Ashville for their grain. There are similar differences between 'producer' and 'consumer' plant residues at sites in Hampshire (Monk and Fasham, 1980). However, there was more than simply local exchange of foodstuffs (Jones, in press). The crop residues at Danebury suggest that semi-processed crops were brought to this major hillfort for final cleaning and were then stored. The presence of weeds from a variety of damp and dry habitats in the material, and combinations of these in individual samples, indicate the bulk processing of a large volume of crops entering the hillfort from satellite farms in different parts of its territory. Furthermore, the fact that the cereals reaching small consumer sites such as Farmoor were at the semi-processed state (as they would have left producer sites like Ashville) and not fully cleaned (as they would have left Danebury) suggests that the hillfort stores which were not consumed by the hillfort community were primarily designed for extra-territorial trade rather than intra-territorial redistribution. Strabo listed the main British exports to the Roman market as corn, cattle, gold, silver, hides, slaves and clever hunting dogs. The trade in foodstuffs which was probably one of the cornerstones of chiefly power in southern England may not, after all, prove to be so completely undetectable as commonly supposed.

One of the most imaginative reconstructions of an iron village has been proposed by Clarke (1972) for Glastonbury in Somerset, a waterlogged settlement excavated between 1892 and 1907 by Bulleid and Gray (1911, 1917). The village was inhabited from *c.* 150 to *c.* 50 b.c., growing in that time from four to seven residence units each occupied by an extended family. Structural and artifactual variations in each unit indicated a major familial and multi-activity area on the one hand and a minor, largely female and domestic area on the other (Fig. 84). Differences in the range and quality of the artifacts suggested that the central unit was occupied by the village head man, with the peripheral units in some kind of client relationship. The community grew spelt, barley and legumes, and kept a substantial flock of sheep (200–1000 head), a herd of perhaps 20–30 cattle, 10–20 ponies and a few dozen pigs and dogs. The flock would have pro-

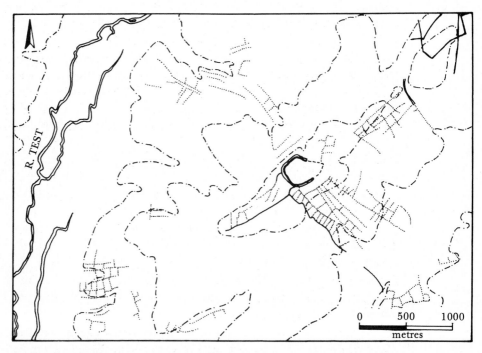

Fig. 83. The agricultural landscape around the Woolbury hillfort in Hampshire, assumed to show the division between arable fields and open pasture. (After Cunliffe, 1974: fig. 11.16)

duced sufficient wool for 40–200 blankets or perhaps the fine woollen cloaks which were a famed export from southwest England to the Roman world (Clarke, 1972: 860). The granary capacities also indicated a modest surplus in grain beyond the requirements of the village and its stock. Glastonbury probably owed its political allegiance and tribute (presumably mainly textiles) to the major hillfort of Maesbury on the winter grazing of the Mendip limestone hills a dozen kilometres away. A further indication of the complexity of the regional economy of Somerset has come from the re-excavation of the Meare 'lake village', now interpreted as some kind of regional fair, a meeting place in the marshes and used intensively by a number of communities for a few weeks each year during the summer (Orme *et al.*, 1981). Elsewhere in lowland England there are hints of regional agricultural systems linking different parts of the local settlement hierarchy, but with nothing like the subsistence detail available in Wessex and Somerset: for example, in Essex (Drury, 1978, 1980), Lincolnshire (May, 1970, 1976), the Trent valley (C. Smith, 1977, 1978; H. Wheeler, 1979), the Yorkshire wolds (Brewster, 1963; Challis and Harding, 1975; Stead, 1968), and the northeastern lowlands (Heslop, in press; van der Veen, 1984).

The Pennines were far less densely populated. In the Derbyshire Peak, blanket peat had spread over the gritstone by *c.* 300 b.c. (Hicks, 1971), so that the agricultural pattern was much as today: the limestone plateau supported small scale mixed farming with a pastoral bias, and the gritstone moors provided supplementary rough grazing for sheep (Hawke-Smith, 1979). Peat growth on the north Yorkshire moors was at much the same rate (Atherden, 1972), and the agricultural system contracted accordingly, with small farms in the valleys using the moors for rough grazing: 'by the end of the Iron Age, it appears that the essential lineaments of the present landscape were clear' (Spratt and Simmons, 1976: 207). In the central and northern Pennines, too, there is a similar settlement record of small dispersed farms at lower elevations and sometimes shielings on the high fells (Jobey, 1966; Raistrick, 1939). There is the strong impression (as Piggott originally pointed out) from site location, structural organisation and the little subsistence data available that, as the modern landscape of dale and moorland took shape, so too did the essential characteristics of British pastoral-based hill farming. At the same

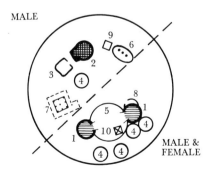

Fig. 84. Model of a residence unit at the late prehistoric village of Glastonbury, Somerset. 1. major house; 2. minor house; 3. ancillary hut (milking parlour/cow house); 4. workshop hut or workfloor; 5. courtyard; 6. baking hut; 7. fenced platform granary; 8. stable; 9. sty or kennel; 10. waggon stance. (Adapted from Clarke, 1972: fig. 21.1)

time, it would be foolhardy to envisage uniform self-sufficiency and pastoral simplicity – Piggott's 'Celtic cowboys and shepherds, footloose and unpredictable, moving with their animals over rough pasture and moorland' (1958: 25) – given the tribal structure that existed at the time of the Roman conquest. The whole of this region was the territory of the Brigantes, whose agricultural system supported kings, nobles and highly skilled craftsmen: the Stanwick hoard of weapons and chariot gear, for example, 'provides a vivid impression of the degree of wealth and display attained by the upper classes of Brigantian society' (Cunliffe, 1974: 112).

There were similar hill-farming societies in most of upland Scotland. In some areas the people lived in small farms but had recourse to large hillforts, in others the farms themselves were fortified (Fairhurst and Taylor, 1971; Feachem, 1966; Small, 1975). At Kilpedhir in eastern Sutherland the density of farms has been taken to imply population levels as high as at the time of the Highland Clearances two centuries ago (Fairhurst, 1971). In coastal regions and in the islands the heavily fortified farm (*broch* or *dun*) was also the norm (Hamilton, 1966); most *brochs* were for single families, probably sustained by crofting (Fig. 85). However, as in the highlands, the agricultural system also supported a highly organised and aristocratic society, and there are occasional large nucleated settlements which must have held 200–300 people (Hedges and Bell, 1980; Lamb, 1980). Little is known of contemporary society in the lowlands, but settlements such as Broxmouth (Hill, 1979) and Dalladies (Watkins, 1978–80) suggest sub-

Fig. 85. The Dun Carloway broch, Lewis, Outer Hebrides, and the typical landscape of the crofting economy: sea and loch, peat-covered hills, and small plots of arable and improved pasture. The black humps by the road are peat stacks, the conical heaps in the first field are stooks of hay drying on wooden racks. (Photograph: author)

stantial mixed farming communities and, perhaps, regional economic structures as complex as in lowland England. Whilst it is true that much of Scotland lacked the political cohesion of other parts of Britain in the late Iron Age, it also seems clear that Cassius Dio's description of the Scots *c*. A.D. 200 'possessing neither walled places nor towns nor cultivated lands, but living by pastoral pursuits and by hunting and on certain kinds of berries . . . they live in tents, naked and shoeless' (Megaw and Simpson, 1979: 491) was, like so much later comment by the outside world on highland culture, a heady mixture of ignorance and wishful thinking.

In Wales, too, the settlement record embraces open settlements and associated field systems in some areas, fortified farmsteads in others, and major nucleated villages in others, but agricultural data for the first two categories of site are very poor (Benson, 1982; Savory, 1980; Wainwright, 1971). Rather more information is available from the large hillforts of the Welsh Marches, once mainly regarded as pastoral enclosures (Alcock, 1965) but now shown to be substantial villages (Gardner and Savory, 1964; Guilbert, 1975, 1976; Musson, 1976; Stanford, 1974). They have all produced evidence for craft production and for mixed farming (the cultivation of spelt and barley, and the rearing of sheep and cattle for secondary products and for meat). Some hillforts have satellite enclosures, and transhumant systems of grazing like those of the historical period are frequently assumed, but the substantial storage facilities at many sites, as well as the evidence that many tribes also controlled mineral ores, traded with the outside world, and sustained a warrior aristocracy and fine craftsmen, imply that a more complex economic system existed than can be discerned from the subsistence data. A recent study comparing the potential agricultural catchments with the size and storage facilities of the Welsh March hillforts concluded that 'grain was probably being sent up to the hillforts from producers located in a wider territory than would be farmed directly from these sites . . . centralised food storage could have been an effective instrument of political policy' (Gent, 1983: 259). In Ireland the commonest form of settlement was the ringfort, normally a fortified farmstead for a single family. There is fragmentary evidence for mixed farming, but the inadequacy of the archaeological record is made abundantly clear by the complexity of Celtic society revealed in the Early Christian sagas: cattle were a major source of wealth for the warrior aristocracy, and their appropriation from neighbours by force of arms the fittest pursuit for heroes.

9

Scandinavia and the eastern Baltic

Geographical introduction

The area discussed in this chapter consists of the countries of northern Europe bordering the Baltic Sea and the Gulf of Bothnia; Denmark; the peninsula of Norway and Sweden; Finland; and the eastern Baltic states of Estonia, Latvia and Lithuania (Fig. 86). The region is very large – some 1500 km west to east and 1750 km from south to north; but much of it, particularly north of about 61° latitude, is inhospitable and sparsely inhabited. Denmark, southern Sweden and the Baltic states have about eighty days of snow a year, whereas there are more than two hundred days of snow north of the Arctic circle and in the central mountains of the Norway/Sweden peninsula. The division is also vegetational: the southern region has mixed deciduous and coniferous forest, whereas in the north are coniferous forests, and tundra in the central mountains.

The Caledonian mountain system forms the backbone of the Norway/Sweden peninsula, reaching in places to about 3000 m above sea level. During the Pleistocene, massive ice sheets covered most of the region. Their final retreat was spasmodic rather than gradual, and resulted in a series of end moraines in an enormous arc running from Denmark to Estonia; the boulder clays of the ground moraines lie inside the arc and the sands of the outwash plains on the outside, the former far more fertile than the latter. The last major deposits were those of transgressional phases of the Baltic, particularly on the coastal margins of Sweden and Finland.

Denmark belongs climatically to western Europe, but in other respects is an integral part of Scandinavia. The western half of the Jutland peninsula is covered by a sandy outwash plain, whereas the eastern half and the main islands of Fünen and Zealand are mantled by boulder clays; there is also a small region of marine clays in the north of Jutland formed at a time of high sea level c. 8000 b.c. The ground moraines of eastern Jutland and the islands provide the basis of Denmark's modern and very successful agricultural industry, contrasting with the poor sandy soils and heaths of western Jutland.

The favourable combination of soils and climate enjoyed by the Danish islands extends across the Oresund channel into the Swedish province of Scania, which has the

Fig. 86. Scandinavia and the eastern Baltic (contours in metres): principal sites and regions mentioned in the text. 1. Komsa; 2. Varanger fjord; 3. Fosna; 4. Bellsås; 5. Tjikkiträsk; 6. Lundvors; 7. Heden; 8. Bjurselet; 9. Norrböle; 10. Ullandhaug; 11. Bjellandsøynae; 12. Oslofjord; 13. Lake Mälaren; 14. Heinola; 15. Antrea; 16. Kunda; 17. Narva; 18. Aggersund; 19. Hvorslev; 20. Ertebølle; 21. Tollund; 22. Ringkloster; 23. Dyrholmen; 24. Meilgaard; 25. Mosegården, Toftum; 26. Vesterlund; 27. Vorbasse; 28. Gadbjerg; 29. Tofting; 30. Satrup Moor; 31. Bundsø; 32. Sarup; 33. Lindebjerg; 34. Langeland island – Lindø, Troldebjerg; 35. Lidsø; 36. Ølby Lyng; 37. Vedbaek.

highest population density and agricultural production in the country as a result. North of this exceptional area, Sweden divides into three regions: the southern peninsula, the central lakeland, and Norrland. In the centre of the southern peninsula are the barren moors and forests of the Småland uplands, but these are girdled by fertile lowlands of marine clay. The central lakeland is the band of country at the head of this peninsula between Göteborg and Stockholm as far north as the Dal river, a mixture of marine clays and morainic material. The natural landscape here is one of forests, swamps and lakes, but over time swamps have been drained and forests cleared for agriculture. Forests still predominate on the less fertile soils. In Norrland (the rest of Sweden north of the Dal river – about 1000 km in length), structure, relief and climate are all unfavourable for settlement. The mountain spine is an expanse of rock, snow and *fjeld* (summer pasture), with enormous coniferous forests at lower elevations. Lakes abound throughout the region, particularly on the edge of the Caledonian mountains. A series of rivers runs northwest to southeast from the central highlands to the Gulf of Bothnia; their lower courses have cut the narrow coastal strip of marine sediments into broad flat terraces, the only soils in Norrland suitable for cultivation.

Norway is even less favoured agriculturally than Sweden and has the lowest population density in Europe. The main region of settlement is the band of marine sediments at the southeastern margin, between Stavanger and Oslo, but even here forests predominate. The influence of the Gulf Stream along the west coast results in relatively mild winters and cool summers, with high precipitation (mostly rain) – up to 2000 mm a year; inland in the mountains winters are much colder and most precipitation falls as snow. Agricultural settlement is possible along the western coast from Stavanger as far north as Trondheim: the traditional fjord economy combined small scale mixed farming with fishing, wintering cattle and sheep in the settlements and taking them up to the *fjeld* summer pastures in the central mountains. Further north, traditional settlement on the coast had to be entirely dependent on the sea. The main spine of the Caledonian mountains in Norway as in Sweden supports a tundra vegetation which can be exploited efficiently only by the reindeer economies of the Lapps, as in their primary zone of settlement in the north of Finland.

Marine sediments on the coast form the major zone of settlement in Finland. The southern belt in particular is favoured because of its warmer climate: the natural zone of mixed deciduous and coniferous forest just extends north to this part of Finland, and today the area supports a thriving dairy industry. Even here, however, the shortness of the growing season is a great limiting factor: 'spring' growth begins only in late June, the hay is cut in late July, the autumn rains return in early September and snow in November (Mead, 1953). Some 75 km inland is the end moraine, and to the north of this is the lake plateau that is the dominant feature of the Finnish landscape and which gave the native name to the country – *Suomi*, the land of lakes and swamps. There are tens of thousands of lakes here set amongst an expanse of coniferous forest, broken only occasionally by pasture clearings and settlements.

Agriculture in Lithuania, Latvia and Estonia, as in southern Finland, has to adapt to a damp climate, a short growing season, and very restricted cultivable soils. Glaciation and its aftermath have left a mosaic of fertile drift, less fertile terminal moraines, and heaths and bogs. The low elevation and confused topography of the moraines have resulted in poor drainage, rivers liable to annual flooding, and innumerable small lakes. The most fertile soils in all three states are on boulder clays. The principal crops are rye, oats, potatoes and flax, but the combination of damp climate and heavy soils is best suited to animal husbandry.

Postglacial foragers in southern Scandinavia

With the rise in temperature at the beginning of the Holocene, the open landscape of the Late Glacial was replaced by forest. In the Pre-Boreal the dominant trees were those able to tolerate relatively low temperatures such as aspen, birch, juniper and willow. The transition to the warmer Boreal was marked in Denmark and southern Sweden by the predominance of hazel and pine, followed by the thermophilous broad-leaved trees – alder, elm, lime, and oak. Alder colonised especially the wetter low ground and lime the higher ground, with elm and oak elsewhere on richer and poorer soils respectively. In the Atlantic, the sands of Jutland still carried an open forest of oak and birch, but mixed oak forest covered much of the rest of southern Scandinavia, although there were innumerable lakes in closed drainage basins and between the forest edge and their open water there was a mixture of alder carr, reed swamp and marshland pasture.

The foragers of southern Scandinavia in the Pre-Boreal and Boreal were equipped with what is termed a Maglemosian technology: flint axes or adzes, wooden bows, wooden arrows armed with flint microliths for game and perhaps fish, one-piece wooden arrows for fowling, bone and antler fish hooks, harpoons and spears and mattocks (Clark, 1975). Most campsites seem to have been occupied by only one or two families, living in simple huts roofed with birch branches and floored with birch bark covered with a sand layer to support the hearth. Some sites were on the coast, but most were on the edge of marshes or on small islets and outcrops of higher ground surrounded by swamp and open water, the preferred habitats of the major game species which dominate Maglemosian faunal samples – aurochs, elk, pig, red deer and roe deer (Anderson, 1961; Bay-Petersen, 1978; Jensen, 1968).

In terms of relative frequencies, red deer and roe deer were the main quarries, but in terms of meat weight the major species were red deer, aurochs and elk. Analysis of tooth eruption and wear stages in red deer mandibles revealed that the Maglemosian hunters were generally selecting animals with the highest meat yields, between two and eight years old. This strategy, by conserving the juveniles which are normally very vulnerable to predation, would have kept the herd at maximum productivity (Bay-Petersen, 1978: 133). Pigs, on the other hand, because of their higher rates of fertility, were normally culled as juveniles (Bay-Petersen, 1975). Game killed infrequently – often primarily for their fur – included bear, beaver, fox, grey seal, lynx, pine marten and wolf (Clark, 1975: 245). Water birds such as ducks, geese and swans were also hunted on a small scale, and fishing (especially for pike) was practised, probably with line and spear rather than net (Clark, 1975: 43). Plant foods were presumably collected, particularly in the summer and autumn. Little is understood of territorial behaviour, but a system of seasonal camps and subsistence variation can perhaps be envisaged rather similar to Price's (1978) model for Holland (Tables 12 and 13, pp. 164 and 165).

Much of the technology used in the Pre-Boreal and Boreal continued more or less unchanged through the Atlantic. However, in the earlier phase of Atlantic settlement (Kongemose: *c.* 5500–4300 b.c.), rhombic arrowheads were developed in place of the microlithic barbs; and in the later phase (Ertebølle: *c.* 4300–3700 b.c.), the technology included transverse arrowheads, fewer bone and antler harpoons, more flake than core axes, and, in the fourth millennium, simple pottery manufactured with the coil technique. The latter consisted of large vessels with pointed bases perhaps used for boiling fish and shellfish (Noe Nygaard, 1967), and small shallow vessels interpreted as fat lamps(Clark, 1975; Troels-Smith, 1966).

Although the Ertebølle shell middens gave rise to the original model of mesolithic 'strand-looping' in the last century, Atlantic subsistence in Denmark was in fact a combination of hunting, fishing, fowling, and gathering. Sites still occurred in the inland basins as before, but were also increasingly on or near the coast and on the smaller islands. Marine and terrestrial fauna are commonly found at both coastal and inland sites. The main game were red deer and pig, with roe deer a frequent kill but providing much less meat; as in the Boreal, hunting strategies were designed to exploit mature deer and young pigs. Evidence for the exploitation of marine resources increases steadily through the Atlantic, with frequent finds of the bones of cod and flounder, and of a variety of sea mammals – common seal, Greenland seal, grey seal, ringed seal, dolphin, killer whale and porpoise (Clark, 1975: 753). Many settlements have produced evidence for short periods of use, in one or two seasons. At Ringkloster, for example, the range of migratory birds and the mortality ages of the pigs and deer indicated winter and spring occupation (S. H. Andersen, 1973–4); Ølby Lyng was a specialised coastal site for hunting Greenland seals (Brinch Petersen, 1970); Aggersund was primarily used for hunting swans in late autumn and winter (S. H. Andersen, 1978; Møhl, 1978). A few sites also seem to have been specialised trapping camps, for badger, otter and wild cat (Brinch Petersen, 1973: 97). However, a critical difference between Boreal and Atlantic foraging was the development (in the late Atlantic at least) of permanent settlements, particularly on the coast, where sites like Ertebølle and Dyrholmen appear to have year-round occupations (Rowley-Conwy, 1981a). The midden at Meilgaard on the eastern coast of Jutland was also used each year on at least a prolonged seasonal basis by a quite substantial community – probably some forty people (Bailey, 1978).

The correlation between settlement expansion and sedentism in the late Atlantic has also been demonstrated by Paludan-Müller (1978) from detailed survey data collected by Mathiassen (1948, 1959) in northwest Zealand. Habitation sites were initially scattered inland, along the coast and on the offshore islands, but in the late Atlantic there was a major expansion of settlement, in part to the islands but in particular along the river estuaries where the wealth of potential food sources (resident and seasonal fish and birds; crabs and shrimps; game; shellfish) made permanent settlement possible. In Denmark in general, subsistence pivoted on 'permanently occupied base camps being maintained only in part by subsistence activities carried out at these sites, and in part by supplies brought back from special purpose, seasonal, sites visited by small groups from the parent settlement' (Rowley-Conwy, 1981a: 52). Furthermore, ethnographic data from recent sedentary hunters such as the Indians of northwestern America indicate that such a system of subsistence can have major social implications: very large band sizes, well defined territories, food storage and control, ceremonial institutions, positions of authority and even a degree of descent in their leadership – all features of tribal rather than band societies (Bender, 1978). In Denmark the remarkable cemetery at Vedbaek, where selected individuals covered in ochre were buried with flint blades, bone daggers, red deer antlers and necklaces of red deer and pig teeth, provides perhaps the clearest indication of such a level of social complexity (normally regarded as typical of agricultural societies) amongst the Atlantic foraging population (Albrethsen and Brinch Petersen, 1976). It is also notable that the evidence for fighting in the form of skeletal injuries clearly increases through time in the mesolithic cemeteries of Denmark and southern Sweden (S . H. Andersen: pers. comm.), presumably in part a reflection of Ertebølle population densities and subsistence or social competition.

For some years the possibility of an agricultural component in Ertebølle subsistence has been the subject of debate (Troels-Smith, 1966). Certainly the late Atlantic population of Denmark was in contact with agricultural settlements to the south in northern Germany; the technique of potting is assumed to have been borrowed from here, and a few perforated stone axes, some of them typical shoe-last celts, are also known from Ertebølle sites (Schwabedissen, 1966). Bones of domestic cattle are reported from several Ertebølle middens, though rarely stratified securely, and occasionally sheep/goat bones. However, it is clear that if any animal husbandry was practised by Ertebølle people in the late Atlantic, it was on a negligible scale. Instead, the rich environment of southern Scandinavia allowed the development of sedentary systems of foraging, with societies 'at a broadly similar level of social complexity to the farmers further south' (Rowley-Conwy, 1981a: 56).

Subsistence trends in southern Sweden were much the same as in Denmark. The population increased substantially during the Atlantic in response to the increasing diversity of game as broad-leaved trees replaced the Boreal forest and of fish and fowl as the inland lakes developed reed marshes on their margins (Welinder, 1978). By the late Atlantic mobility decreased and more sedentary systems of territorial behaviour were established, with the foraging bands using major sites in fen-edge locations for much of the year and smaller hunting or trapping camps further afield.

Although Lithuania, Latvia and (to a lesser extent) Estonia are at the same latitude as Denmark and southern Sweden, the more continental climate meant that coniferous forests prevailed in the Boreal and the Atlantic, and the low diversity of plant species in turn meant a low diversity of game. The region seems to have been first colonised in the eighth millennium b.c. by foragers equipped with stone maceheads, slate chisels, artefacts of local quartz and flint, and bone harpoons, much like those of the Maglemosian groups further west (Indreko, 1964). Simple pottery was manufactured from the late fifth or early fourth millennium b.c. (Ertebølle-like cooking jars and 'lamps'). The principal subsistence activities were hunting elk, beaver, and pig, and fishing (Zvelebil, 1978). Elk, the heaviest species and the main quarry, was well adapted as a browser to withstanding the deep winter snows of the region but was also an animal of relatively low population densities, and although it provided a stable resource, its exploitation – even though augmented by other game and fish – could not support the kind of population levels achieved by the foragers of Denmark and southern Sweden in the late Atlantic.

The colonisation of northern Scandinavia

The colonisation of northern Scandinavia by postglacial foragers can be documented in some detail. As land became available for settlement following the retreat of the polar icecap and associated changes in relative land and sea levels (Fig. 87), so populations expanded into it. As they did so, suitable technologies and modes of seasonal and territorial behaviour were developed to take advantage of the food sources they found. Certain favoured locations in the south allowed the growth of quite substantial populations practising more or less sedentary systems of foraging, but in most of the region the resources supported smaller and more dispersed bands and much more mobile systems of territorial behaviour.

Subsistence models rather like those proposed for mesolithic Zealand have been developed by Cullberg for the province of Bohuslän in western Sweden (Cullberg, 1975). From the analysis of faunal material, variability in lithic assemblages and site catchments, Cullberg argued that the wealth of resources in this region was exploited by substantial bands occupying quite small annual territories, moving some 40–50 km between off-shore islands and inland forests. In winter there was ice fishing on the inland lakes, together with hunting for fur and meat in the surrounding forests; in spring the rivers could be fished for salmon and trout, and the seabirds hunted and their eggs collected on the islands; in summer the same islands provided a base for hunting seals; and in the autumn berries, nuts and roots could be gathered in the forests, game hunted, and the rivers fished before the winter freeze. The main animal hunted was the

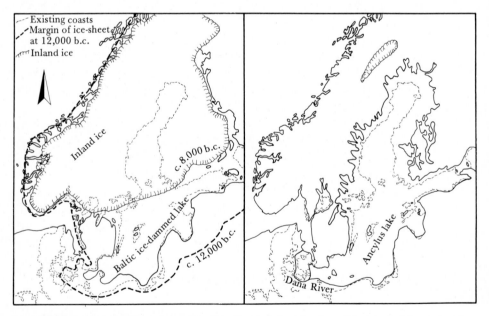

Fig. 87. Early holocene landforms in northern Scandinavia: left, at the close of the late glacial period, and right, *c.* 7500 b.c. (After Clark, 1975: figs. 1 and 2)

elk, the species which is the principal animal represented in the contemporary rock art of the region (Indrelid, 1978: 155). Similar systems of foraging have been proposed by Mikkelsen (1978) for the adjacent part of Norway around the Oslo fjord; the major land mammal hunted was red deer, and this species is again commonly represented in the rock art of the area.

Although the western coast of Norway was freed from ice early in the late glacial and was rapidly colonised by reindeer hunters, the main process of colonisation up the peninsula seems to have begun in the Pre-Boreal, in the eighth millennium b.c. (Indrelid, 1975; Mikkelsen, 1975). In southern Norway, the Hardanger mountains were used in summer and autumn for reindeer and elk hunting, but the people retreated to the coastal areas to the west or southeast for the winter and spring (Mikkelsen, 1978; Moe *et al.*, 1978). The Komsa settlements of the far north are located either on the coast or on the fjord margins, and probably consist of the footings of simple skin tents (Clark, 1975: 212; Odner, 1966). The major encampments at the head of the fjords were devoted to marine fishing and sea mammal hunting (October to May), with satellite camps used on the coast in spring for fowling, by inland rivers in the summer for fishing, and in the hinterland for hunting reindeer (Simonsen, 1973).

Most of northern Sweden was ice-free by *c.* 7000 b.c., and was rapidly colonised by forest – it was not until the first millennium b.c. that temperature lowering created the open *fjall* country in the interior that is now exploited by the reindeer herds of the Lapps. Soon after the retreat of the ice, people from coastal Norway crossed over the Caledonian range and others moved north up the Gulf of Bothnia from southern Sweden. The most common sites in the interior consist of mounds of burnt stones, presumably used for boiling water in pits or in bark containers. The faunal material found with these is invariably dominated by elk bones. At Tjikkiträsk, for example (dated by radiocarbon from *c.* 5000 b.c. to *c.* 3000 b.c.), the large faunal sample consisted of 91% elk, 7% beaver, 1% fish and 1% ringed seal (Meschke, 1967), and that from Bellsås was entirely of elk (Broadbent, 1978: 185). At the former site, seal was represented only by toe bones, probably attached to a seal skin, suggesting that the people who hunted elk during the winter in the interior spent part of the year hunting seals on the coast; the other end of the system is represented by coastal sites such as Lundvors and Heden, the faunal samples of which consist almost exclusively of the bones of the ringed seal (Broadbent, 1978: 184). If this interpretation is correct, the seasonal rhythm was the reverse of that in Norway, with summer reindeer hunting taking place inland in Norway and winter elk hunting in the interior in Norrland.

The earliest evidence for settlement in Finland dates to the seventh millennium b.c., with the appearance of assemblages very like those of the Kunda settlements of Estonia and the coastal settlements of Norway; Fitzhugh (1974) suggests that the slate tools which dominate them were developed particularly because of their suitability for butchering seals, and de-hairing and flensing their blubber. Subsistence depended above all on elk and seal hunting, together with fishing, fowling, and trapping (Forsten, 1972). Something of the scale and technology of offshore fishing at this time is shown by the discovery at Antrea of pieces of a seine net probably 30 m long and 1.5 m high, with the cord made from the bast of willow bark and the floats from pine bark; the net had been lost in some depth of water, clearly suggesting boat fishing(Clark, 1975: 226). On land, too, subsistence technology was well adapted to the inhospitable environment: a pine-wood runner from Heinola probably derives from a substantial sledge using animal traction, presumably dogs (Clark, 1975: 230–1). The subsistence system probably pivoted on the coastal settlements, with fishing expeditions taking place in summer and forays being made inland in winter for elk hunting. The way of life continued unchanged for thousands of years, although the technology was augmented during the fourth millennium by pottery, manufactured in similar forms and with similar techniques to those of Ertebølle pottery, but with local styles of decoration (combed ware).

Initial farming in southern Scandinavia

The beginnings of cereal/stock farming in southern Scandinavia coincide with the appearance of the first TRB or funnel-necked beaker pottery, dated to *c*. 3300–2700 b.c. Much as in other regions of Europe where cultural sequences based on pottery typologies have been dismantled by radiocarbon dating, the stylistic diversity of the earliest TRB material makes it 'very hard to believe that the neolithic culture was the result of the immigration of a new people' (Madsen, 1979: 301–2), a thesis fully supported by the subsistence data.

Probably the most detailed model of early agricultural settlement in Denmark has resulted from Madsen's survey of east central Jutland near Aarhus (Madsen, 1984). The area consists of a series of terminal moraines cross cut by either tunnel valleys formed under ice sheets or glacial river valleys formed at their margins – a landscape today of rivers and lakes separated by low hills. Generally clay predominates near the coast and sand inland, but in any one location gravels, sands and clays can often be found close together. For the earliest agricultural phase, apart from a few possible earth graves and dolmens, Madsen divided the sites into 'catching' and 'residential' locations. Subsistence data from the former were identical to those of Ertebølle sites in the area (game, fowl, fish, shellfish), and locations were also identical – coastal or lakeshore positions, particularly by narrows in the fjords well suited for net fishing and where tidal shifts tended to build up substantial shell banks (Fig. 88). 'Residential' sites were invariably small (less than 500 m^2) and with little cultural material – Mosegården, for example, consisted simply of an open stone hearth surrounded by dumps of ash, with traces of a simple shelter or hut nearby (Madsen, 1979: 307). Preferred locations were areas with a high water table near open water, with easy access to better drained soils on higher ground for cereals and to a range of grazing resources at lower elevations suitable for both game and stock. Sheep/goat bones are represented at a few sites, but pigs and to a lesser extent cattle were the main stock – wild boar had in fact been the principal species at the Ertebølle site of Ringkloster in this region (S. H. Andersen, 1973–4). There is no direct evidence for cereal farming, but plant remains from contemporary sites in Denmark include emmer, einkorn and barley and (in greater quantities) wild fruits, nuts and acorns (Jørgensen and Fredskild, 1978).

In view of the small size and ephemeral nature of the residential camps compared with the substantial domestic sites of ensuing periods, Madsen argues that initial farm-

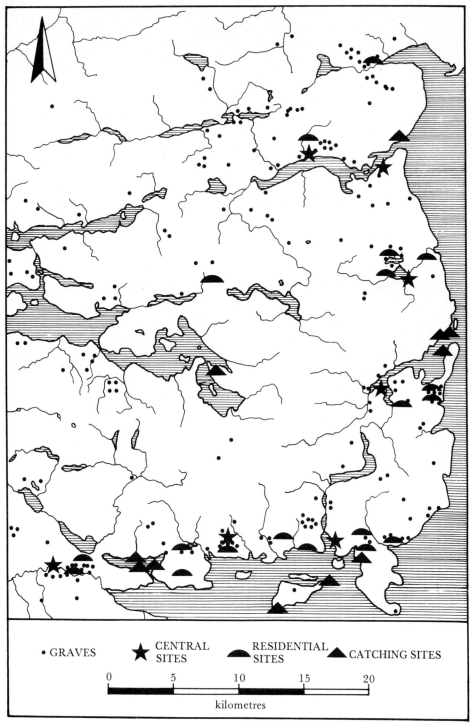

Fig. 88. Neolithic settlement near Aarhus, Denmark. The map is a palimpsest of initial and later TRB settlement, from *c.* 3300 b.c. to the later third millennium; the major central sites and most of the graves belong to the later phase. (After Madsen, 1984: figs. 3 and 4)

ing in east central Jutland must have been on a very small scale, and much less important than foraging: subsistence probably involved much the same short-distance mobility as in the Ertebølle period, but with the population as a whole dispersed into small family groups, at least for most of the year. Early TRB subsistence in the early Sub-Boreal was in greater part the same as Ertebølle subsistence in the late Atlantic in this part of Denmark, but with the critical addition of small scale mixed farming, with small arable plots being managed more or less permanently by simple fallowing and manuring systems. Very similar arguments have been put forward for northwest Zealand at this time, where survey evidence indicates a pattern of early TRB settlement that is essentially an extension of the Ertebølle pattern, with the same development of dispersed family units (Kristiansen, 1982: 6). Initial farming in southern Sweden and Norway seems to have been even more precarious. In Sweden, Welinder's model of agricultural settlement for the Västmanland region north of Lake Mälaren posits (on the somewhat tentative evidence of pollen diagrams and artifact distributions) a short lived phase of initial farming *c.* 3500 b.c. by dispersed families who spent much of the year seal hunting on the coast – further evidence for farming is then absent from the region for several centuries (Welinder, 1975). Mikkelsen and Høeg (1979) argue from palaeobotanical evidence that early husbandry in the Oslofjord area of eastern Norway relied exclusively on stock, with cereal cultivation (in small permanent fields again, not swiddening) developing only after a time lag of several centuries, and both being on a very small scale compared with foraging. The history of initial farming in western Norway was identical (Bakka and Kaland, 1971).

Such arguments are completely at variance with the traditional model of neolithic *landnam* colonisation originally proposed for Denmark by Iversen in 1941 from his analysis of the Ordrup Møse pollen diagram (Fig. 8) and then universally applied to other parts of prehistoric Europe: the concept of pioneering colonists made sense until the late 1960s in terms not only of the cultural models in vogue but also of the general pattern of radiocarbon dates indicating a linear spread of farming (Fig. 5). As I have argued in the preceding regional studies, however, neither the chronology nor the context nor the nature of early farming correlate any longer with such a view. Moreover, a powerful case for the abandonment of the swidden model in Denmark has been assembled by Rowley-Conwy (1981b). First, analogies for the nature of neolithic swiddening were normally drawn from recent or contemporary swidden systems in the tropics or marginal parts of Europe such as northern Scandinavia or the Carpathians (Lewicka, 1972; Sigaut, 1975; Steensberg, 1955); however, tropical swiddening is adapted to completely different soil types and climatic regimes (Jarman and Bay-Petersen, 1976: 181), and in Europe the swidden clearings are invariably outfields in marginal situations where permanent arable and manure are in short supply – neither of which was the case in early farming systems such as those of Denmark. Second, experimental work in Denmark has pointed to the inefficiencies of slash and burn farming in temperate woodlands (Iversen, 1956; Lerche and Steensberg, 1980: 51; Steensberg, 1957), whilst cereal research at places such as Rothamsted Experimental Station has shown that adequate yields could have been obtained by early farmers in temperate Europe without the labour of firing woodland, particularly if manuring and simple fallowing was practised (as seems so often to have been the case). Finally, many neolithic 'clearances' in the Danish pollen record in fact lasted for centuries, not decades as once envisaged, and many phenomena formerly ascribed to *landnam* are likely to be the result of natural causes or statistical bias in the analysis of the pollen grains (Tauber, 1965).

Rowley-Conwy (1982) has also suggested that a small but critical change in the resource base of the Ertebølle foraging system at the end of the Atlantic phase precipitated the adoption of farming in Denmark. In recent years there has been a tendency to minimise the role of shellfish in pre-agricultural subsistence in reaction to the original models of Ertebølle 'strand-looping' (Bailey, 1978), but Rowley-Conwy argues that oysters in particular were probably a critical buffer against starvation in the spring – the other major resources were principally available in the other seasons (summer: cod, mackerel; autumn: ungulates, eels, nuts, acorns; winter: migratory birds, small whales). Oysters need a minimum salinity level of *c.* 23%, and will not grow in Danish inshore waters today because salinity is too low. However, the transgressions of the Litorina Sea allowed more saline waters to enter the Kattegat and oyster beds to form in the inner fjords, where their main growing season in the warmer waters of the period probably coincided with the 'hungry gap' in Ertebølle subsistence: hence 'the oyster achieved an importance out of all proportion to its calorific return rate or its overall contribution to the Ertebølle diet' (Rowley-Conwy, 1982: 28). The major decline in sea level at the end of the Litorina transgression *c.* 3300 b.c. decreased the salinity of the Danish inshore waters, forcing the oysters to retreat to deeper waters offshore. Rowley-Conwy concludes that, as none of the existing resources in Ertebølle foraging can be considered a reliable replacement, and given the coincidence of the disappearance of the oyster, the end of the Ertebølle settlement system, and the inception of farming to augment foraging *c.* 3300 b.c., it is surely reasonable to envisage a direct cause and effect relationship between these events. In this model farming was finally adopted by Danish foragers (after living on the fringe of the farming economy for a thousand years) out of necessity, despite its lower productivity and increased labour requirements.

The technology of initial farming in Denmark, like the scale, was probably rather simple. In the peat of Satrup Moor, several wooden implements have been preserved of the period (Steensberg, 1973). These included two long-handled triangular shovels, and an identical implement with two holes pierced near the upper border of the blade which has been identified as a 'rope traction ard' (Fig. 89). Ropes would be attached to the

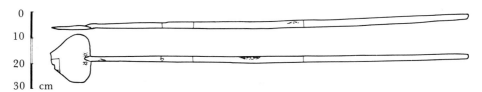

Fig. 89. The 'rope traction ard' from Satrup Moor, Schleswig (northern Germany). The tip has been broken; there are two holes in the blade, presumed to be for pulling ropes, and hand grips half way up the shaft. Implements of similar shape (but without the holes) from mesolithic and neolithic contexts in Denmark were almost certainly paddles, but the identification of this implement as a rope traction ard seems more likely. (After Steensberg, 1976: fig. 3)

blade through the holes, and one person would then pull on the ropes whilst another forced the implement down into the ground. A replica of the device cut a wide shallow drill (13–16 cm wide, 5–6 cm deep) in loose topsoil. Some of the wooden 'paddles' found elsewhere in mesolithic and neolithic Denmark may have been paddle spades like those used today in New Guinea (Steensberg, 1980), although most were probably normal paddles according to wear analysis (Andersen: pers. comm.).

Farming in southern Scandinavia in the third millennium b.c.

A substantial expansion in agricultural settlement can be seen throughout southern Scandinavia during the earlier part of the third millennium b.c. In the Aarhus study, for example, the later TRB phase was marked by considerable growth in the size of settlements, major changes in subsistence, the construction of numerous megalithic tombs, and the development of large central sites including the Toftum causewayed enclosure (Madsen, 1977; Fig. 88). 'Catching' sites were still utilised, but most of the faunal material in the middens now derived from domestic animals (Davidsen, 1978: 140–2). The 'residential' sites were also several times larger than those of the initial TRB phase, with a far richer material culture. The location of the megalithic tombs in the traditional areas of preferred settlement (on the coasts, and on or near the lake and fjord margins) may indicate that they were partly constructed to formalise rights to land using ancestor worship, as competition for the best land developed with the increasing population. The major central sites (10,000–50,000 m²) have internal features and residues suggesting much the same kind of functions (as social, economic and ritual meeting places) as the English causewayed enclosures, and probably reflect the coalescence of the dispersed agricultural families into larger social and territorial units. Very similar processes have been inferred from survey evidence in northwest Zealand by Kristiansen (1982). In general, differential distributions and densities of graves and artifacts indicate that Denmark in the early third millennium can be divided into two socio-economic zones: high population densities and clustered populations on the richer agricultural soils of the east, and low population densities and dispersed populations on the poorer soils of the west (Randsborg, 1975; Fig. 90).

In the main middle neolithic TRB phase later in the third millennium, artifact changes in dolmens and earth graves suggest the emergence of an increasingly stratified society, with wealth being accumulated by high status individuals throughout Denmark. The farmers normally kept cattle, pigs, sheep and goats, in differing proportions according to local ecology: cattle herds consisted of both bullocks and breeding cows, flocks likewise of wethers and ewes, and pigs were killed at about two years old as they approached adult body weight (Higham, 1969; Higham and Message, 1969). Emmer seems to have been by far the most important crop for these farmers (Jørgensen, 1981; Fig. 91). Small permanent fields were maintained by long fallowing and manuring (Jørgensen, 1976; Jørgensen and Fredskild, 1978). At the same time the communities continued to collect wild fruits, berries and nuts, and fishing, fowling and sea mammal hunting were certainly important at many island settlements (Hatting, 1978; Møhl, 1970). Many coastal sites have substantial shell middens.

In southern Sweden and southeastern Norway there were very similar trends in

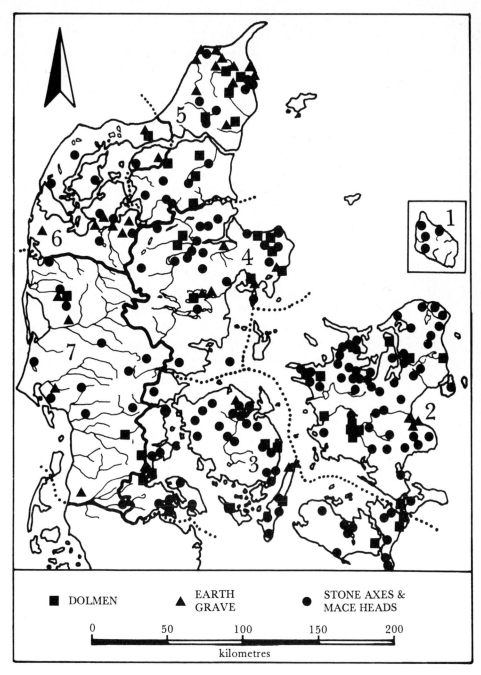

Fig. 90. Settlement in Denmark in the third millennium b.c.: high population densities and clustered populations on the richer agricultural soils of eastern Jutland and the islands, and low population densities and dispersed settlement on the poorer soils of Jutland. Zones: 1. Bornholm; 2. Zealand; 3. Fünen and adjacent islands; 4. eastern Jutland; 5. northeast Jutland; 6. northwest Jutland; 7. western Jutland. (After Randsborg, 1975: figs. 1 and 2)

megalithic and earth burial to those of Denmark during the third millennium, and although subsistence and settlement data are rather poor, the available evidence (together with the pollen record) indicates similar trends in population growth, social change, and agricultural expansion (Larsson, 1981–2; Mikkelsen and Høeg, 1979; Welinder, 1975). At the same time sea mammals and fish remained critical resources for many island and coastal communities (Hagen, 1967; Pira, 1926; Stenberger, n.d.; Welinder, 1977–8).

The process of social transformation and agricultural expansion accelerated dramatically in the last two or three centuries of the third millennium, the period of the 'single grave' barrows. For over a century these barrows were regarded by Scandinavian prehistorians as the graves of a new warrior race: nomads or pastoralists equipped with stone 'battle axes' and cord-decorated beakers, who suppressed existing populations and destroyed their culture. However, as elsewhere in Europe, the complex is not interpreted as evidence of the further consolidation of elite leadership (Malmros and Tauber, 1975; Moberg, 1978). Just as in continental and Atlantic Europe, the emergence of these elites coincided generally with a major expansion in prestige exchange (Randsborg, 1975) and in agricultural technology. Cross-ploughing marks from simple wooden ards pulled by oxen have been found under several barrows (Kjaerum, 1954; Seeberg and Kristensen, 1964; Thrane, 1967a); a wooden yoke from Lower Saxony in Germany probably dates to the same period (Gandert, 1964); oak disc wheels from heavy wagons very like those in Holland have been found in Jutland (Rostholm, 1977); and bones of domestic horses have been found in securely dated con-

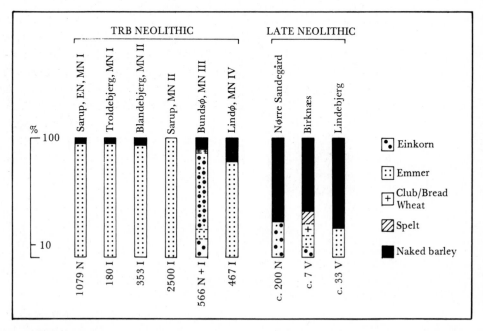

Fig. 91. Cereal changes in neolithic Denmark. N = number of grains; I = number of imprints; V = volume (in litres). (After Jørgensen, 1981: fig. 7)

texts in barrows and settlements (Davidsen, 1978: 142). It may well be that the other main 'secondary products' (milk and wool) were also important at this time, but there is little evidence either way. One clear trend in agriculture at this time seems to have been the replacement of emmer wheat by naked barley as the principal crop (Jørgensen, 1981; Fig. 91). It is difficult to point to climatic reasons for this, and Rowley-Conwy (1978: 169) argues that the reason could well be that emmer was less well adapted than barley to northerly latitudes: it had been adopted as the main crop in initial farming because it was also the principal crop further south, but had extended its range too far north. Another factor may have been the suitability of barley for the wider range of soils being taken into cultivation with the ard.

Survey evidence indicates a substantial expansion of agricultural settlement in Jutland at this time (Mathiessen, 1948), a process confirmed by pollen diagrams (Albrethsen and Street-Jensen, 1963:31). The same trend seems clear from burial and artifact distributions in southern Sweden, again supported by palaeobotanical evidence (Malmer, 1962; Welinder, 1977). In a recent Marxist analysis of this period, Kristiansen argues that contradictions between economic and social organisation resulted in the disintegration of chiefdom organisation at the end of the third millennium and 'the reversion of a chiefly territorial clan organisation into a segmentary organisation suited to predatory expansion', resulting in Jutland in 'the sudden rapid expansion of small pastoral family groups of segmentary tribes . . . onto the light soils' (1982: 15). In fact there is remarkably little hard evidence for the nature of Danish farming at this time – arguments rest principally on inferences drawn from pollen diagrams. However, given the correlation between the adoption of the ard and the pollen evidence for increased clearance, I find it difficult to see much evidence for his thesis of an expansion of predatory pastoralists across the Jutland sands – for which the ard was ideally suited. In eastern Norway a detailed analysis of several pollen diagrams in the Telemark region suggested that it was cereal cultivation rather than stock keeping which increased in importance at this time (Mikkelsen and Høeg, 1979). Most settlements probably consisted of small farmsteads of simple wooden frame buildings (Hvass, 1977; Jensen, 1972).

Later prehistoric farming in Denmark

Well published settlement sites of the second millennium are very rare in Denmark, and the archaeological record for the period is dominated by hundreds of burials. The corpse was placed in a timber coffin (usually a hollowed oak trunk), covered by a small cairn, and then by a turf barrow. The gravegoods appear to consist of the personal equipment of the deceased – jewellery, tools and weapons; in a few burials preservation conditions are such that organic materials have also survived, including woollen clothing, hide shrouds and wooden furniture (Klindt-Jensen, 1957: 63–7). After *c.* 1000 b.c. cremation became the main form of burial. On the basis of the burial record, Kristiansen (1981: 17) described bronze age Denmark (*c.* 1000–500 b.c.) as 'a classic example of theocratic chiefdoms . . . characterised by elaborate communal ritual and feasting, the construction of thousands of impressive tumuli for local chiefly lineages, increased craft production for ritual purposes, and controls over prestige items for the display of rank and wealth'. Regional paramount chiefs are also indicated by centres of unusual wealth such as the Voldtofte cemetery (Jensen, 1967).

Other studies of the gravegoods in the burials have yielded important insights into the nature of bronze age settlement and subsistence as well as social organisation. Randsborg's analysis of about 1000 barrows of the second millennium revealed marked variations in distribution which could not be explained away in terms of differential destruction by later agriculture (Randsborg, 1974). For example, barrows are particularly numerous in northern Zealand and northwest Jutland, and far fewer in the southern parts of the eastern islands and in western Jutland. He compared the numbers of burials in each region with the agricultural potential of the 'settled' parishes (parishes with barrows), measured according to the traditional Danish system of average barley yields ('barrels of hard corn') per hectare. This calculation demonstrated a direct correlation between numbers of graves and agricultural potential, suggesting a broad relationship between agricultural potential and population density (Fig. 92). Furthermore, the degree of stratification evident in the burials implied a rough correlation with population density, with more stratification in the zones of densest settlement. Each zone also registered a steady increase in numbers of graves during the second millennium, still in proportion to the productivity of the settled area – apart from in northwest Jutland, where numbers of graves were far higher than predicted by agricultural potential. Randsborg suggested that here the normal farming system must have been altered to support the high population, either by intensifying agricultural productivity (through shorter fallowing, for example), or by augmenting farming with marine exploitation.

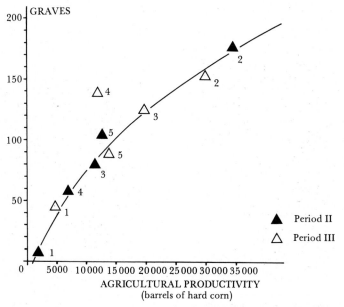

Fig. 92. Settlement in Denmark in the second millennium b.c.: the probable correlation between agricultural potential and population density according to the distribution of burial mounds. Numbers refer to zones: 1. Bornholm; 2. the main islands; 3. northeast Jutland; 4. northwest Jutland; 5. central/southern Jutland. Periods according to the Montelian system. (After Randsborg, 1974: fig. 3)

Comparable inferences about settlement variation have been draw
studies by Kristiansen (1978).

Although these studies imply differences in subsistence as well as se
ficult to characterise these in any detail. Most argument has again been
evidence, particularly for open country and heaths on the sands of western Jutland
(Iversen, 1973), and Danish prehistorians have traditionally envisaged a pastoral
economy here and an arable economy on the heavier soils to the east. Randsborg and
Kristiansen broadly support this model. Randsborg, for example, pointed out that
wealthy female burials were most numerous in the densely settled regions, suggesting a
correlation between plant cultivation, female labour and female status level, with male
dominance and animal husbandry the norm in western Jutland (Randsborg, 1974: 57).
Kristiansen argued that the material poverty of western Jutland arose because the
pastoral economy could not provide the surplus necessary to maintain the supply of
metal, unlike the arable systems elsewhere (1978: 174). However, whilst subsistence
differences clearly existed, we should not envisage a dramatic dichotomy between
nomadic pastoralism on the sands and settled farming on the heavier soils, but, instead,
marked regional biases in the proportion of crops and animals in a mixed farming system. Cereal cultivation with the ard was practised in all regions: ard marks have been
found under several bronze age barrows, especially in Jutland, with the characteristic
cross sections that would be cut by, for example, the ashwood crook ard found at
Hvorslev in Jutland and dated to *c.* 1500 b.c. (Lerche, 1968; Thrane, 1967a, 1967b; Fig.
93). Barley remained the principal crop (Helbaek, 1954; Rowley-Conwy, 1978;
Thrane, 1980).

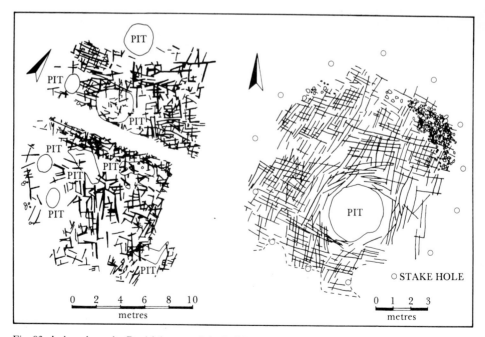

Fig. 93. Ard marks under Danish barrows: left, Gadbjerg, and right, Vesterlund, both in Jutland. (After
Thrane, 1967a: fig. 10, and 1967b: fig. 15)

The climatic deterioration of the first millennium b.c. coincided with major changes in settlement. Barrow distributions indicate that early in the first millennium in every region of Denmark the more marginal soils were abandoned, with settlement contracting to the most productive soils (Kristiansen, 1978: 174). The burial record also suggests that systems of ranking and inheritance became much more concrete, with less emphasis on status rivalry in burial (Randsborg, 1982). At the same time, land ownership altered fundamentally: whereas in the second millennium it had been largely communal, with territory marked symbolically with the ancestral cemeteries, and field divisions marked – if at all – simply by unploughed strips, 'Celtic' field systems were developed in the first millennium with individual fields clearly demarcated with substantial earthen banks and with the layout of complete systems strongly indicative of some kind of central control (Bradley, 1978a). In the same way, the farmsteads of communal longhouses which were the norm in the second millennium were replaced in the first millennium by substantial villages in which ranking differences are very clear: individual farmhouses were small, often equipped with provision for stabling (suggesting direct control of stock by most families), but Hodde in western Jutland is typical in its division between a main compound enclosing about twenty houses with their integral stabling and subsidiary buildings, and a separate enclosure for a much larger house and central storage buildings (Hvass, 1975; Fig. 94).

Subsistence data are again very poor. The settlement contraction was particularly severe on the Jutland sands, and Kristiansen (1978) postulated an increased reliance on

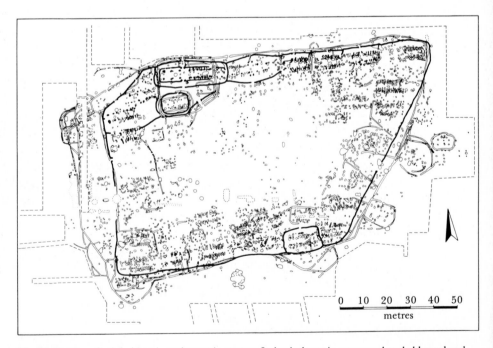

Fig. 94. Hodde, a final prehistoric settlement in western Jutland: the main compound probably enclosed about twenty houses with integral stabling and subsidiary buildings; in the northwestern corner was a separate enclosure for a much larger house and central storage buildings. (After Hvass, 1975: fig. 1)

pastoralism here. Yet from similar distributional evidence Albrectsen (1970) argued that there was a major intensification in arable farming at this time on the island of Fünen, with cattle being stalled and their manure used to raise crop yields. Barley remained the major crop throughout Denmark in the first millennium b.c. (Jensen, 1967; Randsborg, in press); it was only in the late first millennium A.D. that it finally lost its primacy, and then to rye rather than to wheat (Helbaek, 1970). The principal development in animal husbandry was the proliferation in stabling to protect the cattle in the cooler wetter climate and concentrate their manure for cartage to the fields (Fig. 95). There were also important changes in agricultural technology: farmers increasingly had access to iron leaf-knives for fodder collection and iron scythes and rakes for hay making (Steensberg, 1943). By the end of the prehistoric era animal husbandry was increasingly specialised, with clearly defined production goals for wool, meat and/or dairy products evident in the faunal samples (Higham, 1967c). However, whilst broad trends in agricultural intensification can be detected in Denmark during the first millennium b.c., it is impossible to investigate the role of agricultural production in the kind of complex internal relationships between chieftains and clients implied by the structural differences at sites like Hodde.

Later prehistoric farming in southern Sweden and Norway

The archaeological record in the rest of southern Scandinavia is again dominated by funerary remains, studies of which have noted the same evidence as in Denmark for complex ritual life and elaborate status differences, a thesis supported by the symbolism of the rock art of the region (Fredsjö *et al.*, 1969; Levy, 1982). On the island of Ven, in the strait between Denmark and Scania, the distribution of burial mounds, rock carvings and settlement sites suggested a series of social territories, each measuring about 1 km^2 and equipped with a major burial and cult site (Welinder, 1977: 108, 114). In general regional systems of competing chiefdoms are envisaged; warriors on foot or on horseback are also depicted quite commonly in the rock art. The distribution of burial monuments is taken to indicate that settlement concentrated primarily on the Baltic islands such as Gotland and Öland, on the coasts of southern Sweden and Norway, and in discontinuous enclaves in the interior. The settlements consisted of both small villages, built of substantial longhouses with stone footings, and smaller farmsteads with simpler wattle and daub walls (Coles and Harding, 1979: 496–7; Jaanusson, 1971). In addition, traces of smaller huts have been found which are identified as seasonal pastoral or hunting camps (Hyenstrand, 1966; Welinder, 1974). Ard marks have been found under several barrows, and the main crop (as in Denmark) was barley, with emmer and einkorn also being cultivated (Stjernquist, 1969, 1978). Faunal evidence is very poor, but cattle is invariably the main species reported apart from at specialist sites used for fishing, fowling, or hunting sea mammals (Møhl, 1970; Sellstedt, 1965).

As in Denmark, there is widespread evidence for settlement expansion in the second millennium b.c., followed in the deteriorating climate of the first millennium b.c. by major changes in agricultural organisation. In Scania and in Västmanland in Sweden, Welinder (1975, 1977) has argued from pollen evidence that marginal soils were cleared

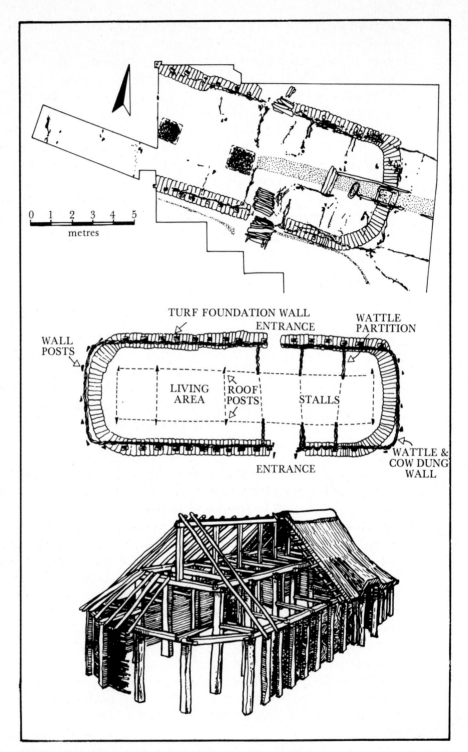

Fig. 95. A reconstruction of the Tofting farmhouse in northern Germany. (After Lund and Thomsen, 1981: figs. 5a, 5b and 5c)

and colonised in the late second and early first millennia b.c., as population levels grew in the primary zones of settlement; following Boserup's thesis of agricultural intensification in the face of population pressure (Boserup, 1965), he suggested that an extensive system of cultivation eventually had to be replaced in the later first millennium b.c. by an intensive infield–outfield system based on the systematic use of manure. The same process has been found in Östergotland, between Scania and Västmanland: in the late first millennium b.c. small settlements with fenced fields were established, identified as farmsteads or hamlets of single families (Lindquist, 1968), and phosphate analysis around two of these clearly indicated an infield system, with intensively cultivated and manured fields and enclosed meadows (Widgren, 1979). As in the historical period, permeable soils were preferred for arable land, clay for hay meadows, and rocky soil or till for pasture (Sjöbeck, 1958). According to medieval land use, such small family farms would have needed three hectares of arable land, thirty hectares of meadow land, and thirty hectares of pasture, stocked with about a dozen cattle (milk cows, heifers and oxen), a dozen sheep and a couple of pigs (Widgren, 1979).

Similar changes in land use at the close of the prehistoric period have been found in southwest Norway. At the end of the first millennium b.c., settlements consisted primarily of small farmsteads with irregular fields marked by clearance cairns; a system of shifting cultivation and long fallow is envisaged (Myrhe, 1978). A few centuries later, however, more substantial farms were built, an organised infield–outfield system laid out, and permanent intensive cultivation and manuring practised. In the Stavanger area, the Ullandhaug farm consisted of two longhouses (one with integral stabling), subsidiary buildings, stock pens, 3–6 hectares of fenced infield land and a fenced droveway leading through these fields to the outfield grazing (Myrhe, 1973, 1978; Fig. 96). The main crop was barley, with oats and flax also being grown. Phosphate studies around a similar farm at Bjellandsøynae indicated intensive manuring systems (Provan, 1973). Like Welinder, Myrhe concluded that the development of intensive permanent agriculture here could best be explained by Boserup's population model, with climatic deterioration perhaps also involved in the process of change.

The functioning of the infield–outfield system of permanent cultivation has been studied with great precision on the island of Gotland by Lindquist (1974). In the district of Rone, a field system some 130 hectares in extent was mapped; excavation found abundant evidence of cross-ploughing, and charcoal in the furrows and in the arable soil above them suggested clearing by burning prior to the fields being taken into cultivation in the last two or three centuries b.c. Most of the fields were small square areas of about 600 m^2 marked out by earth banks; at about four furrows per metre (a density noted here and elsewhere in southern Scandinavia), cross-ploughing each field represented about eight or nine hours' work – a day's work for one man. Preparing the two or three hectares needed for each family would have taken 30–40 man-days, a reasonable task for a single plough team according to nineteenth-century figures for ploughing capabilities (McConnell, 1883). The comparison of the distribution of the prehistoric field systems with land utilisation shown on historical maps suggested that there have been no major changes in the agrarian landscape from the establishment of the prehistoric enclosed fields until recent times (Lindquist, 1974: 10); exactly the same point has been demonstrated for places like Jaeren island in Norway (Myrhe, 1978).

The penetration of farming into the Boreal zone

Conditions for agriculture of course become increasingly marginal with latitude north, and small scale climatic fluctuations in northern Scandinavia had major repercussions for prehistoric farmers, as in later periods. Today in Norway, for example, cereals can be grown with reasonable reliability as far north as the Arctic circle and even further

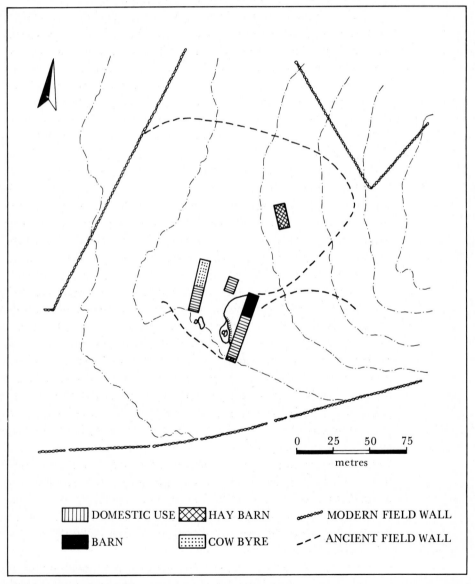

Fig. 96. The Ullandhaug farm, Stavanger: farmhouses and subsidiary buildings, infield land, and a fenced droveway leading to outfield grazing. (After Myrhe, 1973: fig. 8)

north beyond the main limits set by the macroclimate in isolated favoured locations such as sheltered south-facing slopes; in the seventeenth century, however, a small climatic worsening meant a significant reduction in the length of the growing season and a drastic contraction of the northern cereal zones (Vorren, 1979). In general, cereals were never a staple resource in northern Norway during the historic period because of the extreme climatic conditions (Fjaervoll, 1965). Likewise, sheep can be kept on the coast right up to Tromsö, some 300 kilometres north of the Arctic circle, but until the introduction of modern concentrates they had to be kept alive in winter on leaf fodder, such as the bark and twigs of oak, birch and aspen, and seaweed (Brox, 1963).

Pollen diagrams from the Nordland and Troms regions of northern Norway record the development of a more open forest vegetation *c*. 3500 b.c., and from the rise of plantains and fall in tree pollen, Vorren (1979) argues that stock farming based on leaf foddering may have been introduced to the region at this time. The first definite evidence for stock keeping, however, consists of bones of domestic animals in cave deposits dated to the end of the third millennium b.c. (Bakka, 1976), and the first cereal pollen is recorded a few centuries later in the pollen diagrams (Vorren, 1979: 8). Cereal cultivation continued on a small scale along the coast of northern Norway during the second and first millennia b.c., perhaps extending north of the present cereal limit in the optimum period of the second millennium. However, the dominant mode of subsistence for most communities remained foraging and fishing, with a few stock being kept to overcome seasonal scarcities in game (Johansen, 1979). The pollen diagrams all show evidence for a substantial amount of arable and pasture only after the mid first millennium A.D., when pollen curves rise abruptly for cereals, grasses, nettles, buttercups and so on; farmers had probably by now developed the *grindgang* method of manuring which has survived to the present day, whereby stock are moved around within temporary enclosures to manure and trample small plots in succession (Vorren, 1979: 17).

The expansion of agricultural settlement in northern Sweden was broadly contemporary. Late neolithic artifacts from southern Scandinavia such as double-edged battle axes, boat axes and flint daggers have been found as far north as Angermanland, and the earliest cereal pollen recorded in Norrland dates (like the artifacts) to the end of the third millennium b.c. At Norrböle in Angermanland the diagram dated to this period included pollen of wheat, barley, vetch and nettles, as well as plantains (Huttunen and Tolonen, 1972). Cereal pollen has also been found in Västerbotten in contexts dated to the middle of the second millennium b.c. (Königsson, 1970). As in Norway, cereal farming was able to extend beyond its present northern limits for a brief period in the second millennium b.c., but remained a subsidiary activity for the Norrland population. At Bjurselet in Västerbotten, for example, a coastal community grew barley, but in the faunal sample of some 4000 fragments there were only 64 specimens of sheep and five of cattle – the vast majority belonged to the ringed seal: the settlement specialised in seal hunting and fishing, particularly for whitefish (Königsson, 1970; Lepiksaar, 1975). Inland, farming made no impact on the traditional foraging systems.

The pollen diagrams from Angermanland and Västerbotten indicate that cereal cultivation grew steadily in importance for the coastal communities of Norrland in the late second millennium, but that the climatic deterioration of the first millennium then put an end to farming here for many centuries (Engelmark, 1976; Huttunen and Tolonen, 1972). As average summer temperatures decreased and rainfall increased, spruce forest expanded rapidly along the Norrland coast, arable and pasture fields were abandoned, and for a thousand years (*c.* 500 b.c.–*c.* A.D. 500) there is virtually no evidence for farming. The decrease in browse as spruce forest developed on the coast was probably reflected in a decline in numbers of elk, but although a decline in the human population has also been suggested, it is likely that densities here were so low that most communities were able to revert to foraging for their livelihood; most of the prehistoric wooden skis found in Västerbotten have been dated by pollen analysis to this period (Engelmark, 1976: 99).

The middle of the first millennium A.D. marked a climatic amelioration in Scandinavia, and once again the Norrland coastal zone was taken into cultivation. The pollen diagrams show a major increase in open habitat plants such as grasses and plantains as the spruce forests were cleared, and the re-establishment of arable and pasture fields. From that time onward, the record of human influence in the Norrland pollen diagrams has been continuous (Engelmark, 1976: 99; Zackrisson, 1976). This final expansion of agriculture probably involved a northward movement of people from southern Scandinavia rather than, as before, a subsistence change by the indigenous population. Anderson (1981) argues that, as these Scandinavians penetrated into the interior of Norrland, the local foragers (ethnically Lapps) were drawn into supplying furs for them, much as the Canadian Indians around Hudson's Bay supplied European traders in the eighteenth and nineteenth centuries. In both cases, he suggests, the fur trade was instrumental in destroying existing hunting strategies, which were replaced by the localised hunting of small game, fishing, small scale cultivation and eventually, in the open interior, by reindeer herding.

In Finland, some of the coastal foraging and fishing communities began to keep domestic animals on a small scale from the end of the third millennium, the period of the first expansion of farming into northern Scandinavia (Forsten, 1974; Forsten and Alhonen, 1975). The pollen record indicates the presence of pasture land from the same period (Alhonen, 1967), and site catchment data also suggest a preference for clay soils suitable for grazing and fodder production (Zvelebil, 1978: 224). The first cereal pollen dates to the middle of the second millennium b.c., but cereals seem to have been grown on a regular basis by the coastal peoples (still essentially foragers and fishermen) only at the end of the second millennium – and then probably in systems of shifting cultivation and long fallow (Vuorela, 1970, 1972). From this period, too, there is the first consistent evidence for established stock keeping, especially in southwest Finland (Zvelebil, 1978: 226). As in Norway and northern Sweden, farming declined substantially in the later first millennium b.c., and it was not until about A.D. 500 that abandoned land was taken into cultivation again and extensive new areas cleared for agriculture; both swidden clearings and permanent fields were used (Berglund, 1969; Vuorela, 1975). Hunting and fishing, however, remained an essential part of the subsistence system in Finland well into the medieval period.

The climatic warming in the mid-second millennium b.c. responsible for the northern expansion of cereal farming in Norway and Sweden resulted in a decline in suitable grazing grounds for elk in Estonia and Latvia. There is consistent evidence for a decrease in elk body size at this time, and it was in the context of this environmental pressure on a major food resource that animal husbandry began on a substantial scale here, integrated with a cultivation system primarily based on swiddening (Zvelebil, 1978: 216–19). This mode of subsistence continued until the climatic changes of the later first millennium b.c., which allowed the re-establishment of the boreal forests favoured by elk at the expense of the deciduous forests suitable for pig, red deer and cattle. However, exploitation of elk did not increase at this time. Instead, the sub-sistence base was intensified dramatically: an integrated agricultural system was developed with crops (primarily winter rye and spring barley) being grown in rotation in permanent fields, the fertility of the latter being maintained by fallowing and manuring; horses were increasingly kept for traction rather than (as formerly) for meat; and hunting goals changed from food species to fur-bearing species (Zvelebil, 1981). At the same time the existing neolithic technology was replaced by a series of iron tools which made cultivation systems much more productive – axes, ploughs, grain sickles, hay scythes. There was a major increase in settlement density, with the emergence of a settlement hierarchy dominated by fortified villages, and a more stratified society developed which included for the first time specialist craftsmen, and elites who engaged in long distance trade (especially in furs) with Scandinavia and central Europe. Zvelebil (in press) argues that these major transformations in social and economic complexity cannot be explained by any single 'prime mover': significant stimuli probably included contact with external markets, social competition (with the elites promoting surplus production), and stress (both demographic and ecological) on existing systems of subsistence.

...historic farming in Europe:
origins and development

The beginnings of European farming

The beginnings of prehistoric farming in Europe have traditionally been explained by a process of colonisation from the Near East (the 'hearth of domestication'), with neolithic agriculturalists spreading across Europe in the early Holocene from the southeast *c.* 6000 b.c. to the northwest *c.* 3000 b.c., terminating the hunting-gathering way of life which had prevailed there from earliest times. At the close of my initial discussion of the history of research on prehistoric farming, I anticipated one of the principal themes of this book with the comment that the transition to farming in Europe was in fact a far more complex process than ever predicted by the colonisation model. The intervening chapters have presented the evidence for this thesis at some length, and whilst the individual arguments established from the separate data of the different regions need not be repeated, some concluding remarks on the overall process are apposite here. Like two other recent reviews of the origins of European farming (Dennell, 1983; Jarman *et al.*, 1982), I take the view that the phenomenon is best explained by a combination of local and intrusive developments, with the role of migrating colonists being more or less redundant.

The colonisation model has its roots in nineteenth-century archaeology, and in particular in the Victorian concept of an absolute divide between the 'primeval savagery' of the prehistoric hunter and the 'rude barbarism' of the prehistoric farmer (Figs. 2–4), with the way of life of the latter seeming to represent the key stepping stone onto the road to civilisation. Such farming communities were indeed being found in the Fertile Crescent of the Near East and were recognised as being ancestral to the ancient civilisations there, whilst in Europe it seemed impossible to imagine any link between the settled farming of the rather comparable neolithic communities and the aboriginal (mesolithic) population that preceded them, which seemed to epitomise all the worst characteristics of the hunting way of life as perceived by contemporary Victorian ethnography – barbaric, precarious, nomadic and poverty-stricken.

The model was then developed explicitly by Gordon Childe in the 1920s and 1930s: he argued that agriculture began first in the Near East (the 'neolithic revolution'), and whilst one result of the expansion in food production was eventually the 'urban revolution' there, the other was the migration of surplus population into southeast Europe and thence either by sea across the Mediterranean basin or overland up the Danube and ultimately to the furthest regions of temperate Europe. The model neatly explained, on the one hand, the great disparity evident at the time between a small and dispersed mesolithic population in Europe and the pervasive and numerous neolithic populations and, on the other, the clear links in neolithic material culture (particularly pottery) across major regions: the painted pottery of Turkey and Greece, the impressed pottery of the Mediterranean basin, the incised 'Danubian' pottery of the temperate loesslands, the round baggy pottery of western Europe, and so on. At the same time, of course, the model was also an essential prerequisite for establishing the first effective chronology for neolithic Europe (by the typological method of cross-cultural comparisons) which was one of Childe's most remarkable achievements. The process of colonisation was then apparently confirmed by the first main series of radiocarbon dates from early neolithic sites, together with an indication of the rate and direction of movement (Clark, 1965; Fig. 5), and further refined by Ammerman and Cavalli-Sforza's calculation of the 'wave of advance' of neolithic farming from a larger series of radiocarbon dates a few years later (Ammerman and Cavalli-Sforza, 1971).

Until recently the more or less universal acceptance of the colonisation model has largely precluded debate on the possibility that the indigenous mesolithic population of Europe could have developed into neolithic farmers. More seriously, the lack of debate has effectively biased the collection of field data, with the subsistence status of a site often being conferred primarily by assumption rather than by direct data – for example, 'all microlithic assemblages must be mesolithic, mesolithic means foraging, so micro-lithic assemblages are evidence of mesolithic foraging', or 'the evidence for the arrival of the first farmers in this region consists of three polished axes and a megalith'. In fact, apart from the very general directional spread of farming from southeast to northwest across Europe that Clark and then Ammerman and Cavalli-Sforza pointed to (of which more later), there is remarkably little hard evidence for any colonisation movement. In particular, not a shred of evidence has ever been produced (or apparently thought necessary) to demonstrate the existence anywhere in Europe or in the putative home-lands outside Europe of the kind of seething population sump predicted by the model in order to provide ever more land-hungry colonists for service at the expanding agricul-tural frontier. In fact, settlement densities of early agriculturalists seem to have been uniformly low relative to total carrying capacities of the particular region in question both in Europe and in adjacent areas of the Near East (e.g. Cherry, 1981; French, 1970; Kruk, 1980; Levine and McDonald, 1976). At the same time it is now abundantly clear that the indigenous mesolithic populations of Europe were far more substantial than envisaged even quite recently, and as I have argued in the regional chapters, their con-tribution to the first phase of farming in most instances is far more obvious than that of any incoming colonists. Indeed, the most impressive and consistent feature of the first farming systems in different parts of Europe – their successful adaptation to the con-straints and opportunities both of the particular region and also of the immediate locality – betokens detailed local knowledge rather than the tentative experiments of new-comers, unless we have recourse to special pleading (as in the case of Britain currently: Chapter 8, p. 197) that there must be an initial pioneering phase of colonisation as yet undiscovered, which would have been the kind of catalogue of success and failure that characterised initial European farming in north America, southern Africa and Australia in the modern era.

In the face of such evidence, there has been a tendency in recent years to envisage a compromise solution for the beginnings of agriculture: a limited process of neolithic colonisation on the one hand and, on the other, a more widespread process of mesolithic 'acculturation' (or, even worse, 'neolithisation') whereby the native populations adopted the new crops and animals, new technologies and new methods of subsistence from the colonists – although the context of the abandonment of foraging for farming has rarely been discussed beyond a vague consensus that the benefits of farming must eventually have been obvious to even the most obdurate mesolithic hunter. The principal reason for adhering to even these few pathfinding colonists – apart from any unspoken assumptions about innovative and conservative societies (with European mesolithic peoples firmly in the second category) – has been the botanical and zoological evidence that most of the key crops and animals of the first European farming were not native to Europe: that, apart from cattle, dog and pig, the rest of the 'neolithic package' (emmer, einkorn, bread wheat, barley, legumes, sheep and goat) was first domesticated in the Near East. The simplest mechanism for the first entry into and subsequent spread across Europe of these exotic crops and animals was clearly the movement of colonising farmers.

However, it now seems extremely unlikely that the natural distributions of what are today regarded as the wild prototypes ancestral to modern domesticated cereals, legumes, sheep and goats have remained static since the beginning of the Holocene, entirely unaffected by 10,000 years of climatic change and land use. Indeed, there is increasing evidence that some of these distributions extended significantly beyond their present range at that time: for example, wild barley has been reported at the Franchthi cave in Greece in the early mesolithic levels (Hansen and Renfrew, 1978) and was probably present in contemporary levels in the Uzzo cave in Sicily (Piperno: pers. comm.); legumes have been found in the same levels at both sites and in a roughly contemporary context in southern France (Courtin and Erroux, 1974); cereal pollen has been identified in late glacial/early postglacial contexts prior to any evidence for agriculture in northern Greece (Bottema, 1974), the Iron Gates of the Danube (Carciumaru, 1973), and even the Paris basin (Planchais, 1970); and the occurrences of sheep in the late glacial/early postglacial fossil record of Europe – whilst undoubtedly from rather uncertain contexts in some instances – together present a very strong case that sheep inhabited parts of Europe both before and during the last glaciation, surviving in dispersed populations in the Holocene in those regions such as the Mediterranean and Black Sea littorals (and perhaps the middle Danube basin too) least affected by afforestation (Table 19). 'The development of morphologically domestic barley, einkorn, legumes and sheep could have occurred in a "non-centre" that extended from parts of the Mediterranean basin to southeast Europe and the Near East (and possibly eastwards into central Asia and China)' (Dennell, 1983: 163). The two principal resources of European farming for which there is no evidence for their presence in the early Holocene prior to their use by farmers are emmer and bread wheat.

Thus many of the components of European mixed farming may not have been so exotic after all, particularly in southern Europe, and both here and elsewhere an internal change to farming by the resident foraging population seems increasingly to be the major process at work. Furthermore, the very full radiocarbon chronology available

Table 19 *Occurrences of upper pleistocene and early holocene sheep in Europe*

Site	Identification
Upper Pleistocene	
Peche de l'Azé, France	*Ovis fossilis* cf. *aries*
Lunel-Viel, France	*O. tragelaphus*
Balme de Glos, France	*Ovis* sp.
Petershöhle, Austria	*Ovis* sp.
La Bocca del Tasso, Italy	*Ovis* sp.
Certova-Dira, Czechoslovakia	*O. argaloides*
Grotta Bella, Hungary	*Ovis* sp.
Tata, Hungary	*Ovis* sp.
Crvena Stijena, Yugoslovia	*Ovis* sp.
Adzhi Koba III, Crimea	*O.* cf. *ammon*
Mezin, Russia	*O.* cf. *orientalis*
Early Holocene	
La Adam, Rumania	*O. ammon orientalis*
Gramari 7, France	*Ovis* sp.
L'Abri Pages, France	*Ovis* sp.
Grotte Gazel, France	*Ovis* sp.
Abri de Dourgne, France	*Ovis* sp.
Balma Margineda, France	*Ovis* sp.

(After Dennell, 1983: 162, and Geddes, 1983: 58)

today suggests that the spread of farming in Europe was a stop-and-start process, a series of major expansions or explosions followed by substantial pauses, and not the gradual 'wave of advance' inferred in the past from a few radiocarbon dates widely spaced across Europe. These expansions appear to correlate very closely with major climatic changes, and the distinct agricultural systems characterising each of these expansions across the major regions of Europe are also clearly explicable in terms of the regional landscapes resulting from such changes, landscape changes which often seem very likely to have been detrimental to existing systems of foraging. The history of initial farming reconstructed in this book thus totally contradicts Ammerman and Cavalli-Sforza's conclusion from their study that 'environmental factors (climate, soils, forest cover etc) . . . [did not play] . . . a major role in determining the rate of expansion of early farming over Europe' (1971: 686).

   In the Mediterranean, early holocene subsistence was characterised by broadly based foraging organised on a communal basis, harvesting large and small animals, fish, shellfish and plants, probably including cereals, legumes and sheep. The cereals – einkorn and barley – were morphologically wild, with small grains and a brittle rachis, like modern cereals easily harvested, but unpredictable in availability and difficult to process for consumption (Harlan, 1967; Zohary, 1969), and hence unlikely to have been more than a supplementary resource. The nature of sheep exploitation at this time is unclear, but may have involved husbandry of some kind (Geddes, 1983). By *c.* 6000 b.c., permanent settlements were established in Greece (as elsewhere in the eastern Mediterranean) practising mixed farming. A variety of stock, legumes and cereals was used, but these significantly included the new 'exotic' cereals emmer and bread wheat, both far more productive and reliable than the wild cereals previously available because they were large grained and had a tough rachis adapted for efficient harvesting. The new cereals could well have spread from their natural habitats to the east by the same processes of exchange that at that time were carrying obsidian hundreds of kilometres from the sources in central and eastern Turkey (Renfrew *et al.*, 1968), into an environment and subsistence system pre-adapted for them (Fig. 97). However, as Dennell (1983: 167) has pointed out, the cultivation of the new cereals would have had profound implications for the economic and social organisation of Mediterranean foragers. First, their harvesting could not be haphazard but demanded careful cultivation on a labour-intensive basis – establishing permanent fields adjacent to settlements, cultivating the ground, weeding the crop, and above all replenishing the nutrients they extracted from the ground (much more than the other cereals) by following their cultivation with legumes and by manuring. Second, a household rather than a communal system of social organisation would have greatly facilitated the new labour-intensive but more productive system of food procurement.

The subsistence data from the new neolithic settlements of Greece indicate that these agricultural systems were in many respects identical to traditional Mediterranean farming: the cultivation of autumn-sown crops and, in the stock system, a reliance on small stock (particularly sheep) and, probably, quite marked mobility in their husbandry if not the organised transhumance of later prehistory. Similar systems of farming may well have been adopted soon afterwards in restricted parts of the northern Mediterranean, probably precipitated as in Greece by the effects of sea level changes on existing systems of foraging. Elsewhere, foraging or mixed farming/foraging survived in many areas well

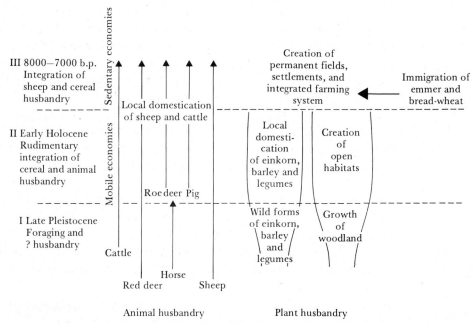

Fig. 97. Suggested developments leading to food production in southeast Europe. (After Dennell, 1983: fig. 27)

into the fourth millennium. North of Greece, the expansion of farming seems to correlate clearly with the increased rainfall and warmer winters of the Atlantic climate beginning in the mid-sixth millennium b.c. which, apparently quite suddenly, made the Mediterranean system of farming viable in the southern Balkans and allowed rather different kinds of plant and animal husbandry to be practised in the northern Balkans and middle Danube basin. One thousand years later a very different form of cereal/stock farming (based on spring-sown crops and cattle keeping) began over a huge area on the optimum soils of temperate Europe, and stock-based husbandry developed in adjacent regions of the continental lowlands just as rapidly; both were clearly well adapted to the environments in which they were practised, with the arable-based farming of the loesslands exploiting the soils best suited for cultivation in the climatic conditions of the time, soils which were also the most marginal for the existing foraging economy. A variety of foraging systems continued to be practised in the surrounding regions of temperate Europe for another thousand years, after which it was replaced to a greater or lesser extent by, again, a variety of quite distinct systems of farming on the alpine foreland, the Atlantic littoral, southern Scandinavia and lowland Britain, surely coinciding significantly with the major landscape changes precipitated by the development of the Sub-Boreal climate. On the northern margins of Europe the adoption of farming was protracted, hesitant and always vulnerable to small scale climatic changes, with foraging and fishing the dominant mode of subsistence for most communities until the mid-first millennium b.c. or even the mid-first millennium A.D.

For virtually all of Europe, therefore, it seems to me most likely that the various systems of initial farming which we can discern were developed by the indigenous populations rather than by newcomers, in the context of some kind of pressure or pressures on their established modes of subsistence, making the adoption of the new resources – along with the enormous technological and social changes normally associated with them – preferable or unavoidable. I would be the first to admit that such 'pressures' are poorly defined. I strongly suspect that the general correlations between initial farming and climatic/ecological changes noted above are a critical part of the equation, although the precise environmental data needed to test such an hypothesis properly are still rarely if ever available. Even less is understood of the demographic status of the indigenous populations of Europe during the adoption of farming, although population pressure on the existing system of food procurement has been commonly regarded as the fundamental trigger in the adoption of farming elsewhere in the world (e.g. Binford, 1968; Cohen, 1977). It is given the same emphasis by both Dennell (1983) and Jarman *et al.* (1982) for Europe. In the case of the British Isles – the strongest redoubt of the colonist model – Dennell postulates that mesolithic populations were probably experiencing population pressure in the early fourth millennium b.c. from an increase in their numbers and/or from an expansion of forest that reduced the amount of plant food available for both people and animals, a problem resolved by woodland clearance to encourage game densities, more intensive use of marine resources, and, ultimately, the adoption of farming (Dennell, 1983: 186). As will have been clear in the regional chapters arguing for the adoption of farming by the existing foraging populations, my own views on the likely role of population pressure are very similar.

Unfortunately, demographic data for the pre-agricultural populations of Europe are almost invariably minimal, and are rudimentary in the extreme for the first agricultural populations, and at present it is quite impossible to evaluate the relationships of local populations to carrying capacities, or the nature and scale of population stress. However, the present lack of demographic data is no justification for continuing to cling to the colonisation model in the face of the very considerable other data that refute it. At the very least, the alternatives must be present in future research designs concerned with the beginnings of European agriculture. One of the most depressing features of previous research has been the manner in which the dominance of the traditional explanation has for decades effectively blighted the chances of objective debate and (most critically) the collection of comparative data on either side of the mesolithic/neolithic divide – witness the rarity of plant remains from 'pre-agricultural' sites; or the intellectual conundrums of 'clearance' interpretation in the pollen record; or, most of all, the paucity of current socio-economic models for the adoption of farming by European foragers. It is very salutary to see the complexity of the models (linking social, ecological and demographic pressures) currently being established in New Guinea to explain why the forest foragers there gradually developed systems of mixed farming between *c.* 5000 and 3000 b.c. without a colonist in sight (Golson, 1976; White and O'Connell, 1982), and the complexity of the relationship between farming and foraging in traditional African societies (Jones, 1984).

Agricultural change in later prehistory
In the final section of Chapter 2, I described the intractable problems of low output from low input that beset most pre-industrial farmers in Europe: it was extremely difficult to break out of the vicious circle of low fertiliser levels (principally manure but also fallowing techniques) resulting in low yields, in turn resulting in low fertiliser levels. These problems can be expected to have been at least as critical for prehistoric farmers. Yet the second theme of this book has been that the later prehistory of European farming witnessed in most regions a succession of major changes in technology, production and organisation rather than the immutable survival of the initial agricultural systems. How can these changes be explained? For the historical period, Grigg (1982) isolates four major stimuli of agricultural change which are just as relevant to prehistoric Europe; they will be discussed here in turn, although in prehistoric as in historic Europe they in fact rarely operated in isolation from one another: climate/environment, technology, population and social organisation.

Climatic and environmental change
It is of course a truism that a farming system is adapted to its environment – the particular choice of crops and animals must suit the constraints and opportunities of the environment immediately around the farm, or the farmer will starve. As all the regional studies have shown, site catchment analysis has repeatedly demonstrated that prehistoric farmers – like all farmers ever since – were well aware of the pros and cons of their locality in terms of soil differences, slope, aspect and so on, and as far as possible adapted their husbandry systems accordingly.

Just as a farming system is adapted to its environment, so it must also adapt to gross environmental change. In historical times much pre-industrial farming (except in marginal situations) was remarkably resilient to long term but gradual climatic trends, yet very vulnerable to periods of increased unpredictability in the weather, when small annual fluctuations in temperature and rainfall could lead to a succession of catastrophic harvest failures (Grigg, 1982). Whilst small scale climatic changes and their effects are extremely difficult to monitor on the prehistoric timescale, the regional studies here contain many examples of the interplay between prehistoric farming and climatic and/or environmental change. On the one hand, there were large scale climatic changes which induced major changes in agriculture on an inter-regional scale, such as the expansion of arable cultivation in temperate Europe in the third millennium and again in the second millennium, and the contractions and transformations induced by the Sub-Atlantic deterioration. The relationship between environmental change and agricultural change is inevitably clearest in marginal situations such as in the most arid parts of the Mediterranean basin or the fenland areas of Britain and Holland, or at the northern limits of cereal cultivation in Scandinavia, where small fluctuations in climate could demand major adjustments in subsistence. In several cases, too, the evidence points towards ecological changes originating at least in part from existing agricultural systems, such as the abandonment of the Balkan tells, or the formation of the heaths and moors of northern Europe.

However, one important point about climatic and environmental change is that adjustments by similar agricultural systems could vary enormously. In the Mediterranean, for example, the more humid climate of the third millennium witnessed the development of polyculture in the Aegean, the major expansion of settlement onto the Garrigues in southern France, and the development of Millaran irrigation and polyculture in southeast Spain, but only a small scale expansion of cultivation in most of peninsular Italy. Again, the return to drier conditions in the second millennium was the context for very different agricultural adjustments: the establishment of the redistributive economies of the Aegean, the development of quite long distance transhumant systems in peninsular Italy and perhaps parts of Spain, the colonisation of the Po plain for permanent settlement, and the contraction of settlement in southern France.

Technological development

The invention of a more efficient technology has frequently been cited as a major stimulus of agricultural change. The major improvements in the efficiency of the technology of prehistoric farming were in cultivation, harvesting and transport. To break up the soil, the earliest farmers had only (we assume) hand implements such as digging sticks, mattocks, hoes and perhaps spades. The next major advance, beginning in the fourth millennium (and perhaps earlier in the Balkans) but mainly adopted in the third millennium, was the ard plough pulled by cattle or oxen; in the right conditions – light soils, and root-free soils – it could be used to cultivate perhaps twice or three times the area that could be turned over with hand tools. Later versions of the ard strengthened with metal tips could be used on a wider range of soils. By the late first millennium b.c. some communities were also using much heavier ploughs, more like the modern mould-board plough which turns the sod right over, enabling them to tackle increasingly heavier soils.

Harvesting technology likewise developed enormously. For millennia the main tool was the composite sickle of wood or bone and flint. This was eventually replaced in the late second millennium b.c. by the bronze sickle, which was probably at least 50% more effective. By the end of the first millennium b.c. heavy metal scythes were also in use in some parts of Europe, much like those still used today. The use of cattle for traction is evidenced from neolithic Rumania in the fifth millennium b.c. (Ghetie and Mateescu, 1973), and carts were certainly used in Europe from the third millennium, although carting was probably only a common element in agricultural technology in the second and in particular in the first millennium b.c.

However, although in all three cases the new technology was much more effective than the old, it only became widespread very slowly – both ards and sickles were still very common in medieval Europe alongside the much more efficient technologies available. The reason was that these technological developments, which now seem to us simply 'better', had in fact many hidden costs for a farming community. Unlike hand tools, the ard required one or two oxen, the maintenance of which in turn needed pasture, stalls, fodder, barns and preferably carts. Heavier ploughs required larger teams of oxen, with all that that entailed. In the same way the flint sickle could normally be made by any household from local materials, whereas the bronze sickle required a community to produce a surplus of some kind to gain access to the bronze market or support the specialist craftsman. Adoption of the scythe, reaping close to the ground (whereas the sickle reaps just below the ear) required further investment in facilities for bulk transport and storage of the straw. In all these cases the true costs to a community might easily outweigh the apparent advantages of technological progress. In medieval Europe, heavy ploughs and scythes were often adopted as part of a complex process of intensification at a time of demographic stress, when more land needed to be cultivated, heavier tools were needed, and the increased investment necessitated by the more efficient technology became worthwhile. The role of technological change in prehistoric Europe seems to have been broadly comparable. It could greatly increase agricultural productivity, but change seems rarely if ever to have been a simple process of invention and immediate universal adoption: technological development was invariably related to major changes in other aspects of society, particularly in population levels and social complexity.

Population increase

The archaeological record frequently implies an increase in the human population of a region: numbers of sites increase, or sizes of sites, or both. When such a trend had to be explained without reference to population immigration, a common explanation put forward was that the invention or adoption of a new technology enabled people to produce more food and hence to raise the ceiling for their numbers. Such an argument was frequently cited to account for the population expansion associated with the earliest agriculture, or that at the end of the second millennium b.c. when bronze became really common in Europe. In 1965, however, Esther Boserup published a study of agricultural change in modern farming systems in tropical Africa that has had an enormous impact on archaeology, putting forward the thesis that population pressure was the key factor in agricultural intensification.

Boserup argued that subsistence farmers, being naturally conservative, will maintain their level of economic output with their existing system of production and technology as long as they can, but as population rises so output efficiency decreases, and eventually they are compelled to increase output by a more productive but more labour-intensive method of farming. In time population pressure will catch up again, and the new system will have to be abandoned for a yet more intensive system of production. Thus in her model the increase in population generates successive intensifications in the agricultural system, not the other way round (Fig. 98).

In a later study, Boserup (1981) has applied her ideas to European agricultural history, arguing that population increase in the later first millennium A.D. was instrumental in forcing the adoption of the mould-board plough, horse rather than cattle traction, and the three course system of rotation in the twelfth and thirteenth centuries. In the later medieval and modern periods, too, the main episodes of agricultural intensification have correlated broadly with periods of population increase, providing some persuasive support for Boserup's thesis even though other factors were clearly involved as well (Grigg, 1982). Many prehistorians, faced with similar evidence for episodes of population increase coinciding with periods of economic change (and normally other cultural change as well), were quick to note the attractions of her model as a powerful generalising explanation for major changes in human behaviour where particularistic explanations had formerly prevailed, notably the change from hunting and gathering to farming, and the intensification in food production associated with the formation of most of the early states.

As the regional studies have made clear, I believe that Boserup's model probably underlies in part at least the major periods of agricultural intensification in prehistoric Europe, given the fact that new technologies normally took so long to become common and that the periods of widespread intensification invariably coincided with population increase. (In the same way the new crops of Mediterranean polyculture were clearly available long before they became important, but their first systematic cultivation

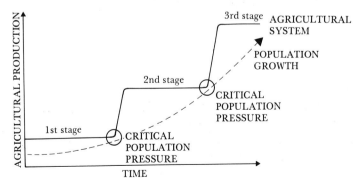

Fig. 98. Boserup's model of population pressure and agricultural change. (From the argument in Boserup, 1965; after Barker, 1981: fig. 52)

invariably coincided with population increase.) However, prehistoric data are such that at present it is impossible to distinguish population increase from population pressure, or to separate cause and effect when on the prehistoric timescale agricultural intensification simply appears as more or less contemporary ('give or take a few centuries') with population increase. Even for the historical period, Boserup conceded that 'it is often difficult or impossible to determine . . . whether the demographic change is the cause or the effect of the change in agricultural methods' (1965: 117).

In addition, agricultural intensification need not be the only solution to population pressure. Migration to new land or diversification in the food base may well be alternatives, as seems likely in several instances in prehistoric Europe. Another alternative is the Malthusian solution – famine and death – and the archaeological record of prehistoric Europe includes several instances (not simply a function of archaeological visibility) of a settlement boom followed by a drastic contraction lasting many centuries, such as those in southern France reminiscent of the population cycles there in historical times (Le Roy Ladurie, 1966; Mills, 1981). Finally, the prime assumption of Boserup's model, that human population growth is a variable independent of the other dynamics of an agricultural system, is highly debatable (e.g. Dahlberg, 1976; Hassan, 1973; Sussman, 1972), and changes in food production in later prehistory brought about by social change could well have resulted in population increase (see below).

Probably the most valuable contribution of Boserup's study to prehistoric archaeology has been not its direct application (although, as I have said, I am sure population stress will emerge most frequently as the fundamental context of agricultural change) but its impact on the general outlook of many archaeologists towards prehistoric farmers. It reminds us that change for low-technology farmers is normally about stress, not opportunism: there has to be a very good reason for them to contemplate change because it might make matters worse. The margin between success and disaster is too narrow for them to countenance idle experiment or some of the rosier speculations offered from the academic armchair (viz: 'there is no mystery about our great extent of prehistoric landscape . . . the people who were using these areas were simply trying to be better farmers', Fowler, 1981b: 30).

Social evolution

Discussing agricultural change in medieval Europe, Grigg (1982: 43) concludes that 'whilst population growth was unquestionably a potent factor in causing agricultural change, there are too many alternative explanations of the events associated with periods of population growth for it to be the only cause'. So too in prehistoric Europe the regional agricultural sequences reconstructed in this book reveal time and time again that changes in agriculture coincided with other major changes in the lives of the human communities – social, economic, technological, even ideological. In particular, the increasing complexity of social organisation in prehistoric Europe meant that communities were increasingly capable of manipulating their technological and economic as well as social environments, and so of setting in train the kind of relationships between technology, food supply and population that are the reverse of the Boserup model. The critical role of elites in the organisation and manipulation of an agricultural surplus is

apparent in many areas of later prehistoric Europe – most r
Aegean because of the wealth of information in the archives
Europe where subsistence data have been well studied on a reg
southern England in the Iron Age.

In earlier agricultural history, too, the role of social structure
have been of considerable significance as the data improve. F
relationships in temperate Europe between social change and the increasing importance
of secondary animal products in the third millennium b.c. have been well shown by
Sherratt (1981), although the process and its origins were probably more complex than
the one- or two-stage Secondary Products Revolution which he argued was caused at
that time by contact with the Russian steppes and Mesopotamia. Dairying was clearly
practised from the very beginning of farming in several parts of Europe, and it would
not be at all surprising to find the physiological adaptation to milk products and
associated husbandry techniques originating in Europe much earlier, in the systems of
animal exploitation practised in Europe in the late Pleistocene. Horse riding was probably also of similar antiquity (Bahn, 1978, 1980), although the horse was then
undoubtedly very rare in Europe until the third millennium; and, as mentioned above,
cattle traction and perhaps ard cultivation could well have been a feature of neolithic
farming in the Balkans. However, the third millennium was clearly the period of the
critical impact of the new technology on much of temperate Europe, associated with
settlement expansion and fundamental social change.

Ethnography suggests that warfare is likely to have been rife amongst many agricultural societies in prehistoric Europe before the prevalence of fortifications (Otterbein,
1970), a thesis which seems increasingly likely to be confirmed by archaeology on the
evidence of neolithic Britain (Mercer, 1980, 1981). The establishment of a social prehistory is still in its infancy, but in Britain we are just beginning to discern the complexities
of the shift from the group alliances and corporate identities of the early farmers to the
power struggles of competing households in the second millennium, accumulating personal wealth by marriage alliances, exchange and, presumably, force of arms. Such
studies of changing social structures have clear implications for changing agricultural
goals amongst prehistoric communities, just as the slave economy of the Roman empire
and the inequalities of land ownership in medieval Europe were integrally related to the
static agricultural technologies of those periods. In addition, it is apparent that one of the
most critical aspects of prehistoric farming for those who had to do it, the division of
labour between the sexes (Fig. 99), is still largely a matter of conjecture, apart from the
consensus view that women probably did most of the work (sowing, weeding, harvesting) in early neolithic hoe-based agriculture, whereas the male role was critical in later
plough agriculture and pastoralism (Sherratt, 1981: 297) – although the continued differences in sex roles in bronze age farming in Denmark (p. 241) suggest that we should
beware of imagining that such a simple linear development was universal.

As Grigg concludes for medieval and modern farming in Europe (1982: 228), it is
impossible to rank models of agricultural change in prehistory in order of usefulness,
and it is very unlikely that there is one model to explain all change at all places at all
times. The story of prehistoric farming described here indicates that those major

changes in agriculture that can be defined – and undoubtedly our present perspective is lamentably sketchy – frequently coincided with other major changes in prehistoric life, and always with population increase, although the role of the latter as cause or effect is never clear. The further investigation of our agricultural prehistory demands the integration of the widest range of archaeological studies: the gaps in the data base from relevant subject areas with a long research history – palaeoenvironmental reconstruction, palaeoeconomy, behavioural studies of technology, social reconstruction – are still immense; and in vital areas such as demography, nutrition and physiology we are still at the pioneering stages of enquiry. However, at least we have reached the stage of discerning a far more complex agricultural prehistory than seemed evident even a decade or so ago, and the explanations we must seek for its development, as for its origins, will undoubtedly turn out to be much more complicated (and I think rewarding) than we have anticipated hitherto: an interplay between the social relations which regulate economic activity on the one hand, and, on the other, the biological principles which prehistoric archaeology indicates to have underpinned so much of the behaviour of our species.

Prehistoric farming in perspective

The third theme of this book stands in stark contrast to the second: that in spite of all the changes in agricultural technology and organisation discussed above, one of the most impressive features of the prehistory and history of European farming is the sur-

Fig. 99. 'Agriculture during the Iron Epoch': the division of labour in prehistoric farming remains very much an open question. (After Figuier, 1876: fig. 263)

vival of regional agricultural traditions. In the Mediterranean or in the Balkans the prehistoric farmer would still recognise much that is familiar in the everyday life of the small farmer today. The traditional system of alpine farming practised in historical times can be traced back to the first prehistoric farming there; fundamentally it did not change until the eighteenth century, when new fodder crops like maize finally enabled farmers to break the constraint of labour-intensive hay production for overwintering stock – yet the foundations of modern alpine farming can still be discerned in the neolithic husbandry of Switzerland. Exactly the same is true of the agricultural systems of northern Scandinavia, or the crofting economy of the Scottish islands. All these areas are of course marginal to the heartland of modern industrial farming on the temperate lowlands where, although medieval practices can often be shown to have been of prehistoric origin (for example *plaggen* culture in Holland), modern farming systems seem light years away from those of antiquity. Yet here most of all I would argue that we have much to learn from the past.

Modern European agriculture ranks as one of the success stories of postwar investment, with constant improvements in productivity being achieved in response to financial encouragement from the E.E.C. governments. However, the huge outputs are essentially the result of vastly increased inputs (Rees, 1983). Cereal yields which would have seemed beyond belief a few decades ago are achieved by lavish inputs of fertilisers, herbicides and fungicides, and experimental work is seeking further advances in high input/high output strains. A test crop in Hampshire in 1983 yielded a world record of 6.33 tonnes per acre (15.65 tonnes per hectare), receiving chemical protection at very high rates and two or three times the level of fertiliser of even today's high norms. Modern dairying is caught in the same sort of spiral: high carrying capacities are dependent on high levels of fertiliser, and high milk yields on high levels of concentrated feeds. Intensive beef production is relying increasingly on large-bodied animals dependent on high energy inputs. The modern factory pig is the prime example of high cost stock keeping. Sheep breeding is less affected than the rest, but research is again concentrating on high yield/high cost animals giving high lambing percentages (twins and triplets per year, or three crops every two years) in response to high feeding levels and close housing.

Profitability in modern arable farming is entirely based on the fragile (indeed almost certainly false) assumption of infinite supplies of relatively cheap chemical dressings and cheap energy, and there has been minimal research on the development of cereal varieties capable of relatively high output on the drastically reduced inputs that will probably be necessary in two or three decades' time. In dairying, constant selection for increased milk per animal has resulted in the development of the modern dairy cow, with a smaller stomach capacity than either her European antecedents twenty years ago or modern Third World cattle, unable to process the large volume of fodder which would be necessary in a return to low-cost feeding regimes. Modern beef cattle are far less efficient converters of traditional bulk feeds than the smaller-bodied breeds common twenty years ago (Meat and Livestock Commission, 1980–1: table 53). This is the context which makes the preservation of today's rare breeds the sensible husbandry of precious genetic resources rather than the sentimental protection of the casualties of progress (Fig. 100). So too the history and prehistory of the crops and animals which have sustained us for the 5000–6000 years of pre-industrial farming (particularly the raw data of archaeobotany and archaeozoology) offer a perspective of success and failure which it is surely sensible to comprehend as best we can.

Fig. 100. 'Don't let them miss the boat': a slogan of the Rare Breeds Survival Trust, on the back cover of their monthly journal *The Ark*, 10 (10), 15 October 1983.

BIBLIOGRAPHY

Acanfora, M. O. (1962–3) Gli scavi di Valle Ottara presso Cittaducale. *Bullettino di Paletnologia Italiana* 71–2, n.s. 14: 73–154.

Albrectsen, E. (1970) Early iron age settlement on Fünen. *Kuml*: 123–44.

Albrethsen, S. E. and Brinch Petersen, E. (1976) Excavating a mesolithic cemetery at Vedbaek, Denmark. *Acta Archaeologica* 47: 1–28.

Albrethsen, S. E. and Street-Jensen, J. (1963) A group of tumuli at Vojens. *Aarbøger for Nordisk Oldkyndighed og Historie*: 29–31.

Alcock, L. (1965) Hillforts in Wales and the Marches. *Antiquity* 39: 184–95.

Alexander, J. (1972) *Yugoslavia Before the Roman Conquest*. London, Thames and Hudson.

Alföldy, G. (1974) *Noricum*. London, Routledge and Kegan Paul (translated by Anthony Birley).

Alhonen, P. (1967) Palaeolimnological investigations of three inland lakes in southwestern Finland. *Acta Botanica Fennica* 76: 1–59.

Aliger, M. (1974–6) Protohistoire de la Vaunage. *Mémoires de l'Academie de Nîmes*, seventh series, 59: 139–67.

Almagro, M. and Arribas, A. (1963) *El Poblade y la Necrópolis Megalíticos de Los Millares*. Madrid, Bibliotheca Praehistorica Hispana.

Ammerman, A. J. and Bonardi, S. (1981) Recent developments in the study of neolithic settlement in Calabria. In G. Barker and R. Hodges (*eds.*) *Archaeology and Italian Society*: 335–42. Oxford, British Archaeological Reports, International Series 102.

Ammerman, A. J. and Cavalli-Sforza, L. L. (1971) Measuring the rate of spread of early farming in Europe. *Man* 6 (1): 674–88.

Ammerman, A. J., Butler, J. J., Diamond, G., Menozzi, P., Pals, J. P., Sevink, J., Smit, A. and Voorrips, A. (1976) Rapporto sugli scavi a Monte Leoni: un insediamento dell'Età del Bronzo in Val Parma. *Preistoria Alpina* 12: 127–54.

Ammerman, A. J., Butler, J. J., Diamond, G., Menozzi, P., Pals, J. P., Sevink, J., Smit, A. and Voorrips, A. (1978) Report on the excavations at Monte Leoni, a bronze age settlement in the Parma valley. *Helinium* 18: 126–66.

Amschler, J. W. (1939) Vorgeschichtliche Tierreste aus den Grabungen von Bludenz. *Mitteilungen den Prähistorisches Kommission der Akademie der Wissenschaft* 3: 217–42.

Amschler, J. W. (1949) Ur- und frühgeschichtliche Haustierfunde aus Österreich. *Archaeologia Austriaca* 3: 1–70.

Anati, E. (1961) *The Camonica Valley*. New York, Knopf.

Anati, E. (1976) *Evolution and Style in Camunian Rock Art*. Centro Camuno di Studi Preistorici (Capo di Ponte, Italy), Archivi 6.

Andel, T. H. van and Shackleton, J. C. (1982) Late paleolithic and mesolithic coastlines of Greece and the Aegean. *Journal of Field Archaeology* 9: 445–54.

Andersen, N. H. (1973–4). Sarup, a fortified neolithic site. *Kuml*: 109–20.

Andersen, S. H. (1973–4) Ringkloster: an inland Ertebølle settlement in Jutland. *Kuml*: 11–108.

Andersen, S. H. (1978) Aggersund. An Ertebølle settlement on the Limfjord. *Kuml*: 7–56.

Anderson, A. (1981) Economic change and the prehistoric fur trade in northern Sweden. *Norwegian Archaeological Review* 14 (1): 1–38.

Anderson, J. (1961) Biology and management of roe deer in Denmark. *La Terre et Vie* 1: 41–53.

Andresen, J. M., Byrd, B. F., Elson, M. D., McGuire, R. H., Mendoza, R. G., Staski, E. and White, J. P. (1981) The deer hunters: Star Carr reconsidered. *World Archaeology* 13: 30–46.

Andrist, D., Flükiger, W. and Andrist, A. (1964) Das Simmental zur Steinzeit. *Acta Bernensia 2*.

ApSimon, A. M. (1976) Ballynagilly and the beginning and end of the Irish Neolithic. In S. J. De Laet (*ed.*) *Acculturation and Continuity in Atlantic Europe*: 15–30. Bruges, Diss. Archaeol. Gandenses 21.

ApSimon, A. M. and Greenfield, E. (1972) The excavation of the bronze age and iron age settlement at Trevisker Round, St. Eval, Cornwall. *Proceedings of the Prehistoric Society* 38: 302–81.

Armitage, P. L. (1983) The early history of the English longwool sheep. *The Ark* (10) 3: 90–7.

Arnal, G. B. (1976) *La Céramique Néolithique dans le Haut-Languedoc*. Lodeve.

Arnal, J. (1973) Le Lebous à St. Mathieu-de-Treviers. *Gallia Préhistoire* 16 (1): 131–200.

Arribas, A. (1968) Las bases economicas del Neolítico al Bronce. In M. Tarradell (*ed.*) *Estudios de Economía Antigua de la Península Ibérica*: 33–60. Barcelona, Vicens Vives.

Arribas, A. (1972) Das Neolithikum Andalusiens. In H. Schwabedissen (*ed.*) *Die Anfänge des Neolithikums vom Orient bis Nordeuropa* 7: 108–27. Cologne, Bohlau.

Arribas, A. (1976) A new basis for the study of the Eneolithic and Bronze Age in south-east Spain. In J. V. S. Megaw (*ed.*) *To Illustrate the Monuments: Essays on Archaeology Presented to Stuart Piggott*: 153–62. London, Thames and Hudson.

Ashbee, P. (1970) *The Earthen Long Barrow in Britain*. London, Dent.

Atherden, M. A. (1972) A contribution to the vegetation and land use history of the eastern-central North York Moors. Durham University, unpublished Ph.D. thesis.

Atkinson, R. J. C. (1968) Old mortality: some aspects of burial and population in neolithic Britain. In J. M. Coles and D. D. A. Simpson (*eds.*) *Studies in Ancient Europe*: 83–94. Leicester, University Press.

Bagolini, B. (1971a) Considerazioni preliminari sull'industria litica dei livelli neolitici di Romagnano (Trento) (scavi 1969–1970). *Preistoria Alpina* 7: 107–33.

Bagolini, B. (1971b) Ricerche sulla tipometria litica dei complessi epipaleolitici della Valle dell'Adige. *Preistoria Alpina* 7: 243–76.

Bagolini, B. (1976) Le attività economiche nella preistoria del Trentino. *Economia Trentina* 4: 105–20.

Bagolini, B. and Biagi, P. (1975a) L'insediamento di Garniga (Trento) e considerazioni sul Neolitico della valle dell'Adige nell'ambito dell'Italia settentrionale. *Preistoria Alpina* 11: 7–24.

Bagolini, B. and Biagi, P. (1975b) Il Neolitico del Vhò di Piadena. *Preistoria Alpina* 11: 77–121.

Bagolini, B. and Biagi, P. (1976) La Vela de Trente de le 'moment de style adriatique' dans la culture des vases à bouche carrée. *Preistoria Alpina* 12: 71–7.

Bagolini, B., Barbacovi, F., Castelletti, L. and Lanzinger, M. (1975) Colbricon (scavi 1973–1974). *Preistoria Alpina* 11: 1–35.

Bahn, P. G. (1977) Seasonal migration in southwest France during the late glacial period. *Journal of Archaeological Science* 4: 245–57.

Bahn, P. G. (1978) The 'unacceptable face' of the west European Upper Palaeolithic. *Antiquity* 52: 183–92.

Bahn, P. G. (1980) Crib-biting: tethered horses in the Palaeolithic? *World Archaeology* 12: 212–17.

Bailey, G. N. (1978) Shell middens as indicators of postglacial economies: a territorial perspective. In P. Mellars (*ed.*) *The Early Postglacial Settlement of Northern Europe*: 37–63. London, Duckworth.

Bailloud, G. (1966) La civilisation du Rhône et le Bronze ancien du Midi de la France. *Revue Archeologique de l'Est et du Centre-Est* 17 (3–3): 131–64.

Bailloud, G. (1973) Les habitations chalcolithiques de Conquette (St. Martin-de-Loudres, Hérault). In *L'Homme Hier et Aujourd'hui*: 493–504. Paris, Cujas.

Bailloud, G. (1974) *Le Néolithique dans le Bassin Parisien*. Paris, CNRS.

Bailloud, G. (1976) Les civilisations néolithiques du Passin Parisien et du Nord de la France. In J. Guilaine (*ed.*) *La Préhistoire Française 2. Civilisations Néolithiques et Protohistoriques*: 375–86. Paris, CNRS.

Bakels, C. C. (1974) Enkele milieu-aspecten van grafhenvel Ia te Hoogkarspel. *West-Frieslands Oud en Nieuw* 41: 259–61.

Bakels, C. C. (1975) Pollen spectra from the late bronze age urnfield at Hilvarenbeek, Prov. Noord-Brabant, Netherlands. *Analecta Praehistorica Leidensia* 8: 45–51.

Bakels, C. C. (1978) Four linearbandkeramik settlements and their environment: a palaeo-ecological study of Sittard, Stein, Elsloo and Hienheim. *Analecta Praehistorica Leidensia* 11: 1–245.

Bakka, E. (1976) Artisk og nordisk i Bronsealderen i Nordskandinavia. *Miscellanea* (Trondheim), 25: 1–58.

Bakka, E. and Kaland, P. E. (1971) Early farming in Hordaland, western Norway. Problems and approaches in archaeology and pollen analysis. *Norwegian Archaeological Review* 4 (2): 1–35.

Bakker, J. A. (1980) Einige Bemerkungen über die niederländische Grossteingräber und deren Erbauer. *Nachrichten aus Niedersachsens Urgeschichte* 49: 31–59.

Bakker, J. A., Brandt, R. W., Geel, B. van, Jansma, M. J., Kujper, W. J., Mensch, P. J. A. van, Pals, J. P. and Ijzereef, G. F. (1977) Hoogkarspel-Watertoren: towards a reconstruction of ecology and archaeology of an agrarian settlement of 1000 B.C. In B. L. van Beek, R. W. Brandt and M. Groenman-van Waateringe (*eds.*) *Ex Horreo*: 187–225. Amsterdam, Albert Egges van Giffen Instituut vour Prae- en Protohistorie.

Balaam, N., Smith, K. and Wainwright, G. J. (1982) The Shaugh Moor project: fourth report – environment, context and conclusion. *Proceedings of the Prehistoric Society* 48: 203–78.

Balkwill, C. J. (1976) The evidence of cemeteries for later prehistoric development in the Upper Rhine valley. *Proceedings of the Prehistoric Society* 42: 187–214.

Bándi, G. (1963) Die Frage der Riementeiler des mittelbronzezeitlichen Pferdegeschirrs im Karpatenbeckens. *Archaeologia Ertesitö* 90: 46–60.

Bandi, H. G. (1964) Birsmatten-Basisgrotte. Eine mittelsteinzeitliche Fundstelle im Unteren Birstal. *Acta Bernensia* 1.

Bandi, H. G. and Müller-Beck, H. (*eds.*) (1963–74) Seeburg, Bürgaschisee-Süd. *Acta Bernensia* 2 (1963), *Acta Bernensia* 4 (1965), *Acta Bernensia* 5 (1967), *Acta Bernensia* 6 (1974).

Bankoff, H. A., Winter, F. A. and Greenfield, H. J. (1980) Archaeological survey in the lower Moravia valley, Yugoslavia. *Current Anthropology* 21 (2): 268–9.

Banner, J. (1955) Research on the Hungarian Bronze Age since 1936 and the bronze age settlement at Békés-Várdomb. *Proceedings of the Prehistoric Society* 21: 123–43.

Barfield, L. H. (1971) *Northern Italy Before Rome*. London, Thames and Hudson.

Barfield, L. H. (1981) Patterns of north Italian trade 5000–2000 b.c. In G. Barker and R. Hodges (*eds.*) *Archaeology and Italian Society*: 27–51. Oxford, British Archaeological Reports, International Series 102.

Barfield, L. H. and Broglio, A. (1965) Nuove osservazioni sull'industria de le Basse di Valcalaona (Colli Euganei). *Revista di Scienze Preistoriche* 20: 307–44.

Barfield, L. H. and Broglio, A. (1966) Materiali per lo studio del neolitico del territorio Vicentino. *Bullettino di Paletnologia Italiana* 75, n.s. 17: 51–95.

Barfield, L. H. and Broglio, A. (1971) Osservazioni sulle culture neolitiche del Veneto e del Trentino nel quadro del Neolitico Padano. *Origini* 5: 21–45.

Barfield, L. H., Biagi, P. and Borrello, M. A. (1975–6) Scavi nella stazione di Monte Covolo (1972–73). Parte 1. *Annali del Museo di Gavardo* 12: 7–160.

Barfield, L. H., Cremaschi, M. and Castelletti, L. (1975) Stanziamento del vaso campaniforme a Sant'Ilario d'Enza (Reggio Emilia). *Preistoria Alpina* 11: 155–99.

Barker, G. (1971) The development of prehistoric copper and bronze metallurgy in Italy, in the light of the metal analyses from the Pigorini museum, Rome. *Bullettino di Paletnologia Italiana* 80, n.s. 22: 12–44.

Barker, G. (1972) The conditions of cultural and economic growth in the Bronze Age of central Italy. *Proceedings of the Prehistoric Society* 38: 170–208.

Barker, G. (1973) Cultural and economic change in the prehistory of central Italy. In C. Renfrew (*ed.*) *The Explanation of Culture Change – Models in Prehistory*: 359–70. London, Duckworth.

Barker, G. (1975a) Prehistoric territories and economies in central Italy. In E. S. Higgs (*ed.*) *Palaeoeconomy*: 111–75. Cambridge, University Press.

Barker, G. (1975b) Stock economy at Tufariello. *Journal of Field Archaeology* 2: 59–72.

Barker, G. (1975c) Early neolithic land use in Yugoslavia. *Proceedings of the Prehistoric Society* 41: 85–104.

Barker, G. (1976a) Early neolithic economy at Vhò. *Preistoria Alpina* 12: 61–70.

Barker, G. (1976b) Animal husbandry at Narce. In T. Potter (*ed.*) *A Faliscan Town in South Etruria: Excavations at Narce 1966–71*: 295–307. London, British School at Rome.

Barker, G. (1976c) An Apennine bronze age settlement at Petrella, Molise. *Papers of the British School at Rome* 44: 133–56.

Barker, G. (1976d) Morphological change and neolithic economies: an example from central Italy. *Journal of Archaeological Science* 3: 71–81.

Barker, G. (1977) Further information on the early neolithic economy of Vhò. *Preistoria Alpina* 13: 99–105.

Barker, G. (1977–9) Prehistoric economy at Monte Covolo: the animal bones. *Annali del Museo di Gavardo* 13: 41–73.

Barker, G. (1981) *Landscape and Society: Prehistoric Central Italy*. London and New York, Academic Press.

Barker, G. (1983) The animal bones from Isbister. In J. Hedges (*ed.*) *Isbister: a Chambered Tomb in Orkney*: 133–48. Oxford, British Archaeological Reports, British Series 115.

Barker, G. (*ed.*) forthcoming *Archaeology and History in a Mediterranean Valley*. Cambridge, University Press.

Barker, G. and Webley, D. P. (1978) Causewayed camps and early neolithic economies in central southern England. *Proceedings of the Prehistoric Society* 44: 161–86.

Barral, L. (1960) La grotte de la Madeleine (Hérault). *Bulletin du Musée d'Anthropologie Préhistorique de Monaco* 7: 5–73.

Barrett, J. G. and Bradley, R. J. (*eds.*) (1980) *Settlement and Society in the British Later Bronze Age*. Oxford, British Archaeological Reports, British Series 83.

Bárta, J. (1973) La Mésolithique en Slovaquie. In S. K. Kozlowski (*ed.*) *The Mesolithic in Europe*: 53–75. Warsaw, University Press.

Battaglia, R. (1943) La palafitta del Lago di Ledro nel Trentino. *Memorie del Museo di Storia Naturale della Venezia Tridentina* 7: 3–63.

Baumann, W. and Quietzsch, H. (1969) Zur ur- und frühgeschichtlichen Besiedlung der Gommatzscher Pflege. *Ausgrabungen und Funde* 14 (2): 64–9.

Bay-Petersen, J. L. (1975) Pre-Neolithic Faunal Exploitation in Southern France and Denmark. University of Cambridge, unpublished Ph.D. thesis.

Bay-Petersen, J. L. (1978) Animal exploitation in mesolithic Denmark. In P. Mellars (*ed.*) *The Early Postglacial Settlement of Northern Europe*: 115–45. London, Duckworth.

Behrens, H. (1973) *Die Jungsteinzeit im Mittelelbe-Saale-Gebiet*. Berlin, VEB Verlag der Wissenschaften.

Behrensmeyer, A. K. and Hill, A. (1979) *Fossils in the Making*. Chicago, University Press.

Bell, M. (1981) Valley sediments and environmental change. In M. Jones and G. Dimbleby (*eds.*) *The Environment of Man: the Iron Age to the Anglo-Saxon Period*: 75–91. Oxford, British Archaeological Reports, British Series 87.

Benac, A. and Brodar, M. (1958) Crvena Stijena. *Glasnik Zemaljskog Muzeja Sarajevo* 13: 43–61.

Bender, B. (1975) *Farming in Prehistory*. London, John Baker.

Bender, B. (1978) Gatherer-hunter to farmer: a social perspective. *World Archaeology* 10: 204–22.

Bender, B. (1981) Gatherer-hunter intensification. In A. Sheridan and G. Bailey (*eds.*) *Economic Archaeology*: 149–57. Oxford, British Archaeological Reports, International Series 96.

Benson, D. (1982) Farming and fighting in iron age Pembrokeshire. *Current Archaeology* 7 (82): 332–5.

Berciu, D. (1967) *Romania*. London, Thames and Hudson.

Berglund, B. (1969) Vegetation and human influence in South Scandinavia during prehistoric times. *Acta Oecologica Scandinavica. Supplementum* 12: 9–29.

Bersu, G. (1940) Excavations at Little Woodbury, Wiltshire. *Proceedings of the Prehistoric Society* 6: 30–111.

Bertrand, J. P. and L'Homer, A. (1975) *Les Deltas de la Méditerranée du Nord*. IXme Congrès International de Sedimentologie, Nice, Excursion 16.

Bettinger, R. L. (1980) Explanatory/predictive models of hunter-gatherer adaptation. In M. Schiffer (*ed.*) *Advances in Archaeological Method and Theory* 3: 189–256. London and New York, Academic Press.

Beug, H. J. (1967) On the forest history of the Dalmatian coast. *Revue Paléobotanique et Palynologique* 2: 271–9.

Beyer, A. I. (1972) *Das Erdwerk der Michelsberger Kultur auf dem Hetzenberg bei Heilbronn-Neckargartach, Teil II, Die Tierknochenfunde*. Stuttgart, Forschungen und Berichte Vor- und Frühgeschichte in Baden-Württemberg 3/II.

Biagi, P. (1976a) Laghi di Ravenole e laghetto Dasdana (Brescia). *Preistoria Alpina* 12: 262–3.

Biagi, P. (1976b) Stazione mesolitica a Provaglio d'Iseo. *Natura Bresciana* 13: 75–92.

Biagi, P. (1980) Some aspects of the prehistory of northern Italy from the final Palaeolithic to the middle Neolithic: a reconsideration of the evidence available to date. *Proceedings of the Prehistoric Society* 46: 9–18.

Binford, L. R. (1962) Archaeology as anthropology. *American Antiquity* 28: 217–25.

Binford, L. R. (1964) A consideration of archaeological research design. *American Antiquity* 29: 425–41.

Binford, L. R. (1965) Archaeological systematics and the study of culture process. *American Antiquity* 31: 203–10.

Binford, L. R. (1968) Post pleistocene adaptations. In S. R. Binford and L. R. Binford (*eds.*) *New Perspectives in Archaeology*: 313–41. Chicago, Aldine.

Binford, L. R. (1981) *Bones – Ancient Men and Modern Myths*. London and New York, Academic Press.

Bintliff, J. L. (1975) Mediterranean alluviation: new evidence in archaeology. *Proceedings of the Prehistoric Society* 41: 78–84.

Bintliff, J. L. (1976) The plain of western Macedonia and the neolithic site of Nea Nikomedeia. *Proceedings of the Prehistoric Society* 42: 241–62.

Bintliff, J. L. (1977a) *Natural Environment and Human Settlement in Prehistoric Greece*. Oxford, British Archaeological Reports, International Series 28.

Bintliff, J. L. (1977b) The history of archaeo-geographic studies of prehistoric Greece, and recent fieldwork. In J. L. Bintliff (*ed.*) *Mycenaean Geography*: 3–16. Cambridge, University Library Press.

Bintliff, J. L. (1980) Settlement patterns, land tenure and social structure: a diachronic model. Paper delivered to SAA meeting, Philadelphia, May 1980.

Blance, B. M. (1961) Early bronze age colonists in Iberia. *Antiquity* 35: 192–201.

Blanchet, J.-C. and Petit, M. (1972) L'habitat néolithiques de Jonquières (Oise): premiers résultats. *Bulletin de la Société Préhistorique Française* 69: 389–407.

Blaxter, K. L., Kay, R. N. B., Scharman, G. A. M., Cunningham, J. M. M. and Hamilton, W. J. (1974) *Farming the Red Deer*. Edinburgh, Department of Agriculture and Fisheries for Scotland.

Bloch, M. (1952) *Les Caractères Originaux de l'Histoire Rurale Française*. Paris, Colin.

Bloemers, J. (1972) Drie Rössen scherven nit Nederlands-Limburg. *Helinium* 12: 47–52.

Board of Agriculture and Fisheries (1918) *Farmyard Manure*. (Leaflet 93). London, H.M.S.O.

Boardman, J. (1976) The olive in the Mediterranean: its culture and use. *Philosophical Transactions of the Royal Society of London* Ser. B, 275: 187–96.

Boatfield, G. (1980a) *Farm Livestock*. Ipswich, Farming Press Ltd.

Boatfield, G. (1980b) *Farm Crops*. Ipswich, Farming Press Ltd.

Bodmer-Gessner, V. (1949–50) Provisorische Mitteilungen über die Ausgrabung einer mesolithischen Siedlung in Schötz ("Fischerhäusen"), Wauwilermoos, Kt. Luzern, durch H. Reinerth im Jahre 1933. *Jahrbuch der Schweizerischen Gesellschaft für Urgeschichte* 40: 108–26.

Boessneck, J. (1962) Die Tierreste aus der Argissa-Magula vom präkeramischen Neolithikum bis zur mittleren Bronzezeit. In V. Milojčić, J. Boessneck and M. Hopf (*eds.*) *Die Deutschen Ausgrabungen auf der Argissa-Magula in Thessalien I: des präkermischen Neolithikum sowie die Tier- und Pflanzenreste*. Bonn, Rudolf Habelt.

Boessneck, J. (1969a) Osteological differences between sheep (*Ovis aries* L.) and goat (*Capra hircus* L.). In D. Brothwell and E. S. Higgs (*eds.*) *Science in Archaeology*: 331–58. London, Thames and Hudson, second edition.

Boessneck, J. (1969b) Restos óseos de animales del Cerro de la Virgen, en Orce, y del Cerro del Real, en Galera (Granada). *Noticario Arqueológico Hispaníco* 10–11 (12): 172–89.

Boessneck, J., Driesch, A. von den, Meyer-Lemppenau, U. and Wechsler-von Ohlen, E. (1971) *Die Tierknochenfunde aus dem Oppidum von Manching*. Wiesbaden, Franz Steiner.

Bognár-Kutzián, I. (1972) *The Early Copper Age Tiszapolgar Culture in the Carpathian Basin*. Budapest, Akadémiai Kiadó.

Bogucki, P. I. (1981) Early Neolithic Economy and Settlement in the Polish Lowlands. Cambridge, Massachusetts, Harvard University Ph.D.

Bogucki, P. I. (1982) *Early Neolithic Subsistence and Settlement in the Polish Lowlands*. Oxford, British Archaeological Reports, International Series 150.

Bogucki, P. I. and Grygiel, R. (1981) The household cluster at Brześć Kujawski 3: small-site methodology in the Polish lowlands. *World Archaeology* 13: 59–72.

Bökönyi, S. (1951) Untersuchung der Haustierfunde aus dem Gräberfeld von Alsonemédi. *Acta Archaeologica Hungarica* 1: 72–8.

Bökönyi, S. (1959) Die Frühalluviale Wirbeltierfauna Ungarns. *Acta Archaeologica* 11: 39–102.

Bökönyi, S. (1964) The vertebrate fauna of the neolithic settlement at Maroslele Pana. *Archaeologia Ertesítö* 91: 87–93.

Bökönyi, S. (1968) Die Wirbeltierfauna der Siedlung von Salgótarján-Pécskó. *Acta Archaeologica* 20: 59–100.

Bökönyi, S. (1970) Animal remains from Lepenski Vir. *Science* 167: 1702–4.

Bökönyi, S. (1973) Stock breeding. In D. R. Theocharis (*ed.*) *Neolithic Greece*: 165–78. Athens, National Bank of Greece.

Bökönyi, S. (1974) *History of Domestic Animals in Central and Eastern Europe*. Budapest, Akadémiai Kiadó.

Bökönyi, S. and Kubasiewicz, M. (1961) *Neolithische Tiere Polens und Ungarns in Ausgrabungen. 1. Das Hausrind*. Szczecin, Szczecińskie Towarzystwo Naukowe.

Bolomey, A. (1973) An outline of the late epipalaeolithic economy at the 'Iron Gates': the evidence of bones. *Dacia* 17: 41–52.

Bona, I. (1960) Clay models of bronze age wagons and wheels in the Middle Danube basin. *Acta Archaeologica Hungarica* 12: 83–111.

Bonatti, E. (1961) I sedimenti del Lago di Monterosi. *Experientia* 17 (252): 1–4.

Bonatti, E. (1963) Stratigrafia pollinica dei sedimenti postglaciali di Baccano, lago craterico del Làzio. *Atti della Società Toscana di Scienze Naturali* Ser. A, 70: 40–8.

Bonatti, E. (1966) North Mediterranean climate during the last Würm glaciation. *Nature* 209 (5027): 984–5.

Bonatti, E. (1970) Pollen sequence in the lake sediments. In G. E. Hutchinson (*ed.*) Ianula – an account of the history and development of the Lago di Monterosi, Latium, Italy. *Transactions of the American Philosophical Society* 60 (4): 26–31.

Bonsall, J. C. (1978) The coastal factor in the mesolithic settlement of northwest England. In B. Gramsch (*ed.*) *Proceedings of the Second International Symposium on the Mesolithic in Europe*: 15–25.

Bonuccelli, G. and Faedo, L. (1968) Il villaggio a ceramica impressa di Capo d'Acqua. *Atti della Società Toscana di Scienze Naturali* Ser. A, 75: 87–101.

Borówko-Długakowa, Z. (1969) Palynological investigations of late glacial and holocene deposits at Konin. *Geographia Polonica* 17: 267–81.

Boşcaiu, N. (1971) L'évolution post würmienne de la végétation du défilé du Danube. *Third International Palynological Conference, Novosibirsk.*

Bosch, P. W. (1979) A neolithic flint mine. *Scientific American* 240 (June): 98–104.

Boserup, E. (1965) *The Conditions of Agricultural Growth*. London, Allen and Unwin.

Boserup, E. (1981) *Population and Technology*. Oxford, Clarendon Press.

Bottema, A. (1967) A late quaternary pollen diagram from Ioannina, north western Greece. *Proceedings of the Prehistoric Society* 33: 26–9.

Bottema, S. (1974) *Late Quaternary Vegetation History of Northwestern Greece*. Groningen, University Press.

Bottema, S. (1975) The interpretation of pollen spectra from prehistoric settlements (with special attention to Liguliflorae). *Palaeohistoria* 17: 17–35.

Bottema, S. (1980) Palynological investigations on Crete. *Review of Palaeobotany and Palynology* 31: 193–217.

Bottema, S. (1981) Pollen analytical investigations in Thessaly (Greece). *Palaeohistoria* 21: 19–40.

Bourdillon, J. (1982) The Faunal Remains from Hamwih (Saxon Southampton). Southampton University, unpublished M.Phil. thesis.

Boureux, M. and Coudart, A. (1978) Implantations des premiers paysans sédentaires dans la vallée d l'Aisne. *Bulletin de la Société Préhistorique Française* 75 (5): 341–60.

Bouzek, J., Jäger, K. D. and Lozek, V. (1976) Climatic and settlement changes in the central European Bronze Age. *IXme Congrès UISPP, Nice (Sect. VII)*: 2. Paris, CNRS.

Bowden, P. (1967) Agricultural prices, farm profits and rents. In J. Thirsk (*ed.*) *The Agrarian History of England and Wales IV. 1500–1640*: 593–695. Cambridge, University Press.

Bozhilova, E. (1975) Changes of vegetation belts in Rila mountains during late and postglacial time. *Biuletyn Geologiczny (Warszawa)* 19: 93–9.

Bozhilova, E. and Filipova, M. (1975) Polenov analyz na Kulturni plastove ot Varnenskoto Ezero. *Izvestia na Narodnia Muzej Varna* 36: 19–25.

Bradford, J. S. P. (1949) 'Buried landscapes' in southern Italy. *Antiquity* 23: 58–72.

Bradford, J. S. P. and Williams-Hunt, P. R. (1946) Siticulosa Apulia. *Antiquity* 20: 191–200.

Bradley, R. J. (1971) Stock raising and the origins of the hillfort on the South Downs. *Antiquaries Journal* 51: 8–29.

Bradley, R. J. (1978a) Prehistoric field systems in Britain and northwest Europe – a review of some recent work. *World Archaeology* 9: 265–80.

Bradley, R. J. (1978b) *The Prehistoric Settlement of Britain*. London, Routledge and Kegan Paul.

Bradley, R. J. (1980) Prestige trade, agriculture and social change – some European examples. Paper delivered to SAA meeting, Philadelphia, May 1980.

Bradley, R. J. and Ellison, A. (1976) *Rams Hill*. Oxford, British Archaeological Reports, British Series 19.

Bradley, R. J., Lobb, S., Richards, J. and Robinson, M. (1980) Two late bronze age settlements on the Kennet gravels: excavations at Aldermaston Wharf and Knight's Farm, Burghfield, Berkshire. *Proceedings of the Prehistoric Society* 46: 217–95.

Braidwood, R. J. (1960) The agricultural revolution. *Scientific American* 203: 130–48.

Braudel, F. (1975) *The Mediterranean and the Mediterranean World in the Age of Philip II*. London, Fontana.

Brea, B. L. (1946) *Gli Scavi nella Caverna delle Arene Candide I*. Bordighera, Istituto di Studi Liguri.

Brea, B. L. (1956) *Gli Scavi nella Caverna delle Arene Candide II*. Bordighera, Istituto di Studi Liguri.

Brewster, T. C. M. (1963) *The Excavation of Staple Howe*. Malton, East Riding Archaeological Committee.

Briard, J. (1965) *Les Dépôts Bretons et l'Age du Bronze Atlantique*. Rennes, Musée de Bretagne.

Briard, J. (1970) Un tumulus du Bronze Ancien, Kernouen en Plouvorn (Finistère). *L'Anthropologie* 74: 5–55.

Briard, J. (1976) *The Bronze Age in Barbarian Europe*. London, Routledge and Kegan Paul.

Briard, J., Guerin, C., Morzadec-Kerfourn, M.-T. and Plusquellec, Y. (1970) Le site de Porsguen en Plouescat (Finistère-Nord). Faune, flore, archéologie. *Soc. Geol. Mineralo. Bretagne* 2: 45–60.

Brinch Petersen, E. (1970) Ølby Lyng: en ost sjaellandsk Kystboplads med Ertebøllekultur. *Aarbøger for Nordisk Oldkyndighed og Historie*: 5–42.

Brinch Petersen, E. (1973) A survey of the late palaeolithic and the mesolithic of Denmark. In S. K. Kozłowski (*ed.*) *The Mesolithic in Europe*: 77–127. Warsaw, University Press.

Brink, F. H. van den (1973) *A Field Guide to the Mammals of Britain and Europe*. London, Collins.

Brinkhuizen, D. C. (1979) Preliminary notes on fish remains from archaeological sites in the Netherlands. *Palaeohistoria* 21: 83–90.

Broadbent, N. D. (1978) Prehistoric settlement in northern Sweden. In P. Mellars (*ed*) *The Early Postglacial Settlement of Northern Europe*: 177–204. London, Duckworth.

Broglio, A. (1969) Considerazioni sui complessi epigravettiani del Veneto. *Scritti sul Quaternario in Onore di Angelo Pasa*: 137–47. Verona, Museo Civico di Storia Naturale.

Broglio, A. (1971) Risultati preliminari delle ricerche sui complessi epipaleolitici della Valle dell'Adige. *Preistoria Alpina* 7: 135–241.

Brongers, J. A. (1976) *Air Photography and Celtic Field Research in the Netherlands*. Amersfort, R.O.B.

Brox, O. (1963) Tradisjonell vinterforing i Nord-Norge. *Ottar* 36: 1–18.

Brukner, B. (1966) Die Tardenoisischen Funde von 'Pereš' bei Hajdakovo und aus Bačka Palanka, und das Problem der Beziehungen in Donaugebiet. *Archaeologica Iugoslavica* 7: 1–12.

Brukner, B. (1968) *Neolit u Vojvodina* (The Neolithic Period in Vojvodina). Beograd–Novi Sad, Vojvodanski Muzej.

Brunhes, J. and Girardin, P. (1906) Les groupes d'habitations du Val d'Anniviers comme types d'établissements humains. *Annales de Géographie* 15: 329–52.

Bryson, R. A., Lamb, H. H. and Donley, D. L. (1974) Drought and the decline of Mycenae. *Antiquity* 48: 46–50.

Bukowski, Z. (1974) Besiedlungscharakter der Lansitzerkultur in der Hallstattzeit am Beispiel Schlesiens und Grosspolens. In B. Chropovsky (*ed.*) *Symp. Problemen der Jüngeren Hallstattzeit in Mitteleuropa*: 15–40. Bratislava, Slovenska Akademia Vied.

Bulleid, A. and Gray, H. St. G. (1911) *The Glastonbury Lake Village I*. Taunton, Glastonbury Antiquarian Society.

Bulleid, A. and Gray, H. St. G. (1917) *The Glastonbury Lake Village II*. Taunton, Glastonbury Archaeological Society.

Burenhult, G. (1980) *The Archaeological Excavation at Carrowmore, Co. Sligo, Ireland, Excavation Seasons 1977–79*. Stockholm, Stockholm University Theses and Papers in North European Archaeology 9.

Burgess, C. (1976) An early bronze age settlement at Kilellan Farm, Islay, Argyll. In C. Burgess and R. Miket (*eds.*) *Settlement and Economy in the Third and Second Millennia b.c.*: 181–207. Oxford, British Archaeological Reports, British Series 33.

Burgess, C. (1980) *The Age of Stonehenge*. London, Dent.

Burkill, M. (1983) The Middle Neolithic of the Paris basin. In C. Scarre (*ed.*) *Ancient France. Neolithic Societies and Their Landscapes 6000–2000 bc*: 34–61. Edinburgh, University Press.

Burstow, G. P. and Holleyman, G. A. (1957) Late bronze age settlement on Itford Hill. *Proceedings of the Prehistoric Society* 23: 167–212.

Buttler, W. (1938) *Der Donauländische und der Westliche Kulturkreis der Jüngeren Steinzeit.* Berlin, de Gruyter.

Buttler, W. and Haberey, W. (1936) *Die Bandkeramische Ansiedlung bei Köln-Lindenthal.* Berlin, de Gruyter.

Butzer, K. (1972) *Environment and Archaeology.* London, Methuen.

Calvi Rezia, G. (1969) L'età neolitica nell'abitato preistorico di Pienza (Siena). *Studi Etruschi* 37: 355–9.

Calvi Rezia, G. (1972) Resti dell'insediamento neolitico di Pienza. *Atti del 14 Riunione del' Istituto Italiano di Preistoria e Protostoria*: 285–99.

Calzoni, U. (1939) Un fondo di capanna scoperto presso Norcia (Umbria). *Bullettino di Paletnologia Italiana* n.s. 3: 37–50.

Calzoni, U. (1954) *Le Stazioni Preistoriche della Montagna di Cetona, Belverde I.* Florence, Olschki.

Calzoni, U. (1962) *Le Stazioni Preistoriche della Montagna di Cetona, Belverde II.* Florence, Olschki.

Cannarella, O. and Cremonesi, G. (1967) Gli scavi nella Grotta Azzurra di Samatorza nel Carso triestino. *Rivista di Scienze Preistoriche* 22: 1–50.

Carciumaru, M. (1973) Analyse pollinique des coprolites livrés par quelques stations archéologiques des deux bords du Danube dans la zone des 'Portes de Fer'. *Dacia* 17: 53–60.

Carrier, E. H. (1932) *Water and Grass.* London, Christophers.

Carter, H. H. (1975) The animal bones. In R. J. Bradley and A. Ellison, *Rams Hill*: 118–22. Oxford, British Archaeological Reports, British Series 19.

Carter, P. L. and Phillipson, D. (1965) Appendix I: faunal report. In F. A. Hastings, Excavation of an iron age farmstead at Hawk's Hill, Leatherhead. *Surrey Archaeological Collections* 62: 1–43.

Case, H. J. (1969) Neolithic explanations. *Antiquity* 43: 176–86.

Case, H. J. (1976) Acculturation and the earlier Neolithic in western Europe. In S. J. de Laet (*ed.*) *Acculturation and Continuity in Atlantic Europe*: 45–58. Bruge, Diss. Archaeol. Gandenses 21.

Casparie, W. A. and Groenman-van Waateringe, W. (1982) Palynological analysis of Dutch barrows. *Palaeohistoria* 22: 7–65.

Casparie, W. A., Mook-Kamps, B., Palfenier-Vegter, R. M., Struijk, P. C. and Zeist, W. van (1977) The palaeobotany of Swifterbant. *Helinium* 17: 28–55.

Cassano, M. and Manfredini, A. (1983) *Studi sul Neolitico del Tavoliere della Puglia.* Oxford, British Archaeological Reports, International Series 160.

Casteel, R. W. (1977) Characterisation of faunal assemblages and the minimum number of individuals determined from paired elements: continuing problems in archaeology. *Journal of Archaeological Science* 4: 125–34.

Castelletti, L. (1974–5) Rapporto preliminare sui resti vegetali macroscopici delle serie neolitico-bronzo di Pienza (Siena). *Rivista Archeologica dell' Antica Provincia e Diocesi di Como* 156–7: 243–51.

Castelletti, L. (1975) Resti vegetali macroscopici di Campo Ceresole – Vhò di Piadena (Neolitico inferiore). *Preistoria Alpina* 11: 125–6.

Cattani, L. (1975) Il Neolitico del Vhò di Piadena – nota palinologica. *Preistoria Alpina* 11: 123–4.

Cattani, L. (1977) Dati palinologici inerenti ai depositi di Pradestel e di Vatte di Zambana nella Valle dell'Adige (TN). *Preistoria Alpina* 13: 21–9.

Caulfield, S. (1978) Neolithic fields – the Irish evidence. In H. C. Bowen and P. J. Fowler (*eds.*) *Early Land Allotment*: 137–43. Oxford, British Archaeological Reports, British Series 48.

Cazzella, A., Cremaschi, M.,Moscoloni, M. and Sala, B. (1976) Siti neolitici in località Razza di Campegine (Reggio Emilia). *Preistoria Alpina* 12: 79–126.

Cernych, E. N. (1978) Aibunar – a Balkan copper mine of the fourth millennium b.c. *Proceedings of the Prehistoric Society* 44: 203–17.

Chadwick, J. (1976) *The Mycenaean World*. Cambridge, University Press.

Chadwick, J. (1977) The interpretation of Mycenaean documents and Pylian geography. In J. Bintliff (*ed.*) *Mycenaean Geography*: 36–9. Cambridge, University Library Press.

Chaix, L. (1976a) *La Faune Néolithique du Valais (Suisse)*. Geneva, Document of the Department of Anthropology, University of Geneva 3.

Chaix, L. (1976b) La faune de la fouille Yverdon – 'Garage Martin'. *Cahiers d'Archéologie Romande de la Bibliothèque Historique Vaudoise* 8: 181–228.

Chaix, L. (1976–7) Les premiers élevages préhistoriques dans les Alpes occidentales. *Bulletin d'Études Préhistoriques Alpines* 8–9: 67–76.

Challis, A. J. and Harding, D. W. (1975) *Later Prehistory from the Trent to the Tyne*. Oxford, British Archaeological Reports, British Series 20.

Chambers, J. D. and Mingay, G. E. (1966) *The Agricultural Revolution 1750–1880*, London, Batsford.

Chapman, R. W. (1978) The evidence for prehistoric water control in south-east Spain. *Journal of Arid Environments* 1: 261–74.

Cherry, J. F. (1979) Four problems in Cycladic prehistory. In J. L. Davis and J. F. Cherry (*eds.*) *Papers in Cycladic Prehistory*: 22–47. University of California, Los Angeles, Institute of Archaeology Monograph 14.

Cherry, J. F. (1981) Pattern and process in the earliest colonisation of the Mediterranean islands. *Proceedings of the Prehistoric Society* 47: 41–68.

Childe, V. G. (1929) *The Danube in Prehistory*. Oxford, Clarendon Press.

Childe, V. G. (1934) Neolithic settlement in the west of Scotland. *Scottish Geographical Magazine* 50: 18–25.

Childe, V. G. (1938–39) A stone age settlement at the Braes of Ringo, Ronsay. *Proceedings of the Society of Antiquaries of Scotland* 73: 6–31.

Childe, V. G. (1951) *Social Evolution*. London, Watts.

Childe, V. G. (1952) *New Light on the Most Ancient East*. London, Routledge and Kegan Paul.

Childe, V. G. (1954) *What Happened in History*. Harmondsworth, Penguin.

Childe, V. G. (1957) *The Dawn of European Civilisation*. London, Routledge and Kegan Paul, sixth edition.

Childe, V. G. (1958) *Prehistory of European Society*. Harmondsworth, Penguin.

Chisholm, M. (1968) *Rural Settlement and Land Use*. London, Hutchinson University Library.

Chowne, P. (1978) Billingborough bronze age settlement: an interim note. *Lincolnshire History and Archaeology* 13: 15–21.

Chowne, P. (1980) Bronze age settlement in south Lincolnshire. In J. C. Barrett and R. J. Bradley (*eds.*) *Settlement and Society in the British Later Bronze Age*: 295–305. Oxford, British Archaeological Reports, British Series 80.

Churchill, D. and Wymer, J. J. (1965) The kitchen midden site at Westward Ho!, Devon, England: ecology, age and relation to changes in land and sea level. *Proceedings of the Prehistoric Society* 31: 74–84.

Clark, C. and Haswell, M. (1964) *The Economics of Subsistence Agriculture*. London, Macmillan.

Clark, G. (1984) Settlement and Economy in Northern Italy 2000–1000 b.c. Sheffield University, unpublished Ph.D. thesis.

Clark, J. G. D. (1936) *The Mesolithic Settlement of Northern Europe*. Cambridge, University Press.

Clark, J. G. D. (1952) *Prehistoric Europe – the Economic Basis*. London, Methuen.

Clark, J. G. D. (1954) *Excavations at Star Carr*. Cambridge, University Press.

Clark, J. G. D. (1965) Radiocarbon dating and the expansion of farming from the Near East over Europe. *Proceedings of the Prehistoric Society* 21: 58–73.

Clark, J. G. D. (1966) The invasion hypothesis in British archaeology. *Antiquity* 40: 172–89.

Clark, J. G. D. (1972) *Star Carr: a Case Study in Bioarchaeology*. Reading, Massachusetts, Addison-Wesley Publishing Company. McCaleb Module in Anthropology 10.

Clark, J. G. D. (1975) *The Earlier Stone Age Settlement of Scandinavia*. Cambridge, University Press.

Clark, J. G. D. (1978) *World Prehistory in New Perspective*. Cambridge, University Press, third edition.

Clarke, D. L. (1968) *Analytical Archaeology*. London, Methuen.

Clarke, D. L. (1972) A provisional model of an iron age society and its settlement system. In D. L. Clarke (*ed.*) *Models in Archaeology*: 801–70. London, Methuen.

Clarke, D. L. (1976) Mesolithic Europe: the economic basis. In G. de G. Sieveking, I. H. Longworth and K. E. Wilson (*eds.*) *Problems in Economic and Social Archaeology*: 449–81. London, Duckworth.

Clarke, D. V. (1976) *The Neolithic Village at Skara Brae, Excavations 1972–73, an Interim Report*. Edinburgh, H.M.S.O.

Clason, A. T. (1966) The animal remains and implements of bone and antler from Niederwil. *Palaeohistoria* 12: 581–5.

Clason, A. T. (1967a) The animal bones found at the Bandkeramik settlement by Bylany. *Archaeologicke Rozhledy* 19 (1): 90–6.

Clason, A. T. (1967b) *Animal and Man in Holland's Past*. Groningen, Wolters.

Clason, A. T. (1968) The animal bones of the Bandkeramik and middle age settlements near Bylany in Bohemia. *Palaeohistoria* 14: 1–17.

Clason, A. T. (1971) The flint mine workers of Spiennes and Rijckholt – St. Geertruid and their animals. *Helinium* 11: 3–33.

Clason, A. T. (1982) Padina and Starčevo: game, fish and cattle. *Palaeohistoria* 22: 141–73.

Clason, A. T. and Brinkhuizen, D. C. (1978) Swifterbant, mammals, birds and fishes. *Helinium* 18: 69–82.

Clough, T. H. McK. and Green, B. (1972) The petrological identification of stone implements from East Anglia. *Proceedings of the Prehistoric Society* 38: 108–55.

Clutton-Brock, J. (1975) Animal remains from the Stones of Stenness, Orkney, Appendix 1. pp. 34–47 in J. N. G. Ritchie, 'The Stones of Stenness, Orkney', *Proceedings of the Society of Antiquaries of Scotland* 107: 1–60.

Clutton-Brock, J. (1979) Report on the mammalian remains other than rodents from Quanterness. In C. Renfrew, *Investigations in Orkney*: 112–34. London, Reports of the Research Committee of the Society of Antiquaries 38.

Clutton-Brock, J. (1981) *Domesticated Animals from Early Times*. London, Heinemann and British Museum (Natural History).

Clutton-Brock, T. H. (1983) Red velvet and venison. *Nature* 303: 754.

Cobbett, W. (1823) *Cottage Economy*. London, Cobbett.

Coblenz, W. (1973) Döbeln-Masten. *Ausgraben und Funde* 18: 70–80.

Coblenz, W. (1974) Die Burgwälle und das Ausklingen der westlichen Lausitzer Kultur. In B. Chropovsky (*ed.*) *Symp. Problemen der Jüngeren Hallstattzeit in Mitteleuropa*: 85–100. Bratislava, Slovenska Akademia Vied.

Cohen, M. N. (1977) *The Food Crisis in Prehistory*. New Haven, Yale University Press.

Cole, J. W. and Wolf, E. R. (1974) *The Hidden Frontier. Ecology and Ethnicity in an Alpine Valley*. London and New York, Academic Press.

Coles, J. M. (1971) The early settlement of Scotland: excavations at Morton, Fife. *Proceedings of the Prehistoric Society* 37 (2): 284–366.

Coles, J. M. and Harding, A. F. (1979) *The Bronze Age in Europe*. London, Methuen.

Coles, J. M. and Hibbert, A. (1975) The Somerset Levels. In P. J. Fowler (*ed.*) *Recent Work in Rural Archaeology*: 12–26. Bradford Upon Avon, Moonraker Press.

Coles, J. M. and Orme, B. J. (1983) *Homo sapiens* or *Castor fiber*? *Antiquity* 57: 95–102.

Coles, J. M., Hibbert, F. A. and Orme, B. J. (1973) Prehistoric roads and tracks in Somerset: 3. the Sweet track. *Proceedings of the Prehistoric Society* 39: 256–93.

Coles, S. (1970) *The Neolithic Revolution*. London, British Museum (seventh edition).

Colini, G. A. (1898) Il sepolcreto di Remedello Sotto nel Bresciano e il periodo eneolitico in Italia. *Bullettino di Paletnologia Italiana* 24: 1–47, 88–110, 206–60, 280–95.

Collis, J. R. (1971) Markets and money. In D. Hill and M. Jesson (*eds.*) *The Iron Age and Its Hillforts*: 97–104. Southampton, University Monograph Series.

Collis, J. (1973) Manching reviewed. *Antiquity* 47: 280–3.

Collis, J. (1975a) *Defended Sites of the Late La Tène*. Oxford, British Archaeological Reports, International Series 2.

Collis, J. R. (1975b) Excavations at Aulnat, Clermont Ferrand. *Archaeological Journal* 132: 1–15.

Collis, J. R. (1979a) Urban structure in the Pre-Roman Iron Age. In B. C. Burnham and J. Kingsbury (*eds.*) *Space, Hierarchy and Society; Interdisciplinary Studies in Social Area Analysis*: 129–36. Oxford, British Archaeological Reports, International Series 59.

Collis, J. R. (1979b) The city and the state in Pre-Roman Britain. In B. C. Burnham and H. B. Johnson (*eds.*) *Invasion and Response: The Case of Roman Britain*: 231–40. Oxford, British Archaeological Reports, British Series 73.

Collis, J. R. (1980) Aulnat and urbanisation in France: a second interim report. *Archaeological Journal* 137: 40–9.

Columeau, P. (1976) Deux cabanes stratifées de l'Age du Bronze final IIIb sur l'oppidum de Roque de Viou à Saint-Dionisy (Gard). Étude de la faune. *Gallia Préhistoire* 19 (1): 261–4.

Comsa, E. (1976) Les quatre agglomérations néolithiques superposées de Radovanu. *Préhist. Ariég.* 31: 63–70.

Cook, S. F. (1972) *Prehistoric Demography*. Reading, Massachusetts, Addison-Wesley. McCaleb Module in Anthropology.

Cooper, M. Mc. G. and Morris, D. W. (1973) *Grass Farming*. Ipswich, Farming Press Ltd.

Corrain, C. and Capitanio, M. (1974) I resti umani della necropoli eneolitici di S. Antonio. In R. R. Holloway (*ed.*) *Buccino: the Eneolithic Necropolis of S. Antonio*: 40–108. Rome, De Luca.

Costantini, G. (1978) *Le Néolithique et le Chalcolithique des Grands Causses*. Millau.

Coste, A. and Maurel, R. (1975) Le Pesquier (Congénies, Gard). Rapport de fouille de sauvetage. *Bulletin du Comité d'Étude et du Sauvetage du Patrimoine de Congénies* 1: 4–14.

Courtin, J. (1967) La grotte de l'Église à Baudinard (Var). *Gallia Préhistoire* 10: 282–300.

Courtin, J. (1974a) *La Néolithique de la Provence*. Paris, Klincksieck.

Courtin, J. (1974b) Les habitats du plein air du Néolithique ancien cardial en Provence. *Revue d'Études Ligures* 38 (3–4): 227–43.

Courtin, J. (1976) Les civilisations néolithiques en Provence. In J. Guilaine (*ed.*) *La Préhistoire Française 2. Civilisations Néolithiques et Protohistoriques*: 255–66. Paris, CNRS.

Courtin, J. (1977) Les animaux domestiques du néolithique provençal. In *L'Élevage en Méditerranée Occidentale*: 67–76. Actes du Colloque International de l'Institut de Recherches Méditerranéenes, Marseilles, CNRS.

Courtin, J. and Erroux, J. (1974) Aperçu sur l'agriculture préhistorique en Provence. *Bulletin de la Société Préhistorique Française* 71 (1): 321–34.

Courtin, J., Gagnière, S., Granier, J., Ledoux, J. C. and Onoratini, G. (1970–2) La Grotte du Cap Ragnon, commune du Rove (Bouches-du-Rhône). *Bulletin de la Société d'Étude des Sciences Naturelles, Vaucluse*: 113–70.

Cowie, R. (1985) Production and Exchange of Neolithic Pottery in Central Europe. Sheffield University, unpublished M.Phil. thesis.

Cremonesi, G. (1962) I resti degli ultimi Mesolitici del Fucino. *Atti della Società Toscana di Scienze Naturali* Ser. A, 69: 447–56.

Cremonesi, G. (1965) Il villaggio di Ripoli alla luce dei recenti scavi. *Rivista di Scienze Preistoriche* 20: 85–155.

Cremonesi, G. (1966) Il villaggio Leopardi presso Penne in Abruzzo. *Bullettino di Paletnologia Italiana* 75, n.s. 17: 27–49.

Cremonesi, G. (1976) *La Grotta dei Piccioni di Bolognano nel Quadro delle Culture dal Neolitico all'Età del Bronzo in Abruzzo*. Pisa, Giardini.

Cremonesi, G. (1978) L'Eneolitico e l'Età del Bronzo in Basilicata. *Atti della XX Riunione Scientifica dell'Istituto Italiana per la Preistoria e Protostoria*: 63–86. Florence, Parenti.

Crumley, C. (1974) *Celtic Social Structure: The Generation of Archaeologically Testable Hypotheses from Literary Evidence*. Michigan, Museum of Anthropology, University of Michigan. Anthropological Paper 54.

Cullberg, C. (1975) Prospecting the west Swedish Mesolithic. *Norwegian Archaeological Review* 8: 36–53.

Cunliffe, B. W. (1974) *Iron Age Communities in Britain*. London, Routledge and Kegan Paul.

Cunliffe, B. W. (1976) The origins of urbanisation in Britain. In B. W. Cunliffe and T. Rowley (*eds.*) *Oppida in Barbarian Europe*: 135–61. Oxford, British Archaeological Reports, International Series 11.

Cunliffe, B. W. and Phillipson, D. W. (1968) Excavations at Eldon's Seat, Encombe, Dorset, England. *Proceedings of the Prehistoric Society* 34: 191–237.

Dahlberg, F. (1976) More on mechanisms of population growth. *Current Anthropology* 17: 164–6.

Damas, D. (1972) The Copper Eskimo. In M. G. Bicchieri (*ed.*) *Hunters and Gatherers Today*: 3–50. New York, Holt.

Daniel, G. E. (1958) *The Megalith Builders of Western Europe*. London, Hutchinson.

Daniel, G. E. (1964) *The Idea of Prehistory*. Harmondsworth, Penguin.

Daniel, G. E. (1967) *The Origins and Growth of Archaeology*. Harmondsworth, Penguin.

Dansgaard, W., Johnsen, S. J., Møller, J. and Langway, C. C. (1969) One thousand centuries of climatic record from Camp Century on the Greenland ice sheet. *Science* 166: 377–81.

Darling, F. F. (1937) *A Herd of Red Deer*. Oxford, University Press.

Davidsen, K. (1978) *The Final TRB Culture in Denmark*. Copenhagen, Akademisk Forlag (Arkaeologiske Studier 5).

Davidson, D. A., Jones, R. L. and Renfrew, C. (1976) Palaeoenvironmental reconstruction and evaluation – a case study from Orkney. *Transactions of the Institute of British Geographers* 1 (3): 346–61.

Davidson, I. (1972) The animal economy of La Cueva del Volcan del Faro, Spain. *Transactions of the Cave Research Group of Great Britain* 14: 23–31.

Davidson, I. (1976) Los Mallaetes and Monduvier: the economy of a human group in prehistoric Spain. In G. de G. Sieveking, I. H. Longworth and K. E. Wilson (*eds.*) *Problems in Economic and Social Archaeology*: 483–99. London, Duckworth.

Davies, S. M. (1981) Excavations at Old Down Farm, Andover. Part II. Prehistoric and Roman. *Proceedings of the Hampshire Field Club* 37: 81–163.

Degerbøl, M. (1963) Prehistoric cattle in Denmark and adjacent areas. In A. E. Mourant and F. E. Zeuner (*eds.*) *Man and Cattle*: 68–79. London, Occasional Paper of the Royal Anthropological Institute 18.

De Laet, S. J. (1962) *The Low Countries*. London, Thames and Hudson, second edition.

Delano-Smith, C. (1972) Late neolithic settlement and land use, and *garrigue* in the Montpellier region, France. *Man* 7 (3): 397–407.

Delano-Smith, C. (1979) *Western Mediterranean Europe*. London and New York, Academic Press.

Delibrias, G., Guillier, M.-T., Evin, J., Thommeret, J. and Thommeret, Y. (1976) Datations absolues des dépôts post-glaciaires et des gisements pré- et protohistoriques par la méthode du Carbone 14. In J. Guilaine (*ed.*) *La Préhistoire Française 2. Civilisations Néolithiques et Protohistoriques*: 859–99. Paris, CNRS.

Dennell, R. W. (1972) The interpretation of plant remains. In E. S. Higgs (*ed.*) *Papers in Economic Prehistory*: 149–60. Cambridge, University Press.

Dennell, R.W. (1974a) Botanical evidence for prehistoric crop processing activities. *Journal of Archaeological Science* 1: 275–84.

Dennell, R. W. (1974b) The purity of prehistoric crops. *Proceedings of the Prehistoric Society* 40: 132–5.

Dennell, R. W. (1974c) Neolithic flax in Bulgaria. *Antiquity* 48: 220–2.

Dennell, R. W. (1976a) The economic importance of plant resources represented on archaeological sites. *Journal of Archaeological Science* 3: 229–47.

Dennell, R. W. (1976b) Prehistoric crop cultivation in southern England: a reconsideration. *Antiquaries Journal* 56: 11–23.

Dennell, R. W. (1978) *Early Farming in South Bulgaria from the VI to the III Millennia b.c.* Oxford, British Archaeological Reports, International Series 45.

Dennell, R. W. (1983) *European Economic Prehistory*. London and New York, Academic Press.

Dennell, R. W. and Webley, D. (1975) Prehistoric settlement and land use in southern Bulgaria. In E. S. Higgs (*ed.*) *Palaeoeconomy*: 97–109. Cambridge, University Press.

Detev, P. (1960) Razkopki na selishnata mogila Yasa-tepe v Plovdiv 1959g. *Giodisnik na Muzeite v Plovdivski Okrug* 4: 5–55.

Di Cicio, P. (1966) Il problema della Dogana delle Pecore nella seconda metà del XVIII secolo. *La Capitanata* 4: 63–72.

Dimbleby, G. W. (1962) *The Development of British Heathlands and Their Soils*. Oxford, Forestry Memoir 23.

Dixon, P. (1981) Crickley Hill. *Current Archaeology* 7 (76): 145–7.

Dohrn-Ihmig, M. (1976) Die jüngere Bandkeramik im Rheinland und ihre Beziehungen zum Westen. In S. J. De Laet (*ed.*) *Acculturation and Continuity in Atlantic Europe*: 95–106. Brugge, Diss. Archaeol. Gandenses 21.

Dohrs, F. E. (1971) Nature versus ideology in Hungarian agriculture: problems of intensification. In G. W. Hoffman (*ed.*) *Eastern Europe: Essays in Geographical Problems*: 271–95. London, Methuen.

Dolukhanov, P. (1979) *Ecology and Economy in Neolithic Eastern Europe*. London, Duckworth.

Drack, W. (*ed.*) (1971) *Ur- und Frühgeschichtliche Archäologie der Schweiz. Band 3. Die Bronzezeit.* Basel, Verlag Schweizerische Gesellschaft für Ur- und Frühgeschichte.

Drewett, P. L. (1977) The excavation of a neolithic causewayed enclosure on Offham Hill, East Sussex, 1976. *Proceedings of the Prehistoric Society* 43: 201–42.

Drewett, P. L. (1978) Neolithic Sussex. In P. L. Drewett (*ed.*) *Archaeology in Sussex to AD 1500*: 23–9. London, Council for British Archaeology Research Report 29.

Drewett, P. L. (1980) Black Patch and the later Bronze Age in Sussex. In J. C. Barrett and R. J. Bradley (*eds.*) *Settlement and Society in the Later British Bronze Age*: 337–96. Oxford, British Archaeological Reports, British Series 80.

Drewett, P. L. (1982) Late bronze age downland economy and excavations at Black Patch, East Sussex. *Proceedings of the Prehistoric Society* 48: 321–400.

Driesch, A. von den (1972) *Osteoarchäologische Untersuchungen auf der Iberischen Halbinsel*. Munich, Institut für Palaeoanatomie, Domestikationsforschung und Geschichte der Tiermedizen.

Driesch, A. von den (1976) *A Guide to the Measurement of Animal Bones from Archaeological Sites*. Harvard, Peabody Museum, Museum Bulletin 1.

Driesch, A. von den and Morales, Y. (1977) Los restos animales del gacimento de terrera Ventura (Tabernas, Almeria). *Cuadernos de Prehistoriá Arquelogia* 4: 15–34.

Drury, P. J. (1978) *Excavations at Little Waltham, 1970–71*. London, Council for British Archaeology Research Report 26.

Drury, P. J. (1980) The early and middle phases of the Iron Age in Essex. In G. Buckley (*ed.*) *Archaeology in Essex to AD 1500*: 47–54. London, Council for British Archaeology Research Report 34.

Duchaufour, P. (1970) *Précis de Pédologie*. Paris, Masson.

Ducos, P. (1957) Étude de la faune du gisement néolithique de Roucadour (Lot). II. La faune. *Bulletin du Musée d'Anthropologie Préhistorique de Monaco* 7: 5–73.

Ducos, P. (1976) Quelques documents sur les débuts de la domestication en France. In J. Guilaine (*ed.*) *La Préhistoire Française 2. Civilisations Néolithiques et Protohistoriques*: 165–7. Paris, CNRS.

Ducos, P. (1977) Le mouton de Châteauneuf-les-Martigues. In *L'Élévage en Méditerranée Occidentale*: 77–86. Actes du Colloque International de l'Institut de Recherches Méditerranéenes. Marseilles, CNRS.

Dudal, R., Tavernier, R. and Osmond, D. (1966) *Soil Map of Europe*. Rome, Food and Agricultural Organisation of the United Nations.

Duday, H. (1976) Les sépultures des hommes du Mésolithique. In H. de Lumley (*ed.*) *La Préhistoire Française* 1, 1: 734–7. Paris, CNRS.

Duerst, U. (1923) Kulturhistorische Studien zur schweizerischen Haustierzucht. *Schweizerische Landwirtschaftliche Monatshefte (Bern-Bümpliz)*: 25–9, 52–6, 76–81, 102–6, 128–33, 157–61.

Dumitrescu, V. (1961) *Necropola de incineratie din epoca bronzului de la Cîrna*. Bucharest, Edit. Acad. R.S.R.

Dumitrescu, V. (1965) Cascioărele: a late neolithic settlement in the lower Danube. *Archaeology* 18: 34–40.

Dumitrescu, V. and Bănăţeanu, T. (1965) À propos d'un sol de charrue primitive en bois de cerf, découvert dans la station néolithique de Cascioărele. *Dacia* 9: 59–67.

Dumont, R. (1957) *Types of Rural Economy. Studies in World Agriculture*. London, Methuen.

Dzambazov, N. (1963) Loveshkiti peshteri. *Izvestia Archeologicheskaya Institut* 23: 229–42.

Earle, T. K. and Ericson, J. E. (*eds.*) (1977) *Exchange Systems in Prehistory*. London and New York, Academic Press.

Effentere, H. van (1980) *Le Palais de Mallia*. Rome, Edizioni dell'Ateneo.

Ehrich, R. W. (1956) Homolka: a fortified neolithic village in Bohemia. *Archaeology* 9 (4): 233–40.

Ellison, A. (1978) The Bronze Age. In P. Drewett (*ed.*) *Archaeology in Sussex to AD 1500*: 30–7. London, Council for British Archaeology Research Report 29.

Ellison, A. and Drewett, P. L. (1971) Pits and post-holes in the British Early Iron Age: some alternative explanations. *Proceedings of the Prehistoric Society* 37: 183–94.

Ellison, A. and Harriss, J. (1972) Settlement and land use in the prehistory and early history of southern England: a study based on locational models. In D. L. Clarke (*ed.*) *Models in Archaeology*: 911–62. London, Methuen.

Elster, E. S. (1976) The chipped stone industry (Anza). *Monumenti Archaeologica* 1: 257–78.

Emery, F. (1967) The farming regions of Wales. In J. Thirsk (*ed.*) *The Agrarian History of England and Wales. IV. 1500–1640*: 113–60. Cambridge, University Press.

Engelmark, R. (1976) The vegetational history of the Umeå area during the past 4000 years. *Early Norrland* 9: 75–111.

Ente, P. J. (1976) The geology of the northern part of Flevoland in relation to the human occupation in the Atlantic time. *Helinium* 16: 15–35.

Ericson, J. E. and Earle, T. K. (*eds.*) (1982) *Contexts for Prehistoric Exchange*. London and New York, Academic Press.

Ernle, Lord (1936) *English Farming, Past and Present*. London, Longman.

Erroux, J. (1976) Les débuts de l'agriculture en France: les cereales. In J. Guilaine (*ed.*) *La Préhistoire Française 2. Civilisations Néolithiques et Protohistoriques*: 186–91. Paris, CNRS.

Es, W. A. van (1967) Wijster, a native village beyond the imperial frontier. *Palaeohistoria* 11.

Es. W. A. van (1968) Paddepoel, excavations of frustrated terps, 200 BC–AD 250. *Palaeohistoria* 14: 187–352.

Escalon de Fonton, M. (1966) 'La Baume de Montclus'. Circonscription de Languedoc-Roussillon. *Gallia Préhistoire* 9: 578.

Escalon de Fonton, M. (1968) 'La Baume de Montclus'. Circonscription de Languedoc-Roussillon. *Gallia Préhistoire* 11: 484–92.

Escalon de Fonton, M. (1970) 'La Baume de Montclus'. Circonscription de Languedoc-Roussillon. *Gallia Préhistoire* 13: 531–6.

Evans, J. D. (1968) Neolithic Knossos: the growth of a settlement. *Proceedings of the Prehistoric Society* 37 (2): 95–117.

Evans, J. D. and Renfrew, C. (1968) *Excavations at Saliagos near Antiparos*. London, British School at Athens Supplementary Volume 5.

Evans, J. G. (1971a) Notes on the environment of early farming communities in Britain. In D. D. A. Simpson (*ed.*) *Economy and Settlement in Neolithic and Bronze Age Britain and Europe*: 11–26. Leicester, University Press.

Evans, J. G. (1971b) Habitat changes on the calcareous soils of Britain: the impact of neolithic man. In D. D. A. Simpson (*ed.*) *Economy and Settlement in Neolithic and Bronze Age Britain and Europe*: 27–73. Leicester, University Press.

Evans, J. G. (1975) *The Environment of Early Man in the British Isles*. London, Elek.

Evett, D. (1975) A preliminary note on the typology, functional variability and trade of Italian neolithic ground stone axes. *Origini* 9: 35–54.

Evett, D. and Renfrew, J. M. (1971) D'agricoltura neolitica italiana: una nota sui cereali. *Rivista di Scienze Preistoriche* 26: 403–9.

Fairhurst, H. (1971) Kilpedhir and hut circle sites in northern Scotland. *Scottish Archaeological Forum* 3: 1–10.

Fairhurst, H. and Taylor, D. B. (1971) A hut circle settlement at Kilpedhir, Sutherland. *Proceedings of the Society of Antiquaries of Scotland* 103: 65–9.

Farrugia, J. P., Kuper, R., Lüning, J. and Stehli, P. (1973) Untersuchungen zur neolitischen Besiedlung der Aldenhovener Platte III. *Bonner Jahrbucher* 173: 226–56.

Fasham, P. and Monk, M. (1978) Sampling for plant remains: some results and implications. In J. F. Cherry, C. Gamble and S. Shennan (*eds.*) *Sampling in Contemporary British Archaeology*: 363–71. Oxford, British Archaeological Reports, British Series 50.

Feachem, R. W. (1966) The hill forts of northern Britain. In A. L. F. Rivet (*ed.*) *The Iron Age in Northern Britain*: 59–87. Edinburgh, University Press.

Feachem, R. W. (1973) Ancient agriculture in the highland zone of Britain. *Proceedings of the Prehistoric Society* 39: 332–53.

Fedele, F. (1973) Una stazione vaso a bocca quadrata sul Monfenera, Valsesia (scavi 1969–72). *Preistoria Alpina* 9: 151–222.

Fenton, A. (1976) *Scottish Country Life*. Edinburgh, John Donald.

Ferguson, C. W., Huber, B. and Suess, H. E. (1966) Determination of the age of Swiss lake dwellings as an example of dendrochronologically calibrated radiocarbon dating. *Zeitschrift für Naturforschung* 21 (a): 1173–7.

Fernandez-Miranda, M. and Moure, A. (1974) Verdelpino (Cuenca): nuevas fechas de C-14 para el neolítico peninsular. *Trabajos de Prehistoria* 31: 311–16.

Field, N. H., Matthews, C. L. and Smith, I. F. (1964) New neolithic sites in Dorset and Bedfordshire, with a note on the distribution of neolithic storage pits in Britain. *Proceedings of the Prehistoric Society* 30: 352–81.

Figuier, L. (1876) *Primitive Man*. London, Chatto and Windus.

Finley, M. I. (1957) The Mycenaean tablets and economic history. *Economic History Review* 10: 128–41.

Firbas, F. (1949) *Waldgeschichte Mitteleuropas*. Jena, Gustav Fischer.

Fisher, P. F. (1982) A review of lessivage and neolithic cultivation in southern England. *Journal of Archaeological Science* 9: 299–304.

Fitzhugh, W. (1974) Ground slates in the Scandinavian Younger Stone Age, with reference to circumpolar maritime adaptations. *Proceedings of the Prehistoric Society* 40: 45–58.

Fjaervoll, K. (1965) Korndyrking i Troms fylke i 1700-åra med tilknytning til ngare tid. *Tilleggsbok til Håløygminne*.

Flannery, K. V. (1965) The ecology of early food production in Mesopotamia. *Science* 147: 1247–56.

Flannery, K. V. (1969) Origins and ecological effects of early domestication in Iran and the Near East. In P. Ucko and G. Dimbleby (*eds.*) *The Domestication and Exploitation of Plants and Animals*: 73–100. London, Duckworth.

Flannery, K. V., Kirby, A. V., Kirby, M. J. and Williams, A. W. (1967) Farming systems and political growth in ancient Oaxaca. *Science* 158: 445–54.

Fleming, A. M. (1971) Territorial patterns in bronze age Wessex. *Proceedings of the Prehistoric Society* 37: 138–66.

Fleming, A. M. (1978) The prehistoric landscape of Dartmoor. Part I. South Dartmoor. *Proceedings of the Prehistoric Society* 44: 97–123.

Fleming, A. M. (1979) The Dartmoor reaves: boundary patterns and behaviour patterns in the second millennium b.c. *Proceedings of the Devon Archaeological Society* 37: 115–31.

Fleming, A. F. (in press) Land tenure, productivity and field systems. In G. Barker and C. Gamble (*eds.*) *Beyond Domestication: Subsistence Archaeology and Social Complexity in Ancient Europe*. New York, Academic Press.

Fleming, A. M. and Collis, J. R. (1973) A late prehistoric reave near Cholwich Town, Dartmoor. *Proceedings of the Devon Archaeological Society* 31: 1–21.

Follieri, M. (1971) Researches on prehistoric agriculture. Paper presented at the Third International Congress of the Museum of Agriculture, Budapest.

Forsten, A. (1972) The refuse fauna of the mesolithic Suomusjärvi period in Finland. *Finskt Museum* 79: 74–85.

Forsten, A. (1974) A bronze age refuse fauna from Käkar, Åland. *Finskt Museum* 81: 56–60.

Forsten, A. and Alhonen, P. (1975) The subfossil seals of Finland. *Boreas* 4: 143–55.

Fowler, P. J. (1971) Early prehistoric agriculture in western Europe: some archaeological evidence. In D. D. A. Simpson (*ed.*) *Settlement and Economy in Neolithic and Bronze Age Britain and Europe*: 153–82. Leicester, University Press.

Fowler, P. J. (1981a) Later prehistoric Britain. In S. Piggott (*ed.*) *The Agrarian History of England and Wales I, I*: 63–298. Cambridge, University Press.

Fowler, P. J. (1981b) Wildscape to landscape: 'enclosure' in prehistoric Britain. In R. Mercer (*ed.*) *Farming Practice in British Prehistory*: 9–54. Edinburgh, University Press.

Fowler, P. J. and Evans, J. G. (1967) Plough-marks, lynchets, and early fields. *Antiquity* 41: 289–301.

Fox, A. (1973) *South West England, 3500 BC–AD 600*. London, Newton Abbot.

Fox, C. F. (1932) *The Personality of Britain*. Cardiff, National Museum of Wales.

Frank, A. H. E. (1969) Pollen stratigraphy of the lake of Vico (Central Italy). *Palaeogeography, Palaeoclimatology, Palaeoecology* 6: 67–85.

Frankenstein, S. and Rowlands, M. J. (1978) The internal structure and regional context of early iron age society in south-western Germany. *Institute of Archaeology Bulletin* 15: 73–112.

Fredsjö, A., Janson, S. and Moberg, C. A. (1969) *Hällristningar i Sverige*. Oskarshamn, Forum.

French, D. H. (1970) Notes on site distribution on the Çumra area. *Anatolian Studies* 20: 139–48.

Frenzel, B. (1966) Climatic change in the Atlantic/Subboreal transition in the northern hemisphere: botanical evidence. In J. S. Sawyer (*ed.*) *Proceedings of the International Symposium of World Climate 8000–0 B.C.*: 99–123. London, Royal Meteorological Society.

Frey, O. H. (1966) Der Ostalpenraum und die antike Welt in der frühen Eisenzeit. *Germania* 44: 48–66.

Frey, O. H. (1969) *Die Entstehung der Situlenkunst*. Berlin, de Gruyter.

Frierman, J. (1969) The Balkan graphite ware. *Proceedings of the Prehistoric Society* 35: 42–4.

Furger, A., Orcel, A., Stöckli, W. and Suter, P. (1977) *Die Neolithischen Ufersiedlungen von Twann*. Bern, Vorbericht 1.

Gabołowna, L. (1966) Ze studiów nad grupą Brzesko-Kujawską kultury lendzielskiej. *Lodz, Acta Archaeologica Lodzensia.*

Gagnière, S. (1967) La faune. In J. Courtin, 'La grotte de l'Église à Baudinard (Var)'. *Gallia Préhistoire* 10 (2): 299–300.

Gamble, C. S. (1978) Optimising information from studies of faunal remains. In J. F. Cherry, C. Gamble and S. Shennan (*eds.*) *Sampling in Contemporary British Archaeology*: 321–53. Oxford, British Archaeological Reports, British Series 50.

Gamble, C. S. (1979) Surplus and self-sufficiency in the Cycladic subsistence economy. In J. L. Davis and J. F. Cherry (*eds.*) *Papers in Cycladic Prehistory*: 122–34. University of California, Los Angeles, Institute of Archaeology Monograph 14.

Gamble, C. S. (1981) Social control and the economy. In A. Sheridan and G. Bailey (*eds.*) *Economic Archaeology*: 215–29. Oxford, British Archaeological Reports, International Series 96.

Gardiner, J. (1980) Land and social status: a case study from eastern England. In J. C. Barrett and R. J. Bradley (*eds.*) *Settlement and Society in Later Bronze Age Britain*: 101–14. Oxford, British Archaeological Reports, British Series 83.

Gardner, W. and Savory, H. N. (1964) *Dinorben: A Hillfort Occupied in Early Iron Age and Roman Times.* Cardiff, National Museum of Wales.

Garner, H. V. and Dyke, G. V. (1969) The Broadbank yields. *Rothamsted Experimental Station Report for 1968*: 26–49. Harpenden, Lawes Agricultural Trust.

Gaudert, O.-F. (1964) Zur Frage der Rinderauschirrung im Neolithikum. *Jahrbuch der Römisch-Germanischen Zentral Museums* 11: 34–56.

Gautier, A. (1968) The animal remains of the La Tène settlement Nekkerspoel (Malines, Prov. Antwerp). *Helinium* 8: 241–58.

Geddes, D. S. (1981a) Les mouton mésolithiques dans le Midi de la France: implications pour les origines de l'élevage en Méditerranée occidentale. *Bulletin de la Société Préhistorique Française* 78 (8): 227.

Goddes, D. S. (1981b) Les débuts de l'élevage dans la vallée de l'Aude. *Bulletin de la Société Préhistorique Française* 78 (8): 370–8.

Geddes, D. S. (1983) Neolithic transhumance in the Mediterranean Pyrenees. *World Archaeology* 15 (1): 51–66.

Gedl, M. (1962) *Kultura Łuzycka na Gornym Śląsku.* Warsaw, Ossolineum.

Geist, V. (1971) *Mountain Sheep: A Study in Behavior and Evolution.* Chicago, University Press.

Gejvall, N.-G. (1969) *Lerna: A Preclassical Site in the Argolid. 1. The Fauna.* Princeton, American School of Classical Studies at Athens.

Gent, H. (1983) Centralised storage in later prehistoric Britain. *Proceedings of the Prehistoric Society* 49: 243–67.

Georgiev, G. I. (1961) Kulturgruppen der Jungsteinzeit und Kupferzeit in der Ebene von Thracien. In J. Böhm and S. J. de Laet (*eds.*) *L'Europe à la Fin de l'Age de la Pierre*: 45–100. Prague, Académie Tchécoslovaque de Sciences.

Georgiev, G. I. (1965) The Azmak mound in southern Bulgaria. *Antiquity* 39: 6–8.

Ghetie, B. L. and Mateescu, C. N. (1973) L'utilisation des bovins à la traction dans la Néolithique Moyen. *VIII Congrès International des Sciences Préhistoriques et Protohistoriques* (Beograd, 1971): 454–61.

Giffen, A. E. van (1936) Der Warf in Ezinge. *Germania* 20: 40–7.

Gilman, A. (1976) Bronze age dynamics in southeast Spain. *Dialectical Anthropology* 1: 307–19.

Gilman, A. (1981) The development of social stratification in bronze age Europe. *Current Anthropology* 22 (1): 1–8.

Gimbutas, M. (1965) *Bronze Age Cultures in Central and Eastern Europe.* The Hague, Mouton.

Gimbutas, M. (1970) Obre, Yugoslavia. Two neolithic sites. *Archaeology* 23: 287–97.

Gimbutas, M. (1972) Excavations at Anza, Macedonia. *Archaeology* 25: 112–23.

Gimbutas, M. (1974a) Achilleion: a neolithic mound in Thessaly. *Journal of Field Archaeology* 1: 277–302.

Gimbutas, M. (1974b) Anza, *c.* 6500–5000 bc. A cultural yardstick for the study of neolithic southeast Europe. *Journal of Field Archaeology* 1: 25–66.

Gimbutas, M. (1974c) *The Gods and Goddesses of Old Europe 7000–3500 B.C.* London, Thames and Hudson.

Gimbutas, M. (1976) *Neolithic Macedonia*. Berkeley, UCLA, Monumenta Archaeologica 1.

Giot, P. R. (1960) *Brittany*. London, Thames and Hudson.

Gjerstad, E. (1966) *Early Rome IV*. Lund, Skrifter utgivna av Svenska Institutet i Rom 17 (4).

Glick, T. F. (1970) *Irrigation and Society in Medieval Valencia*. Cambridge, Massachusetts, Harvard University Press.

Glob, P. V. (1951) *Ard og Plov i Nordens Oldtid*. Aarhus, University Press.

Glob, P. V. (1971) *The Bog People*. London, Paladin.

Golson, J. (1976) Archaeology and agricultural history in the New Guinea Highlands. In G. de G. Sieveking, I. H. Longworth and K. E. Wilson (*eds.*) *Problems in Economic and Social Archaeology*: 201–20. London, Duckworth.

Gonzenbach, V. von (1949) *Die Cortaillodkultur in der Schweiz*. Basel, Monographien zur Ur- und Frühgeschichte der Schweiz 7.

Goodwin, D. H. (1979) *Sheep Management and Production*. London, Hutchinson.

Goody, J. (1976) *Production and Reproduction*. Cambridge, University Press.

Gould, R. A. (1980) *Living Archaeology*. Cambridge, University Press.

Gramsch, B. (1973) Das Mesolithikum in Mecklenburg und Brandenburg – zeitliche Gliederung und Formengruppen. In S. K. Kosłowski (*ed.*) *The Mesolithic in Europe*: 209–35. Warsaw, University Press.

Gramsch, B. (1976) Bemerkungen zur Palökologie und zur Besiedlung während des jüngeren Boreals und des älteren Atlantikums im nördlichen Mitteleuropa. *IX Congrès International des Sciences Préhistoriques et Protohistoriques, Nice*, Coll. 19: 114–19. Paris, CNRS.

Grayson, D. K. (1978) Minimum numbers and sample size in vertebrate faunal samples. *American Antiquity* 43: 53–65.

Grayson, D. K. (1979) On the quantification of vertebrate archaeofaunas. In M. Schiffer (*ed.*) *Advances in Archaeological Method and Theory* 2: 200–39. London and New York, Academic Press.

Green, H. S. (1976) The excavation of a late neolithic settlement at Stacey Bushes, Milton Keynes, and its significance. In C. Burgess and R. Miket (*eds.*) *Settlement and Economy in the Third and Second Millennia b.c.*: 11–77. Oxford, British Archaeological Reports, British Series 33.

Greig, J. R. A. and Turner, J. (1974) Some pollen diagrams from Greece and their archaeological significance. *Journal of Archaeological Science* 1: 177–94.

Grigg, D. B. (1976) *Agricultural Systems of the World*. Cambridge, University Press.

Grigg, D. B. (1982) *The Dynamics of Agricultural Change*. London, Hutchinson.

Grigson, C. (1966) The animal remains from Fussell's Lodge long barrow, including a possible ox-hide burial. pp. 63–73 in P. Ashbee, The Fussell's Lodge long barrow. Excavations 1957. *Archaeologia* 100: 1–80.

Grigson, C. (1978) The craniology of four species of Bos 4. The relationship between *Bos primigenius* Boj. and *Bos taurus* L. and its implications for the phylogeny of the domestic breeds. *Journal of Archaeological Science* 5: 132–52.

Grigson, C. (1980) The animal bones. pp. 161–71 in M. E. Robertson-Mackay, A 'head and hooves' burial beneath a round barrow with other neolithic and bronze age sites, on Hemp Knoll, near Avebury, Wiltshire. *Proceedings of the Prehistoric Society* 46: 123–76.

Grigson, C. (1981) Mammals and man on Oronsay: some preliminary hypotheses concerning mesolithic ecology in the Inner Hebrides. In D. Brothwell and G. Dimbleby (*eds.*) *Environ-*

mental Aspects of Coasts and Islands: 163–80. Oxford, British Archaeological Reports, International Series 94.

Grigson, C. (1982) Porridge and pannage: pig husbandry in neolithic England. In S. Limbrey and M. Bell (*eds.*) *Archaeological Aspects of Woodland Ecology*: 297–314. Oxford, British Archaeological Reports, International Series 146.

Groenman-van Waateringe, W. (1970–1) Hecken im westeuropäischen Frühneolithikum. *Berichten R.O.B.* 20–1: 295–9.

Groenman-van Waateringe, W. (1978) Are we too loud? *The Third Beatrice de Cardi Lecture, 1978*. London, Council for British Archaeology.

Groenman-van Waateringe, W. and Pals, J. P. (1982) Newgrange, Co. Meath: pollen and seed analysis. In M. J. O'Kelly, *Newgrange*: 219–23. London, Thames and Hudson.

Grüger, E (1977) Pollenanalytische Untersuchung zur Würmzeitlichen Vegetationsgeschichte von Kalabrien (Süditalien). *Flora* 166: 475–89.

Grygiel, R. and Bogucki, P. (1979) Excavations at Brześć Kujawski, Poland. *Current Anthropology* 20 (2): 400–1.

Gubler-Gross, R. (1962) Moderne Transhumanz in der Schweiz. Zürich, unpublished Ph.D. thesis.

Guilaine, J. (*ed.*) (1976a) *La Préhistoire Française 2. Civilisations Néolithiques et Protohistoriques*: 165–7. Paris, CNRS.

Guilaine, J. (*ed.*) (1976b) *Premiers Bergers et Paysans de l'Occident Méditerranéen*. Paris, Mouton.

Guilaine, J. (1977) Sur les débuts de l'élevage en Méditerranée occidentale. In J. Guilaine (*ed.*) *L'Élevage en Méditerranée Occidentale*: 39–48. Actes du Colloque International de l'Institut de Recherches Méditerranéennes. Marseilles, CNRS.

Guilaine, J. and Vaquer, J. (1973) Le site Chasséen d'Auriac, commune de Carcassonne (Aude). *Bulletin de la Société Préhistorique Française* 70: 367–86.

Guilbert, G. C. (1975) Planned hillfort interiors. *Proceedings of the Prehistoric Society* 41: 203–21.

Guilbert, G. C. (1976) Moel y Gaer (Rhosesmor) 1972–3: an area excavation in the interior. In D. W. Harding (*ed.*) *Hillforts: Later Prehistoric Earthworks in England and Ireland*: 303–17. London and New York, Academic Press.

Guilbert, G. C. (1981) Hill-fort functions and populations: a sceptical viewpoint. In G. C. Guilbert (*ed.*) *Hill-fort Studies*: 104–21. Leicester, University Press.

Guyan, W. H. (1955) Das jungsteinzeitliche Moordorf von Thayngen-Weier. In W. H. Guyan (*ed.*) *Das Pfahlbauproblem*: 223–72. Basel, Monographien zur Ur- und Frühgeschichte der Schweiz 2.

Guyan, W. H. (1966) Zur Herstellung und Funktion einiger jungsteinzeitlicher Holzgeräte von Thayngen-Weier. In R. Deger, W. Drack and R. Wyss (*eds.*) *Helvetia Antiqua*: 21–32. Zürich, Schweizerisches Landesmuseum.

Haarnagel, W. (1979) *Die Grabung Feddersen Wierde*. Wiesbaden, Franz Steiner Verlag.

Hagen, A. (1967) *Norway*. London, Thames and Hudson.

Hajnalova, E. (1973) Prispevok k štúdiu, analýze a interpretácii nálezov Kultúrnych rastlin na Slovenska. *Slovenska Archeologica* 21 (1): 211–18.

Hallegouet, B., Giot, P.-R. and Briard, J. (1971) Habitat et dépôt de l'Age du Bronze au Lividic en Plounéour-Trez (Finistère). *Annales de Bretagna* 78: 59–72.

Halstead, P. (1977) Prehistoric Thessaly: the submergence of civilisation. In J. L. Bintliff (*ed.*) *Mycenaean Geography*: 23–9. Cambridge, University Library Press.

Halstead, P. (1981) Counting sheep in neolithic and bronze age Greece. In I. Hodder, G. Isaac and N. Hammond (*eds.*) *Pattern of the Past: Studies in Memory of David Clarke*: 307–39. Cambridge, University Press.

Halstead, P., Hodder, I. and Jones, G. (1978) Behavioural archaeology and refuse patterns: a case study. *Norwegian Archaeological Review* 11 (2): 118–31.

Hamilton, J. R. C. (1966) Forts, brochs, and wheel-houses in northern Scotland. In A. L. F. Rivet (*ed.*) *The Iron Age in Northern Britain*: 111–30. Edinburgh, University Press.

Handley, J. E. (1953) *Scottish Farming in the Eighteenth Century.* London, Faber and Faber.

Hansen, J. and Renfrew, J. M. (1978) Palaeolithic–neolithic seed remains at Franchthi Cave, Greece. *Nature* 271: 349–52.

Harcourt, R. A. (1971) Animal bones from Durrington Walls. In G. J. Wainwright and I. H. Longworth, *Durrington Walls: Excavations 1966–1968*: 338–50. London, Research Report of the Society of Antiquaries of London 29.

Harcourt, R. A. (1974) The dog in prehistoric and early historic Britain. *Journal of Archaeological Science* 1: 151–76.

Harcourt, R. A. (1979a) The animal bones. In G. J. Wainwright, *Mount Pleasant, Dorset: Excavations 1970–1971*: 214–23. London, Research Report of the Society of Antiquaries of London 37.

Harcourt, R. A. (1979b) The animal bones. In G. J. Wainwright *(ed.) Gussage All Saints: An Iron Age Settlement in Dorset*: 150–60. London, H.M.S.O. (DOE Archaeological Report 10).

Harding, A. F. (1975) Mycenaean Greece and Europe: the evidence of bronze tools and implements. *Proceedings of the Prehistoric Society* 41: 183–202.

Harding, A. F. (1976) Bronze agricultural implements in bronze age Europe. In G. de G. Sieveking, I. H. Longworth and K. A. Wilson *(eds.) Problems in Economic and Social Archaeology*: 513–22. London, Duckworth.

Harding, A. F. *(ed.)* (1982) *Climatic Change in Later Prehistory.* Edinburgh, University Press.

Harding, A. F. and Warren, S. E. (1973) Early bronze age faience beads from central Europe. *Antiquity* 47: 64–6.

Harlan, J. R. (1967) A wild wheat harvest in Turkey. *Archaeology* 20 (3): 197–201.

Hart, C. R. (1981) *The North Derbyshire Archaeological Survey.* Chesterfield, North Derbyshire Archaeological Trust.

Hartmann-Frick, H. (1960) Die Tierwelt des prähistorischen Siedlungsplatzes auf dem Eschner-Lutzengüetle Fürstentum Liechtenstein (Neolithikum bis La Tène). *Jahrbuch des Historischen Vereins für das Fürstentum Liechtenstein* 59: 9–223.

Haselgrove, C. C. (1976) External trade as a stimulus to urbanisation. In B. W. Cunliffe and T. Rowley *(eds.) Oppida: The Beginnings of Urbanisation in Barbarian Europe*: 25–49. Oxford, British Archaeological Reports, International Series 11.

Hassan, F. A. (1973) On mechanisms of population growth during the Neolithic. *Current Anthropology* 14: 535–42.

Hatt, J. J. (1970) *Celts and Gallo-Romans.* Geneva, Nagel.

Hatting, T. (1978) Lidsø: zoological remains from a neolithic settlement. In K. Davidsen, *The Final TRB Culture in Denmark*: 193–207. Copenhagen, Akademisk Forlag (Arkaeologiske Studier 5).

Hawkes, J. (1968) The proper study of mankind. *Antiquity* 42: 255–62.

Hawke-Smith, C. F. (1979) *Man-Land Relations in Prehistoric Britain: The Dove-Derwent Interfluve, Derbyshire.* Oxford, British Archaeological Reports, British Series 64.

Hawke-Smith, C. F. (1981) Land use, burial practice and territories in the Peak District *c.* 2000–1000 b.c. In G. Barker *(ed.) Prehistoric Communities in Northern England: Essays on Social and Economic Reconstruction*: 57–72. Sheffield, Sheffield University, Department of Prehistory and Archaeology.

Heath, M. C. (1958) Early Helladic clay sealings from the House of the Tiles at Lerna. *Hesperia* 27: 81–121.

Hedges, J. W. (1983) *Isbister: A Chambered Tomb in Orkney.* Oxford, British Archaeological Reports, British Series 115.

Hedges, J. W. and Bell, B. (1980) That tower of Scottish prehistory – the broch. *Antiquity* 54: 87–94.

Hedges, J. and Buckley, D. (1978) Excavations at a neolithic causewayed enclosure, Orsett, Essex. *Proceedings of the Prehistoric Society* 44: 194–233.

Heer, O. (1866) Die Pflanzen der Pfahlbauten. *Neujahrsblatt der Naturforschenden Gesellschaft in Zürich* 68: 1–54.

Heim, J. (1978) L'environment vegetal de l'habitat néolithique du rubane à Reichstett par l'étude du contenu pollinique des fosses. *Revue Archéologique de l'Est et du Centre-Est* 29: 56–62.

Helbaek, H. (1952a) Early crops in southern England. *Proceedings of the Prehistoric Society* 18: 194–233.

Helbaek, H. (1952b) Preserved apples and panicum in the prehistoric site at Nøore Sandegaard in Bornholm. *Acta Archaeologica* 28: 107–15.

Helbaek, H. (1952c) Spelt (*Triticum spelta* L.) in bronze age Denmark. *Acta Archaeologica* 28: 97–107.

Helbaek, H. (1954) Prehistoric food plants and weeds in Denmark. *Danmarks Geologiske Undersøgelse* 11 (80): 250–61.

Helbaek, H. (1959) Domestication of food plants in the Old World. *Science* 130: 365–72.

Helbaek, H. (1970) The arrival of rye in Denmark. *Kuml*: 279–96.

Herity, M. and Eogan, G. (1977) *Ireland in Prehistory*. London, Routledge and Kegan Paul.

Herlihy, D. (1967) *Medieval and Renaissance Pistoia*. Yale, University Press.

Hescheler, K. and Rüeger, J. (1942) Die Reste der Haustiere aus den neolithischen Pfahlbaudörfen Egolzwil 2 (Wauwilersee, Kt. Luzern) und Seematte-Gelfingen (Baldeggersee, Kt. Luzern). *Vierteljahrsschrift der Naturforschenden Gesellschaft in Zürich* 87: 383–486.

Heslop, D. (in press) *The Excavations at Thorpe Thewles, Cleveland*. London, Council for British Archaeology Research Report.

Hibbs, J. (1983) The Neolithic of Brittany. In C. Scarre (*ed.*) *Ancient France. Neolithic Societies and Their Landscapes 6000–2000 bc*: 271–323. Edinburgh, University Press.

Hicks, S. P. (1971) Pollen analytical evidence for the effect of prehistoric agriculture on the vegetation of north Derbyshire. *New Phytologist* 70: 647–67.

Higgs, E. S. (*ed.*) (1972) *Papers in Economic Prehistory*. Cambridge, University Press.

Higgs, E. S. (*ed.*) (1975) *Palaeoeconomy*. Cambridge, University Press.

Higgs, E. S. and Jarman, M. R. (1969) The origins of agriculture: a reconsideration. *Antiquity* 43: 31–41.

Higgs, E. S. and Jarman, M. R. (1972) The origins of animal and plant husbandry. In E. S. Higgs (*ed.*) *Papers in Economic Prehistory*: 3–13. Cambridge, University Press.

Higgs, E. S. and Vita-Finzi, C. (1972) Prehistoric economies: a territorial approach. In E. S. Higgs (*ed.*) *Papers in Economic Prehistory*: 27–36. Cambridge University Press.

Higgs, E. S., Vita-Finzi, C., Harris, D. R. and Fagg, A. E. (1967) The climate, environment and industries of stone age Greece: part III. *Proceedings of the Prehistoric Society* 33: 1–29.

Higham, C. F. W. (1967a) Stock rearing as a cultural factor in prehistoric Europe. *Proceedings of the Prehistoric Society* 33: 84–106.

Higham, C. F. W. (1967b) The earliest neolithic culture in Switzerland. *Vierteljahrsschrift der Naturforschenden Gesellschaft in Zürich* 112: 123–36.

Higham, C. F. W. (1967c) The economy of iron age Veileby (Denmark). *Acta Archaeologica* 38: 222–41.

Higham, C. F. W. (1969) The economic basis of the Danish Funnel-Necked Beaker (TRB) culture. *Acta Archaeologica* 40: 200–9.

Higham, C. F. W. and Message, M. (1969) An assessment of a prehistoric technique of bovine husbandry. In D. Brothwell and E. S. Higgs (*eds.*) *Science in Archaeology*: 315–30. London, Thames and Hudson, second edition.

Hill, P. (1979) *Broxmouth (Lothian) Hillfort Excavations 1977–8: an Interim Report*. Edinburgh, University, Department of Archaeology Occasional Paper 2.

Hillman, G. C. (1973) Crop husbandry and food production: modern models for the interpretation of plant remains. *Anatolian Studies* 23: 241–4.

Hillman, G. C. (1981) Crop husbandry practices from charred remains of crops. In R. Mercer (*ed.*) *Farming Practice in British Prehistory*: 123–62. Edinburgh, University Press.

Hills, M. and Liddon, A. (1981) The Vale of Belvoir survey. *Transactions of the Thoroton Society of Nottinghamshire* 85: 13–25.

Hnízdóva, I. (1953) Postoloprty. *Archeologiche Rozhledy* 5: 380–92, 431–2.

Hodder, I. and Orton, C. (1976) *Spatial Analysis in Archaeology*. Cambridge, University Press.

Hodson, F. R. and Rowlett, R. M. (1974) From 600 BC to the Roman conquest. In S. Piggott, G. Daniel and C. McBurney (*eds.*) *France Before the Romans*: 157–91. London, Thames and Hudson.

Holloway, R. R. (1975) Buccino: the early bronze age village of Tufariello. *Journal of Field Archaeology* 2: 11–81.

Holloway, R. R. (1976) Gaudo and the east. *Journal of Field Archaeology* 3: 143–58.

Hopf, M. (1962a) Bericht über die Untersuchung von Samen und Holzkohlenresten von der Argissa-Magula. In V. Milojčić, J. Boessneck and M. Hopf (*eds.*) *Die Deutschen Ausgrabungen auf der Argissa-Magula in Thessalien I*: 101–10. Berlin, Rudolf Habelt.

Hopf, M. (1962b) Nutzpflanzen von Lernäischen Golf. *Jahrbuch des Römisch-Germanischen Zentral Museums, Mainz* 9: 1–19.

Hopf, M. (1964) *Triticum monococcum* L. y *Triticum dicoccum* Schübl., en el Neolitico antiguo español. *Archivo de Prehistoria Levantina* 11: 53–73.

Hopf, M. (1973) Frühe Kulturpflanzen aus Bulgarien. *Jahrbuch des Römisch-Germanischen Zentral Museums, Mainz* 20: 1–47.

Hopf, M. (1977) Pflanzenreste aus der bandkeramischen Siedlung Poigen, Ger.- Bez. Horn, NÖ. *Prähistorischen Forschungen* 8: 97–9.

Hopf, M. and Pellicer, M. (1970) Neolitische Getreidefunde in der Höhle von Nerja (prov. Malaga). *Madrider Mitteilungen* 11: 18–34.

Horowitz, A. (1975) Holocene pollen diagrams and palaeoenvironments of the Valcamonica, northern Italy. *Bullettino del Centro Camuno di Studi Preistorici* 12: 39–48.

Howell, J. M. (1983a) *Settlement and Economy in Neolithic Northern France*. Oxford, British Archaeological Reports, International Series 157.

Howell, J. (1983b) The late Neolithic of the Paris basin. In C. Scarre (*ed.*) *Ancient France. Neolithic Societies and Their Landscapes 6000–2000 bc*: 62–90. Edinburgh, University Press.

Hubbard, R. N. L. B. (1976) On the strength of the evidence for prehistoric crop processing activities. *Journal of Archaeological Science* 3: 257–65.

Hubbard, R. N. L. B. (1979) Ancient agriculture and ecology at Servia. *Annual of the British School at Athens* 74: 226–8.

Hubert, F. (1971a) Neue Ausgrabungen im Michelsbergen Erdwerk in Boitsfort (Belgien). *Germania* 49: 214–18.

Hubert, F. (1971b) Fosses néolithiques à Spiennes. *Archaeologica Belgica* 136: 5–68.

Hundt, H.-J. (1958) *Katalog Straubing I. Die Funde der Glockenbecherkultur und der Straubinger Kultur*. Kallmünz/Opf, Lassleben.

Hundt, H.-J. (1964) *Katalog Straubing II. Die Funde der Hügelgräber der Bronzezeit und der Urnfelderzeit*. Kallmünz/Opf, Lassleben.

Huttunen, P. and Tolonen, M. (1972) Pollen analytical studies of prehistoric agriculture in northern Angermanland. *Early Norrland* 1: 9–34.

Hvass, S. (1975) Das Eisenzeitliche Dorf bei Hodde, Westjutland. *Acta Archaeologica* 46: 142–58.

Hvass, S. (1977) A house of the Single-Grave culture excavated at Vorbasse in central Jutland. *Acta Archaeologica* 48: 219–32.

Hyenstrand, A. (1966) Igelsta i Östertälje (A bronze age complex in Södermanland). *Forvännen* 61: 90–8.

Ijzereef, G. F. (1981) *Bronze Age Animal Bones from Bovenkarspel*. Amersfort, Rijksdienst voor het Oudheidkundig Bodemonderzoek.

Ilett, M. (1983) The early Neolithic of northeastern France. In C. Scarre (*ed.*) *Ancient France. Neolithic Societies and Their Landscapes 6000–2000 bc*: 6–33. Edinburgh, University Press.

Indreko, R. (1964) *Mesolithische und Frühneolithische Kulturen in Osteuropa und West Sibiren.* Stockholm, Almquist and Wiksell.

Indrelid, S. (1975) Problems relating to the early mesolithic settlement of southern Norway. *Norwegian Archaeological Review* 8 (1): 1–18.

Indrelid, S. (1978) Mesolithic economy and settlement patterns in Norway. In P. Mellars (*ed.*) *The Early Postglacial Settlement of Northern Europe*: 147–76. London, Duckworth.

Ingold, T. (1980) *Hunters, Pastoralists and Ranchers. Reindeer Economies and their Transformations.* Cambridge, University Press.

Ingold, T. (1981) The hunter and his spear: notes on the cultural mediator of social and ecological systems. In A. Sheridan and G. Bailey (*eds.*) *Economic Archaeology*: 119–30. Oxford, British Archaeological Reports, International Series 96.

Isaenko, V. F. (*ed.*) (1970) *Očerki po arkheologii Belorussii.* Minsk.

Iterson Scholten, F. R. van (1977) Rope and fishing tackle. In B. L. van Beek, R. W. Brandt and W. Groenman-van Waateringe (*eds.*) *Ex Horreo*: 135–43. Amsterdam, Albert Egges van Giffen Instituut fur Prae- en Protohistorie.

Itten, M. (1970) *Die Horgener Kultur.* Basel, Monographien zur Ur- une Frühgeschichte der Schweiz 17.

Iversen, J. (1941) Land occupation in Denmark's Stone Age. *Danmarks Geologiske Undersøgelse* 2 (66): 1–68.

Iversen, J. (1956) Forest clearance in the Stone Age. *Scientific American* 194: 36–41.

Iversen, J. (1973) The development of Denmark's nature since the last glacial. *Danmarks Geologiske Undersøgelse* 5 (7–8): 7–126.

Jaanusson, H. (1971) Bronsålderboplatsen vid Hallunda (A late bronze age settlement at Hallunda). *Forvännen* 66: 173–85.

Jacobi, G. (1974) *Werkzeug und Gerät aus dem Oppidum von Manching.* (Manching 5). Wiesbaden, Franz Steiner.

Jacobi, R. M. (1976) Britain inside and outside mesolithic Europe. *Proceedings of the Prehistoric Society* 42: 67–84.

Jacobi, R. M. (1978) Northern England in the eighth millennium b.c.: an essay. In P. Mellars (*ed.*) *The Early Postglacial Settlement of Northern Europe*: 295–332. London, Duckworth.

Jacobsen, T. W. (1969) Excavations at Porto Cheli and vicinity. Preliminary report II: the Franchthi Cave 1967–1968. *Hesperia* 38: 343–81.

Jacobsen, T. W. (1973) Excavations in the Franchthi Cave, 1969–1971, parts I and II. *Hesperia* 42: 45–8, 253–83.

Jacobsen, T. W. (1976) 17,000 years of Greek prehistory. *Science* 234: 76–87.

Janssen, C. R. (1960) On the late glacial and postglacial vegetation of South Limburg, Nederland. *Wentia* 4: 1–112.

Jarman, H. N. (1972) The origins of wheat and barley cultivation. In E. S. Higgs (*ed.*) *Papers in Economic Prehistory*: 15–26. Cambridge, University Press.

Jarman, H. N. and Bay-Petersen, J. L. (1976) Agriculture in prehistoric Europe – the lowlands. *Philosophical Transactions of the Royal Society of London* Ser. B, 275: 175–86.

Jarman, H. N. and Gamble, C. (1975) Plant remains from Fiavè: preliminary report. *Preistoria Alpina* 11: 75–6.

Jarman, H. N., Legge, A. J. and Charles, J. A. (1972) Retrieval of plant remains from archaeological sites by froth flotation. In E. S. Higgs (*ed.*) *Papers in Economic Prehistory*: 39–48. Cambridge, University Press.

Jarman, M. R. (1969) The prehistory of Upper Pleistocene and recent cattle. Part I: east Mediterranean, with reference to northwest Europe. *Proceedings of the Prehistoric Society* 35: 236–66.

Jarman, M. R. (1970) Isera (Trentino), Cava Nord: fauna report. *Studi Trentini di Scienze Naturali* Sez. B. 47: 78–80.

Jarman, M. R. (1971) Culture and economy in the north Italian Neolithic. *World Archaeology* 3: 255–65.

Jarman, M. R. (1972a) European deer economies and the advent of the Neolithic. In E. S. Higgs (*ed.*) *Papers in Economic Prehistory*: 125–47. Cambridge, University Press.

Jarman, M. R. (1972b) The fauna. In P. Warren, *Myrtos: An Early Bronze Age Settlement in Crete*: 318–20. London, British School of Archaeology at Athens.

Jarman, M. R. (1975) The fauna and economy of Fiavè. *Preistoria Alpina* 11: 65–73.

Jarman, M. R. (1976) Prehistoric economic development in sub-Alpine Italy. In G. de G. Sieveking, I. H. Longworth and K. E. Wilson (*eds.*) *Problems in Economic and Social Archaeology*: 523–48. London, Duckworth.

Jarman, M. R., Bailey, G. N. and Jarman, H. N. (1982) *Early European Agriculture. Its Foundations and Development*. Cambridge, University Press.

Jarman, M. R. and Jarman, H. N. (1968) The fauna and economy of early neolithic Knossos. *Annual of the British School at Athens* 63: 741–64.

Jarman, M. R. and Webley, D. (1975) Settlement and land use in Capitanata, Italy. In E. S. Higgs (*ed.*) *Palaeoeconomy*: 177–221. Cambridge, University Press.

Jarman, M. R. and Wilkinson, P. F. (1972) Criteria of animal domestication. In E. S. Higgs (*ed.*) *Papers in Economic Prehistory*: 83–96. Cambridge, University Press.

Jensen, J. A. (1967) Voldtoften and late bronze age settlement archaeology in Denmark. *Aarbøger for Nordisk Oldkyndighed og Historie*: 91–154.

Jensen, J. A. (1972) Myrhøj. Three houses with Bell Beaker pottery. *Kuml*: 61–122.

Jensen, P. (1968) Food selection of the forests in northern Europe in epipalaeolithic times. *Det Kongelige Danske Videnskabesnes Selskab Biologiske Meddelelser* 12: 1.

Jobey, G. (1966) A field survey in Northumberland. In A. L. F. Rivet (*ed.*) *The Iron Age in Northern Britain*: 89–109. Edinburgh, University Press.

Jochim, M. A. (1976) *Hunter-Gatherer Subsistence and Settlement. A Predictive Model*. London and New York, Academic Press.

Joffroy, R. (1972) Informations archéologiques. Circonscription de Champagne-Ardenne. *Gallia Préhistoire* 15: 399–411.

Johansen, O. S. (1979) Early farming north of the Arctic Circle. *Norwegian Archaeological Review* 12 (1): 22–31.

Johnson, A. E. (1975) Experiments made on Stackyard Field, Woburn, 1877–1974. *Rothamsted Experimental Station Report for 1974*: 29–44. Harpenden, Lawes Agricultural Trust.

Jones, G. (1981) Crop processing at Assiros Toumba – a taphonomic study. *Zeitschrift für Archäologie* 15: 105–11.

Jones, M. (1980) Carbonised cereals from Grooved Ware contexts. *Proceedings of the Prehistoric Society* 46: 61–3.

Jones, M. (1981) The development of crop husbandry. In M. Jones and G. W. Dimbleby (*eds.*) *The Environment of Man from the Iron Age to the Anglo-Saxon Period*: 95–127. Oxford, British Archaeological Reports, British Series 87.

Jones, M. (in press) Archaeobotany beyond subsistence reconstruction. In G. Barker and C. Gamble (*eds.*) *Beyond Domestication: Subsistence Archaeology and Social Complexity in Ancient Europe*. New York, Academic Press.

Jones, P. (1966) Italy, in Chapter 7, 'Medieval agrarian society in its prime'. In M. A. Postan (*ed.*) *Cambridge Economic History of Europe 1. The Agrarian Life of the Middle Ages*: 341–431. Cambridge, University Press.

Jones, P. A. (1984) The social geography of early agriculture in sub-Saharan Africa. Sheffield University, unpublished Ph.D. thesis.

Jones, R. L. (1979) Vegetation studies. In C. Renfrew, *Investigations in Orkney*: 21–8. London, Report of the Research Committee of the Society of Antiquaries of London 38.

Jong, J. de (1970–1) Pollen and C14 analysis of Holocene deposits in Zijderveld and environs. *Berichten van de Rijksdienst voor het Oudheidkundig Bodemonderzoek* 20–1: 75–88.

Joos, M. (1976) Die Sedimente der neolitischen Station Feldmeilen-Vorderfeld. *Antiqua* 5: 105–32 (Basel).

Jordan, B. (1975) *Die Tierknochenfunde aus der Magula Pevkakia in Thessalien*. Munich, Institut für Palaeoanatomie, Domestikationsforschung und Geschichte der Tiermedizin der Universität München.

Jørgensen, G. (1975) *Triticum aestivum* s.l. from the neolithic site of Weier in Switzerland. *Folia Quaternaria* 46: 7–21.

Jørgensen, G. (1976) A corn-hoard from Sarup. A contribution to the agriculture of the TRB culture. *Kuml*: 62–4.

Jørgensen, G. (1981) Cereals from Sarup. With some remarks on plant husbandry in neolithic Denmark. *Kuml*: 221–31.

Jørgensen, G. and Fredskild, B. (1978) Plant remains from the TRB culture, period MN V. In K. Davidsen, *The Final TRB Culture in Denmark*: 189–92. Copenhagen, Akademisk Forlag (Arkaeologiske Studier 5).

Jorns, W. (1960) Zur Salzgewinnung in Bad Nauheim während der Spätlatènezeit. *Germania* 38: 178–84.

Josien, T. (1955) Station lacustre d'Auvernier (Lac de Neuchâtel). Étude de la faune de la station. *Bulletin de la Société Préhistorique Française* 52: 57–75.

Jourdan, L. (1976) Les complexités de l'élevage et de l'alimentation au Mésolithique et au Néolithique ancien en Provence. In J. Guilaine (*ed.*) *La Préhistoire Française 2. Civilisation Néolithiques et Protohistoriques*: 168–71. Paris, CNRS.

Jovanovic, B. (1973) Chronological frames of the Iron Gate group of early neolithic period. *Archaeologica Iugoslavica* 10: 23–38.

Jovanovic, B. and Ottoway, B. S. (1976) Copper mining and metallurgy in the Vinča group. *Antiquity* 198: 104–13.

Kaenel, G. (1976) Le site néolithique de Châble-Perron VD (stations I et II). *Jahrbuch der Schweizerischen Gesellschaft für Urgeschichte* 59: 7–29.

Kahlke, D. (1954) *Die Bestattungssitten des Donauländischen Kulturkreises der Jüngeren Steinzeit*. Berlin, Mutten und Loening.

Kalicz, N. (1963) *Die Badener (Pecele) Kultur und Anatolien*. Budapest, Akadémiai Kiadó.

Kalicz, N. (1968) *Die Frühbronzezeit in Nordostungarn*. Budapest, Akadémiai Kiadó.

Keesing, R. M. (1975) *Kin Groups and Social Structure*. New York, Holt.

Keller, F. (1878) *The Lake Dwellings of Switzerland and Other Parts of Europe*. London, Longmans, Green and Co.

Killen, J. T. (1964) The wool industry of Crete in the Late Bronze Age. *Annual of the British School at Athens* 59: 1–15.

Kimmig, W. (1975) Early Celts on the Upper Danube. In R. Bruce-Mitford (*ed.*) *Recent Archaeological Excavations in Europe*: 32–64. London, Routledge and Kegan Paul.

Kingery, W. D. and Frierman, J. D. (1974) The firing temperature of a Karanovo sherd and inferences about southeast European chalcolithic refracting technology. *Proceedings of the Prehistoric Society* 40: 204–5.

Kjaerum, P. (1954) Plough furrows under a stone age barrow in Jutland. *Kuml*: 27–9.

Klichowska, M. (1970) Neolityzne Szczatki Roślinne z Radziejuwa Kujawskiego. *Prace i Materialy Muzeum Archeologicznego i Etnograficznego w Lodzi* 17: 165–77.

Klindt-Jensen, O. (1957) *Denmark*. London, Thames and Hudson.

Knörzer, K.-H. (1971a) Pflanzliche Grossreste aus der rössenerzeitlichen Siedlung bei Langmeiler, Kr. Jülich. *Bonner Jahrbucher* 171: 9–33.

Knörzer, K.-H. (1971b) Eisenzeitliche Pflanzenfunde im Rheinland. *Bonner Jahrbucher* 171: 40–58.

Knörzer, K.-H. (1972) Subfossile Pflanzenreste aus der bandkeramischen Siedlung Langweiler 3 und 6, Kreis Jülich, und ein urnenfelderzeitlicher Getreidefund innerhalb dieser Siedlung. *Bonner Jahrbucher* 172: 395–403.

Koenigswald, W. von (1972) Die Faunenwandel an der Pleistozän-Holozän-Grenze in der steinzeitliche Schichtenfolge vom Zigeunerfels bei Sigmaringen. *Archäologische Information* 1.

Königsson, L. K. (1970) *Traces of Neolithic Human Influence upon the Landscape Development of the Bjurselet Settlement, Västerbotten, Northern Sweden*. Umea, Skytteanska Samfundets Handlingar 7.

Kooi, P. B. (1979) *Pre-Roman Urnfields in the North of the Netherlands*. Groningen, Wolters–Noordhoff.

Korek, J. (1951) Ein Gräberfeld der Badener Kultur bei Alsónémedi. *Acta Archaeologica Hungarica* 1: 35–91.

Kossack, G. (1956–7) Zur den Metallbeigaben des Wagengrabes von Ca' Morta. *Sibrium* 3: 41–54.

Kosse, K. (1979) *Settlement Ecology of the Köros and Linear Pottery Cultures in Hungary*. Oxford, British Archaeological Reports, International Series 64.

Kowalezyk, J. (1969) The origins of the neolithic age in Polish territories. *Wiadomósci Archeologiczne* 34: 3–69.

Kral, F. (1979) *Spät- und Postglaziale Waldgeschichte der Alpen auf Grund der Bisherigen Pollenanalysen*. Veröffentlichung des Institutes für Waldbau an der Universität für Bodenkultur in Wien. Wien, Kommissionsverlag Österr. Agrarverlag.

Krämer, W. (1960) The oppidum of Manching. *Antiquity* 34: 191–200.

Krämer, W. and Schübert, F. (1970) *Die Ausgrabungen in Manching 1955–1961. Einführing und Fundstellungübersicht*. Wiesbaden, Franz Steiner.

Kratochvil, A. (1972) Knochenüberreste von der neolithischen Siedlung Jeleni Lonka bei Mikulov. *Prehled Vyzkumñ* (1971): 24–7.

Kristiansen, K. (1978) The consumption of wealth in bronze age Denmark. A study in the dynamics of economic process in tribal societies. In K. Kristiansen and C. Paludan-Müller (*eds.*) *New Directions in Scandinavian Archaeology*: 158–90. Copenhagen, National Museum of Denmark.

Kristiansen, K. (1981) Economic models for bronze age Scandinavia – towards an integrated approach. In A. Sheridan and G. Bailey (*eds.*) *Economic Archaeology*: 239–303. Oxford, British Archaeological Reports, International Series 96.

Kristiansen, K. (1982) The formation of tribal systems in later European prehistory. Northern Europe 4000–500 bc. In C. Renfrew, M. Rowlands and B. Seagraves (*eds.*) *Theory and Explanation in Archaeology*: 271–80. New York, Academic Press.

Kroll, H. J. (1975) *Ur- und Frühgeschichtlicher Ackerbau in Archsum auf Sylt*. Kiel.

Kruk, J. (1973) *Studia Osadnicze nad Neolitem Wyzyn Lessowych*. Warsaw, Polska Akademia Nauk, Instytut Historii Kultury Materialnej.

Kruk, J. (1980) *The Neolithic Settlement of Southern Poland*. Oxford, British Archaeological Reports, International Series 93.

Kruta, V. (1975) Les habitats et nécropoles Laténiens en Bohème. In P. M. Duval and V. Kruta (*eds.*) *L'Habitat et la Nécropole a l'Âge du Fer en Europe Occidentale et Centrale*: 95–102. Paris, Libraire Honoré Champion.

Kubiena, W. L. (1953) *The Soils of Europe*. London, Thomas Murby and Co.

Kuhn, E. (1932) Beiträge zur Kenntnis der Säugetierfauna der Schweiz seit dem Neolithikum. *Revue Suisse de Zoologie* 39: 531–768.

Kulczycka-Leciejewiczowa, A. (1969) Nowa Huta-Pleszów osada neolityczna kultury ceramiki wstegowej rytej i lendzielskiej. *Materialy Archeologiczne Nowej Huty* 2: 7–124.

Kulczycka-Leciejewiczowa, A. (1970) The linear and stroked pottery cultures. In T. Wiślański (*ed.*) *The Neolithic in Poland*: 14–75. Warsaw, Ossolineum.

Kuper R. H. and Piepers, W. (1966) Eine Siedlung der Rössener Kultur in Inden (Kr. Jülich) und Lamersdorf (Kr. Düren), Vorbericht. *Bonner Jahrbucher* 166: 370.

Kuper, R. H., Löhr, J., Lüning, J. and Stehli, P. (1974) Untersuchungen zur neolithischen Besiedlung der Aldenhovener Platte IV. *Bonner Jahrbucher* 174: 424–508.

Kutzian, I. B. (1947) *The Köros Culture*. Budapest, Dissertationes Pannonicae.

Lamb, H. H. (1966) Atmospheric circulation and the main climatic variables between 8000 and

0 BC: meteorological evidence. In J. S. Sawyer (*ed.*) *World Climate from 8000–0 BC*: 174–217. London, Royal Meteorological Society.

Lamb, H. H. (1977) *Climate: Past, Present and Future 2. Climatic History and the Future*. London, Methuen.

Lamb, R. G. (1980) *Iron Age Promontory Forts in the Northern Isles*. Oxford, British Archaeological Reports, British Series 79.

Lambert, J. B., Szpunar, C. B. and Buikstra, J. E. (1979) Chemical analysis of excavated human bone from middle and late Woodland sites. *Archaeometry* 21 (2): 115–29.

Lambrick, G. and Robinson, M. (1979) *Iron Age and Roman Riverside Settlements at Farmoor, Oxfordshire*. London, Council for British Archaeology Research Report 32.

Larsson, L. (1981–2) A causewayed enclosure with Valby pottery at Stävie, western Scania. *Meddelanden från Lunds Universitets Historiska Museum* 4: 65–114.

Lee, R. B. and DeVore, I. (*eds.*) (1968) *Man the Hunter*. Chicago, Aldine.

Legge, A. J. (1972) Prehistoric exploitation of the gazelle in Palestine. In E. S. Higgs (*ed.*) *Papers in Economic Prehistory*: 119–24. Cambridge, University Press.

Legge, A. J. (1981a) Aspects of cattle husbandry. In R. Mercer (*ed.*) *Farming Practice in British Prehistory*: 169–81. Edinburgh, University Press.

Legge, A. J. (1981b) The agricultural economy. In R. Mercer (*ed.*) *Excavations at Grimes Graves*: 79–103. London, H.M.S.O.

Leisner, G. and Leisner, V. (1943) *Die Megalithgräber der Iberischen Halbinsel: Der Süden*. Berlin, Walter de Gruyter.

Lepiksaar, J. (1975) *The Analysis of the Animal Bones from the Bjurselet Settlement, Västerbotten, Northern Sweden*. Umea, Skytteanska Samfundets Handlingar 8.

Lerche, G. (1968) The radiocarbon-dated Danish ploughing implements. *Tools and Tillage* 1: 56–60.

Lerche, G. and Steensberg, M. (1980) *Agricultural Tools and Field Shapes*. Copenhagen, National Museum of Denmark.

Le Roy Ladurie, E. (1966) *Les Paysans de Languedoc*. Paris, S.E.V.P.E.N.

Le Roy Ladurie, E. (1978) *Montaillou*. London, Scolar.

Levine, L. S. and McDonald, M. M. A. (1976) The neolithic and chalcolithic periods in the Mahidasht. *Iran* 15: 39–50.

Levy, J. E. (1982) *Social and Religious Organisation in Bronze Age Denmark*. Oxford, British Archaeological Reports, International Series 124.

Lewicka, A. (1972) Brandwirtschaft und Brandrodung in den Polnischen Karpathen. In I. Balassa(*ed.*) *Getreideban in Ost- und Mitteleuropa*: 119–42. Budapest, Akadémiai Kiadó.

L'Helgouach, J. (1965) *Les Sepultures Megalithiques en Armorique*. Rennes, Travaux du Laboratoire d'Anthropologie Préhistorique de la Faculté des Sciences.

L'Helgouach, J. (1976) Les civilisations néolithiques en Armorique. In J. Guilaine (*ed.*) *La Préhistoire Française 2. Civilisations Néolithiques et Protohistoriques*: 365–74. Paris, CNRS.

Lies, H. (1974) Zur neolithischen Siedlungsintensität im Magdeburger Raum. *Jahresschrift für Mitteldeutsche Vorgeschichte* 58: 57–111.

Lindquist, S. O. (1968) *Det förhistoriska Kulturlandskapet i Östra Östergotland*. Stockholm, Acta Universitatis Stockholmiensis. (Studies in North European Archaeology 2.)

Lindquist, S. O. (1974) The development of the agrarian landscape on Gotland during the early Iron Age. *Norwegian Archaeological Review* 7: 6–32.

Louwe Kooijmans, L. P. (1974) The Rhine/Meuse delta. Four studies in its prehistoric occupation and holocene geology. *Analecta Praehistorica Leidensia* 7.

Louwe Kooijmans, L. P. (1980) Archaeology and coastal change in the Netherlands. In F. H. Thompson (*ed.*) *Archaeology and Coastal Change*: 106–33. London, Society of Antiquaries of London Occasional Paper 1.

Lowe, V. P. W. (1969) Population dynamics of the red deer (*Cervus elaphus*) on Rhum. *Journal of Animal Ecology* 38: 475–7.

Ložek, V. (1966) Die quatäre Klimaentwicklung in der Tschechoslowakei. *Quartär* 17: 1–20.

Lüdi, W. (1954) Beitrag zur Kenntnis der Vegetationsverhältnisse im Schweizerischen Alpen-vorland während der Bronzezeit. In W. Guyan (*ed.*) *Das Pfahlbauproblem*: 92–109. Schaf-fhausen, Monographien zür Ur- und Frühgeschichte der Schweiz 10.

Lund, J. and Thomsen, V. (1981) On the reconstruction of an iron age house. *Kuml*: 187–205.

Lüning, J. (1967) Die Michelsberger Kultur und ihre Funde in zeitlicher und raümlicher Gliederung. *Bericht der Römisch-Germanischen Kommission* 48: 1–350.

Lüning, R. J. (1976) Un nouveau modèle de l'habitat du Néolithique ancien. *IX Congrès du Union International des Sciences Préhistoriques et Protohistoriques, Nice, Section VI.* Paris, CNRS.

Lurati, O. (1969) Alwesen und Alpbewirtschaftung im Tessin mit besonderer Berücksichtigung der genossenschaftlichen Sennerei. In L. Földes (*ed.*) *Viehwirtschaft und Hirtenkultur*: 756–77. Budapest, Akadémiai Kiadó.

Luttrell, A. (1971) Two templar-hospitaller preceptories north of Tuscania. *Papers of the British School at Rome* 39: 90–124.

Lynch, A. (1981) *Man and Environment in S.W. Ireland*. Oxford, British Archaeological Reports, British Series 85.

Machin, M. L. (1973) Further excavations at the enclosure of Swine Sty. *Transactions of the Hunter Archaeological Society* 10 (2): 204–11.

McConnell, P.V. (1883) *An Agricultural Notebook*. London, Crosby Lockwood and Co.

McInnes, I. J. (1971) Settlement in late neolithic Britain. In D. D. A. Simpson (*ed.*) *Economy and Settlement in Neolithic and Early Bronze Age Britain and Europe*: 113–30. Leicester, University Press.

McNeal, R. A. (1972) The Greeks in history and prehistory. *Antiquity* 46: 19–28.

MacNeish, R. S. (1964) Ancient Mesoamerican civilisation. *Science* 143: 531–7.

MacNeish, R. S. (1965) The origins of American agriculture. *Antiquity* 39: 87–94.

McPherron, A. and Srejović, D. (1971) *Early Farming Cultures in Central Serbia*. Kragujevac, Naroden Muzej.

Madsen, T. (1977) Toftum near horsens. A causewayed camp from the transition between early and middle Neolithic. *Kuml*: 161–84.

Madsen, T. (1979) Earthen long barrows and timber structures: aspects of the early neolithic mortuary practice in Denmark. *Proceedings of the Prehistoric Society* 45: 301–20.

Madsen, T. (1984) The settlement system of the early agricultural societies in east Jutland, Denmark. A regional study. In K. Kristensen (*ed.*) *New Directions in Scandinavian Archaeology* 3 (in press). Copenhagen, National Museum of Denmark.

Malmer, M. P. (1962) *Jungneolithische Studien*. Acta Archaeologica Lundensia 2.

Malmros, C. and Tauber, H. (1975) Radiocarbon dates of the Danish Single Grave culture. *Aarbøger for Nordisk Oldkyndighed og Historie*: 78–95.

Maltby, M. (1979) *The Animal Bones From Exeter*. Sheffield, Sheffield University (Department of Prehistory and Archaeology).

Maltby, M. (1981) Iron age, Romano-British and Anglo-Saxon animal husbandry – a review of the faunal evidence. In M. Jones and G. Dimbleby (*eds.*) *The Environment of Man: the Iron Age to the Anglo-Saxon Period*: 155–203. Oxford, British Archaeological Reports, British Series 87.

Manby, T. G. (1963) The excavation of the Willerby Wold long barrow, East Yorkshire. *Proceedings of the Prehistoric Society* 29: 173–205.

Manby, T. G. (1976) The excavation of the Kilham long barrow, East Riding of Yorkshire. *Proceedings of the Prehistoric Society* 42: 111–59.

Manfredini, A. (1972) Il villaggio trincerato di Monte Aquilone nel quadro del Neolitico dell'Italia meridionale. *Origini* 6: 29–154.

Markgraf, V. (1969) Moorkundliche und vegetationsgeschichtliche Untersuchungen an einem Moorsee an der Waldgrenze im Wallis. *Botanische Jahrbücher für Systematik Pflanzengeschichte und Pflanzengeographie* 87: 1–63.

Markovic, C. (1974) The stratigraphy and chronology of the Odmut Cave. *Archaeologica Iugoslavica* 15: 7–12.

Mateescu, C. N. (1975) Remarks on cattle breeding and agriculture in the middle and late Neolithic on the Danube. *Dacia* 19: 13–18.

Mathiassen, T. (1948) *Studier Ovor Vestjyllands Oldtidsbebyggelse*. Copenhagen, Nationalmuseets Skrifter, Arkaeologisk-Historick Raekke 2.

Mathiassen, T. (1959) *Nordwestjaellands Oldtidsbebyggelse*. Copenhagen, National Museum of Denmark.

Matley, I. M. (1968) Transhumance in Bosnia and Herzegovina. *The Geographical Review*, 58: 231–61.

Matthias, W. and Schultze-Motel, J. (1971) Kulturpflanzenabdrücke an Gefässen der Schnurkeramik und der Aunjetitzer Kultur aus Mitteldeutschland. *Jahresschrift für Mitteldeutsche Vorgeschichte* 55: 113–34.

May, J. (1970) Dragonby – an interim report on excavations of an iron age and Romano-British site near Scunthorpe, Lincolnshire. *Antiquaries Journal* 50: 222–45.

May, J. (1976) *Prehistoric Lincolnshire*. Lincoln, History of Lincolnshire Committee.

Mead, W. R. (1953) *Farming in Finland*. London, Athlone Press.

Meadow, R. H. (1975) Mammal remains from Hajii Firuz: a study in methodology. In A. T. Clason (*ed.*) *Archaeozoological Studies*: 265–83. Amsterdam, North Holland Publishing Company.

Meat and Livestock Commission (1980–1) *Beef Production Year Book*.

Megaw, J. V. S. (1976) Gwithian, Cornwall: some notes on the evidence for neolithic and bronze age settlement. In C. B. Burgess and R. Miket (*eds.*) *Settlement and Economy in the Third and Second Millennia B.C.*: 51–79. Oxford, British Archaeological Reports, British Series 33.

Megaw, J. V. S. and Simpson, D. D. A. (1979) *Introduction to British Prehistory*. Leicester, University Press.

Mellaart, J. (1960) Anatolia and the Balkans. *Antiquity* 34: 270–8.

Mellars, P. A. (1974) The Palaeolithic and Mesolithic. In C. Renfrew)*ed.*) *British Prehistory: a New Outline*: 41–99. London, Duckworth.

Mellars, P. A. (1975) Ungulate populations, economic patterns and the mesolithic landscape. In J. G. Evans, S. Limbrey and H. Cleere (*eds.*) *The Effect of Man on the Landscape: the Highland Zone*: 49–56. London, Council for British Archaeology Research Report 11.

Mellars, P. A. (1976) Fire ecology, animal populations and man: a study of some ecological relationships in prehistory. *Proceedings of the Prehistoric Society* 42: 15–45.

Mellars, P. A. (1978) Excavation and economic analysis of mesolithic shell middens on the island of Oronsay (Inner Hebrides). In P. Mellars (*ed.*) *The Early Postglacial Settlement of Northern Europe*: 371–96. London, Duckworth.

Mellars, P. A. and Wilkinson, M. R. (1980) Fish otoliths as evidence of seasonality in prehistoric shell middens: the evidence from Oronsay (Inner Hebrides). *Proceedings of the Prehistoric Society* 46: 19–44.

Menendez Amor, J. and Florschütz, F. (1963) Sur les éléments stéppiques dans la vegetation quatenaires de l'Espagne. *Boletín de la Real Sociedad Española de Historia Natural* 62: 251–5.

Menendez Amor, J. and Florschütz, F. (1964) Results of the preliminary palynological investigation of samples from a 50 m boring in southern Spain. *Boletín de la Real Sociedad Española de Historia Natural* 62: 251–5.

Mensch, P. J. A. van and Ijzereef, G. F. (1975) Animal remains from a bronze age settlement near Andijk, Province of North Holland. *Berichten van de Rijksdienst voor het Oudheidkundig Bodemonderzoek* 25: 55–68.

Mercer, J. (1971) A regression-time stone-workers' camp, 33 ff O.D., Lassa River, Isle of Jura. *Proceedings of the Society of Antiquaries of Scotland* 103: 1–32.

Mercer, R. (1980) *Hambledon Hill: A Neolithic Landscape*. Edinburgh, University Press.

Mercer, R. (*ed.*) (1981) *Farming Practice in British Prehistory*. Edinburgh, University Press.

Meroc, M. L. (1967) St Michel-du-Touch. Circonscription de Midi-Pyrenees. *Gallia Préhistoire* 10: 393–8.

Meroc, L. and Simmonet, G. (1970) Le Chasséen de la haute et de la moyenne vallée de la Garonne. In J. Guilaine (*ed.*) *Les Civilisations Néolithiques du Midi de la France*: 38–47. Carcassonne, Actes du Colloque de Narbonne.

Meschke, C. (1967) *En Norrländsk Stenåldersboplats Med Skärvstensvall*. Antikvariskt Arkiv 31.

Mikkelsen, E. (1975) Mesolithic in southeastern Norway. *Norwegian Archaeological Review* 8: 19–35.

Mikkelsen, E. (1978) Seasonality and mesolithic adaptation in Norway. In K. Kristiansen and C. Paludan-Müller (*eds.*) *New Directions in Scandinavian Archaeology*: 79–119. Copenhagen, National Museum of Denmark.

Mikkelsen, E. and Høeg, H. I. (1979) A reconsideration of neolithic agriculture in eastern Norway. *Norwegian Archaeological Review* 12 (1): 33–47.

Mikov, V. and Dzambazov, N. (1960) *Devetashkata Peshtera*. Sofia.

Milisauskas, S. (1976) Olszanica: an early farming village in Poland. *Archaeology* 29 (1): 31–41.

Milisauskas, S. (1978) *European Prehistory*. London and New York, Academic Press.

Mills, N. T. W. (1976) Exploitation and settlement patterns in western Provence, 7500–2000 bc. Sheffield University, unpublished M.A. thesis.

Mills, N. T. W. (1981) Prehistoric agriculture in southern France – case studies from Provence and Languedoc. Sheffield University, unpublished Ph.D. thesis.

Mills, N. T. W. (1983) The Neolithic of southern France. In C. Scarre (*ed.*) *Ancient France. Neolithic Societies and Their Landscapes 6000–2000 bc*: 91–145. Edinburgh, University Press.

Mills, N. T. W. (in press) Regional survey and settlement trends: studies from prehistoric France. In G. Barker and C. Gamble (*eds.*) *Beyond Domestication: Subsistence Archaeology and Social Complexity in Ancient Europe*. New York, Academic Press.

Milojčić, V. (1965) Die Tontafeln von Tartaria und die absolute Chronologie des mittel-europäischen Neolithikum. *Germania* 43: 261–8.

Mišić, V., Colić, D. and Dinić, A. (1972) Ecological-phytocenological investigation. In D. Srejović, *Lepenski Vir*: 171–81. London, Thames and Hudson.

Mitchell, G. F. (1976) *The Irish Landscape*. London, Collins.

Moberg, C.-A. (1978) Some developments in north European prehistory in the period 1969–1976. *Norwegian Archaeological Review* 11: 6–26.

Modderman, P. J. R. (1955) Woonsporen uit de bronstijd en de ijzertijd op de Margijnen Enk onder Deventer, Overijssel. *Berichten van de Rijksdienst voor het Oudheidkundig Bodemonderzoek* 6: 22–31.

Modderman, P. J. R. (1958–9a) Die geographische Lage der bandkeramischen Siedlungen in den Niederlanden. *Palaeohistoria* 6–7: 1–6.

Modderman, P. J. R. (1958–9b) Bandkeramische Siedlungsspuren in Elsloo. *Palaeohistoria* 6–7: 27–31.

Modderman, P. J. R. (1958–9c) Die bandkeramische Siedlung von Sittard. *Palaeohistoria* 6–7: 33–120.

Modderman, P. J. R. (1964) Bijzettingen en bewonigssporen uit de Bronstijd te Zwangdijk, gem. Wervershoof. *West-Frieslands Oud en Nieuw* 31: 209–27.

Modderman, P. J. R. (1970) Linearbandkeramik aus Elsloo und Stein. *Analecta Praehistorica Leidensia* 3.

Modderman, P. J. R. (1977) Die neolithische Besiedlung bei Hienheim, Ldkr. Kelheim – I: Die Ausgrabungen am Weinberg 1965–1970. *Analecta Praehistorica Leidensia* 10.

Moe, D., Indrelid, S. and Kjos-Hanssen, O. (1978) A study of environment and early man in the southern Norwegian highlands. *Norwegian Archaeological Review* 11 (2): 73–83.

Mogoşanu, H. and Bitiri, M. (1961) Asupra prozentei Campignianului in Romîna. *Studi şi Cercetări de Istorie Veche* 12 (2): 215–26.

Møhl, U. (1970) Seal and whale hunting on the Danish coasts. *Kuml*: 297–329.

Møhl, U. (1978) Zoological analysis of the Aggersund settlement: a special-purpose camp for hunting swans? *Kuml*: 57–75.

Monk, M. A. and Fasham, P. J. (1980) Carbonised plant remains from two iron age sites in central Hampshire. *Proceedings of the Prehistoric Society* 46: 321–44.

Moore, A. M. T. (1982) Agricultural origins in the Near East: a model for the 1980's. *World Archaeology* 14 (2): 224–36.

Moore, P. D. (1973) The influence of prehistoric cultures upon the initiation and spread of blanket bog in upland Wales. *Nature* 241 (5388): 350–3.

Mordant, C. and Mordant, D. (1972) L'enceinte néolithique de Noyen-sur-Seine (Seine-et-Marne). *Bulletin de la Société Préhistorique Française* 69: 554–69.

Mörner, N. A. and Wallin, B. (1977) A 10,000 year temperature record from Gotland, Sweden. *Palaeogeography, Palaeoclimatology, Palaeoecology* 21: 113–38.

Morzadec-Kerfourn, M.-T. (1969) Variations de la ligne de rivage au cours du Post-glaciare le long de la côte nord du Finistère. Analyses polliniques de tourbes et de dépôts organiques littoraux. *Bullétin de l'Association Française pour l'Étude du Quaternaire* 4: 285–318.

Morzadec-Kerfourn, M.-T. (1974) Variations de la ligne de rivage armoricaine au Quaternaire: analyses polliniques de dépôts organiques littoraux. *Mémoires de la Société Géologique et Minéralogique de Bretagne* 17.

Morzadec-Kerfourn, M.-T. (1976) L'évolution de la végétation en Armorique à partir du Néolithique. In J. Guilaine (*ed.*) *La Préhistoire Française 2. Civilisations Néolithiques et Protohistoriques*: 88–94. Paris, CNRS.

Mounteney, G. (1981) Faunal attrition and subsistence reconstruction at Thwing. In G. Barker (*ed.*) *Prehistoric Communities in Northern England: Essays in Social and Economic Reconstruction*: 73–86. Sheffield, Sheffield University, Department of Prehistory and Archaeology.

Müller, H. H. (1964) *Die Haustiere der Mitteldeutscher Bandkeramiker*. Berlin, Schriften der Sektion für Vor- und Frühgeschichte der Deutschen Akademie der Wissenschaften zu Berlin 17.

Muñoz, A. M. (1965) *La Cultura Neolítica Catalana de los Sepulcros de Fosa*. Barcelona, Istituto de Arqueologia, Universidad.

Munro, R. (1890) *The Lake Dwellings of Europe*. London, Cassell.

Murphy, P. L. (1977) Early agriculture and environment in the Hampshire chalklands. Southampton University, unpublished M.Phil. thesis.

Murray, J. (1970) *The First European Agriculture*. Edinburgh, University Press.

Musson, C. R. (1976) Excavations at the Breiddin 1969–1973. In D. W. Harding (*ed.*) *Hillforts: Later Prehistoric Earthworks in Britain and Ireland*: 293–302. London and New York, Academic Press.

Myrhe, B. (1973) The iron age farm in southwest Norway. *Norwegian Archaeological Review* 6: 14–41.

Myrhe, B. (1978) Agrarian development, settlement history and social organisation in southwest Norway in the Iron Age. In K. Kristiansen and C. Paludan-Müller (*eds.*) *New Directions in Scandinavian Archaeology* 1: 224–71. Copenhagen, National Museum of Denmark.

Nandris, J. (1970) Groundwater as a factor in the first temperate neolithic settlement of the Körös region. *Zbornik Naroden Muzej Beograd* 6: 59–71.

Necrasov, O. (1964) Sur les restes de faunes subfossiles datant de la culture Starčevo-Criş, et la problème de la domestication. *Analele Stiintifice Ale Universitaţii Din Jaşi* n.s. 11 (10): 167–81.

Nemeskéri, J. (1976) La structure paléodémographique de la population épipaléolithique-prénéolithique de Vlasac (Yougoslavia). *IXe Congrès de l'Union Internationale des Sciences Préhistoriques et Protohistoriques, Nice* section 5. Paris, CNRS.

Netting, R. McC. (1971) Of men and meadows: strategies of alpine land use. *Anthropological Quarterly* 45: 132–44.

Netting, R. McC. (1976) The system nobody knows. Village irrigation in the Swiss Alps. In T. E. Downing and McG. Gibson (*eds.*) *Irrigation's Impact on Society*: 67–75. Tucson, Arizona, Anthropological Papers of the University of Arizona 25.

Neustupny, E. and Neustupny, J. (1961) *Czechoslovakia (Before the Slavs)*. London, Thames and Hudson.

Newell, R. P. (1973) The postglacial adaptations of the indigenous populations of the northwest European plain. In S. K. Kozłowski (*ed.*) *The Mesolithic in Europe*: 399–440. Warsaw, University Press.

Nilsson, S. (1868) *The Primitive Inhabitants of Scandinavia*. London, Longman.

Noe-Nygaard, N. (1967) Recent 'kokkenmøddinger' in Ghana. *Geografisk Tidsskrift* 66: 179–97.

Noe-Nygaard, N. (1975) Two shoulder blades with healed lesions from Star Carr. *Proceedings of the Prehistoric Society* 41: 10–16.

Noe-Nygaard, N. (1977) Butchering and marrow fracturing as a taphonomic factor in archaeological deposits. *Paleobiology* 3: 218–37.

O'Connor, T. P. (1982) *Animal Bones From Flaxengate, Lincoln, c. 870–1500 A.D.* Archaeology of Lincoln 17/1. London, Council for British Archaeology.

Odner, K. (1964) Erhverv og bosetning i Komsakulturen. *Viking* 28: 117–28.

Orme, B. J., Coles, J. M., Caseldine, A. E. and Bailey, G. N. (1981) Meare Village West 1979. In J. M. Coles (*ed.*) *Somerset Levels Papers* 7: 12–69. Somerset Levels Project.

Östenberg, C. E. (1967) Luni sul Mignone e problemi della preistoria d'Italia. *Acta Instituti Romani Regni Sueciae* 4 (75).

Ostoja-Zagorski, J. (1974) Studies on the economic structure and the decline of the Bronze Age and the Hallstatt period in the north and western zone of the Odra and Vistula basins. *Przeglad Archeologiczny* 22: 123–50.

Otterbein, K. (1970) *The Evolution of War*. New Haven, Human Relations Area Files Press.

Ottoway, B. (1973) The earliest copper ornaments in northern Europe. *Proceedings of the Prehistoric Society* 39: 294–331.

Ottoway, B. and Strahm, C. (1975) Swiss neolithic copper beads: currency, ornament or prestige items? *World Archaeology* 6 (3): 307–21.

Paco, A. do (1954) Sementes prehistóricas do castro di Vila Nova de Saô Pedro. *Accademia Portuguesa da Historia, Anais* 5: 281–359.

Palmer, L. R. (1963) *The Interpretation of Mycenaean Greek Texts*. Oxford, University Press.

Palmer, S. (1976) The mesolithic habitation site at Culver Well, Portland, Dorset: interim note. *Proceedings of the Prehistoric Society* 42: 324–7.

Pals, J. P. and Voorrips, A. (1977–9) Seeds, fruit and charcoal. *Annali del Museo di Gavardo* 13: 31–40.

Paludan-Müller, C. (1978) High Atlantic food gathering in northwestern Zealand. Ecological conditions and spatial representation. In K. Kristiansen and C. Paludan-Müller (*eds.*) *New Directions in Scandinavian Archaeology*: 120–57. Copenhagen, National Museum of Denmark.

Parrington, M. (1978) *The Excavation of an Iron Age Settlement, Bronze Age Ring-ditches and Roman Features at Ashville Trading Estate, Abingdon (Oxfordshire) 1974–1976*. London, Council for British Archaeology Research Report 28.

Pasquinucci, M. (1979) La transumanza nell'Italia Romana. In E. Gabba and M. Pasquinucci, *Strutture Agrarie e Allevamento Transumante nell'Italia Romana*: 79–182. Pisa, Giardini.

Patterson, T. C. (1971) The emergence of food production in central Peru. In S. Struever (*ed.*) *Prehistoric Agriculture*: 181–207. New York, American Museum of Natural History.

Păunescu, Al. (1963) Perežitki Tardennazko kulturi v drevnei neolite v Ciumeşti (Beria). *Dacia* 7: 467–75.

Pavuk, J. (1972) Neolithisches Gräberfeld in Nitra. *Slovenská Archeológia* 20 (1): 5–105.

Payne, S. (1972a) Partial recovery and sample bias: the results of some sieving experiments. In E. S. Higgs (*ed.*) *Papers in Economic Prehistory*: 49–64. Cambridge, University Press.

Payne, S. (1972b) On the interpretation of bone samples from archaeological sites. In E. S. Higgs (*ed.*) *Papers in Economic Prehistory*: 65–91. Cambridge, University Press.

Payne, S. (1973) Kill-off patterns in sheep and goats: the mandibles from Aşvan Kale. *Journal of Anatolian Studies* 23: 281–303.

Payne, S. (1975) Faunal change at Franchthi cave from 20,000 b.c. to 3000 b.c. In A. T. Clason (*ed.*) *Archaeozoological Studies*: 120–31. Amsterdam, North Holland Publishing Co.

Peet, T. E. (1909) *The Stone and Bronze Ages in Italy*. Oxford, University Press.

Pellicer, M. (1963) Estratigrafía prehistórica de la Cueva de Nerja. *Excavaciones Arqueológicas en España* 16.

Pennington, W. (1969) *The History of British Vegetation*. London, Unibooks.

Pequart, M. L. N., Pequart, S. J., Boule, M. and Vallois, H. V. (1937) Téviec – station-nécropole mésolithique du Morhiban. *Archives de l'Institut de Paléontologie Humaine, Mémoires* 18.

Percival, J. (1921) *The Wheat Plant*. London.

Percival, J. (1936) *Agricultural Botany: Theoretical and Practical*. London, Duckworth, eighth edition.

Perini, R. (1971) I depositi preistorici di Romagnano-Loc (Trento). *Preistoria Alpina* 7: 7–106.

Perini, R. (1975) La palafitta di Fiavè-Carera. *Preistoria Alpina* 11: 25–64.

Perini, R. (1983) Der frühbronzezeitliche Pflug von Lavagnone. *Archäologisches Korrespondenzblatt* 13 (2): 187–95.

Peroni, R. (1971) *L'Età del Bronzo nella Penisola Italiana 1. L'Antica Età del Bronzo*. Florence, Olschki.

Pešić, B. R. (*ed.*) (1967) *Soils of the Velika Morava and Mlava Basin*. Beograd, Nolit Publishing House.

Pharr, C. (1952) *The Theodosian Code*. Princeton, University Press.

Phillips, P. (1975) *Early Farmers of West Mediterranean Europe*. London, Hutchinson University Library.

Phillips, P. (1980) *The Prehistory of Europe*. London, Allen Lane.

Phillips, P. (1982) *The Middle Neolithic in Southern France: Chasseen Farming and Culture Process*. Oxford, British Archaeological Reports, International Series 147.

Phippen, W. L. (1975) Vegetal remains (at Tufariello). *Journal of Field Archaeology* 2: 79–80.

Pierpoint, S. (1980) *Social Patterns in Yorkshire Prehistory, 3500–750 B.C.* Oxford, British Archaeological Reports, British Series 74.

Pierpoint, S. (1981) Land, settlement and society in the Yorkshire Bronze Age. In G. Barker (*ed.*) *Prehistoric Communities in Northern England: Essays in Social and Economic Reconstruction*: 41–56. Sheffield, Sheffield University, Department of Prehistory and Archaeology.

Piggott, S. (1958) Native economies and the Roman occupation of north Britain. In I. A. Richmond (*ed.*) *Roman and Native in North Britain*: 1–27. Edinburgh, Nelson.

Piggott, S. (1965) *Ancient Europe*. Edinburgh, University Press.

Pilcher, J. R. and Smith, A. G. (1979) Palaeoecological investigations at Ballynagilly, a neolithic and bronze age settlement in county Tyrone, Northern Ireland. *Philosophical Transactions of the Royal Society* 286: 345–69.

Piningre, J. F. and Vuaillat, D. (1976) L'abri épipaléolithique-néolithique et protohistorique de la Roche aux Gours, Longeville (Doubs). *Revue Archéologique de l'Est et du Centre-Est* 27: 43–80.

Pira, A. (1926) On bone deposits in the cave of 'Stora Förvar' on the isle of Stora Karlsö, Sweden. *Acta Zoologica* 7: 123–217.

Pittioni, R. (1954) *Urgeschichte des Österreichischen Raumes*. Wien, Denticke.

Pitts, M. (1979) Hides and antlers: a new look at the gatherer-hunter site at Star Carr, North Yorkshire, England. *World Archaeology* 11: 32–42.

Planchais, N. (1970) Tardiglaciaire et postglaciaire à Mur-de-Sologne (Loir-et-Cher). *Pollen et Spores* 12 (3): 381–428.

Planchais, N. (1976) La végétation pendant le Post-Glaciaire: aspects de la végétation holocène dans les plaines françaises. In J. Guilaine (*ed.*) *Préhistoire Française 2. Civilisations Néolithiques et Protohistoriques*: 35–43. Paris, CNRS.

Planchais, N., Renault-Miskovsky, J. and Vernet, J.-L. (1977) Les facteurs d'évolution de la végétation dans la sud de la France (côte à moyenne montagne) depuis la tardiglaciaire d'après l'analyse pollinique et les charbons de bois. In H. Laville and J. Renault-Miskovsky (*eds.*) *Écologie de l'Homme Fossile*: 373–5. Paris, Association Française pour l'Étude de Quaternaire.

Planson, E. (1979) La camp-refuge néolithique de Marcilly-sur-Tille. *Revue Archéologique de l'Est et du Centre-Est* 30: 47–56.

Platt, M. I. (1934) Report on the animal bones. pp. 348–50 in J. G. Callander and W. G. Grant, A long stalled chambered cairn or mausoleum (Ronsay type) near Midhowe, Ronsay, Orkney. *Proceedings of the Society of Antiquaries of Scotland* 68: 320–50.

Platt, M. I. (1934–5) Report on the animal bones, pp. 341–3 in J. G. Callander and W. G. Grant, A long stalled cairn, the Knowe of Yarso, in Ronsay, Orkney. *Proceedings of the Society of Antiquaries of Scotland* 69: 325–51.

Platt, M. I. (1935–6) Report on the animal bones found in the chambered cairn, Knowe of Ramsay, Ronsay, Orkney. pp. 415–19 in J. G. Callander and W. G. Grant, A stalled chambered cairn, the Knowe of Ramsay, at Hullion, Ronsay, Orkney. *Proceedings of the Society of Antiquaries of Scotland* 70: 407–19.

Platt, M. I. (1936–7a) Report on the animal bones. pp. 307–8 in J. G. Callander and W. G. Grant, A long stalled cairn at Blackhammer, Ronsay, Orkney. *Proceedings of the Society of Antiquaries of Scotland* 71: 297–308.

Platt, M. I. (1936–7b) Report on the animal bones. pp. 152–4 in J. G. Callander and W. G. Grant, A neolithic double-chambered cairn of the stalled type and late structures on the Calf of Eday, Orkney. *Proceedings of the Society of Antiquaries of Scotland* 71: 115–54.

Platt, M. I. (1936–7c) Report on the animal bones. pp. 317–21 in J. G. Callander and W. G. Grant, Hower, a prehistoric structure on Papa Westray, Orkney. *Proceedings of the Society of Antiquaries of Scotland* 71: 309–21.

Plog, F. (1975) Demographic studies in southwestern prehistory. In A. G. Swedland (*ed.*) *Population Studies in Archaeological and Biological Anthropology*: 94–103. Washington, Society for American Archaeology, Memoir 3.

Pop, E., Boşcaiu, N. and Lupşa, V. (1970) Analisa sporopolinaca a sedimentelor de la Cuina Turcului-Dubovica. *Ştudii Şi Cercetări de Istorie Veche* 21 (1): 31–4.

Poplin, F. (1975) La faune danubienne d'Armeau (Yonne, France): ses données sur l'activité humaine. In A. T. Clason (*ed.*) *Archaeozoological Studies*: 179–92. Amsterdam, North Holland Publishing Co.

Popović, C. D. (1971) Les migrations des troupeaux en Bosnie et Herzégovine. *Wissenschaftliche mitteilungen des Bosnisch-Herzegowinischen Landesmuseums* 1 (B): 99–116.

Potter, T. W. (*ed.*) (1976) *A Faliscan Town in South Etruria – Excavations at Narce 1966–71.* London, British School at Rome.

Potter, T. W. (1979) *The Changing Landscape of South Etruria.* London, Paul Elek.

Poulain, T. (1966) Le gisement néolithique d'Escanin II, Bouches-du-Rhône. Étude de la faune. *Cahiers Rhodaniens* 13: 100–9.

Poulain, T. (1970) Étude de la faune. In H. Carré, Les dernières découvertes du Bronze Final à Vinneuf (Yonne). *Bulletin de la Société Préhistorique Française* 67: 370–1.

Poulain, T. (1973) Étude de la faune. In J. Arnal, Le Lébous à St. Mathieu-De-Treviers (Hérault). *Gallia Préhistoire* 16 (1): 195–8.

Poulain, T. (1974) Étude de la faune. In J.-L. Rondil, F. Brazile and M. Sonlier, L'habitat campaniforme de St. Côme-et-Marnéjols (Gard). *Gallia Préhistoire* 17 (1): 215–17.

Poulain, T. (1975) Fosses nèolithiques d'Entzheim: étude de la faune. *Revue Archéologique de l'Est et du Centre-Est* 26: 69–94.

Poulain, T. (1976a) La faune sauvage et domestique en France du néolithique à la fin de l'Age du Fer. In J. Guilaine (*ed.*) *La Préhistoire Française 2. Civilisations Néolithiques et Protohistoriques*: 104–15. Paris, CNRS.

Poulain, T. (1976b) Le dolmen Angevin de Pierre-Folle à Thiré (Vendée). Étude de la faune. *Gallia Préhistoire* 19: 61–7.

Poulain, T. (1977) Le Bois des Refuges à Misy-sur-Yonne: étude des vestiges osseux. *Bulletin de la Société Préhistorique Française* 74: 463–71.

Poulain, T. (1978) Site néolithique de Reichstett: étude de la faune. *Revue Archéologique de l'Est et du Centre-Est* 29: 45–56.

Pounds, N. J. G. (1974) *An Economic History of Medieval Europe*. London, Longman.

Preuschen, E. (1973) Estrazione mineraria dell'Età del Bronzo nel Trentino. *Preistoria Alpina* 9: 113–50.

Price, T. D. (1975) Mesolithic settlement in the Netherlands. University of Michigan, unpublished Ph.D. thesis.

Price, T. D. (1978) Mesolithic settlement systems in the Netherlands. In P. Mellars (*ed.*) *The Early Postglacial Settlement of Northern Europe*: 81–113. London, Duckworth.

Primas, M. (1976) Frühe Metallverarbeitung und Verwendung im alpinen und zirkumalpinen Bereich. *Colloque XXIII Union Internationale des Sciences Préhistoriques et Protohistoriques, Nice*: 81–117.

Prinke, A. (1973) A note on the Mesolithic of Eastern Great Poland and Kujavia. In S. K. Kosłowski (*ed.*) *The Mesolithic in Europe*: 477–83. Warsaw, University Press.

Prošek, F. and Ložek, V. (1952) Mesoliticke sidlištĕ v Zatyni u Dubé. *Anthropozoikum* 2: 93–172.

Protopopescu-Pake, E., Mateescu, C. and Grosso, A. (1970) Formation des couches de civilisation de la station de Vădastra en rapport avec le sol, la faune palaeocologique et le climat. *Quartär* 20: 135–62.

Provan, D. M. J. (1973) The soils of an iron age farm site – Bjellandsøynae, southwestern Norway. *Norwegian Archaeological Review* 6: 53–64.

Prummel, W. (1979) Environment and stock-raising in Dutch settlements of the Bronze Age and the Middle Ages. *Palaeohistoria* 21: 91–107.

Pryor, F. (1974) *Excavations at Fengate, Peterborough. The First Report*. Toronto, Royal Ontario Museum, Archaeological Monographs 3.

Pryor, F. (1976) Fen-edge land management in the Bronze Age: an interim report on excavations at Fengate, Peterborough, 1971–5. In C. Burgess and R. Miket (*eds.*) *Settlement and Economy in the Third and Second Millennia b.c.*: 29–49. Oxford, British Archaeological Reports, British Series 33.

Pryor, F. (1978) *Excavations at Fengate, Peterborough, England: the Second Report*. Toronto, Royal Ontario Museum, Archaeological Monographs 5.

Pryor, F. (1980) *Excavation at Fengate, Peterborough, England: the Third Report*. Toronto, Royal Ontario Museum, Archaeological Monographs 6.

Pyrgala, J. (1970) Settlement microregion between the Vistula and the lower Wkra in the La Tène and Roman Period. *Archaeologia Polana* 12: 335–49.

Quitta, H. (1970) Zur Lage und Verbreitung der bandkeramischen Siedlungen im Leipziger Land. *Zeitschrift für Archäologie* 4 (2): 155–76.

Rackham, O. (1972) Charcoal and plaster impressions. In P. Warren, *Myrtos, an Early Bronze Age Settlement on Crete*: 299–304. London, British School of Archaeology at Athens.

Radley, J., Tallis, J. H. and Switsur, V. R. (1974) The excavation of three 'narrow blade' mesolithic sites in the southern Pennines, England. *Proceedings of the Prehistoric Society* 40: 1–19.

Radulescu, C. and Samson, P. (1962) Sur un centre de domestication du mouton dans le mésolithique de la grotte 'La Adam' en Dobrogea. *Zeitschrift für Tierzuchtung und Zuchtungsbiologie* 76: 282–320.

Raistrick, A. (1939) Iron age settlements in West Yorkshire. *Yorkshire Archaeological Journal* 34: 115–50.

Rajewski, Z. (1970) *Biskupin: Osiedle Obronne Wspúlnot Pierwotnych Sprzed 2500 Lat*. Warsaw, Arkady.

Ralph, N. G. A. S. A. (1982) An assessment of ancient land use in abandoned settlement and fields: a study of prehistoric and medieval land use and its influence on soil properties on Holne Moor, Dartmoor, England. Sheffield University, unpublished Ph.D. thesis.

Randsborg, K. (1974) Social stratification in early bronze age Denmark: a study in the regulation of cultural systems. *Praehistorische Zeitschrift* 49: 38–61.

Randsborg, K. (1975) Social dimensions of early neolithic Denmark. *Proceedings of the Prehistoric Society* 41: 105–18.

Randsborg, K. (1982) Ranks, rights and resources – an archaeological perspective from Denmark. In C. Renfrew and S. Shennan (*eds.*) *Ranking, Resource and Exchange*: 132–9. Cambridge, University Press.

Randsborg, K. (in press) Subsistence and settlement in the North Sea–Baltic area in the first millennium A.D. In G. Barker and C. Gamble (*eds.*) *Beyond Domestication: Subsistence Archaeology and Social Complexity in Ancient Europe*. New York, Academic Press.

Rankine, W. F. (1961) The mesolithic age in Dorset. *Proceedings of the Dorset Natural History and Archaeological Society* 83: 91–9.

Reaney, J. (1968) Beaker burials in north Derbyshire. *Derbyshire Archaeological Journal* 32: 147–51.

Rees, J. (1983) Reaping the profits of greed. *The Guardian* 23 June 1983: 13.

Rees, S. (1981) Agricultural tools: function and use. In R. Mercer (*ed.*) *Farming Practice in British Prehistory*: 66–84. Edinburgh, University Press.

Regteren Altena, J. F. van, Bakker, J. A., Clason, A. T., Glasbergen, W., Groenman-van Waateringe, W. and Pons, L. J. (1962) The Vlaardingen culture. *Helinium* 2: 3–35, 97–103, 215–43.

Regteren Altena, J. F. van, Bakker, J. A., Clason, A. T., Glasbergen, W., Groenman-van Waateringe, W. and Pons, L. J. (1983) The Vlaardingen culture. *Helinium* 3: 39–54, 97–120.

Reinerth, H. (1936) *Das Federseemoor als Siedlungsgebiet*. Leipzig, Führer Zur Urgeschichte (Neuauflage) 9.

Rellini, U (1931) Le stazioni enee delle Marche di fase seriore e la civiltà italiana. *Monumenti Antichi* 34: 129–280.

Renault-Miskovsky, J. (1976) Les flores quaternaires dans le bassin occidental de la Méditerranée. In *Chronologie et Synchronisme dans la Préhistoire Circum-Méditerranéenne*. Nice, Union Internationale des Sciences Préhistoriques et Protohistoriques, 9. Congrés, Colloque 2.

Renfrew, C. (1967) Colonialism and megalithismus. *Antiquity* 41: 276–88.

Renfrew, C. (1969) The autonomy of the southeast European Copper Age. *Proceedings of the Prehistoric Society* 35: 12–47.

Renfrew, C. (1972) *The Emergence of Civilisation*. London, Methuen.

Renfrew, C. (1973a) *Before Civilisation*. London, Jonathan Cape.

Renfrew, C. (1973b) Monuments, mobilization and social organization in neolithic Wessex. In C. Renfrew (*ed.*) *The Explanation of Culture Change – Models in Prehistory*: 539–58. London, Duckworth.

Renfrew, C. (1976) Megaliths, territories and populations. In S. J. de Laet (*ed.*) *Acculturation and Continuity in Atlantic Europe*: 198–220. Bruges, Dissertationes Archaeologicae Gandenses 21.

Renfrew, C. (1978) The Varna cemetery. *Antiquity* 52: 199–206.

Renfrew, C. (1979) *Investigations in Orkney*. London, Report of the Research Committee of the Society of Antiquaries 38.

Renfrew, C., Dixon, J. E. and Cann, J. R. (1968) Further analysis of Near Eastern obsidians. *Proceedings of the Prehistoric Society* 34: 319–31.

Renfrew, C. and Wagstaff, M. (*eds.*) (1982) *An Island Polity: The Archaeology of Exploitation on Melos*. Cambridge, University Press.

Renfrew, J. M. (1966) A report of recent finds of carbonised cereal grains and seeds from prehistoric Thessaly. *Thessalika* 5: 21–36.

Renfrew, J. M. (1969) The archaeological evidence for the domestication of plants: methods and problems. In P. Ucko and G. Dimbleby (*eds.*) *The Domestication and Exploitation of Plants and Animals*: 149–72. London, Duckworth.

Renfrew, J. M. (1972) The plant remains. In P. Warren, *Myrtos: An Early Bronze Age Settlement on Crete*: 315–17. London, British School of Archaeology at Athens.

Renfrew, J. M. (1973) *Palaeoethnobotany*. London, Methuen.

Reverdin, L. (1960) Étude de la faune, p. 67 in M. R. Sauter and A. Gallay, Les materiaux néolithiques et protohistoriques de la station de Génissiat (Ain, France). *Geneva* 8: 63–111.

Reynolds, P. (1974) Experimental iron age storage pits. *Proceedings of the Prehistoric Society* 40: 118–31.

Reynolds, P. (1979) *Iron Age Farm: The Butser Experiment*. London, British Museum Publications.

Reynolds, P. (1981) Deadstock and livestock. In R. Mercer (*ed.*) *Farming Practice in British Prehistory*: 97–122. Edinburgh, University Press.

Riedel, A. (1976a) La fauna del villaggio eneolitico delle Colombare di Negrar (Verona). *Bullettino del Museo Civico di Storia Naturale, Verona* 3: 205–38.

Riedel, A. (1976b) La fauna del villaggio preistorico di Barche di Solferino. *Atti del Museo Civico di Storia Naturale, Trieste* 29 (4): 215–318.

Riedel, A. (1976c) La fauna del villaggio preistorico di Ledro. Archeozoologia e paleoeconomia. *Studi Trentini di Scienze Naturale* 53: 3–120.

Riedel, A. (1977) The fauna of four prehistoric settlements in northern Italy. *Atti del Museo Civico di Storia Naturale, Trieste* 30 (1): 65–122.

Ritchie, A. (1970) Palisaded sites in north Britain: their context and affinities. *Scottish Archaeological Forum* 2: 48–67.

Ritchie, A. (1975) The Knap of Howar. *Discovery and Exploration in Scotland*: 35–7.

Roberts, N. (1979) The location and environment of Knossos. *Annual of the British School at Athens* 74: 231–40.

Roche, J. (1965) Observations sur la stratigraphie et la chronologie des amas coquilliers de Muge (Portugal). *Bulletin de la Société Préhistorique Française* 62: 130–8.

Rodden, R. J. (1962) Excavations at the early neolithic site at Nea Nikomedeia, Greek Macedonia. *Proceedings of the Prehistoric Society* 28: 267–88.

Rodden, R. J. (1965) The early neolithic village in Greece. *Scientific American* 212 (4): 83–91.

Roever, J. P. de (1976) Excavations at the river dune sites S21–S22. *Helinium* 16: 209–21.

Rostholm, H. (1977) Neolithic disc wheels from Kideris and Bjerregårde, central Jutland. *Kuml*: 185–222.

Rothamsted Experimental Station (1970) *Details of the Classical and Long-term Experiments up to 1967*. Harpenden, Lawes Agricultural Trust.

Rowlands, M. J. (1973) Modes of exchange and the incentives for trade, with reference to later European prehistory. In C. Renfrew (*ed.*) *The Explanation of Culture Change – Models in Prehistory*: 589–600. London, Duckworth.

Rowlands, M. J. (1980) Kinship, alliance and exchange in the European Bronze Age. In J. C. Barrett and R. J. Bradley (*eds.*) *Settlement and Society in the British Later Bronze Age*: 15–55. Oxford, British Archaeological Reports, British Series 83.

Rowlett, R. M., Rowlett, E. S. J. and Boureux, M. (1969) A rectangular early La Tène Marnian house at Chassemy (Aisne). *World Archaeology* 1: 106–35.

Rowley-Conwy, P. (1978) Carbonised grain from Lindebjerg. *Kuml*: 167–71.

Rowley-Conwy, P. (1981a) Mesolithic Danish bacon: permanent and temporary sites in the

Danish mesolithic. In A. Sheridan and G. Bailey (*eds.*) *Economic Archaeology*: 51–5. Oxford, British Archaeological Reports, International Series 96.

Rowley-Conwy, P. (1981b) Slash and burn in the temperate European Neolithic. In R. Mercer (*ed.*) *Farming Practice in British Prehistory*: 85–96. Edinburgh, University Press.

Rowley-Conwy, P. (1982) The laziness of the short-distance hunter: final hunters and first farmers in Denmark. In K. Kristiansen (*ed.*) *New Directions in Scandinavian Archaeology* 3. Copenhagen, National Museum of Denmark.

Rozoy, J. G. (1973) The Franco-Belgian epipalaeolithic. In S. K. Kozłowski (*ed.*) *The Mesolithic in Europe*: 503–30. Warsaw, University Press.

Rüeger, J. (1942) Die Tierreste aus der spät(mittel)-bronzezeitlichen Siedlung Crestaulta (Kanton Graubünden) nach den Grabungen 1935–38. *Revue Suisse de Zoologie* 49 (18): 251–67.

Russell, E. J. and Voelcker, J. A. (1936) *Fifty Years of Field Experiments at the Woburn Experimental Station*. London, H.M.S.O.

Russell, E. W. (1961) *Soil Conditions and Plant Growth*. London, Longman, ninth edition.

Rütimeyer, L. (1862) Die Fauna der Pfahlbauten der Schweiz. *Neue Denkschriften der Allgemeinen Schweizerischen Gesellschaft für die Gesammten Naturwissenschaften* 19: 1–248.

Ruttkay, E., Wessely, G. and Wolff, P. (1976) Eine Kulturschicht der ältesten Linearbandkeramik in Prellen Kirchen, p.B. Bruck, Niederösterreich. *Annalen des Naturhistorischen Museums in Wien* 80: 843–61.

Ryder, M. J. (1969) Changes in the fleece following domestication. In P. J. Ucko and G. W. Dimbleby (*eds.*) *The Domestication and Exploitation of Plants and Animals*: 495–521. London, Duckworth.

Ryder, M. J. (1981) Skins and fleeces. In R. Mercer (*ed.*) *Farming Practice in British Prehistory*: 182–209. Edinburgh, University Press.

Säflund, G. (1939) *La Terremare delle Provincie di Modena, Reggio Emilia, Parma e Piacenza*. Lund, Acta Instituti Romani Regni Sueciae 7.

Sahlins, M. D. (1963) Poor man, rich man, big-man, chief: political types in Melanesia and Polynesia. *Comparative Studies in Society and History* 5: 285–303.

Sakellaridis, M. (1979) *The Mesolithic and Neolithic of the Swiss Area*. Oxford, British Archaeological Reports, International Series 67.

Sala, B. (1977) Il popolamento floristico e faunistico dei dintorni di Trento nell'Olocenico antico. *Preistoria Alpina* 13: 7–10.

Sandars, N. K. (1978) *The Sea Peoples*. London, Thames and Hudson.

Saussol, A. (1970) *L'Élevage Ovin en Languedoc Central (Hérault, Gard, Lozère)*. Montpellier, Faculté des Lettres.

Sauter, M.-R. (1976) *Switzerland*. London, Thames and Hudson.

Savory, H. N. (1968) *Spain and Portugal*. London, Thames and Hudson.

Savory, H. N. (1980) The early Iron Age in Wales. In J. A. Taylor (*ed.*) *Culture and Environment in Prehistoric Wales*: 287–320. Oxford, British Archaeological Reports, British Series 76.

Scarre, C. (1980) Neolithic camps around the Marais Poitevin. *Current Archaeology* 72: 23–5.

Scarre, C. (1982) Settlement patterns and landscape change: the late Neolithic and the Bronze Age of the Marais Poitevin area of western France. *Proceedings of the Prehistoric Society* 48: 53–73.

Scarre, C. (*ed.*) (1983a) *Ancient France. Neolithic Societies and Their Landscapes 6000–2000 bc*. Edinburgh, University Press.

Scarre, C. (1983b) The Neolithic of west-central France. In C. Scarre (*ed.*) *Ancient France. Neolithic Societies and Their Landscapes 6000–2000 bc*: 223–70. Edinburgh, University Press.

Schietzel, K. (1965) *Müddersheim, eine Ansiedlung der jungeren Bandkeramik in Rheinland*. Köln, Böhlau.

Schiffer, M. B. (1972) Archaeological context and systemic context. *American Antiquity* 37 (2): 156–65.

Schindler, C. (1971) Geologie von Zürich und ihre Beziehung zu Seespiegelschwankungen. *Vierteljahrsschrift der Naturforschenden Gesellschaft in Zürich* 116: 284–315.

Schmid, P. (1978) New archaeological results of settlement structures (Roman Iron Age) in the northwest-German coastal area. In B. Cunliffe and T. Rowley (*eds.*) *Lowland Iron Age Communities in Europe*: 123–45. Oxford, British Archaeological Reports, International Series 48.

Schmidt, R. R. (1945) *Die Burg Vučedol.* Zagreb, Der Kroatische Archäologische Staatmuseum in Zagreb.

Schmitt, G. (1974) Le transition entre le Néolithique moyen et le Néolithique final en Basse-Alsace. *Revue Archéologique de l'Est et du Centre-Est* 25: 277–364.

Schüle, W. (1967) Feldbewässerung in Alt-Europa. *Madrider Mitteilungen* 8: 79–99.

Schwab, H. and Müller, R. (1973) *Die Vergangenheit des Seelandes in Neuen Licht. Über die Wasserstände der Juraseen.* Freiburg.

Schwabedissen, H. (1966) Ein horizontierter 'Breitkeil' aus Satrup und die mannigfachen Kulturverbindungen des beginnenden Neolithikums im Nordern und Nordwestern. *Palaeohistoria* 12: 409–68.

Schwidetsky, I. von (1972) Vorgleichendstatistische Untersuchungen zur Anthropologie der Eisenzeit (Letztes Jahrtausend v.d.z.). *Homo* 23 (3): 245–72.

Scott, J. G. (1970) A note on neolithic settlement in the Clyde region of Scotland. *Proceedings of the Prehistoric Society* 36: 116–24.

Seeberg, P. and Kristensen, H. H. (1964) Many criss-cross furrows. *Kuml*: 7–14.

Sellstedt, H. (1966) Djurbensmaterial från järnåldersboplatserna vid Ormöga och Sörby-tall på Öland. *Forvännen* 61: 1–13.

Semenov, S. A. (1964) *Prehistoric Technology.* London, Adams and Dart.

Seymour, J. and Seymour, S. (1973) *Self-Sufficiency.* London, Faber and Faber.

Shackleton, M. R. (1964) *Europe – A Regional Geography.* London, Longman, seventh edition.

Shackleton, N. (1970) Stable isotope study of the palaeoenvironment of the neolithic site of Nea Nikomedeia, Greece. *Nature Land* 227: 943–4.

Shennan, S. (1975) The social organisation at Branč. *Antiquity* 59: 279–88.

Shennan, S. J. (1976) Bell beakers and their context in central Europe. In J. N. Lanting and J. D. van der Waals (*eds.*) *Glockenbecker Symposium, Oberried, 1974*: 231–9.

Shennan, S. J. (1981) Settlement history in East Hampshire. In S. J. Shennan and R. T. Schadla Hall (*eds.*) *The Archaeology of Hampshire*: 106–21. Southampton, Hampshire Field Club and Archaeological Society, Monograph 1.

Shepherd, I. A. G. (1976) Preliminary results from the Beaker settlement at Rosinish, Benbecula. In C. Burgess and R. Miket (*eds.*) *Settlement and Economy in the Third and Second Millennia b.c.*: 209–19. Oxford, British Archaeological Reports, British Series 33.

Sherratt, A. G. (1972) Socio-economic and demographic models for the Neolithic and Bronze Ages in Europe. In D. L. Clarke (*eds.*) *Models in Archaeology*: 477–542. London, Methuen.

Sherratt, A. G. (1976) Resources, technology and trade: an essay in early European metallurgy. In G. de G. Sieveking, I. H. Longworth and K. A. Wilson (*eds.*) *Problems in Social and Economic Archaeology*: 558–81. London, Duckworth.

Sherratt, A. G. (1980) Water, soil and seasonality in early cereal cultivation. *World Archaeology* 11 (3): 313–30.

Sherratt, A. G. (1981) Plough and pastoralism: aspects of the secondary products revolution. In I. Hodder, G. Isaac and N. Hammond (*eds.*) *Pattern of the Past: Studies in Memory of David Clarke*: 261–305. Cambridge, University Press.

Sherratt, A. G. (1982–3) Neolithic and copper age settlement on the Great Hungarian plain. *Oxford Journal of Archaeology* 1 (1): 287–316.

Sherratt, A. G. (1983) The secondary exploitation of animals in the Old World. *World Archaeology* 15 (1): 20–104.

Sielmann, B. (1971) Zur Interpretationsmöglichkeit ökologischer Befunde im Neolithikum Mitteleuropas. *Germania* 49: 231–8.

Sigaut, F. (1975) *L'Agriculture et le Feu*. Paris and The Hague, Mouton.

Silver, I. A. (1969) The ageing of domestic animals. In D. Brothwell and E. S. Higgs(*eds.*) *Science in Archaeology*: 283–302. London, Thames and Hudson, second edition.

Simmons, I. G. (1969a) Environment and early man on Dartmoor, Devon, England. *Proceedings of the Prehistoric Society* 35: 203–19.

Simmons, I. G. (1969b) Evidence for vegetation changes associated with mesolithic man in Britain. In P. J. Ucko and G. W. Dimbleby (*eds.*) *The Domestication and Exploitation of Plants and Animals*: 111–19. London, Duckworth.

Simmons, I. G. (1975) The ecological setting of mesolithic man in the highland zone. In J. G. Evans, S. Limbrey and H. Cleere (*eds.*) *The Effect of Man on the Landscape: the Highland Zone*: 57–63. London, Council for British Archaeology, Research Report 11.

Simmons, I. G. and Dimbleby, G. W. (1974) The possible role of ivy (*Hedera helix* L.) in the mesolithic economy of western Europe. *Journal of Archaeological Science* 1: 291–6.

Simmons, I. G., Dimbleby, G. W. and Grigson, C. (1981) The Mesolithic. In I. G. Simmons and M. J. Tooley (*eds.*) *The Environment in British Prehistory*: 82–124. London, Duckworth.

Simmons, I. G. and Tooley, M. J. (*eds.*) (1981) *The Environment in British Prehistory*. London, Duckworth.

Simonsen, P. (1973) Jaeger og nomade i Finnmark. *Tromsø Museums Skrifter* 14: 174–83.

Simpson, D. D. A. (1976) The later neolithic and Beaker settlement at Northton, Isle of Harris. In C. Burgess and R. Miket (*eds.*) *Settlement and Economy in the Third and Second Millennia b.e.*: 221–31. Oxford, British Archaeological Reports, British Series 33.

Sjöbeck, M. (1958) *Landskapets Odlingsarv*. Stockholm, Natur i Västmanland.

Slicher Van Bath, B. H. (1963) *The Agrarian History of Western Europe AD 500–1850*. London, Arnold.

Sloan, R. E. and Duncan, M. A. (1978) Zooarchaeology of Nichoria. In G. Rapp and S. E. Schenbrenner (*eds.*) *Excavations at Nichoria in Southwest Greece 1*: 60–77. Minneapolis, University of Minnesota Press.

Small, A. (1975) The hillforts of the Inverness area. *Inverness Field Club Centenary Volume*: 78–89.

Smith, A. G. (1970) The influence of mesolithic and neolithic man on British vegetation: a discussion. In D. Walker and R. G. West (*eds.*) *Studies in the Vegetational History of the British Isles*: 81–96. Cambridge, University Press.

Smith, A. G. (1975) Neolithic and bronze age landscape changes in northern Ireland. In J. G. Evans, S. Limbrey and H. Cleere (*eds.*) *The Effect of Man on the Landscape: the Highland Zone*: 64–74. London, Council for British Archaeology, Research Report 11.

Smith, A. G., Grigson, C., Hillman, G. and Tooley, M. J. (1981) The Neolithic. In I. G. Simmons and M. J. Tooley (*eds.*) *The Environment in British Prehistory*: 125–209. London, Duckworth.

Smith, C. (1977) The valleys of the Tame and middle Trent – their populations and ecology during the late first millennium b.c. In J. Collis (*ed.*) *The Iron Age in Britain – A Review*: 51–61. Sheffield, Sheffield University, Department of Prehistory and Archaeology.

Smith, C. (1978) The landscape and natural history of iron age settlement on the Trent gravels. In B. Cunliffe and T. Rowley (*eds.*) *Lowland Iron Age Communities in Europe*: 91–101. Oxford, British Archaeological Reports, International Series 48.

Smith, I. F. (1965) *Windmill Hill and Avebury: Excavations by Alexander Keiller 1925–1930*. Oxford, University Press.

Smith, I. F. (1966) Windmill Hill and its implications. *Palaeohistoria* 12: 469–82.

Smith, K., Coppen, J., Wainwright, G. J. and Beckett, S. (1981) The Shaugh Moor project: third report – settlement and environmental investigations. *Proceedings of the Prehistoric Society* 47: 205–73.

Soergel, E. (1969) Stratigraphische Untersuchungen am Tierknochen – Material von Thayngen-Weier. *Archäologie und Biologie, Deutsche Forschungsgemeinschaft* 15: 157–71.

Soudsky, B. (1962) The neolithic site of Bylany. *Antiquity* 36: 190–200.

Soudsky, B. (1975) *Les Fouilles Protohistoriques dans la Vallée de l'Aisne. Rapport d'Activité 3, 1975*. Paris, Centre de Recherche Protohistorique de l'Université de Paris 1.

Soudsky, B. and Pavlu, I. (1972) The linear pottery culture settlement patterns of central Europe. In P. J. Ucko, R. Tringham and G. W. Dimbleby (*eds.*) *Man, Settlement and Urbanism*: 317–28. London, Duckworth.

Speedy, A. W. (1980) *Sheep Production: Science into Practice*. London, Longman.

Spratt, D. A. (1981) Prehistoric boundaries on the North Yorkshire moors. In G. Barker (*ed.*) *Prehistoric Communities in Northern England: Essays in Social and Economic Reconstruction*: 87–104. Sheffield, Sheffield University, Department of Prehistory and Archaeology.

Spratt, D. A. and Simmons, I. G. (1976) Prehistoric activity and environment on the North York Moors. *Journal of Archaeological Science* 3: 193–210.

Srejović, D. (1972) *Lepenski Vir*. London, Thames and Hudson.

Srejović, D. (1974) The Odmut cave – a new facet of the mesolithic culture of the Balkan peninsula. *Archaeologica Jugoslavica* 15: 3–6.

Stamp, L. D. (1965) *Land Use Statistics of the Countries of Europe*. World Land Use Survey Occasional Paper 3.

Stamp, L. D. and Beaver, S. H. (1963) *The British Isles. A Geographic and Economic Survey*. London, Longman.

Stampfli, H. R. (1965) Tierreste der Grabung Müddesheim, Kr. Düren. In K. Schietzel, *Müddersheim, eine Ansiedlung der Jungeren Bandkeramik in Rheinland*: 115–23. Köln, Böhlau.

Stampfli, H. R. (1976) Die Tierknochen von Egolzwil 5. Osteoarchäologische Untersuchungen. In R. Wyss, Das jungsteinzeitliche Jäger-Bauerndorf vom Egolzwil 5 im Wauwilermoos. *Archaeologische Forschungen*: 125–40.

Stampfli, H. R. (1979) Die Tierreste des mesolithischen Siedlungsplatzes von Schötz 7 im Wauwilermoos (Kanton Luzern). In R. Wyss, Das mittelsteinzeitliche Hirschjägerlager von Schötz 7 im Wauwilermoos. *Archaeologische Forschungen*: 97–111.

Stanford, S. C. (1974) *Croft Ambrey*. Herefordshire, Luston.

Stead, I. M. (1968) An iron age hillfort at Grimthorpe, Yorkshire, England. *Proceedings of the Prehistoric Society* 34: 148–90.

Steensberg, A. (1943) *Ancient Harvesting Implements*. Copenhagen, National Museets Skrifter: Archaeologisk-Historick Raekke 1.

Steensberg, A. (1955) Mit Braggender Flamme. *Kuml*: 63–130.

Steensberg, A. (1957) Some recent Danish experiments in neolithic agriculture. *Agricultural History Review* 5: 66–73.

Steensberg, A. (1973) A 6000 year old ploughing implement from Satrup moor. *Tools and Tillage* 2: 105–18.

Steensberg, A. (1976) The husbandry of food production. *Philosophical Transactions of the Royal Society of London* Ser. B, 275: 43–54.

Steensberg, A. (1980) *New Guinea Gardens. A Study of Husbandry with Parallels in Prehistoric Europe*. London and New York, Academic Press.

Stenberger, M. n.d. *Sweden*. London, Thames and Hudson.

Sterud, E. L. (1978) Prehistoric populations of the dinaric alps: an investigation of inter-regional interaction. In C. L. Redman, M. J. Berman, E. V. Curtin, W. T. Langhorne, N. M. Versaggi and J. C. Wanser (*eds.*) *Social Archaeology: Beyond Subsistence and Dating*: 381–408. London and New York, Academic press.

Stjernquist, B. (1969) *Beiträge zum Studium von Bronzezeitlichen Siedlungen*. Bonn, Habelt; Lund, Gleerups.

Stjernquist, B. (1978) Studies of structure, continuity and change in iron age settlements in

Sweden. In B. Cunliffe and T. Rowley (*eds.*) *Lowland Iron Age Communities in Europe*: 167–85. Oxford, British Archaeological Reports, International Series 48.

Sturdy, D. A. (1975) Some reindeer economies in prehistoric Europe. In E. S. Higgs (*ed.*) *Palaeoeconomy*: 55–95. Cambridge, University Press.

Sulimirski, T. (1960) Remarks concerning the distribution of some varieties of flint in Poland. *Swiatowit* 22: 281–307.

Sussman, R. W. (1972) Child transport, family size and increase in human population during the Neolithic. *Current Anthropology* 13: 258–67.

Tabaczyński, S. (1970) *Neolit Środkowo Europejski: Podstawy Gospodarcze*. Warsaw, Ossolineum.

Tauber, H. (1965) Differential pollen dispersion and the interpretation of pollen diagrams. *Danmarks Geologiske Undersøgelse* 2 (89): 7–69.

Tauber, H. (1981) ^{13}C evidence for dietary habits of prehistoric man in Denmark. *Nature* 292: 332–3.

Taylor, J. A. (1975) The role of climatic factors in environmental and cultural changes in prehistoric times. In J. G. Evans, S. Limbrey and H. Cleere (*eds.*) *The Effect of Man on the Landscape: the Highland Zone*: 6–19. London, Council for British Archaeology Research Report 11.

Tempir, Z. (1964) Beitrage zu ältesten Geschichte des Pflanzenbaus in Ungarn. *Acta Archaeologica* 16: 65–98.

Tempir, Z. (1971) Einige Ergebnisse der archäoagrobotanischen Untersuchungen des Anbaus von kulturpflanzen auf dem Gebiet der ČSSR. *Actes du VIII Congrès International des Sciences Préhistoriques et Protohistorique* 2: 1326–132. L'Académie Tchécoslovaque des Sciences.

Ters, M. (1976) Les lignes de rivage holocène, le long de la côte atlantique française. In J. Guilaine (*ed.*) *La Préhistoire Française 2. Civilisations Néolithiques et Protohistoriques*: 27–30. Paris, CNRS.

Teunissen, D. and Teunissen-van Oorschot, H. G. C. M. (1980) The history of the vegetation in southwest Connemara (Ireland). *Acta Botanica Neerlandica* 29 (4): 285–306.

Thevenot, J.-P. and Carré, H. (1976) Les civilisations néolithiques de la Bourgogne. In J. Guilaine (*ed.*) *La Préhistoire Française 2. Civilisations Néolithiques et Protohistoriques*: 402–14. Paris, CNRS.

Thirsk, J. (1967) Farming technique. In J. Thirsk (*ed.*) *The Agrarian History of England and Wales IV. 1500–1640*: 161–99. Cambridge, University Press.

Thrane, H. (1967a) Neolithic graves under a bronze age barrow at Gadbjerg in southeast Jutland. *Aarbøger for Nordisk Oldkyndighed og Historie*: 82–90.

Thrane, H. (1967b) Ein bronzezeitlicher Grabhügel bei Vesterlund, Jütland. *Kuml*: 7–35.

Thrane, H. (1980) Five grain vessels from Kirkebjerg at Voldtoften bronze age site, southwest Funen. *Aarbøger for Nordisk Oldkyndighed og Historie*: 73–84.

Tine, S. (1970) Notizario. *Revista di Scienze Preistoriche* 25: 427–8.

Tinsley, H. M. (1981) The Bronze Age. In I. G. Simmons and M. J. Tooley (*eds.*) *The Environment in British Prehistory*: 250–81. London, Duckworth.

Titow, J. Z. (1972) *Winchester Yields: A Study in Medieval Agricultural Productivity*. Cambridge, University Press.

Todorova, H. (1978) *The Eneolithic in Bulgaria*. Oxford, British Archaeological Reports, International Series 49.

Tooley, M. J. (1974) Sea level changes during the last 9000 years in northwest England. *Journal of Geography* 140: 18–42.

Tozzi, C. (1978) Un aspetto della corrente culturale della ceramica dipinta in Abruzzo: il villaggio di Catignano (Pescara). *Quaderni de la Ricerca Scientifica* 100: 95–111.

Triat, H. (1978) Contribution pollenanalytique à l'histoire tardi et post-glaciaire de la végétation de la basse vallée du Rhône. Marseilles, Université d'Aix-Marseille III, unpublished Docteur du Sciences thesis.

Tringham, R. (1968) A preliminary study of the early neolithic and latest mesolithic blade industry in southeast and central Europe. In J. Coles and D.D. A. Simpson (*eds.*) *Studies in Ancient Europe*: 45–70. Leicester, University Press.

Tringham, E. (1971) *Hunters, Fishers and Farmers of Eastern Europe 6000–3000 B.C.* London, Hutchinson University Library.

Tringham, R. (1980) The early agricultural site of Selevac, Yugoslavia. *Archaeology* 33 (2): 24–32.

Troels-Smith, J. (1956) The neolithic period in Switzerland and Denmark. *Science* 124: 876–9.

Troels-Smith, J. (1960) Ivy, mistletoe and elm. Climate indicators – fodder plants. *Danmarks Geologiske Undersøgelse* 4 (4): 1–32.

Troels-Smith, J. (1966) The Ertebølle culture and its background. *Palaeohistoria* 12: 505–28.

Trow-Smith, R. (1951) *English Husbandry, from the Earliest Times to the Present Day*. London, Faber and Faber.

Turner, J. (1975) The evidence for land use by prehistoric farming communities: the use of three-dimensional pollen diagrams. In J. G. Evans, S. Limbrey and H. Cleere (*eds.*) *The Effect of Man on the Landscape: the Highland Zone*: 86–95. London, Council for British Archaeology Research Report 11.

Turner, J. (1981) The Iron Age. In I. G. Simmons and M. J. Tooley (*eds.*) *The Environment in British Prehistory*: 250–81. London, Duckworth.

Turner, J. and Grieg, J. R. A. (1975) Some Holocene pollen diagrams from Greece. *Review of Palaeobotany and Palynology* 20: 171–204.

Turrill, W. B. (1929) *The Plant Life of the Balkan Peninsula: A Phytogeographical Study*. Oxford, University Press.

TV Vet (anon.) (1980) *The TV Vet Sheep Book: Recognition and Treatment of Common Sheep Ailments*. Ipswich, Farming Press Ltd.

Tyler, A. (1976) *Neolithic Flint Axes from the Cotswold Hills*. Oxford, British Archaeological Reports, British Series 25.

Vallet, G. (1962) L'introduction de l'olivier en Italie centrale. In M. Renard (*ed.*) *Hommages à Albert Grenier*: 1554–63. Brussels, Collection Latomus 58.

Veen, M. van der (1984) Sampling for seeds. In W. van Zeist and W. A. Casperie (*eds.*) *Plants and Ancient Man: Studies in Palaeoethnobotany*: 193–9. Rotterdam, A. A. Balkema.

Veen, M. van der and Fieller, N. (1982) Sampling seeds. *Journal of Archaeological Science* 9: 287–98.

Velde, P. van de (1979) On Bandkeramik social structure. *Analecta Praehistorica Leidensia* 12: 1–242.

Vencl, S. L. (1971) The topography of mesolithic sites in Bohemia. *Archeologicke Rozhledy* 23 (2): 169–87.

Ventris, M. and Chadwick, J. (1956) *Documents in Mycenaean Greek*. Cambridge, University Press.

Vermeersch, P. and Walters, R. (1974) Troisième campagne de fouilles à Thiensies. *Archéologie: Chronique Semestrielle* 96.

Vermeule, E. (1972) *Greece in the Bronze Age*. Chicago, University Press.

Vernet, J.-L. (1976) La flore et la végétation mediterranéennes à propos de leur mise en place en Europe de l'ouest. In *Chronologie et Synchronisme dans la Préhistoire Circum-Méditerranéenne*. Nice, Union International des Sciences Préhistoriques et Protohistoriques, 9. Congrès, Colloque 2.

Verron, G. (1976) Les civilisations néolithiques en Normandie. In J. Guilaine (*ed.*) *La Préhistoire Française 2. Civilisations Néolithiques et Protohistoriques*: 387–401. Paris, CNRS.

Vértes, L. (1960) Die Altsteinzeit der südlichen Donaugebiete. *Quartär* 12: 53–105.

Vértes, L. (1964) Eine prähistorische Silexgrabe am Mog Yorósdomb bei Sumeg. *Acta Archaeologica Hungaricae* 16: 187–215.

Vetters, H. and Piccotini, G. (1969) Die Ausgrabungen auf dem Magdalensberg, 1965–8. *Carinthia I* 159: 285–422.

Vicent, A. A. and Munoz, A. M. (1973) Segunda campaña de excavaciones. La Cueva de los Murciélagos, Zuheros (Córdoba) 1969. *Excavaciones Arquéologicas en Espana* 77.

Villaret-von Rochow, M. (1967) Frucht- und Samenreste aus der neolithischen Station Seeberg, Burgäschisee-Sud. *Acta Bernensia* 2 (4): 21–64.

Visset, L. (1973) La Butte aux Pierres (Grande Brière L.A.), étude pollinique. *Bull. Soc. Scient. Bretagne* 47: 219–23.

Vita-Finzi, C. and Higgs, E. S. (1970) Prehistoric economy in the Mount Carmel area of Palestine: site catchment analysis. *Proceedings of the Prehistoric Society* 36: 1–37.

Vizdal, I. (1972) Erste bildiche Darstellung eines zweirädigen Wagens vom Ende der mittleren Bronzezeit in der Slowakei. *Slovenska Archaeologica* 20: 233.

Vladar, J. (1972) Vorbericht über die systematische Ausgrabung der befestigten Siedlung der Otomani-Kultur in Spišsky Štvrtok. *Archeologicke Rozhledy* 24: 18–25.

Vogel, R. (1933) Tierreste aus vor- und frühgeschichtlichen Siedlungen Schwabens. 1. Die Tierreste aus den Pfahlbauten der Bodensees. *Zoologica* 31 (82): 1–109.

Vogt, E. (1951) Das steinzeitliche Uferdorf Egolzwil 3. *Zeitschrift für Schweizerische Archäologie und Kunstgeschichte* 12 (4): 193–215.

Vogt, E. (1969) Siedlungswesen. In W. Drack (*ed.*) *Ur- und Frühgeschichtliche Archäologie der Schweiz 2. Die Jüngere Steinzeit*: 157–174. Basel, Schweizerische Gesellschaft für Ur- und Frühgeschichte.

Vonbank, E. (1952) Die Krinne bei Koblack. *Vorarlberger Golsblatt* (6 June): 90–2.

Vörös, I. (1982) The animal bones from the late La Tène and Roman settlement of Szakály-Réti Földek. In D. Gabler, E. Patek and I. Vörös (*eds.*) *Studies in the Iron Age of Hungary*: 129–79. Oxford, British Archaeological Reports, International Series 144.

Vorren, K. D. (1979) Anthropogenic influence on the natural vegetation in coastal north Norway during the Holocene. Development of farming and pastures. *Norwegian Archaeological Review* 12 (1): 1–21.

Vuorela, I. (1970) The indication of farming in pollen diagrams from southern Finland. *Acta Botanica Fennica* 87: 1–40.

Vuorela, I. (1972) Human influence on the vegetation of Katinhäntä bog, southern Finland. *Acta Botanica Fennica* 98: 1–21.

Vuorela, I. (1975) Pollen analysis as a means of tracing settlement history in southwestern Finland. *Acta Botanica Fennica* 104: 1–48.

Waals, J. D. van der (1963) *Prehistoric Disc Wheels in the Netherlands*. Groningen, Wolters.

Waals, J. D. van der (1967) Graven en bewoningssporen uit Neolithicum en Bronstijd te Ahgelsloo. *Nieuwe Drentse Volksalmanak* 85: 209–14.

Waals, J. D. van der (1977) Excavations at the natural levee sites S2, S3/5 and S4. *Helinium* 17: 3–27.

Waals, J. D. van der and Waterbolk, H. T. (1976) Excavations at Swifterbant – discovery, progress, aims and methods. *Helinium* 16: 3–14.

Wainwright, G. J. (1971) The excavation of a fortified settlement at Walesland Rath, Pembroke-shire. *Britannia* 2: 48–108.

Wainwright, G. J. (1972) The excavation of a neolithic settlement on Broome Heath, Ditchingham, Norfolk. *Proceedings of the Prehistoric Society* 38: 1–97.

Wainwright, G. J. and Longworth, I. H. (1971) *Durrington Walls: Excavations 1966–1968*. London, Research Report of the Society of Antiquaries of London 29.

Waldren, W. H. (1982) *Balaeric Prehistoric Ecology and Culture*. Oxford, British Archaeological Reports, International Series 149.

Walker, D. S. (1967) *A Geography of Italy*. London, Methuen.

Walker, M. J. (1967) Aspects of the Neolithic and Copper Ages in the basins of the rivers Segura and Vinalopo, southeast Spain. Oxford University, unpublished D.Phil. thesis.

Walker, M. J. (1972) Cave dwellers and cave artists of the neothermal period in southeast Spain. *Transactions of the Cave Research Group of Great Britain* 14 (1): 1–22.

Wallace, J. (1883) *A Description of the Isle of Orkney*. Edinburgh, William Brown. Reprinted from the original of 1693.

Warren, P. (1972) *Myrtos: An Early Bronze Age Settlement on Crete*. London, British School of Archaeology at Athens.

Warren, P. (1975) *The Aegean Civilizations*. London, Phaidon.

Warren, P. and Tzedhakis, J. (1974) Debla, an early Minoan settlement in western Crete. *Annual of the British School at Athens* 69: 299–342.

Waterbolk, H. T. (1956) Pollen spectra from neolithic grave monuments in the northern Netherlands. *Palaeohistoria* 5: 39–51.

Waterbolk, H. T. (1960) Preliminary report on the excavations at Anlo. *Palaeohistoria* 8: 59–90.

Waterbolk, H. T. (1962) Hauptzüge der eisenzeitlichen Besiedlung der nördlichen Niederlande. *Offa* 19: 9–46.

Waterbolk, H. T. (1964) The bronze age settlement of Elp. *Helinium* 4: 97–131.

Waterbolk, H. T. (1965–6) The occupation of Friesland in the prehistoric period. *Berichten R.O.B.* 15–16: 13–35.

Waterbolk, H. T. (1975) Evidence of cattle stalling in excavated pre- and protohistoric houses. In A. T. Clason (*ed.*) *Archaeozoological Studies*: 383–94. Amsterdam, North Holland Publishing Co.

Waterbolk, H. T. (1977) Walled enclosures of the Iron Age in the north of the Netherlands. *Palaeohistoria* 19: 97–172.

Waterbolk, H. T. and Harsema, O. H. (1979) Medieval farmsteads in Gasselte (province of Drenthe). *Palaeohistoria* 21: 227–65.

Waterbolk, H. T. and Zeist, W. van (1966) Preliminary report on the neolithic bog settlement of Niederwil. *Palaeohistoria* 12: 559–80.

Waterbolk, H. T. and Zeist, W. van (1978) *Niederwil, eine Siedlung der Pfyner Kultur*. Bern and Stuttgart, Verlag Paul Haupt; Academica Helvetica 1.

Watkins, T. (1978–80) Excavation of an iron age open settlement at Dalladies, Kincardineshire. *Proceedings of the Society of Antiquaries of Scotland* 110: 122–64.

Watrous, L. V. (1977) Aegean settlements and transhumance. In P. P. Betancourt (*ed.*) *Temple University Aegean Symposium* 2: 2–6. Philadelphia, Temple University.

Watson, D. M. S. (1931) The animal bones from Skara Brae. In V. G. Childe, *Skara Brae: A Pictish Village in Orkney*: 198–204. London, Kegan Paul.

Watson, J. P. N. (1979) Faunal remains (from neolithic Servia). *Annual of the British School at Athens* 74: 228–9.

Webley, D. P. (1976) How the west was won: prehistoric land use in the southern Marches. In G. C. Boon and J. M. Lewis (*eds.*) *Welsh Antiquity, Essays Presented to H. N. Savory*: 19–35. Cardiff, National Museum of Wales.

Webley, D. P. and Dennell, R. (1978) Palaeonematology: some recent evidence from neolithic Bulgaria. *Antiquity* 52: 136–7.

Welinder, S. (1974) Den norrländska stenålderns sydgräns. *Forvännen* 69: 185–93.

Welinder, S. (1975) *Prehistoric Agriculture in Eastern Middle Sweden*. Acta Archaeologica Lundensia 8, 4.

Welinder, S. (1977) *Ekonomiska Processor I Förhistorisk Expansion*. Acta Archaeologica Lundensia 8, 7.

Welinder, S. (1977–8) The acculturation of the Pitted Ware culture in eastern Sweden. *Meddelanden från Lunds Universitets Historiska Museum* n.s. 2: 98–110.

Welinder, S. (1978) The concept of 'ecology' in mesolithic research. In P. Mellars (*ed.*) *The Early Postglacial Settlement of Northern Europe*: 11–25. London, Duckworth.

Welldon-Finn, R. (1967) Devonshire. In H. C. Darby and R. Welldon-Finn (*eds.*) *The Domesday Geography of Southwest England*: 223–95. Cambridge, University Press.

Wells, P. S. (1980) *Culture Contact and Culture Change: Early Iron Age Central Europe and the Mediterranean World*. Cambridge, University Press.

Welten, M. (1955) Pollenanalytische Untersuchungen über die neolithischen Siedlungsverhältnisse am Burgäschisee. In W. Guyan (*ed.*) *Das Pfahlbauproblem*: 61–80. Basel, Monographien zur Ur- und Frühgeschichte der Schweiz 11.

Welten, M. (1977) Résultats palynologiques sur le développement de la végétation et sa dégradation par l'homme a l'étage inférieur du Valais Central (Suisse). In H. Laville and J. Renault-Miskovsky (*eds.*) *Approche Écologique de l'Homme Fossile*: 303–7. Paris, Supplément au Bulletin de l'Association Française pour l'Étude du Quaternaire.

Werner, J. (1953) Keltisches Pferdegeschirr der spätLaTènezeit. *Saalburger Jahrbuch* 12: 42–52.

Westropp, H. (1872) *Prehistoric Phases*. London, Bell and Daldy.

Whallon, R. (1978) The spatial analysis of mesolithic occupation floors: a reappraisal. In P. Mellars (*ed.*) *The Early Postglacial Settlement of Northern Europe*: 27–35. London, Duckworth.

Whallon, R. and Price, T. D. (1976) Excavations at the river dune sites S11–13. *Helinium* 16: 222–9.

Wheeler, A. (1979) The fish bones. In C. Renfrew, *Investigations in Orkney*: 144–9. London, Report of the Research Committee of the Society of Antiquaries of London 38.

Wheeler, H. (1979) Excavation at Willington, Derbyshire, 1970–1972. *Derbyshire Archaeological Journal* 99: 58–220.

Wheeler, R. E. M. (1954) *Archaeology from the Earth*. London, Pelican.

Wheeler, R. E. M. and Richardson, K.M. (1957) *Hill Forts of Northern France*. London, Research Report of the Society of Antiquaries of London 19.

White, K. D. (1970) *Roman Farming*. London, Thames and Hudson.

White, P. J. and O'Connell, J. F. (1982) *A Prehistory of Australia, New Guinea and Sahul*. London and New York, Academic Press.

Whitehead, G. K. (1964) *The Deer of Great Britain and Ireland*. London, Routledge and Kegan Paul.

Whitehouse, R. (1971) The last hunter-gatherers in southern Italy. *World Archaeology* 2: 239–54.

Whitehouse, R. (1973) The earliest towns in peninsular Italy. In C. Renfrew (*ed.*) *The Explanation of Culture Change – Models in Prehistory*: 617–24. London, Duckworth.

Whitehouse, R. and Renfrew, C. (1974) The Copper Age in peninsular Italy and the Aegean. *Annual of the British School at Athens* 69: 343–90.

Whittle, A. W. R. (1977a) *The Earlier Neolithic of Southern England and its Continental Background*. Oxford, British Archaeological Reports, International Series 35.

Whittle, A. W. R. (1977b) Earlier neolithic enclosures in northwest Europe. *Proceedings of the Prehistoric Society* 43: 329–48.

Whittle, A. W. R. (1978) Resources and population in the British Neolithic. *Antiquity* 52: 34–42.

Whittle, A. W. R. (1982) Climate, grazing and man. In A. Harding (*ed.*) *Climatic Change in Later Prehistory*: 192–203. Edinburgh, University Press.

Wickham, C. (1981) *Early Medieval Italy: Central Power and Local Society*. London, Macmillan.

Widgren, M. (1979) A simulation model of farming systems and land use in Sweden during the early Iron Age *c.* 500 B.C.–A.D. 550. *Journal of Historical Geography* 5 (1): 21–32.

Wijnen, M. H. J. N. W. (1981) The early neolithic I settlement at Sesklo: an early farming community in Thessaly, Greece. *Analecta Praehistorica Leidensia* 14.

Wijngaarden-Bakker, L. H. (1974) The animal remains from the Beaker settlement at New Grange, Co. Meath: first report. *Proceedings of the Royal Irish Academy* 74: 313–83.

Wijngaarden-Bakker, L. H. (1981) *An Archaeozoological Study of the Beaker Settlement at Newgrange, Ireland*. Amsterdam.

Wilkes, J. J. (1969) *Dalmatia*. London, Routledge and Kegan Paul.

Wilkinson, M. R. (1982) Fish remains on British archaeological sites. Sheffield University, unpublished Ph.D. thesis.

Wilkinson, T. J. (1982) The definition of ancient manured zones by means of extensive sherd-sampling techniques. *Journal of Field Archaeology* 9: 323–3.

Willerding, U. (1980) Zum Ackerbau der Banderkeramiker. *Beiträge zur Archäologie Nordwest-*

deutschlands und Mitteleuropas: 471–56. Materialhefte zu Ur- und Frühgeschichte Niedersachsens 16.

Wilson, B., Grigson, C. and Payne, S. (1982) *Ageing and Sexing Animal Bones from Archaeological Sites*. Oxford, British Archaeological Reports, British Series 109.

Winiger, J. (1976) Feldmeilen-Vorderfeld. Die Ausgrabungen 1970–1. *Antiqua* 5: 1–100.

Wobst, H. M. (1974) Boundary conditions for palaeolithic social systems: a simulation approach. *American Antiquity* 39: 147–78.

Wojciechowski, W. (1966) Janowek. *Silesia Antiqua* 8: 42.

Wolff, P. (1977a) Die Jagd- und Haustierfauna der spätneolithischen Pfahlbauten des Mondsees. *Jahrbuch des Oberösterreichischen Musealvereines* 122 (1): 269–347.

Wolff, P. (1977b) Die Tierresten aus den bandkeramischen Siedlungen Poigen und Frauenhofen, Ger. Bez. Hörn, NÖ. *Prähistorische Forschungen* 8: 99–102.

Woodman, P. C. (1978a) *The Mesolithic in Ireland*. Oxford, British Archaeological Reports, British Series 58.

Woodman, P. G. (1978b) The chronology and economy of the Irish Mesolithic: some working hypotheses. In P. Mellars (*ed.*) *The Early Postglacial Settlement of Northern Europe*: 333–69. London, Duckworth.

Würgler, F. (1962) Veränderungen der Haustierbestandes während der bronze- und Eisenzeit in zwei schweizerischen "Melauner"-Stationen, Montlingerberg und Mottata-Ramosch. *Zeitschrift für Tierzüchtung und Züchtungsbiologie* 77 (1): 35–46.

Wyss, R. (1968) Das Mesolithikum. In W. Drack (*ed.*) *Ur- und Frühgeschichtliche Archäologie der Schweiz 1. Die Altere und Mittlere Steinzeit*: 124–44. Basel, Schweizerische Gesellschaft für Ur- und Frühgeschichte.

Wyss, R. (1969) Wirtschaft und Technik. In W. Drack (*ed.*) *Ur- und Frühgeschichtliche Archäeologie der Schweiz 2. Die Jüngere Steinzeit*: 117–18. Basel, Schweizerische Gesellschaft für Ur- und Frühgeschichte.

Wyss, R. (1970) *Die Pfyner Kultur*. Berne.

Wyss, R. (1971) Siedlungswesen und Gekehrswege. In W. Drack (*ed.*) *Ur- und Früh geschichtliche Archäologie der Schweiz 3. Die Bronzezeit*: 103–22. Basel, Schweizerische Gesellschaft für Ur- und Frühgeschichte.

Wyss, R. (1979) *Das mittelsteinzeitliche Hirschjägerlager con Schötz 7 im Wauwilermoos*. Zürich, Schweizerische Landesmuseum, Archäologische Forschungen 7.

Y'Edynak, G. (1978) Culture, diet and dental reduction in mesolithic forager-fishers of Yugoslavia. *Current Anthropology* 19 (3): 616–18.

Zackrisson, O. (1976) Vegetation dynamics and land use in the lower reaches of the River Umeälven. *Early Norrland* 9: 7–74.

Zaharia, E. (1962) Considération sur la civilisation de Criş à la lumière des sondages de Let. *Dacia* 6: 5–51.

Zeist, W. van (1955) Pollen analytical investigations in the northern Netherlands. *Acta Botanica Neerlandica* 4: 1–81.

Zeist, W. van (1958–9) Palynologische Untersuchungen eines Torfprofils bei Sittard. *Palaeohistoria* 6–7: 19–24.

Zeist, W. van (1964) A palaeobotanical study of some bogs in western Brittany (Finistère), France. *Palaeohistoria* 10: 157–80.

Zeist, W. van (1967) Archaeology and palynology in the Netherlands. *Review of Palaeobotany and Palynology* 4: 45–64.

Zeist, W. van (1968) Prehistoric and early historic food plants in the Netherlands. *Palaeohistoria* 14: 41–173.

Zeist, W. van (1974) Palaeobotanical studies of settlement sites in the coastal area of the Netherlands. *Palaeohistoria* 16: 223–383.

Zeist, W. van (1975) Preliminary report on the botany of Gomolava. *Journal of Archaeological Science* 2: 315–25.

Zeist, W. van (1976) Two early rye finds from the Netherlands. *Acta Botanica Neerlandica* 25: 71–9.

Zeist, W. van and Bottema, S. (1971) Plant husbandry in early neolithic Nea Nikomedeia, Greece. *Acta Botanica Neerlandica* 20 (5): 524–38.

Zeist, W. van and Casparie, W. A. (1974) Niederwil, a palaeobotanical study of a Swiss neolithic lake shore settlement. *Geologie en Mijnbouw* 53 (6): 415–78.

Zeist, W. van, Hoorn, T. C. van, Bottema, S. and Woldring, H. (1976) An agricultural experiment in the unprotected salt marsh. *Palaeohistoria* 18: 111–53.

Zeist, W. van and Spoel-Walvius, M. R. van der (1982) A palynological study of the late glacial and the postglacial in the Paris Basin. *Palaeohistoria* 22: 67–109.

Zimmerman, H. W. (1966) Zur postglaziale Sedimentation im Greitenzee. *Vierteljahrsschrift der Naturforschenden Gesellschaft in Zürich* 111: 1–22.

Zimmerman, W. H. (1978) Economy of the Roman iron age settlement at Flögen (Kr. Cuxhaven), Lower Saxony. In B. Cunliffe and T. Rowley (*eds.*) *Lowland Iron Age Communities in Europe*: 147–65. Oxford, British Archaeological Reports, International Series 48.

Zohary, D. (1969) The progenitors of wheat and barley in relation to domestication and dispersal in the Old World. In P. J. Ucko and G. W. Dimbleby (*eds.*) *The Domestication and Exploitation of Plants and Animals*: 47–66. London, Duckworth.

Zólyomi, B. (1964) Pannonische Vegetationprobleme. *Verhandlungen der Zoologisch-Botanischen Gesellschaft in Wien* 103: 144–51.

Zvelebil, M. (1978) Subsistence and settlement in the northeastern Baltic. In P. Mellars (*ed.*) *The Early Postglacial Settlement of Northern Europe*: 205–41. London, Duckworth.

Zvelebil, M. (1981) *From Forager to Farmer in the Boreal Zone*. Oxford, British Archaeological Reports, International Series 115.

Zvelebil, M. (in press) Iron age transformations in northern Russia and the northeast Baltic. In G. Barker and C. Gamble (*eds.*) *Beyond Domestication: Subsistence Archaeology and Social Complexity in Ancient Europe*. New York, Academic Press.

SITE INDEX

314

GENERAL INDEX